EMORY UPTON

C&C

CAMPAIGNS & COMMANDERS

GREGORY J. W. URWIN, SERIES EDITOR

EMORY UPTON
Misunderstood Reformer

DAVID J. FITZPATRICK

UNIVERSITY OF OKLAHOMA PRESS | NORMAN

Publication of this book is made possible through the generosity of Edith Kinney Gaylord.

Elements from two previously published articles appear, in substantially revised form, in chapters 2, 4, 6, 7, and 9 of this book: "Emory Upton and the Citizen Solider," *Journal of Military History* (April 2001): 355–89; and "Emory Upton and the Army of a Democracy," *Journal of Military History* (April 2013): 463–90.

Library of Congress Cataloging-in-Publication Data

Name: Fitzpatrick, David J., 1958– author.
Title: Emory Upton : misunderstood reformer / David J. Fitzpatrick.
Other titles: Emory Upton, misunderstood reformer
Description: Norman, OK : University of Oklahoma Press, [2017] | Series: Campaigns and commanders ; volume 60 | Includes bibliographical references and index.
Identifiers: LCCN 2016049877 | ISBN 978-0-8061-5720-7 (hardcover : alk. paper)
Subjects: LCSH: Upton, Emory, 1839–1881. | United States—History, Military—To 1900. | Generals—United States—Biography. | United States. Army—Organization.
Classification: LCC E181.U73 F57 2017 | DDC 355.0092 [B] —dc23
LC record available at https://lccn.loc.gov/2016049877

Emory Upton: Misunderstood Reformer is Volume 60 in the Campaigns and Commanders series.

The paper in this book meets the guidelines for permanence and durability of the Committee on Production Guidelines for Book Longevity of the Council on Library Resources, Inc. ∞

1 2 3 4 5 6 7 8 9 10

Interior layout and composition: Alcorn Publication Design

For John and Arlene Shy

Contents

Illustrations

Figures

Maps

Acknowledgments

O ne does not undertake a project such as this without incurring many debts, intellectual and otherwise. This book is no exception. Generous grants from the Horace H. Rackham School of Graduate Studies at the University of Michigan; from the Upton Foundation of St. Joseph, Michigan; and from the U.S. Army Center for Military History have supported my work. I owe a particular debt of gratitude to Dr. John Dann, the now-retired director of the William L. Clements Library at the University of Michigan, to Mr. David Upton of the Upton Foundation, and to Brig. Gen. (Ret.) Jack Mountcastle and Dr. Jeffrey Clarke at the Center for Military History. I also wish to thank the Board of Trustees at Washtenaw Community College in Ann Arbor, Michigan, for granting me sabbatical so that I might finally see this undertaking to publication.

The staffs of various manuscript libraries played important roles in the successful completion of this work. Tim Nenninger and Mike Pilgrim at the National Archives were invaluable in helping sift through the volumes of relevant material located there. Dr. Richard Summers and Mr. David Keough at the U.S. Army's Military History Institute provided indispensable help during my visits. I am particularly grateful to Dr. Summers for directing me to the Francis Parker Papers and to a poem Lieutenant Parker wrote in 1879 entitled "Upton's Lament." Other manuscript librarians who provided valuable help include Marge MacNinch at the Hagley Museum and Library, Al Aimone at the U.S. Military Academy Library, Suzanne Christoff of the U.S. Military Academy Archives, Susan Conklin at the Genesee County History Department, Rob Cox at the Clements Library, and Mike Kline at the Manuscript Division of the Library of Congress.

Over the course of my research, numerous friends and colleagues have asked pointed questions, suggested different research paths, provided valuable insights, or allowed me to bore them about Emory Upton. Herman Hattaway provided early encouragement and suggestions. Mark Grandstaff recommended that I look at the John Tidball manuscript in the U.S. Military Academy Library's Special Collections for an account of Upton's funeral and for speculation regarding Upton's motives in committing suicide. Sal Cilella pointed me toward the correspondence between Upton and his wife, Emily, that is in the Princeton University Library. Jerry Cooper's criticisms of a paper I delivered at a meeting of the Society of Military History, the subject of which was the Asian portion of Upton's around-the-world journey, have made that chapter much better than it otherwise would have been. Charles Royster suggested looking at the letters William T. Sherman had exchanged with the mother of his aide-de-camp Joseph Audenried for insightful references to Upton. "Mac" Coffman and Carol Reardon have provided valuable advice over the years as has Brian Linn, the latter's counsel usually being offered over a much needed beer or three. Katie Stimac, a former student, was indispensable in transcribing Emily Upton's letters and diary as well as Upton's letters to her. And I want to thank Joe Fischer, Rick Herrera, and Kathy Barbier for their never-ending support.

Numerous members of the staff at the Center for Military History, among them Andrew Birtle and Dave Hogan, provided encouragement. I fear that the members of the Friday afternoon Military Discussion Group at the University of Michigan have heard more about General Upton than they ever wanted to know, and yet they were always receptive and their criticisms thoughtful and incisive. I particularly appreciate the insights of Gerald Linderman, Tom Collier, Jonathan Marwil, Sheldon Levy, Hal Friedman, and Bryn Roberts. Bruce Vandervort and the *Journal of Military History*'s referees greatly improved the two articles I wrote on Upton that appeared in that publication and, hence, as portions of chapters in this book.

Were it not for the leaders of the Department of History at the U.S. Military Academy, I never would have started this project. My introduction to graduate-level history came about because they asked me to return to my alma mater as an active-duty officer to teach military history. For this I am grateful to Brig. Gen. (Ret.) Robert Doughty, Col. (Ret.) Ken Hamburger, and Brig. Gen. (Ret.) Roy Flint. After I resigned from active duty, these officers, along with Brig. Gen. (Ret.) Casey Brower, Col. (Ret.) Jim Johnson, and Col. (Ret.) Scott Wheeler, offered encouragement and supported my efforts. Their dedication to the study of military history is exemplary of "Uptonian" professionalism in that term's most positive connotation.

Bradford Perkins and Sidney Fine, both of whom were on my dissertation committee, provided valued advice and offered a collegial atmosphere for my work. Their criticisms were always constructive and given in a manner that conveyed faith in me and in this project. These two scholars, both of whom were truly great historians, always treated me as a colleague rather than as a student, and for this I will be forever grateful.

The support and advice of the staff at the University of Oklahoma Press were invaluable. Chuck Rankin enthusiastically supported this project from the moment we met and shepherded it to completion. Bethany Mowry and Stephanie Evans were a tremendous assistance in moving the manuscript toward publication, and Kevin Brock's copyediting improved substantially the final product. Erin Grieb's maps add much to the book's narrative; I am indebted to her. Finally, I owe tremendous thanks to Greg Urwin, who exhibited interest in my work years ago when we first met at the annual conference of the Society for Military History. Greg put me in contact with the University of Oklahoma Press, provided sage advice, and always offered encouragement.

I could write a chapter regarding my debts to John and Arlene Shy. John has been more than my academic advisor, dissertation chairman, and intellectual mentor—he has been my good friend. John has always shown great patience toward my rather eclectic interests, having encouraged work on the eighteenth-century sieges of Louisbourg, the militia movement of the late twentieth century, the Gerald Ford administration's response to the arms embargo Congress imposed on Turkey in 1974, the Soviet navy's role in the Indian Ocean in the 1970s, civil-military relations in the era of Colin Powell, and finally, Emory Upton. Through all of these projects, he has given me his complete support, wisdom, and subtle, well-taken criticisms. John also took it upon himself to help me secure financial support from the University of Michigan as well as from other sources. But his aid has gone far beyond the academic realm. He and Arlene made my family part of their own, and they have always been deeply interested in my children's escapades and adventures. They are my best friends. For all of John's work in the field of military history, his dedication to encouraging its study no doubt will be his greatest legacy. If I can carry on his passion for learning, for not ignoring aspects of history we might find unpleasant, and for encouraging the development of a new generation of historians as dedicated to teaching and to research as he, I might repay him in some small way.

Finally, I want to thank my children, Liz, Bill, and Jim, for their love and support throughout what to them must have seemed a never-ending endeavor. Still, they endured, always expressing interest in and concern for my work and for, as Bill calls him, "Mr. Upton." They all have become, to one degree or another, experts on the general, and he has come to be almost as large a part of their lives as he has of mine. For their patience with my impatience, for their encouragement when I was discouraged, and for their elation at my completion of this book, I am eternally thankful. I could not have finished this without their love and complete support.

A Note on Sources

For many years, Peter Michie's *Life and Letters of Emory Upton* has been the sole source of much of the general's correspondence because many of the letters reproduced in that volume had simply disappeared. Recently, the Holland Land Office Museum in Batavia, New York, came into possession of nearly one hundred letters Upton had written. Most were "new" in that they had not been available either through a manuscript library nor published anywhere. A large minority, however, had been published in *Life and Letters.* Michie had edited some of these letters, most in innocuous ways, but in some he changed fundamentally Upton's thrust. In any event, where the original letter is now available, I have cited the original, not Michie's transcription. It is also worth noting that some (but not all) editions of *Armies of Asia and Europe* contain letters Upton wrote while on the Asian portion of his around-the-world journey in 1875–76.

The Martin-Throop Papers at Princeton University contain more than sixty letters Upton wrote to his wife, Emily, in late 1868 and early 1869. For most of that period, Emily was convalescing in either Key West or Nassau from what very likely was tuberculosis. Numerous letters make clear that Upton was concerned about the logistics of getting them to his wife, and he had to consider the schedules of ships leaving New Orleans, Baltimore, and New York destined for those ports. This is the likely explanation for his sometimes writing two letters on the same date, sending one to one port and the second to another. Unfortunately, the letters often are different in their content, and there is no clear way to differentiate them in a citation. I have chosen to do so by either the letters' salutations or their closings.

Finally, to say that Emory Upton's handwriting is atrocious is to give it too much credit. When I first started work on this project more than twenty years ago, I called the county historian in Genesee County, New York, to arrange a visit. When I told her I was working on Upton, she asked, "Have you seen his handwriting?" "No," I answered. "You might want to consider another topic," she replied. Dealing with his scrawl has been a journey. I have done my best to make sense of his letters, and many people have helped me in that effort. Still, I acknowledge that I likely have made errors in my transcriptions, and for that I alone am responsible.

EMORY UPTON

INTRODUCTION

His life was pure and upright, his bearing chivalric and commanding, his conduct modest and unassuming, and his character absolutely without blemish.
History cannot furnish a brighter example of unselfish patriotism, or of ambition unsullied by an ignoble thought or an unworthy deed. He was a credit to
the State and family, which gave him birth, to the Military Academy which
educated him, and to the army in which he served. So long as the Union has
such soldiers as he to defend it, it will be perpetual.[1]

So wrote Emory Upton's wartime commander and longtime friend, James H.
Wilson, in the introduction to Peter Michie's *The Life and Letters of Emory
Upton*. That Upton was a patriot and war hero there is little doubt, but his legacy
to the U.S. Army went far beyond his Civil War exploits. The infantry-tactics
manual he wrote in the early 1870s was the basis for the army's tactical doctrine
for nearly twenty years. More importantly, Upton's two great works, *The Armies
of Asia and Europe* and *The Military Policy of the United States* (published by the
War Department twenty-three years after his death), provided the intellectual
justification for those officers, politicians, and civilians who desired to reform
the army's organization and, in some respects, its relationship with the state
and federal governments. Many of his proposals, including the development of
a general staff, the creation of a system of "graduate" schools for army officers,
and the formation of a reserve force subject to a degree of federal control, constituted the core of the so-called Root Reforms of the early twentieth century.[2]

Yet today Upton is, though frequently mentioned, an enigmatic, almost
elusive figure. Allan Millett and Peter Maslowski argue that he and his more
famous naval counterpart, Alfred Thayer Mahan, were the most influential military officers of their time within their respective services. One author has even
declared Upton to be "The Army's Mahan."[3] Still, his detractors were many, and
their criticisms have influenced modern views of Upton. Some contemporaries,
officers included, believed his proposals were "too Prussian" and did not make
sense in the American context.[4] Later critics thought Upton had purposely den-
igrated the role the militia and volunteers had played in America's wars in order
to further the fortunes of the Regular Army. John McAuley Palmer, a graduate
of West Point and member of John J. Pershing's staff during the First World War

and that of George C. Marshall twenty years later, was especially critical in this regard. He argued Upton had misrepresented George Washington's opinion of the militia in order to minimize its contributions during the Revolution while maximizing its liabilities, thereby completely discrediting it.[5]

The Life and Letters of Emory Upton does little to clear away the haze. Its author, who graduated from West Point two years after Upton and served as the academy's professor of natural and experimental philosophy during Upton's tenure as commandant of cadets in the 1870s, portrays the general as a God-fearing, apolitical, professional army officer who acted only from what he saw as his duty to God, the United States, and the army. Unfortunately, Michie's work, though providing valuable correspondence, is more hagiography than biography and provides little true insight regarding Upton's character and motivation.

Historians have tended to echo the sentiments of earlier critics. In *Towards an American Army,* Russell Weigley argues, "Upton proposed a military system . . . which even he scarcely expected to work in the American context." He continues:

> [Upton] ended in deep pessimism, and he did so in part because he failed to acknowledge that military policy must reflect the general policy of the nation and, more than that, reflect the general spirit of the nation. While one of his persistent themes in his treatment of American military history was the recurrent failure of American civil leaders to devote the country in peace to preparation for war, he never attempted to discover the motives and the possible merits of their views. . . . *Because Upton never really attempted to understand the civilian view of military policy, he failed utterly to formulate a policy in harmony with the American national genius.* . . . Instead, he began with fixed views of military policy and then despaired because he could not shape the nation in accord with their demands.[6]

From this damning indictment, Weigley proceeds one step further. Believing Upton to have been a "militaristic zealot," he contends the general's contempt for civilian leadership "suggests the Henry Wilsons, Douglas Haigs, Henri Pétains, and the Ferdinand Foches of the First World War sneering at the 'frocks.'" Thanks to this, Weigley concludes, officers became convinced that a democracy could not maintain an effective military and therefore was largely responsible for the "Uptonian pessimism" that allegedly pervaded the U.S. Army in the late nineteenth and early twentieth centuries.[7]

Stephen Ambrose's *Upton and the Army* builds a biography based largely on Weigley's critique. Ambrose contends that the general's attempts to "transform Prussian ideas into American practice" were unsuccessful because his "inability to understand the interrelationship between politics and war in a democratic state prevented him from fashioning a democratic system." Upton, he argues, "was trying to stand the [one clear] lesson [of the Civil War] on its head. The Civil War proved that in future wars civilians . . . would lead the masses into combat while the professional soldiers would serve only as *one* of the tools used by civilians. Stanton and Lincoln . . . were not 'usurpers'; they were part of an historical development—a development Upton refused to acknowledge." When Congress rejected his reforms in 1879, "Upton convinced himself that no one really agreed with his ideas, and he began to see himself as a misunderstood prophet," according to Ambrose, "standing alone against a hostile world."[8]

Weigley's and Ambrose's critical interpretations have provided the point of departure for numerous other historians. These studies contend that the army was "suffocating in Uptonian pessimism" in the early 1900s and that Upton's disciples, "rather than seeking a military system in accord with American traditions and institutions, clung suicidally to the Uptonian model as the *only* solution. Failure brought despair, and from despair came a deep pessimistic attitude which (dangerously) questioned the capacity of a democracy to perform its military imperative." They also contend that Upton's proposals, as well as those of Commanding General William Sherman, "revealed a dangerous spirit in postwar military reform." Andrew Bacevich goes so far as to argue that Upton was responsible for the mistaken belief, one held by many scholars and career soldiers, that a professional regular army cannot exist comfortably in the American political and social systems.[9] More recently, Brian McAlister Linn has taken great pains to show that Weigley's portrait of the army's intellectual climate in the late nineteenth century is incorrect. Still, the Weigley-Ambrose appraisal of Upton and of his influence remains prominent into the early twenty-first century.[10]

When I began my work on Upton, I was fully aware of the Weigley-Ambrose critique and had no expectation of challenging it. Instead, my goal was to provide a fuller biography of the general, one that would make him a three-dimensional figure and place his ideas in their contemporary context. I believe I have accomplished this goal. But my research also took me in an unanticipated direction. Expecting to find that Upton was the nemesis of citizen-soldiers, I found him to have been their advocate. Presuming that he had called for a larger regular army, I discovered that he had argued for a smaller, more efficient force. Anticipating that Upton had been a militarist and had held anti-democratic proclivities, I found him to have been concerned about the threat to republicanism posed by a politicized army led alternately by appointees over whom the president could exert no influence or by a president who might have aspirations to become a military dictator. These conclusions surprised me, as did my findings regarding his intellectual influence. It seems clear that there was little pessimism in the late-nineteenth- and early-twentieth-century army, Uptonian or otherwise. Instead, Upton, along with others, helped provoke an intellectual outpouring among army officers, one that significantly influenced reform measures that were adopted early in the twentieth century.

This biography, then, is an effort to put Upton and his reforms in their proper context and to reevaluate his subsequent influence.

CHAPTER 1

EARLY LIFE AND EDUCATION

Emory Upton was born on August 27, 1839, in Batavia, New York, the tenth of thirteen children of Daniel and Electa Upton. Though the family had resided in Batavia only twenty-two years, it was prominent in the village. Daniel's parents had settled there in 1817, and two years later, while working as a cooper in nearby Stafford, Daniel met Electa Randall. The couple was married on September 30, 1821, after which they established their home in a log cabin on the outskirts of Batavia. "At the time," according to the family history, "Batavia was nothing but a virgin forest. However, during Daniel Upton's own lifetime, and in no small share due to his own efforts, Batavia became a flourishing community." Family pride, no doubt, influenced this judgment, but it contains much truth. Between them, Electa and Daniel had little money, but they had a piece of property that, with hard work, promised one day to be a productive farm. Within twenty years the couple's diligence had transformed a "virgin forest" into 225 acres of valuable farmland and the log cabin into a large white, frame farmhouse, surrounded by several outbuildings.[1]

The Uptons almost certainly participated in the Christian revivals that swept the area in the 1830s. Upstate New York had been in a state of religious ferment since the late eighteenth century, and the Uptons, because they were strict Methodists, likely adopted the teachings of Charles G. Finney. The revivals he led, according to Paul Johnson, "marked the acceptance of an activist and millennialist evangelism as the faith of the northern middle class." Finney preached to his followers that "if they were united all over the world the Millennium might be brought about in three months." This was not, however, the apocalyptic millennium many thought the Book of Revelations predicted. Rather, it was one in which "Utopia would be realized on earth, and it would be made by God with the active and united collaboration of His people."[2]

Such a philosophy placed people in charge of their spiritual universe. No longer were men and women condemned to eternal damnation through election and predestination. They were instead moral free agents who would be judged by their actions in this life. Finney's theology, according to Johnson, taught "that virtue and order were products not of external authority but of choices made by morally responsible individuals." This meant that man was responsible for leading a pure, exemplary life, one that would help prepare the way for the millennium. It was not a great leap for Finney's followers to move from his theology's emphasis on the saving of the individual to a more activist role in society at large. Slavery, alcohol, and other excesses were all evil, for "they wasted men's time and clouded their minds and thus blocked the millennium"; utopia could come only with their eradication.[3]

Much about the Uptons suggests that they were intent on preparing for the millennium. Daniel was devoted to promoting harmony between different Christian denominations, seeking to bring them together in the Methodist Church, and he served as a lay delegate at national conventions in Cincinnati, Ohio, in 1846 and in 1866 dedicated to that cause. In particular, he "was known for his tolerance of the religious views of others." Daniel was "zealously opposed to slavery" and was an active participant in the "Underground Railroad," routinely sheltering runaway slaves at his farm while he sought passage for them to Canada. Local legend also held that he was "a radical teetotaler" who had been "the first man in Batavia to raise a building without using alcoholic beverages."[4]

It was into this "family of devout, freedom-loving, militant people of Puritan inheritance" that Emory was born. The Uptons were stern parents who did not tolerate mischief or thoughtlessness from any of their children. As a young adult Emory came to appreciate the value of this discipline. "None of us can reproach our father and mother for neglect of duty," he wrote to a younger sister, probably Sara, during his last year as a cadet at West Point. "I can now appreciate the effect of the discipline under which we were trained. Rigid though it was at times, yet the chastisement was always given in love rather than in anger. Our characters were formed early; and, hence, none of us when thrown upon our own resources have thus far disgraced our name." Many years later Upton wrote to his mother that his father had been correct "to chastise me for acts which to a juvenile mind appeared perfectly proper."[5]

The Uptons stressed the importance of education, all of their children attending school and several going to college. In 1851 Daniel acquired scholarships at Oberlin College for two of his sons, John and James, both of whom enrolled there between 1851 and 1853, though only John graduated. That he was able to secure "scholarships" for his sons suggests his success as a farmer and as a businessman. For a donation of $150, a donor "was entitled perpetually to the privileges of the school for a single pupil." This money did not go toward tuition, room, or board but merely secured a spot in the school for any person the donor wished to send there; the student was expected to meet all of their expenses.[6]

Before leaving for Ohio, James had suggested to Emory that he might consider attending the U.S. Military Academy. It was an idea that almost immediately sparked the younger brother's interest, and reading about the life and campaigns of Napoleon encouraged him further. Not yet sixteen, Emory applied to Rep. Benjamin Pringle for an appointment to West Point in 1855. Pringle doubted that the young man was properly prepared for the academy's course of instruction and suggested that he continue his education elsewhere. Because both John and James had departed Oberlin the previous year, Daniel agreed to send Emory and his older brother Henry there.[7]

The student body at Oberlin during Upton's time there was among the most diverse of any college or university in the nation. The 490 students who attended between 1852 and 1854 ranged in age from eleven to thirty-six, the average age being under nineteen. The largest number of students came from New York, most from the western part of the state known as "Burned Over District"; the majority of the remainder were from Ohio and New England. Most were children of farmers and, according to a student who transferred there from Yale in 1836, were "coarse & green . . . but noble, good hearted and pious." Prof. John Morgan of Oberlin observed that they were "genuine Yankees of the best class of plain farmers. . . . The students, though many of them crude, are a fine set of young men."[8]

The unique aspect of Oberlin's student body was its multiracial and coeducational composition. Of the more than 11,000 students who attended Oberlin from 1833 to 1866, 42 percent were women. The college was equally famous for its admission of African Americans, though they were a much smaller percentage of the student population, consisting of less than 3 percent of the 8,800 students who attended prior to 1861. Oberlin's official policy was, as Reverend Henry Cowles elaborated: "The white and colored students associate together in this college very much as they choose. Our doctrine is that *mind* and *heart*, not *color*, make the man and woman too. We hold that neither men [n]or women are much better or much the worse for their *skin*. . . . We believe in treating men according to their intrinsic merits—not according to distinctions over which they have no control." White students were not required to socialize with blacks, though Oberlin fully integrated the latter into its academic, religious, and social activities. And due to the small, if prominent, number of blacks at the school as well as its relative proximity to Canada, the campus community was a vital link in the Underground Railroad.[9]

Women and blacks often went to Oberlin because other institutions would not admit them. The school's manual-labor system, on the other hand, attracted many of its male students. Oberlin needed a mechanism to enable its students to pay for their education since so many came from modest means. The manual-labor system met this need. It required each student to work an average of three hours per day, the men working on the college farm and most women serving in some capacity in the boarding house. Depending on the task, students received from 2.75 to 10 cents per hour, though those who worked in the fields were paid 25 cents per bushel of potatoes or oats they harvested.[10]

The manual-labor system also existed because Oberlin's leadership believed strenuous physical activity would help students to maintain their health. A typical day for an Oberlin student began with wake-up at 5:00 A.M. and ended with "bedtime" at 9:30 P.M. In between every minute of the day was filled either with academic activities or with duties (for example, "milking"). By the time Upton attended Oberlin, however, few students were performing tasks that required vigorous physical exertion because the school's population had expanded so quickly through the sale of scholarships, such as those Daniel Upton had bought for his sons, that there was not enough work to provide meaningful employment for all students.[11]

Most students led a Spartan life. The college required those who lived in rooms it provided to furnish them at their own expense, though the school did provide a stove; this meant the average dorm room was nearly barren of furniture. The diet was bland, according to Oberlin historian Robert Fletcher. "Bread with water," he writes, "bread with salt, bread with gruel, bread with gravy made from flour and water mixed with pot liquor, and occasionally bread with butter too ancient to tempt the most ravenous appetite were the commonest fare." And despite the college's efforts to promote a vigorous lifestyle, many students fell victim to the ravages of typhoid and dysentery, caused no doubt by the open sewer that flowed through the campus square.[12]

Oberlin hoped that its entrants might have academic qualifications that were on a par with those of Harvard or Yale, but its students' backgrounds meant this was nearly unattainable, and the faculty seldom expected entering students to have "more . . . than a knowledge of the 'three R's.'" As a result, piety and morality were the most important qualifications for any candidate's admission. Oberlin required all potential students to present "testimonials of good character" and refused to admit anyone discovered to have traveled on the Sabbath.[13]

Religion was a very important aspect of student life. Explaining to his parents his reasons for founding a religious colony at Oberlin, John Shipherd wrote in 1832:

> I have been deeply impressed of late with the certainty that the world will never be converted till it received from the Church *a better example, more gospel laborers, and more money*. . . . Something *must* be done, or a millennium will never cheer our benighted world. The Church must be restored to gospel simplicity and devotion. As a means which I hope God would bless to the accomplishment of some part of this work, I propose through His assistance

to plant a colony somewhere in this region, whose chief aim shall be to glorify God, and do good to men, to the utmost of their ability.[14]

Many thus saw Oberlin as a means to an end, as its students would do the work of God and prepare the way for the millennium. By the mid-1850s the school was a hotbed of religious revivalism, evangelism, and abolitionism. The entire community, not just the college, took part in these activities, and the resultant fervor swept up many. Charles Finney was Oberlin's president during Upton's brief time there, and the school's religious philosophy therefore reflected Finney's own, especially the rejection of Calvinist doctrine and preparation for the coming millennium. Achieving this state would be hard and continuous work, for there was "no clear dividing line between sanctified and unsanctified Christians." The speakers who came to Oberlin and preached this doctrine were some of the most influential of the time, including Henry Ward Beecher, Calvin Stowe, Arthur and Lewis Tappan, John Shipherd, Asa Mahan, and most frequently during the time of Upton's attendance, Finney himself.[15]

The rigid interpretation of Finney's doctrine led to strict rules of behavior for Oberlin's students as well as for members of the greater community. The church often served as a court and tried citizens for "Unchristian conduct," "Tattling," "Slander," and "Falsehood." Other offenses included heresy, atheism, "the neglect of reading the Holy Scriptures and prayers in his family," and "the neglect of meeting with God's people on the Sabbath and on other days of worship." The rules imposed on Oberlin's students reflected this Puritanical morality. Students were subject to disciplinary action for, among other things, failing to pay bills in a timely manner, missing class or prayers, entering another student's room without permission, failure to pay library fines, and sweeping the dust out of one's room after 4:00 P.M. on Saturday or at any time on Sunday. Some of the more serious offenses included participating in "games of chance," use of tobacco or alcoholic beverages, possession of firearms, and visiting the room of a student of the opposite sex. Those who violated these rules had to confess their sin in public in the college's chapel. The scene at such a confession, according to one of the school's historians, "must have been impressive and singularly reminiscent of old Puritan New England." Confession, however, did not guarantee that the penitent would be allowed to remain at Oberlin. Indeed, if the crime were severe enough, the student might be excommunicated from the church.[16]

Austere and demanding, Oberlin well suited Emory Upton's needs and predispositions. Unlike many students attending in the 1850s, both Emory and Henry participated in the manual-labor system, working at a lumber mill in town for eight cents per hour. This meant hard physical labor, but both were accustomed to this from working on their father's farm. A good friend later reminisced that Emory never seemed to participate in any form of recreation, nor did he ever take part "in the foolish freaks of the boys," instead spending all of his free time studying. Even when he took a rare break to wander through a nearby forest, Upton did so with a friend with whom he would study and read while there. At one time he considered joining a literary society, but upon discovery it was "an infidel affair," he declined membership. Upton's sense of morality was apparent in his daily actions. "I never knew Emory Upton to use profane language," a friend remembered, "or speak with the least disrespect of religion, its ministers, or members as such. The only useless phrase he used was 'confound it.' This served all occasions. I never knew him to speak with the least levity of a woman, nor take any pleasure in jests or stories that inclined to anything disrespectful of the sex."[17]

Through it all, Upton remained focused on his goal of entering West Point, so much so that he refused to sleep with a pillow out of fear of becoming "round-shouldered" and thereby unfit for the service. He had little use for things he thought inconsequential in the pursuit of his goal, and he therefore preferred "practical education" rather than the study of music and literature. The course of instruction in the Preparatory Department, where Upton was enrolled, did much to ready him for West Point's academic rigors. The average student took Latin, Greek, English grammar, geography, orthography, ancient geography, arithmetic, algebra, geometry, natural philosophy, physiology, reading and oratory, Bible recitations, composition, and declamations and discussions. Upton was uninterested in liberal-arts courses, believing science-based courses more pertinent for a future army officer. When informed that he was not a good public speaker, Upton replied that "a soldier did not need to be an orator, for that, if he ever had to speak, it would be to his men in the face of the enemy, and on such occasions an oration must necessarily be short, and he thought he would be able for that."[18]

Upton seldom participated in the great demonstrations against slavery that often occurred on the Oberlin campus and was unimpressed with those few in which he did partake. Even the rhetoric of John Brown failed to move him. This does not mean Upton was uninterested in the cause of abolition. Rather, he felt that the students were wasting their time by participating in those rallies. "I am sick of such stuff," he is reported to have said. "Let those fellows learn their lessons now while at school, and by-and-by, if they have any brains, they may be able to do some good." How might they be able to do good? Upton was certain that the issue of slavery was driving the nation to a civil war, and the young men of Oberlin, himself included, had to be prepared to fight. He also doubted the efficacy of "protracted" prayer meetings that resulted in the conversion of its participants. "[Y]oung and inconsiderate persons often catch the enthusiasm of an excited minister," he wrote to his sister Maria, "and believe they have found religion; but as soon as the meetings cease, their enthusiasm subsides, from the want of a thorough conviction, and they revert to their primitive state."[19]

In 1856 Upton again applied to Representative Pringle for admission to the U.S. Military Academy. Not yet seventeen, his year at Oberlin apparently had provided Upton with the educational background Pringle thought necessary for success at West Point. "I selected you for the place," he wrote the young appointee,

> because, from representations made by your friends concerning you, and from my slight acquaintance with you, I believed that you possessed sufficient talent and ability; honesty and integrity, industry, energy, and perseverance to enable you to pass the ordeal at West Point creditably. Should you fail, it will be mortifying to me and to your other friends, but I trust there will be no failure. . . . You can hardly imagine the interest that I feel and shall continue to feel for your success. By doing well for yourself you will honor me. The place to which you are appointed has been sought by many and supported by influential friends, but I thought best to choose you, and you must prove to the world that I have made a good choice.[20]

Such an admonition, though it might have been given to all of the congressman's appointees to the military academy, certainly struck a responsive chord. Five years later, as Upton prepared to graduate from West Point and go off to war, he told his sister: "Remember me most kindly to Judge Pringle. I owe all to him. His motive in appointing me seldom actuates other Congressmen. Most appointments are political favors. I told you the reason he assigned for appointing me." Upton's motives for attending the academy? He was quite clear about that. "I would not leave the Academy for the $5000 that [brother] Jim spoke about," he wrote to one of his sisters only a few days after arriving there. "If I should graduate, one million dollars would not place me in the position I would then occupy had I not rec'd the appointment. My reason[s] are hidden, but set it *down* if I should graduate and there should be civil war, the north might be somewhat benefitted by me." By attending and graduating from West Point and then serving his nation in the civil war that he knew was coming, Upton could prove to Pringle he indeed had been a proper choice. When in March 1856 he accepted the appointment, the young man had taken a giant step toward his life's goal of serving his nation in a holy crusade.[21]

Upton arrived at West Point on June 3, 1856. Over the next few weeks, he and his prospective classmates undertook a rigorous set of examinations designed to ferret out those who had little chance of measuring up to the school's academic standards. Of the one hundred young men who had been granted appointments, the academy admitted only seventy-three. The Academic Board rejected sixteen for having failed one or more of the entrance exams, and four more failed their physicals.[22] The apparent pettiness of the exams appalled Upton. Some of those not admitted, he wrote, "were as fine fellows as there is in the corps, and are rejected on the most trivial of mistakes particularly in spelling." Several potential cadets failed, he claimed, simply because they were unable to spell "privilege" and "conferred." "I however spelled them correctly," he reported.[23]

For Upton, the most disconcerting experience during his first days at the academy came when he and thirty other potential cadets were marched off to the hospital. He was convinced that they were going there to be reexamined, a fate he believed to be "about the same as dismissal." All were relieved when, upon arrival, they discovered they were to be vaccinated. At a parade the next day, Upton and seventy-two other young men were informed they had passed the examinations and were officially "New Cadets." "I am admitted, by gosh," he reported to his family. "I am considerably elated."[24]

The class of May 1861 was relatively diverse in socioeconomic terms.[25] Of the seventy-three cadets admitted to the academy in the summer of 1856, twenty-six came from cities, twenty-eight lived in towns, and nineteen came from the country. Sixty-three came from families of "moderate" means (Upton was one of these), nine from "affluent" families (Henry A. du Pont, for example), and one from "reduced" means. The number of cadets whose fathers were farmers (eighteen) was more than double that of any other occupational grouping. West Point's classes during the late antebellum period, according to James Morrison, had a distinctly middle-class, small-town nature, and he concludes that their demography shows academy graduates were not, as has been charged, an American aristocracy.[26] Contrary to the contention of many of the academy's post–Civil War critics, Upton's class, like others of the antebellum era, was overwhelmingly northern in its complexion, with almost 60 percent of its members coming from free states and territories. It is more difficult to gauge its religious makeup as no records were kept of that statistic, but the school's atmosphere was overwhelmingly Protestant: though there were separate services for Episcopalians and Catholics, the academy required all other cadets, including Jews and atheists, to attend Protestant chapel.[27]

The new cadets' first task was to survive the summer encampment on the Plain at West Point. Not yet known as "Beast Barracks," the encampment still was a grueling period that tested a young man's mental and physical mettle. The day began at 5:00 A.M. and did not end until 9:45 P.M., with typical activities

consisting of inspections, guard mounts, meals, roll calls, and most importantly, several periods of infantry and artillery drill (the first one at 5:30 A.M.)
and two parades. When a new cadet was not occupied with official activities, he
was to be in his tent cleaning his weapon or repairing equipment and clothing.
There was little opportunity for extracurricular activity, though some took part
in dance lessons, and Henry du Pont found time to visit the library and read.[28]

Upperclassmen's hazing of the new cadets added to this rigorous sched-
ule. Morris Schaff, who graduated from West Point in 1862, claimed that more-
senior cadets spoke to their new charges "with voices boiling with indignation,
and eyes glaring with panther-like readiness to jump on us and tear us to bits,
as though we had seriously meditated the overthrow of West Point, and possibly of the Christian religion itself." New cadets often spent their "free" time in
the guard tent as punishment for minor infractions. Upton reported to his family that he had been placed there three times for stepping out of his tent without
a hat on his head. "I presume father will not like the guard tent, or will not like
to have me in it," he wrote to his sister Rachel. "But the old Cadets are bound
to have a time with us, and so they put us in the tent." Upperclassmen also
"hazed" Upton after a drill period by making him do "the Shanghai Step." This
consisted of "raising knees parallel to the hips and stepping as fast as you can."
"I took a moderate step," he reported, "& consequently did not have it hard."
Nighttime proved to be anything but restful. "The *animals* don't get much sleep
here nights," Upton reported to his family. "They are pulled out of bed 2, 3, or
six times a night. Some times they get a pail of water thrown on them." Despite
these annoyances, he recognized that camp was preferable to life in the barracks, where he and the others would be much more confined.[29]

The new cadets moved from their tents into rooms in the cadet barracks
when the academic year began in September. Upton likely found his accom-
modations at West Point similar to those at Oberlin. Four or five cadets usually lived in a room that was twelve feet long by twelve feet wide. The quarters
were poorly lit, sweltering hot in the summer, and frigid cold in the winter.
Hot and cold running water had been installed in the barracks only recently,
and with that amenity, the academy required cadets to bathe once a week "but
not oftener without special permission from the superintendent." The furniture
in the rooms was "neither decorative nor comfortable," and cadets were not
allowed to decorate them in any manner. It was a bleak existence.[30]

Upton's class was one of only three that participated in the five-year course
of instruction that existed at the time. Joseph Totten, the chief of engineers,
had ordered then-Superintendent Robert E. Lee to implement the program
in 1854 in the hope that it would allow more humanities courses, particularly
English and foreign languages, to be incorporated into the curriculum. Much

grumbling ensued from cadets and faculty alike, and as a result Secretary of War John B. Floyd, in the fall of 1858, abruptly ordered the program reduced to four years. He reversed this decision the following spring, probably under pressure from Sen. Jefferson Davis, who was the chairman of the Senate Military Affairs Committee and had been the secretary of war when the program began. The outbreak of war in 1861 and the subsequent demand for trained officers forced West Point to return to a four-year program. Upton's class, which graduated in May 1861, was the last five-year class. Other classes at the academy that spring had their course of instruction reduced by one year, with what would have been the Class of 1862 graduating in June 1861 instead.[31]

There can be little doubt that the school's academic program was demanding, maybe too demanding. "A candidate for admission to West Point in the years between 1846 and 1861," according to Morrison, "could scarcely have gained a hint of the academic rigors he was about to face from the lax entrance requirements." In 1857 the academy's Board of Visitors complained that only thirty-eight cadets graduated of the ninety-six who had been admitted as members of that year's class. "It would be a violent supposition," the board declared, "to assume that the fifty-eight members who entered with those now graduating were all wanting in mental capacity to become efficient and educated officers." The cause of the high failure rate, it concluded, was "that the amount of study required to compass the course laid down is excessive in quantity. . . . The most unremitting intellectual effort seems to be required during the entire term of the cadet at the academy. No mental relaxation comparatively is allowed."[32] The so-called Thayer System, the curriculum and pedagogic methods Sylvanus Thayer had implemented when he was the academy's superintendent from 1817 to 1833, caused much of this pressure. Thayer had effected a series of reforms designed to bring the school's method of instruction into line with that then used at French military schools. These had included the arrangement of classes into sections that consisted of a small number of cadets who were, according to Morrison, "academically homogenous": that is, the first section of any subject consisted of the top ten to twelve cadets in that subject; the second section consisted of the next ten to twelve, on down to the last section, which was made up of the lowest-ranking cadets. Thayer also instituted the concept of the "daily recitation," by which all students in almost every class meeting were required to answer their instructor's questions and were given a grade based on their answers. Finally, at the end of the semester, cadets undertook comprehensive oral examinations on every subject. Failure of an exam meant failure of that specific course, and course failure meant that the cadet could be expelled.[33]

Despite the avowed intention of the five-year program to increase the exposure of cadets to literature and language, math and engineering remained the most important subjects at West Point. Between 1846 and 1861, science-based courses never constituted less than 54 percent of the cadets' total academic work, while the study of tactics never counted more than 14 percent.[34] During Upton's first year at the academy, he took English studies and mathematics, both of which met on a daily basis, as well as fencing, which met every other day. His second-year curriculum consisted of daily meetings in math and French and meetings every other day in fencing and English studies. Upton's third year's program consisted of alternating meetings of French and Spanish during the first semester, daily classes in philosophy both semesters, daily meetings of Spanish during the second semester, and alternating classes in riding and drawing for both semesters. The course in drawing continued into his fourth year, and courses in riding, chemistry, civil engineering, and "Moral Science, History of Philosophy, Logic, etc" rounded out that year's curriculum.

Upton's senior year appears to have been his busiest in academic terms. Courses in ordnance and gunnery and in cavalry, artillery, and infantry tactics gave him his first academic look at the military profession, while classes in the history of law, mineralogy and geology, and practical engineering furthered his education in the arts and sciences. The capstone of the West Point academic program was Dennis Hart Mahan's course in military engineering. Unlike the other classes during a cadet's final year, all of which were one semester or less in duration and met every other day, Mahan's course met every day for the entire year. As such, it carried more weight than any other in determining a cadet's order of merit.[35]

Mahan's course focused on practical aspects of military engineering—fortification drawing, terrain sketches, and the construction of entrenchments—yet also contained a subcourse in the science of war that employed history to teach cadets about generalship and the conduct of battle. Some historians argue that in his instruction Mahan presented war in a very mechanical manner and therefore was in part responsible for the lack of innovation displayed on Civil War battlefields. They contend Henry Halleck's *Elements of Military Art and Science*, which many officers in the antebellum army had read, and William Hardee's *Rifle and Light Infantry Tactics*, which was the army standard manual in 1861, reflected Mahan's adherence to the ideas of French theorist Antoine Henri Jomini.[36] These works, because they presented war in limited terms and prescribed scientific principles that should be followed, allegedly prevented American generals from understanding the complexities that emerged during the Civil War. It was not Ulysses S. Grant's West Point education but his common sense, according to T. Harry Williams, "that enabled him to rise above the dogmas of traditional warfare," dogmas Mahan had taught at West Point.[37]

There can be little doubt that Jomini's works had influenced Mahan. The military theorist had emphasized scientific analysis in an effort to deduce the reasons for Napoleon's success, finding interior lines, lines of communication, movement into the enemy's rear, and the necessity of bringing "the maximum possible force to bear against the decisive point in the theater of operations" as the secrets behind the Corsican's victorious campaigns. This formulation of Napoleonic strategy became the basis for the teaching of military history at West Point under Mahan. Jomini's interpretation of Napoleon included one other important tenet: according to John Shy, his scientific explanation presented "a skillful disconnecting of the political and social upheaval of the [French] Revolution from the causes and consequences of his victories," thus allowing conservatives after 1815 to "think about warfare without being troubled by its possible relationship to revolution." The forces that the French Revolution had unleashed had greatly disturbed Jomini, and his sterile analysis of Napoleon was an effort to explain his greatness without taking into account the period's popular movements. These influences are evident in Mahan's own writings and in those of disciples like Hardee and Halleck, and it is clear that other students of the West Point professor admired his Jominian analytical framework.[38]

Nevertheless, the degree to which Mahan's Jominian perspective dictated the outlook and future careers of antebellum graduates of West Point is open to debate. The ability of one course in a five-year academic program to have had significant influence on its students many years after their graduation is highly doubtful. Morrison has pointed out that such an argument totally overlooks the role West Point's environment may have played in shaping its graduates' personalities and ignores differences in cadets' intellect and their experiences after graduation. He instead suggests that it was West Point's emphasis on strict obedience to orders and regulations, no matter how senseless, that fostered a lack of mental agility on the battlefields of the 1860s.[39]

Moreover, Mahan's biographer contends that such an interpretation of the professor's ideas and of their influence on his students is far too simplistic. "It is true," Thomas Griess argues, "that he [Mahan] believed there were certain principles important to the successful waging of war and he adapted some of Jomini's ideas; but he also insisted upon injecting common sense, the practical approach, into the art of war." Mahan recognized the importance of morale, leadership, planning, and fighting on one's home territory in the outcome of battles and campaigns. He also stressed the role generalship played— that is, he understood that not everyone had the ability to lead an army into battle. Principles were important, but an officer's education, experience, intellectual capacity, and to a certain degree innate abilities also dictated the outcome of battle. In addition, he stressed the need to maintain one's flexibility in the conduct of military operations. Though repeatedly emphasizing the importance of identifying a "main attack" that "should be directed against the point which would lead to most decisive results," he also advocated the conduct of demonstrations and secondary attacks whose purpose was to tie down potential enemy reinforcements; Mahan believed that a commander needed to be prepared to exploit any success these secondary efforts might achieve.[40]

More importantly, it is apparent that Mahan's philosophy concerning the nature of war had evolved over time. The emphasis in his course began to shift gradually after 1845 from the "science of war" and "the investigation of pure principles" to the history of the military art and its attendant philosophy that war is relatively unstructured. Mahan, according to Griess, "looked upon war as embodying the elements of both a science and an art but with the latter being more important." Though he never rejected the validity of scientific principles in the analysis of past military campaigns or in the planning and conduct of contemporary operations, he also stressed the importance of common sense in their application as well as the necessity for flexibility on the part of the commander.[41]

It is also too convenient to blame the military academy, and especially Mahan and his teachings, for regular-army officers' contempt of the militia.[42] This disdain predated his tenure at West Point, going back to before the outbreak of the War of 1812. Jacksonian rhetoric of the 1830s alleging that the military academy was authoritarian and elitist had fed this disdain, which led to officers not only denouncing the militia but also convincing them that civilians were more antimilitary than they probably were. Officers often believed that politicians were "adversaries—'demagogues' who appealed to the 'mob' by attacking the army," according to William Skelton, "and who placed party and sectional loyalties over the nation's welfare, defined of course as a strong military establishment." Political hostility to West Point had long been a bone of contention within the officer corps, and by the 1840s, many had come to see politicians as antagonists rather than allies. Graduates who subsequently taught at West Point inculcated this belief into their impressionable charges. Such an analysis of political leaders fit well with Upton's own predispositions and with those of many cadets, among them Henry du Pont, who doubted the ability of civilian leaders to appoint qualified officers to the army, fearing instead that they would commission political hacks. Upton had similar fears and believed that he was one of a few who had been appointed to the academy for "correct" reasons; others were unworthy of their status as cadets at West Point.[43]

The resultant suspicion of the militia was a fixed part of the officer corps' ideology by the late 1840s. The militia, though it had its problems, was not as hopeless as the vehemence of officers' complaints suggested. Rather, "the amateur soldiers served as a foil for the emerging professional consciousness of the officer corps." This, however, is not a wholly satisfactory explanation of the reasons for the regulars' hostility, for it overlooks the very real problems inherent in the militia and minimizes valid concerns about its ability to perform its mission.[44] More importantly, Mahan took a somewhat different tack. Though a staunch advocate of military professionalism, he was also a realist and understood that the Jeffersonian influence in American politics never would allow the existence of a large standing army, nor was he ignorant of the threat such a force posed to a republic and to individual rights. Mahan therefore "believed that the militia played an important part in the defensive posture of the nation."[45]

This does not mean that Mahan failed to recognize the militia's deficiencies. Indeed, he believed that they lacked discipline and were careless on the battlefield. These shortcomings could be remedied, he thought, if the militia were used to augment the small regular army as a means of expansion; if its officers were "men competent in military matters," most of whom would probably be academy graduates who had resigned from the service; and if it operated from entrenchments while the regular regiments maneuvered in the open field. Finally, Mahan believed that the militia needed to be trained in peacetime, and to this end he hoped that his two great works, *Out-Post* and *Field Fortification*, would be used as training manuals.[46] Clearly, he had not given up on the militia as had many of his fellow army officers. Though it is impossible to draw a direct link between Mahan's beliefs regarding the militia and the proposals Upton developed in the 1870s, the parallels are unmistakable, and the latter's experiences as the commander of the 121st New York Infantry—a regiment of raw, militia-like volunteers—in 1862 and 1863 probably confirmed their efficacy to the recent West Point graduate.

Upton found his senior year's studies to be "very interesting," no doubt in part because of Mahan's "charismatic" nature. His academic performance during the second semester was among his best while at the academy, ranking fourth in Mahan's engineering course, third in ordnance, and seventh in ethics. Upton's record during his final year at West Point is typical of his entire academic career, for it reveals a predisposition for science and math rather than the arts and letters. As had been true at Oberlin, he hated public speaking. During the winter of 1857, he wrote to his brother John, "My studies all Geometry & History (U.S.) [and] Elocution[,] the first two are very agreeable but hang the latter." The cadet displayed a knack for Spanish and French, ranking twenty-first and fifteenth, respectively, in those classes. Despite his preference for the scientific, Upton performed very poorly in the three drawing courses in which he enrolled, ranking thirty-third, twenty-ninth, and thirty-ninth. Most impressive about his performance at the academy was his steady progress up the ladder of the General Order of Merit. Though he ranked thirty-fourth out of the sixty cadets in his class at the end of his first semester at West Point, by June 1860 he had climbed to fifth. Despite the fact that he subsequently fell to eighth, his overall improvement is a testament both to Upton's tenaciousness and to his intellectual growth.[47]

Upton's disciplinary record was similarly meritorious. By the end of his first year at the academy, he had accumulated only sixty-five demerits, a very small total for a first-year cadet, and ranked thirty-first overall in conduct out of the 191 cadets. His second year was somewhat less successful: he was "awarded" one hundred demerits, all of which were for relatively minor offenses such as "Trifling in Ranks," "laughing in ranks," and "late at roll-call," none of which earned him more than four demerits. He was not above committing more serious offenses such as throwing a snowball in the mess hall, an indicator, perhaps, that he was not quite as humorless as often is thought. His sister apparently thought that his disciplinary problems represented some form of moral failure. The young cadet tried to disabuse her of that notion. "You use the term 'bad marks,'" he wrote to her. "*Bad* signifies to you, evil, wrong, immoral, and wicked, which placed before *marks* signifies that I have been doing something wrong or immoral—something which conscience disapproves. That is wrong, not only in the sight of a military man, but of God. Now, what moral wrong is there in 'laughing in ranks,' 'late at roll call,' 'not stepping off at command,' 'not having coat buttoned throughout,' and kindred reports? Now, is that wrong in the sight of God? I say, No!" By the time he was a second classman, Upton had mastered the art of avoiding trouble, receiving no demerits in one semester and only five in another. As a result, along with only a handful of other cadets, he received extended privileges numerous times during his final two years that allowed him to depart academy grounds after his last class on Saturday and to return by 10:45 P.M. that evening.[48] Upton also was awarded with the temporary rank of cadet lieutenant during his fourth year at the academy, though he graduated as a "high private."[49]

More important to Upton's cadet life than his academic studies and his personal conduct were his religious experiences. West Point did not initially impress him as a place that respected God. "[T]his is the most unhallowed place man ever set foot in," he wrote to his sister Rachel in the summer of 1856. "Just think of the desecrations of the Sabbath, Parading, *marching* to church and the like." He complained that "the Bible is not read much" and that three new cadets had been placed in the guard tent for doing so. "The army is a hard place to practice religion," he noted later, "though few scoff at it, yet a great majority totally disregard it."[50] The Board of Visitors concurred with Upton and strongly criticized "the limited provision made by regulation, and by actual practice, for the religious instruction of cadets." This atmosphere did not deter Upton from the pursuit of his beliefs. "I take the Bible as the standard of morality," he wrote to his sister during the spring of his first year, "and try to read two chapters in it daily." Other cadets admired him for "being conscientiously consistent in profession and in life," and he was one of the fifteen or twenty regular participants in prayer meetings and Bible classes led by Capt. O. O. Howard, an instructor at the academy at that time.[51]

Though West Point failed to shake Upton's religious convictions, his brother Le Roy's grave illness in the winter of 1859 challenged them severely. Informed in early February that his brother was ailing, Upton wrote to a sister that Le Roy should "not delay in making his peace with God." Yet he must have had his own doubts and probably expressed them to his family when he went home for his brother's funeral, for at the end of March he wrote: "Dear Le Roy's request to me shall not go unheeded. I have resolved, yes, begun to seek the Lord, and shall continue till I find him."[52] Within weeks of his brother's death, Upton's activist beliefs again came to the fore. "What is the length of life," he wrote to a cousin, "compared with never ending eternity? Infinitely small. Yet our actions during this instant are to determine our future condition through eternity. Let us strive to show ourselves worthy of the kingdom of heaven. Let us be true to the trust confided in us. We must necessarily encounter difficulties. We may have to bear the scoffs of the world, but we should recollect that the Son of God not only had to bear this, but he was crucified, and his blood was shed for us."[53]

As it became ever more apparent that civil war was soon to engulf the nation, Upton's religious convictions reinforced his belief that he would be doing God's work in that conflict. "If he intends me to occupy a high position," he wrote in January 1860, "he will raise me to it; if not, I shall be happy in having done my duty and in meeting his approval. There will be no limit for doing good in the army. There will be wounded soldiers to minister to, and the dying to comfort. These remarks may be premature; but the conviction strengthens that we must have war. I thank God that none of my relatives will feel its horrors; but I pity those where the conflict must occur." Upton believed that Christians had an important role to play in the nation's army. "I do not think that Christians have ever disgraced the profession of arms," he wrote. "[O]n the contrary, they are those who have most ennobled it."[54] Christians, then, would provide the army with the moral tone—that of a crusade—that otherwise might be lacking.

Indeed, Upton's religious beliefs provided the prism through which he viewed the secession crisis. "We are living in perilous times," he wrote home in January 1860.

Government, society, and everything seem to be on the verge of revolution. The passions of the people are being waked up, and they must have vent. God is directing the storm, and all is for the best. We may ask, How have we incurred his displeasure? The answer is easy. Mormonism, spiritualism, intemperance, slavery, corruption in politics, either of which is almost sufficient to curse a people. Few there are who have not bowed a knee to Baal. We must have reform. We must return to reason and virtue. Why should we expect tolerance when God suffered such calamities to befall his own chosen people? He scourged them with war, and he will punish us likewise. If we are to have war, I shall have no conscientious scruples as to engaging in it, for I believe I shall be on the side of right. I am ambitious; but I shall strive to limit it to doing good. It will profit a man nothing to gain the whole world and lose his own soul.[55]

This letter reveals that many of Upton's beliefs that came to the forefront later in his life had been present prior to his graduation from West Point. That he apparently placed political corruption on the same moral plane as slavery says a great deal about his later opinions of politicians and what he believed was their betrayal of the democratic process.

The growing sense of sectionalism became apparent at West Point after John Brown's raid on Harpers Ferry in 1859, and Upton found himself in the center of the furor. Many in the Corps of Cadets were aware that Upton supported abolition and that he had previously attended Oberlin, an institution especially odious to southerners for its advocacy of abolition as well as for its admission of black students. "Upton's sincere declaration of his position," according to Morris Schaff, "obnoxious in the last degree to the South—at once made him a marked man." His background was particularly repugnant to Wade Hampton Gibbes, a cadet from South Carolina and a member of the Class of 1860. In a private meeting with other cadets, Gibbes hinted that Upton had had sexual relations with black women while a student at Oberlin. Schaff doubted that Gibbes thought Upton would know of the remark, but upon hearing about it Upton, after a battalion formation, demanded an explanation. When Gibbes was not forthcoming, Upton challenged him to a duel that was to be fought on the first floor of the First Division of the cadet barracks. After the two protagonists entered the division, a crowd surrounded the stairwell, thus preventing the cadet guard from entering the building and breaking up the fight. The events of the melee that ensued are unclear, for cadets outside the division heard only a shuffling of feet, though they cheered wildly. In the confusion one was heard to demand that Upton and Gibbes use bayonets. When the fight was over, Upton emerged from the building looking the worse for wear, his face bleeding rather profusely. Behind him his roommate and second, Cadet John Rogers, proclaimed, "If there are any more of you down there who want anything, come right up." Schaff observed that Rogers's "eyes were glowing like a panther's."[56]

The Upton-Gibbes fracas altered substantially the relationship between northern and southern cadets. Schaff believed that it convinced the southern cadets of the "iron and steel there was in Northern blood when once it was up," though he also thought it was "but the prelude of that mightier collision between the States." And while sectionalism at West Point seemed to die after the duel, apparently out of embarrassment, this deceptive tranquility was short lived. The debate between northern and southern cadets became a permanent fixture in the corps after February 1860, when Jefferson Davis submitted a number of resolutions to the Senate designed to protect the "peculiar institution" by declaring that, when it came to the issue of slavery, states were virtually sovereign republics. The dispute over the sectional issue broke out once again within the corps.[57]

In October 1860, less than a month before the presidential election, what Schaff describes as an "evil spirit" visited a roomful of southerners, and by the next morning a box had been placed in a barracks hall for the purpose of conducting a straw vote. "A better scheme than this straw ballot to embroil the corps, and to precipitate the hostilities between individuals which soon involved the States, could not have been devised," he later observed. The result of the election quickly became a subject of great dispute. Abraham Lincoln's strength in the straw poll (Schaff claims he garnered 64 of the 218 votes) dismayed many southerners, and "with almost astounding effrontery, the self constituted supervisors of the election appointed tellers for each division to smoke out those whom some of them saw fit to designate luridly as 'the Black Republican Abolitionists in the Corps.'" A second count subsequently revealed John C. Breckinridge to have been the overwhelming winner, with 99 votes, whereas Stephen Douglas received 47, John Bell 44, and Lincoln 24. The results of the informal election infuriated northern cadets, particularly Upton, who charged that northerners had been prevented from voting.[58] The result was an even deeper split in the corps.

The only break in the tension came later that month when Edward, Prince of Wales, visited West Point. While there, the future king of England sat in on classes and watched a demonstration in the riding hall, where one cadet "was thrown almost off his horse, but he regained his seat with such skill and address as to make the prince clap his hands." The cadets had planned to hold a ball in Prince Edward's honor, but he declined, and the weather prevented holding a parade. Nevertheless, Edward reviewed the corps on the day of his arrival, after which Upton met him. "I can now say that my rustic hand has grasped the hand of royalty," the New Yorker later wrote. He found the accompanying entourage to be "perfect gentlemen" and was struck by the fact that they spoke "*pure* English." The prince apparently impressed most cadets just as they impressed him, but within a few weeks any good feelings Edward's visit had generated dissipated as the secession of several southern states became imminent.[59]

Lincoln's election and South Carolina's subsequent defection made it apparent to all at West Point that war soon would ensue. Upton was certain South Carolina would attack Fort Moultrie in Charleston Harbor, which would provoke a federal military response, and which in turn would alienate most of the southern states that had not yet left the Union. Initially, at least, he believed, as did most in the North, that the Union would quickly defeat the South in any conflict. His certainty regarding the war's course had weakened, however, within a few weeks. "Truly troubling times have come upon us," he wrote his sister Maria. "We are at sea with no chart to guide us. What the end will be our wisest statesmen can't foresee. The south is gone, & the question is whether the government will coerce her back. The attempt I think must be made, but we cannot tell what will be the result yet. Southern men are brave & will fight well, but their means for prosecuting a long war are wanting."[60] His confidence waned even further as he watched the administration of Pres. James Buchanan founder. "Your remarks as to Tories were very appropriate," he wrote his sister-in-law Julia.

> There is a large class at [*sic*] the North & they will seriously affect the power of the Gov't. They are so servile that they would prefer to accept the terms of Jeff Davis rather than fight for the honor of the North. I am entirely out of patience with them. . . . I am impatient with the conduct of the North. The South is making ample preparations for war, while we "are lying supinely on our backs." Why are no steps taken to defend the Union? If we have war (*mark my words*) Jeff. Davis will be successful for one or two campaigns. . . . Every victory for him at the outset will require three defeats to offset.[61]

Upton equated the president's failure to address the crisis with treason. "The papers say, Buchanan has ordered the commandant of Fort Moultrie to surrender if attacked," he wrote to one of his sisters in late December 1860. "[I]f true, what a traitor. [Secretary of War] Floyd has sent 250,000 stand of arms to different Southern posts within the past year, and for what—certainly not for the use of soldiers garrisoning them. What, then, is the inference? That they should be convenient for *secession*. The administration must be deeply implicated in this plot to destroy the govern't, its conduct cannot be explained otherwise." "I heartily rejoice that 'Old Abe' is elected," he concluded the letter, "& I heartily rejoice that we have got such a noble set of republicans at Wash-n at the present critical time."[62]

Upton in fact had always been deeply distrustful of the desire and ability of *any* Democratic administration to deal adequately with the sectional crisis. Less than a year after entering West Point, he had written his brother John that Pres. Franklin Pierce had been "subservient to southern interests" and that Buchanan had to "deal justly with the north or ruin the Democratic Party." By 1861 it was evident to Upton that no Democrat could be entrusted to safeguard the Republic, and as a result he never again had confidence in the motivations of Democratic politicians. Twenty years later he wrote his sister-in-law Julia that he "would scarcely alter now" the letter that had accused Buchanan of treason.[63]

His evolving evaluation of the ever-deepening crisis is instructive for a number of reasons. First, still a cadet at West Point, Upton predicted that the war would be longer than most in the Union leadership thought, which belies, to some degree, the criticism of the instruction at West Point for its emphasis on a limited, Jominian outlook. Second, his analysis foreshadowed that of *The Military Policy of the United States*, in which he blamed the defeat at First Bull Run and the subsequent cost of the prosecution of the war on inadequate preparation on the part of the federal government. The seeds of Upton's later ideas, then, had been planted before the outbreak of the Civil War, and his experiences in that conflict simply nourished those beliefs. Finally, his disdain of politicians, and especially of Democrats, had been set in stone before his graduation from West Point.

Upton became less and less tolerant of his southern counterparts and of anyone who might be construed as sympathetic with their cause. "They [the South Carolina legislature] are wild on the subject of a Southern confederacy," he wrote one of his brothers, "and they have resolved to establish it at the price of a revolution. If this is the real cause of secession, the door to compromise should forever be closed, and the South should be completely subjugated. In the Union their property is and ought to be protected; out of the Union, slavery is overthrown. I hope some day to see it abolished *peaceably*; but, if they go out, they of themselves overthrow it in blood." In April 1861 a petition circulated among Upton's classmates requesting that the secretary of war graduate and commission them at once. Thirty members of the class signed the petition, but another eighteen, at least initially, demurred. Upton believed these cadets to be traitors and thought that the petition would show the government who was loyal to the Union and who was treasonous. It never seems to have occurred to him that many cadets who had not signed the petition were having a "crisis of conscience" over the question of duty to the federal government versus obligation to their state. Upton, however, had no doubts where his duty lay. "If the worst is to come and war follow, *I am ready*," he wrote to a sister. "I will take for my motto, '*Dieu et mon droit.*' I will strive to fulfill my duty to God and to my country, and willingly abide the consequences."[64]

The chief of the Engineer Branch, Joseph Totten, initially took no action when the petition arrived on his desk, but the pace of events quickly overtook the army. In late April the new secretary of war, Simon Cameron, ordered the Class of 1861 graduated immediately.[65] The Academic Board recommended that Upton, who ranked eighth in his class, for assignment in either the "Engineers, Top[ographical] Eng[inee]rs, Ordnance, Artillery, Dragoons, Mounted Riflemen or Cavalry." In a small ceremony that took place in the academy's library on May 6 as the rest of the corps marched off to lunch, a local justice of the peace swore in Upton's class. Afterward the newly commissioned officers went to the mess hall, where the Corps of Cadets gave them a tumultuous greeting, after which they marched down the hill to the train station near South Dock on the Hudson River. Secretary of War Cameron's orders had specified that they would "repair to Washington City without delay and report in person to the Adjutant General"; there was a train to catch.[66] The U.S. Military Academy's Class of May 1861 was off to war, and Emory Upton, age twenty-one, was embarking on his crusade.

CHAPTER 2

Upton's Civil War, 1861–1863

After a brief stop in New York City, where Upton and his classmates received their personal weapons, the new West Point graduates continued on to Washington, D.C. Their journey was delayed unexpectedly upon arrival in Philadelphia. A rumor had circulated there that southern cadets who had recently resigned from the academy were en route to the Confederacy, carrying weapons hidden in their luggage. The appearance of Upton and the others, still wearing dress gray and with their just-issued weapons, seemed to confirm the rumor. Officials pulled the entire class off the train and took the men to the city's "Rogues' Gallery." After many anxious minutes the mayor arrived and, having seen that the War Department had issued their orders, "which, of course, was sufficient evidence of our character," ordered the young men released and their weapons returned. Because they had missed the night's last train for Washington, the mayor had the officers billeted in one of Philadelphia's better hotels at the city's expense.[1]

Upton reported to the army's adjutant general when he arrived in the capital. Though he made clear that he wished to be assigned to the Third U.S. Infantry, he instead found himself drilling volunteer units in the Washington area. Upton eventually became a member of the Fourth U.S. Artillery but remained in the service of Brig. Gen. Joseph Mansfield, the commander of all troops in and around the capital. Mansfield sent him to help drill Col. Daniel Butterfield's regiment, the Twelfth New York Volunteer Infantry, and to prepare it for battle. The young officer found the duty thankless and unrewarding, and he feared it might cause him to miss the war's first battle. Having heard that a sizable Union force had crossed the Potomac River at Long Bridge, Upton wrote his family: "This move is the initiative of the war. How soon a pitched battle will be fought I know not, but one must come soon. I am trying my best to be present, but I fear I shall be unsuccessful."[2]

Upton also had other, more mundane concerns on his mind. Shortly after his arrival in the capital, he wrote to a sister: "I now really have commenced life. No longer a cadet I am now my own master." What might this newfound freedom portend? He hoped to have a "prosperous and useful career." In the meantime, however, he expected to attend a party at Secretary of State William

Seward's home. "We shall go in full dress," Upton wrote. "It will be my debut in W[ashingto]n society. I am very desirous of making some lady acquaintances." No wonder that, at this early point in his career, he concluded, "I like Army life." Yet his focus remained on the coming battle, and he intended to be an important part of it. "We hope to celebrate the *Fourth* of *July* at Fairfax Court House," Upton wrote his sister Maria on July 1. "Whether the move will involve battle I know not but I hope it will. . . . I think we shall have fighting soon beyond a doubt. I have been where I expected a fight but have not been satisfied as yet." In response to his sister's plans to visit him in Washington, he replied, "I should like to accompany you at any other time than this; but you know an opportunity will soon present itself for me to be under fire, & I would not miss it for all the world."[3]

After serving less than a month as a drill instructor for new regiments, Upton became an aide-de-camp on the staff of Brig. Gen. Daniel Tyler, the commander of the First Division of the Army of Northeastern Virginia. Here too Upton had many opportunities to work with volunteers, and what he saw did not impress him. He was particularly scornful of their officers. In one instance prior to the First Battle of Bull Run, Upton found a regiment of Zouaves whose pickets had been poorly placed. He took it upon himself to move them, reported to the regimental commander he had done so, and then asked that one of the regiment's majors accompany him to see the results. "The major did not like my interference," Upton reported, "but he said but little." After observing the Seventeenth New York Infantry, he reported that it was in "a miserable condition" while also observing, "The Col. is not a military man, the commissary knows nothing of his business; the consequences is there is no discipline."[4]

Upton's yearning for battle was satisfied on the morning of July 21, 1861. That day Tyler's division moved down the Warrenton Turnpike from the vicinity of Centerville, its mission being to threaten the Confederate position at the Stone Bridge on Bull Run, while the bulk of Brig. Gen. Irvin McDowell's army moved down the Manassas–Sudley Road toward Manassas Junction and into the enemy rear. As the division came into contact with Confederates on the far side of the creek, Upton sighted and fired "the first gun" of the battle near Blackburn's Ford. He subsequently participated in the charge of the Second and Third Michigan and the First Massachusetts above Stone Bridge, where he was wounded in the left side and arm. Later in the day, shortly after leading the Sixty-Ninth New York across the creek and while riding a horse at the head of the column of New Yorkers, Upton encountered a Rebel regiment. Because it was early in the war and both sides were wearing various styles of uniforms, the young officer asked the soldiers their allegiance. Discovering they were secessionists, he tried to move quickly to the rear in order to give his infantry a clear line of fire, but his horse was shot out from under him. After a brief skirmish, the Union troops pushed on to the south.[5]

Without a horse, Upton went to the rear to find another mount. Near a Union aid station, he found one that was unattended and asked for its owner. When Rep. Owen Lovejoy appeared, the officer explained his predicament and asked if he could borrow the animal. Lovejoy, who had been tending to the wounded, permitted him to take the horse, after which the young lieutenant spent the day carrying messages between General Tyler and his subordinates. Upton was appalled by the lack of leadership he saw. "Our troops fought well," he wrote his sister the day after the battle, "but were badly managed." Yet Upton had impressed his superiors with his actions at Bull Run, and his courage distinguished him from many other officers on that bleak day for the Union army. Tyler lauded Upton's bravery in his report, and on the eve of Upton's funeral in 1881, William T. Sherman, who had commanded one of Tyler's brigades, remembered fondly his performance at Bull Run.[6]

The conduct of volunteer soldiers during the battle had favorably impressed Upton, but his opinion of them and of their officers dropped precipitously over time. After participating in a brief excursion across the Potomac, he complained:

> The conduct of our troops was disgraceful beyond expression. They burned buildings, destroyed furniture, stole dishes, chairs, etc., killed chickens, pigs, calves, and everything they could eat. They would take nice sofa-chairs, which they had not the slightest use for, and ten minutes after throw them away. Talk about the barbarity of the rebels! I believe them to be Christians compared to our thieves. . . . One of our volunteer majors walked up to a looking glass . . . and deliberately put his foot through it. I wish I had witnessed it. He would have had the benefit of a court-martial.[7]

Upton's presumptions about the nature and conduct of the war would change as the conflict wore on, and by 1865 he would be participating in the destruction of private and public property in a way that he could not have imagined in 1861. Still, at this early stage of the war, such a practice was abhorrent, and for Upton it was yet another indicator of the poor quality of volunteers and of their officers.

In the aftermath of Bull Run, Upton came to believe even more fervently in the cause for which he was fighting and in the righteousness of his role in it. When a sister wrote him that she feared he would perish in the war, he replied that she should quit worrying. "If I am to be killed in battle," he told her, "no earthly power can avert it. My fate I know not. Whatever it may be I am ready & willing to meet it. I am fighting for right, & trust in God to defend me. If it be his will I desire no more happy or glorious death than on the battlefield in the defense of our flag. I owe all to the Government, and, in return, the Gov't shall have all."[8]

One month later Upton responded to a disturbing letter his sister-in-law Julia had written. "I must confess that I was surprised at the sentiment contained," he wrote. "They certainly were revolutionary. By your appeal to me & the officers of the Army you I understand would have us determine the action of the government or make it the execution of *our* wills instead of being the executors of *its* will. You evidently would inaugurate a military despotism if thereby your views could be enforced." Having rejected the suggestion of what amounted to a military coup, he moved on to address the war's object. "I am opposed to Southern slavery in every form," he explained, "but I will not become a rebel to overthrow it. I have taken an oath to 'bear truth faith & allegiance to the United States' & I hope to observe that oath. Would you have me break it? Slavery is the cause of the rebellion & I believe it is God's providence that it shall be overthrown—it will be the consequence not the object of the war." He concluded: "The rebels wish to establish a monarchy, and are fighting for that object. We are fighting for the Government, and against that object."[9] Though Upton was fighting to eradicate the sin of slavery, he would not sacrifice the nation's republican government to accomplish that goal. He had, in fact, come to the conclusion that the destruction of slavery went hand in hand with that of the South's monarchical government. As it did here, Upton's belief in the value of republican government would shape his views on military policy later in his life.

Less than a month after Bull Run, the lieutenant was assigned to Battery D, Second U.S. Artillery. Almost immediately he developed a "miserable" relationship with his new commander. "I can't agree with [Capt. Edward] Platt," he wrote his sister, "& I am bound to leave his company. . . . I will not serve with him. . . . I would resign before I would serve with Platt during the war." He then described his numerous efforts to move to a different command or even to a headquarters staff. "I will accept [a staff position]," he wrote, "before I will remain with Platt long." Upton believed that he had impressed his superiors in his brief career and hoped that fact might help his quest. "I got [a] considerable reputation in Army circles at Bull Run, & in the next battle I would like to get Upton's battery a name."[10]

By the time the Peninsula Campaign had begun in the spring of 1862, Upton had risen to command of Battery D (Platt had become the division's chief of artillery) and, without participating in battle, had succeeded in making a name for himself within McDowell's First Corps of what had become the Army of the Potomac. While reviewing the corps that winter, the general had asked, "Which is Upton's battery?" The fact that the corps commander apparently thought well of him pleased Upton, though he still yearned to lead his men in battle. "Give me one chance," he wrote, "& I shall be quite contented—if I don't acquit myself with honor, you will never see me again." Yet it must have appeared to Upton that he would miss the upcoming campaign because in mid-March, when the bulk of the Army of the Potomac, under the command of Maj. Gen. George B. McClellan, moved to the tip of the peninsula formed by the James and York Rivers in Virginia, the First Corps remained behind to defend Washington. It was not until mid-April that President Lincoln and Secretary of War Edwin Stanton assented to the transfer of Brig. Gen. William B. Franklin's division to the Peninsula, and with it Upton's battery, one of four under Franklin's command.[11]

McClellan was undertaking a "siege" of the Confederate fortifications that stretched from the James to the York near Yorktown when Franklin's division joined the campaign. After a sharp engagement near Williamsburg on May 5, the Confederates manning those lines pulled out and retreated toward Richmond. McClellan then conceived a bold plan that, if properly executed, might have produced an important victory for the Union: he proposed to move a division up the York River and to land it in the Confederate rear, thereby cutting their line of retreat. McClellan selected Franklin's division for the mission because it had been training to conduct amphibious assaults.[12]

"The missing ingredient" in this amphibious end run, according to Stephen W. Sears, "as was so often the case with McClellan's Army of the Potomac—was timing." Franklin landed his command on the south bank of the York River at the Eltham plantation, opposite West Point, before dawn on May 7. Had this operation taken place on May 5, it is likely that all of Gen. Joe Johnston's Confederate army would have been cut off from Richmond. Two days later, however, Johnston's main body was only five miles away from the Eltham plantation, at Barhamsville, and Franklin no longer had any real chance to cut its line of retreat. Johnston, desiring only to cover his withdrawal, ordered Brig. Gen. John Hood's brigade of Texans to delay any attack Franklin might make. Hood, with an aggressiveness for which he became famous, conducted a furious attack at mid-morning on May 7 that broke several Union regiments.[13]

Upton's battery was in reserve when the Texans made their initial attack, and it was almost noon before his battery engaged the Rebels. From the center of a large field "on a point commanding the approach of the enemy," his guns fired on Confederate soldiers who were occupying a woods fourteen hundred yards away. Upton initially engaged them with fused rounds, but two exploded less than nine hundred yards away, not far from another Union battery. He then switched to solid shot, and as the battle continued he moved his battery to within six hundred yards of the Confederate position. From this exposed location Upton's guns fired spherical-case rounds until the enemy retired from the field. The commander of a Union infantry brigade lauded Upton for his "skill and efficiency," and the division's new chief of artillery, Capt. Richard Arnold, praised the battery's accurate fire, which, he said, "contributed greatly to the repulse of the enemy, and gave all our troops on this flank increased confidence."[14]

Upton continued to distinguish himself through the remainder of the Peninsula Campaign. At the Battle of Gaines's Mills on June 27, Battery D served with Brig. Gen. John Newton's brigade of Brig. Gen. Henry Slocum's division in the Sixth Corps, remaining assigned to Slocum for the remainder of the Seven Days' Battles. Slocum was particularly pleased with the support Upton's and Capt. Josiah Porter's batteries had provided his command. "The officers and men of both these batteries," he later wrote, "have on all occasions manifested that coolness and bravery so necessary to this branch of the service."[15]

After the Peninsula Campaign's ignominious end, Upton's battery, along with the remainder of the Army of the Potomac, withdrew from the vicinity of Richmond and moved to Washington. As Gen. Robert E. Lee's Army of Northern Virginia marched into Maryland following its victory over Maj. Gen. John Pope at Second Bull Run, McClellan moved warily to meet the Confederate invaders. Upton, now a captain and the chief of artillery for Slocum's division, distinguished himself at the Battle of Crampton's Gap on September 14, 1862, and at the Battle of Antietam three days later.[16] As had been the case during the encounter at Eltham plantation, at Antietam Upton quickly forsook spherical case in favor of solid shot, which he found to be "great demoralizers." The Confederates, he reported, "did not appreciate our kindness, and entertained us in a like manner." Rebel sharpshooters took aim at Upton several times during the battle. Late in the afternoon, in an effort to steady his field glasses so he could get a better view of the action, he leaned against a wooden post, which a Minié ball immediately struck. At one critical point in the battle, the captain supervised the placement of an artillery battery whose ensuing volleys broke up an impending Rebel charge against an exposed portion of the Sixth Corps line.

The carnage at Antietam appears to have both appalled and fascinated Upton. "The infantry fighting was terrible," he wrote his sister. "I do not believe there has been harder fighting this century than that between [Maj. Gen. Joseph] Hooker and the rebels in the morning. I have heard of the 'dead lying in heaps,' but never saw it till at this battle. Whole ranks fell together. The trials of the wounded were horrible." Still, he also wrote, "From the time we left Alexandria . . . [after returning from the Peninsula] till the close of the battle of Antietam, I never spent any hours more agreeably or enjoyed myself better." Upton had reason to feel exhilarated, for afterward General Slocum lauded his performance on the field of battle as did his corps commander, Major General Franklin.[17]

Despite his accomplishments and conspicuous bravery, it appeared to Upton as if Antietam might be his last combat for some time, having received orders in August to report to West Point as an instructor. Fortune intervened during the Antietam Campaign, however, and Upton's career took a distinctly different path. Several new regiments had joined the Sixth Corps after it had returned to the Washington area from the Virginia Peninsula, one of which was the 121st New York Volunteer Infantry. Commanded by Col. Richard Franchot, who was also a member of the U.S. House of Representatives, the 121st had been raised in Otsego and Herkimer Counties in August 1862. In the aftermath of the disaster at Second Bull Run, it had been rushed to Washington, D.C. The regiment subsequently had participated in the Battle of Crampton's Gap, though it had not been heavily engaged, and had remained there during the Battle of Antietam.[18]

Afterward the 121st made camp near Bakersville, Maryland. Colonel Franchot's brief time in command, barely a month, had been disastrous. "The unit suffered irreparably from his poor leadership," according to Salvatore Cilella. "Forced marches, severely cold nights without blankets or tents, and a lack of experience crippled the 121st physically and psychologically." Franchot, who for good reason was unpopular with his men, had seen enough of war and was desirous of returning home so he could campaign for reelection; the army discharged him on September 25, 1862. Upton, a fellow New Yorker who himself did not wish to return to West Point, seemed the perfect candidate for the vacant command. On the recommendation of General Slocum and with the intervention of Rep. Reuben Fenton of New York, Upton's orders to West Point were revoked, and he assumed command of the 121st on October 25, 1862. Charles H. Clark had commanded the regiment during the month between Franchot's discharge and Upton's assumption of command. Under Clark the 121st, for the first time, began drilling on a regular basis. His leadership, according to Cilella, resulted in the regiment being brought "into fighting form." These efforts, he concludes, meant that Clark "turned over to Upton a far more disciplined, soldierly regiment" than he had inherited from Franchot.[19]

The 121st's soldiers experienced a "change for the better" almost immediately upon Upton's assumption of command, according to Isaac Best, a soldier in the regiment. Dr. Daniel Holt, the regiment's assistant surgeon, commented similarly, observing that Franchot's resignation and return to New York had come as a great relief. Though the new commander was an unknown quantity, Holt was hopeful that Upton's background as a regular-army officer might mean better times for the regiment. He was especially pleased that the new commander appeared to be a stern disciplinarian. "I think from the general appearance of the man," the doctor wrote his wife, "that when he sets his foot down upon a matter he intends to carry it out. So I live in hope."[20]

The 121st lacked shelters and endured much sickness in its ranks when Upton took command. "Unless a change takes place soon," Dr. Holt believed, "deaths will be as frequent as the most cruel enemy could wish." Upton's first priority, then, was to see that his hospitalized soldiers received proper cared and to procure tents and blankets for the men. These endeavors were somewhat successful, but poor health bedeviled his soldiers throughout Upton's time in command. Similarly, the lack of adequate equipment remained a constant problem. As winter drew near, and despairing of receiving gloves from the army quartermaster, Upton wrote the Ladies Aid Society of Little Falls, New York, requesting that the women of Otsego and Herkimer Counties knit eight hundred pairs of mittens for his solders. When the regiment arrived at Belle Plain, Virginia, in mid-December just prior to the Battle of Fredericksburg, its supply situation had not improved and in fact had grown worse. The 121st's wagons had not yet arrived, its soldiers had little food, and they lacked tents. Upton asked his brigade commander, Col. Henry L. Cake, for permission to place the regiment in a nearby woods that offered some shelter from the elements, but Cake refused the request. The regiment therefore slept in a wind-driven, freezing rain on open ground during a night that was so cold that by morning, the mud had frozen solid. After the Battle of Fredericksburg, Upton wrote his sister Louisa that his soldiers had "but a thin 'shelter tent' & a blanket each—how they manage to keep warm is a mystery," and he declared that such circumstances meant that the army would lose fifteen thousand men to sickness if it did not go into winter quarters soon. Through all of this, Upton earned his soldiers' respect by suffering through the same privations as they. "Our Colonel," one member of the regiment wrote home, "sleeps on the ground without any tent the same as the rest of us do and is always on duty."[21]

Part of Upton's success in reducing the regiment's sick list can be attributed to his emphasis on discipline. The 121st's camp was in poor condition when Upton took command, but through his efforts it "was newly ordered and cleaned up." Noncommissioned officers who failed to ensure their soldiers' cleanliness and the serviceability of their equipment faced certain demotion. The young colonel also insisted that routine inspections become more exacting and held his officers strictly accountable for any shortcomings. This emphasis on discipline went hand in hand with Upton's predilection for drill, for he believed that the regiment would not acquit itself well in battle unless it drilled well and would not drill well without discipline. The 121st engaged in drill incessantly whenever it stayed in place for more than a day or two. Indeed. judged by the diary of Dean Pierce, in March and April 1863 the regiment did little else but drill, undergo inspection, and perform picket duty. The men spent a typical morning in company drill, battalion drill began at 1:00 P.M., regimental parade was at 4:00 P.M., and officers attended a "School of Instruction" at 6:00 P.M. "At first some of the boys thought he was severe in discipline and drill," Maj. Douglas Campbell remembered of Upton sixteen years later, "but when people began flocking from distant encampments to witness our dress parades, and when in battle they saw the regiment standing like a solid wall, these very men thanked the colonel." Both officers and soldiers became enthusiastic about their regiment, and they were particularly pleased when they became known as "Upton's Regulars" within the Army of the Potomac, a designation that certainly flattered their colonel too.[22]

Still, the 121st had its share of disciplinary problems. In some instances, such as that of a sentinel who lost his musket while on duty, the punishment was a wicked tongue-lashing by Upton that, in this case, left the private believing he "would rather spend a month in the guard-house than have him [Upton] talk and look so." Upton dealt with more serious crimes much more sternly. The day after the Battle of Fredericksburg, six soldiers "committed an offense," he informed the regiment, "the punishment of which is death." Upton attributed the unspecified infraction to the fact that the soldiers, who had been in the service only four months, "did not comprehend the magnitude of the crime before committing it." He punished the soldiers, four privates and two corporals, by requiring them to do ten extra tours of guard duty over the next month and demoted the corporals to privates.[23]

Desertion was a very serious problem in the 121st during the winter of 1862–63. When it reached near-epidemic proportions in mid-January 1863, Upton's regimental adjutant wrote the editor of the *Herkimer County Journal* requesting that the paper publish the names of thirteen soldiers who were "cowards and deserters," having left "immediately after the Regt. had received the usual orders to provide itself with three days [*sic*] rations and sixty rounds of cartridges preparatory to meeting the enemy."[24] The day after he dispatched this letter, nineteen more soldiers "took leg bail." In late-February Upton charged three sergeants and two corporals with desertion. The subsequent court-martial found all guilty, ordered them reduced in rank to private, and sentenced them to eighteen months' hard labor. An even more serious incident happened in March, when a private began spreading the rumor that the regiment had never been mustered into the service of the United States and its soldiers therefore were being illegally held. The private's remedy for this "crime" was for the men to stack arms and refuse to drill. Upton charged him with sedition, and a general court-martial sentenced him to one years' confinement at hard labor at Dry Tortugas, the forfeiture of ten dollars per month during the confinement, and having his head shaved upon return to the 121st.[25]

Upton's most troubling disciplinary problem involved one of the regiment's assistant surgeons, Stephen B. Valentine. Shortly after taking command Upton reported to the Sixth Corps medical director that Valentine was "a surgeon of very little experience, no energy and no disposition to do his duty." He complained that the doctor had failed to procure enough medical supplies to support the regiment's movement from Maryland to Virginia and seldom appeared concerned with the comfort or cleanliness of the soldiers. "From the large sick report we have had," he concluded sarcastically, "I am constrained to believe that he is not stifled [sic] in his profession." Despite Upton's request that Valentine appear before a medical board to determine his fitness for his position, the doctor remained with the regiment.[26]

After the collapse of the Army of the Potomac's "Mud March" in January 1863, Valentine sent more than seventy 121st soldiers to the hospital at Aquia Creek because, Dr. Holt believed, he was too lazy to be bothered with seeing them during morning sick call. "This wholesale sending off of the men," Holt observed, "made Col. Upton rear like a mad bull." Shortly after this incident Valentine again ran afoul of his colonel, and this time the surgeon could not escape serious consequences. In late-January Upton received a sworn statement from a soldier who charged that the assistant surgeon had forced another man to pay $150 before he would sign the latter's medical discharge. In a subsequent letter to the New York adjutant general, Upton recounted the doctor's prior performance, stating that Valentine had "neglected the sick and been faithless to his trust." But now Valentine had gone too far. "This last act of his, so dishonorable to himself & prejudicial to the interests of the Government," Upton wrote, "demands prompt punishment, & it is but due to the honor of his Regiment that his name be stricken in disgrace from its rolls." Charged with fraud and incompetence, Valentine was dismissed from the service.[27]

Though Upton was a strict disciplinarian, he also developed a system of rewards for those who performed their duties well. He promoted those in his regiment who had been good soldiers in camp and on the march or had been brave in battle, and he took pains to ensure that his men understood promotion was a matter of competition, not favoritism. Upton did not tolerate incompetent officers or noncommissioned officers, but he rewarded enlisted men who were "deserving, efficient, and meritorious." Early in his tenure as the commander of the 121st, the colonel made it known that soldiers who showed promise could be promoted to the rank of lieutenant. At the same time he had little tolerance for officers who did not measure up to his standards. By the beginning of the Chancellorsville Campaign, so many of the regiment's original officers had resigned or had transferred that there was "a crisis in leadership."[28]

Despite the resultant shortage of officers, Upton resisted politicians' efforts to influence promotions in *his* regiment. When Charles Evans, New York's assistant adjutant general, requested that a sergeant be promoted to lieutenant, Upton replied that the man in question was "a good soldier & will undoubtedly earn a commission, but I cannot at present recommend him." The colonel informed Evans that he had established a policy within the regiment that no soldier would be promoted until he passed "a thorough examination." Its purpose, he explained, was "to bring the Regt. to the highest state of discipline and efficiency and to accomplish this end the greatest care must be shown for the selection of officers." Upton then indicated he had been swamped with petitions from "influential men" in Otsego and Herkimer Counties seeking commissions for friends and relatives. He had not filled those requests "because I have not found the men with the requisite energy, fitness & intelligence to make good Officers." "I trust His Excellency Governor Seymour will allow me to fill the vacancies in the manner proposed," he concluded, "& when filled, I will promise a Regt. which shall be not only an honor to the State, but to the whole Country."[29]

Yet Upton was not entirely immune to political pressure in the appointment of officers to his regiment. In June 1863 Dr. Holt was dismayed to discover that he had not been selected to be the 121st's chief surgeon and that the position had been given to Dr. John Slocum, the brother of General Slocum.[30] "You ask *why* I am not promoted," he wrote to his wife:

> I will tell you in a very few words—*favoritism*. . . . General [*sic*] Upton owes his promotion from *Lieutenant* in the *regular* service, to Colonel of *Volunteers*, to the influence of General Slocum, a regular army officer, and he (Upton) to reciprocate the favor, recommends Slocum's brother, who is an Assistant in the 122nd N.Y. to Surgeon in this regiment. Having none to press my claims or in any way to interest themselves in my behalf, I remain where I started with all the work to do—responsibility to carry and none of the advantages arriving from the increase of labor.[31]

Holt's complaints have the ring of truth, but it is almost certain that his poor health also factored into Upton's decision to appoint Slocum. Holt was very sick at the time and in fact had never been well during his time of service with the regiment.[32] In any event Upton, as a twenty-three-year-old regimental commander, not only had implemented a promotion system that stressed competency as measured by examinations as well as through performance of duty but also resisted, if not altogether successfully, the pressure politicians had placed on him in an effort to secure promotions for soldiers under his command. Both experiences likely influenced the promotion reforms he later recommended for the army.

Upton's religious beliefs were ever-present throughout the time he commanded the 121st. The regiment's soldiers knew he was "strictly temperate, and decidedly religious in conduct." Isaac Best observed that the colonel "was not ashamed to keep a well worn Bible on his desk, and his conversation was always clean and without profanity." This religiosity, Best believed, helped him earn the respect of his officers and men.[33] Upton's convictions reflected of those of many of his soldiers. "How can we, as a nation," Dr. Holt wrote to his wife in April 1863,

> expect the smiles of heaven when we hold in bondage, sell and chastise our fellow man for the simple reason that the color of his skin is not like our own, though created by the same hand and sustained by the same power. I tell you Louisa, *we never shall succeed until we let the oppressed go free. Never, never, never will God Grant us the victory and establish our government until it can be done in righteousness.* We cannot roll the sin of slavery under our tongue as a sweet morsel and claim the divine flavor. It is impious to call upon God for a blessing while we dare have such cruelty in our hearts. Then let us put away the evil from among us to be really what we profess—a God-fearing and brother-loving people. Then and not until then, will peace flow in our land like a mighty river.[34]

Dr. Holt, like Upton, was participating in a holy crusade, his aim being to rid the land of a terrible sin, thereby preparing the way for God. Because Otsego and Herkimer Counties bordered the Burned Over District, it seems likely most soldiers in the 121st New York held similar convictions. Still, Upton's religious beliefs seldom entered into his day-to-day conduct of regimental business. One of the few instances it did was in the celebration of Thanksgiving in November 1862, when he asked the men of his regiment to "invoke His blessing upon our country and the success of our arms. He alone can give us safety through our troubles, and to him the giver of all good let us look for deliverance in this hour of our national peril."[35]

The events that transpired in the weeks after that holiday must have caused Upton to wonder whose side God was on. Maj. Gen. Ambrose Burnside, who had replaced McClellan as the commander of the Army of the Potomac in early November, moved his command to the banks of the Rappahannock River opposite Fredericksburg, Virginia. There he hoped to cross the river unopposed and force Lee's Army of Northern Virginia to retreat toward Richmond. Poor staff work, however, prevented the necessary pontoon bridges from arriving in a timely manner. By the time they did show up, so had Lee's army, occupying the formidable terrain west and south of the town. Still, Burnside was determined to cross and take on the Confederates there.[36]

During the ill-fated battle that followed, the 121st New York remained in the Sixth Corps's First Division, now commanded by Maj. Gen. William "Baldy" Smith and Brig. Gen. William Brooks, respectively, and was a part of Major General Franklin's "Grand Division." Franklin began crossing the Rappahannock south of Fredericksburg on December 11 and engaged Lt. Gen. Thomas "Stonewall" Jackson's corps during the subsequent battle on December 13. Positioned on the Franklin's right flank, the Sixth Corps played but a small role in the fighting, and the 121st was relegated to picket duty near Deep Run. The regiment remained there for several days afterward under almost constant harassing fire. At one point Upton personally directed a Union battery in an effort to suppress Confederate artillery. Though the regiment had not participated in the slaughter that took place at the foot of Marye's Heights, the army's rumor mill kept the men informed of the disaster that had occurred there. Afterward the 121st, along with the remainder of Franklin's Grand Division, withdrew across the Rappahannock.[37]

After the brief respite that followed the debacle at Fredericksburg, the regiment took part in the Army of the Potomac's Mud March in January 1863. Burnside hoped to turn Lee's left flank at Fredericksburg by marching his army up the north bank of the Rappahannock and crossing the river at Banks' Ford. The 121st was one of the few Union units to reach that location because two days of near-continuous rain had mired supply wagons and artillery caissons in knee-deep mud. Horses and mules collapsed and died, their bodies sinking into the mud, and soldiers exhausted themselves while marching only a few hundred yards. Burnside eventually called off the maneuver, and the army established its winter camp across the river from Fredericksburg.[38]

The first true test of the 121st's mettle and of that of its commander came in May 1863 during the Chancellorsville Campaign. By then Maj. Gen. Joseph Hooker was the Army of the Potomac's new commander, and he proposed to move the bulk of his force up the Rappahannock to a point nearly twenty miles above Fredericksburg. From there he expected to cross both the Rappahannock and Rapidan Rivers, after which the army would move east and into rear of the Army of Northern Virginia, which he hoped would still be in its entrenchments near Fredericksburg. Maj. Gen. John Reynolds's First Corps and the Sixth Corps, now under the command of Maj. Gen. John Sedgwick, remained behind facing Fredericksburg from across the Rappahannock, their mission being to distract Lee from the army's move to the west. Hooker designated Sedgwick overall commander of the roughly thirty-five thousand soldiers in both corps;

the Sixth Corps remained there when Reynolds's corps subsequently followed the route of Hooker's main body.

It initially appeared that Hooker's plan had succeeded in surprising the Confederates, but Lee pulled the majority of his army out of its Fredericksburg entrenchments and halted the Union advance as it emerged from the Wilderness near Chancellorsville Tavern on May 1. The next day he sent Stonewall Jackson's corps on its famous flank march, which resulted in the collapse of the Army of the Potomac's right wing. Hooker then withdrew into a defensive position in front of the Rapidan and Rappahannock and ordered Sedgwick to assault the few Confederates who remained in the entrenchments near Fredericksburg. Once Sedgwick had forced the Rebels there to retreat, Hooker expected him to move west down the Orange Plank Road and into Lee's rear.[39]

Because Maj. Gen. Jubal Early's division was the sole Confederate unit occupying the position at the foot of Marye's Heights, the assault was a far cry from the bloody repulse there of the previous December. Brig. Gen. William Brooks's division, to which the 121st New York still belonged, had crossed the Rappahannock in the early morning hours of April 29 and had occupied a position on the southern edge of Fredericksburg. The Sixth Corps's remaining two divisions, commanded by Brig. Gen. Albion Howe and Maj. Gen. John Newton, followed during the evening of May 2 and seized the town itself. The next morning Howe's and Newton's divisions assaulted the Rebel position and pushed Early out of his entrenchments, forcing the Confederates to flee west toward Lee's main body near Chancellorsville. Brooks's division followed those of Howe and Newton through the breach and up the heights that dominate Fredericksburg from the west. Marching quickly and without a halt, the soldiers of the Sixth Corps were nearly exhausted by the time they reached the crest of this substantial hill mass five miles west of town, the day's heat and the weight of eight days' rations having taken their toll.

The corps's movement west continued after a short rest, with Brooks's division in the lead, Brig. Gen. Joseph Bartlett's brigade of that division posted to the left side of the Orange Plank Road. The 121st New York deployed immediately to the left of the Plank Road and, led by a heavy skirmish line, formed the brigade's right flank. Bartlett encountered scattered resistance from Confederate skirmishers and from some artillery, but his advance was unchecked until the brigade was roughly one-half mile east of Salem Church. There his men encountered Confederates who had taken cover in woods behind a rail fence. Beyond the trees, just west of Salem Church, a substantial Rebel force occupied entrenchments that had been dug the previous December. Bartlett ordered the 121st to continue moving forward, which it did despite heavy fire. Upton later commented that his soldiers advanced "without creating the slightest

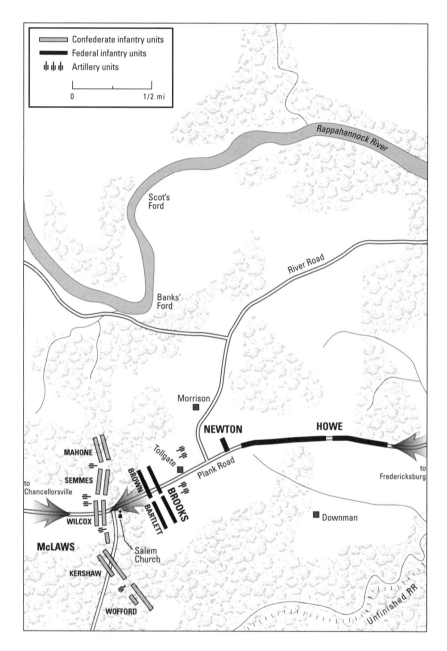

Battle of Salem Church, 4:00 P.M., May 3, 1863. Map by Erin Greb. Copyright © 2017 by the University of Oklahoma Press.

confusion." At the height of the battle, the colonel's horse bolted toward the enemy lines after being struck by a Minié Ball, and Upton had to throw "himself from the saddle to avoid being captured." Still, the regiment advanced, at one point forcing the Confederates out of their position near the church, but the Rebels rallied twenty or thirty yards farther back. "They poured volley after volley into us," one of the New Yorkers wrote home the next day, "but the 121st did not retreat until the old Regiments did for the reason of flank fire. . . . We did not have any panic in our ranks but retired until we came to a fence then rallied & the grape and canister strewed the ground with rebels. . . . If our whole brigade had remained steady we might have drove them." But it was not to be. With both of its flanks exposed and devastated by a withering fire, the regiment withdrew. The repulse of Sedgwick's assault at Salem Church and his corps's subsequent withdrawal across the Rappahannock at Banks' Ford, along with the remainder of the Army of the Potomac at U.S. Ford, brought the Chancellorsville Campaign to an end.[40]

The 121st New York had suffered grievously from the engagement at Salem Church—48 soldiers had been killed, 49 died later of their wounds, 124 others were wounded, and 55 were missing in action, a total of 276 casualties in a regiment that numbered but 453 soldiers that day, a 60.9 percent casualty rate. Included in these numbers were Dr. Holt and Upton's brother, Henry, a lieutenant in the regiment. Both had been captured, and Henry had been severely wounded, shot in the right shoulder and in the upper portion of his right lung.[41] "There is not half the Regiment left," a soldier wrote in his diary, "the most wounded I ever saw." Dr. Holt concurred, observing, "we were almost totally annihilated." In a war infamous for decimating units that attacked over open ground, this was the twenty-second-highest casualty rate incurred by any Union regiment in a single battle, while the 97 soldiers killed gives the 121st New York the distinction of having suffered the tenth-largest number of deaths in a Union regiment during one battle.[42]

These losses combined with New York's helter-skelter recruiting policies to present Upton with a true crisis. The regiment, with an effective strength of fewer than two hundred soldiers, badly needed an infusion of replacements. These came from five other New York regiments that had been recruited for two years' service and whose period of service had expired but had a number of three-year soldiers in their ranks. These soldiers, though still having a year remaining, had signed on with the understanding that they would remain in the same regiment for the duration of their enlistment. Many believed their transfer to the 121st New York constituted a breach of those terms. "They are disposed to be mutinous," one of Upton's officers wrote, " I am fearful we shall see trouble with them as they say they will not go into a fight." The colonel confronted this problem by appealing to the soldiers' patriotism while also telling them he intended to enforce rigidly the orders that brought them to his command. "After that they worked with us," Isaac Best wrote, "and they never kicked or flinched in any field." They did, however, appeal their case to a board of investigation that ruled in their favor. On review, though, Secretary of War Edwin Stanton dismissed the case with the remark, "Might as well disband the Army"—or so said the regiment's rumor mill.[43]

Upton's 121st New York Infantry performed the unenviable task of being the rear guard when Sedgwick's Sixth Corps marched north in June 1863 in response to Lee's invasion of Maryland and Pennsylvania. The regiment began its move at midnight on the evening of June 14–15, leaving its camp at White Oak Church, Virginia, during a driving rainstorm punctuated "by vivid flashes of lightening with accompanying peals of thunder." It was a miserable night for the regiment's soldiers as they marched along roads that had been traveled before them by tens of thousands of men as well as by thousands of horses, wagons, and artillery limbers, the downpour turning the roadways into quagmires. The next two days proved little better, for the heat of the Virginia summer quickly dried the red-clay roads, and the soldiers' marching created a thick layer of dust that caused "a choking thirst." Water was scarce, and because they were bringing up the rear, not only of the corps but of the entire army, the New Yorkers found the surrounding countryside "had been stripped of everything that would sustain troops." After two days' hard marching, the regiment rested for a day at Fairfax Station, where according to one of its officers, a rainstorm "greatly refreshed us, so that on the morning on the 18th of June when we moved out again it was with lighter steps and more cheerful feelings." After a short march the regiment stopped at Fairfax Court House, staying there for nine days.[44]

The 121st began moving north once again on June 27, but rather than joining the pursuit of Lee's army, it moved toward the Washington defenses. The next day it renewed its march north, arriving in Manchester, Maryland, on June 30. Late the following evening, Upton received two startling pieces of news. First, he heard that two Union corps had clashed with Lee's army twenty-two miles to the northwest near Gettysburg, Pennsylvania, that day, and that the remainder of the army was moving there to join the battle. Second, he learned that his brigade commander, General Bartlett, had been promoted to command of the division and that he, Colonel Upton, had been appointed commander of the Second Brigade. Ordered to close up with the main body of the Army of the Potomac, the brigade, which consisted of the Fifth Maine, the Ninety-Fifth and Ninety-Sixth Pennsylvania, and the 121st New York, was on the road almost immediately, departing Manchester at 10:00 P.M. on July 1.[45]

The brigade did not take the most direct route from Manchester to Gettysburg because initially it had been ordered to Taneytown, Maryland. As a result, the men covered thirty-two miles before arriving on the battlefield late in the afternoon of July 2. It had been a grueling march of almost sixteen hours with only brief stops; the soldiers were exhausted. After a three-hour rest the brigade moved to the extreme left of the Union line near Round Top, where it reinforced those elements of the Third and Fifth Corps that John Hood's assault had so sorely tested there earlier that afternoon. Writing to a sister afterward, Upton badly exaggerated the role his soldiers played in the day's action. "We arrived just in time to reinforce our left," he reported, "which was hard pressed by Longstreet & slowly giving way. Ten minutes later & the battle had been lost." As the brigade occupied its position, General Bartlett returned to its command, and Upton reverted to command of the 121st New York. Though July 3 proved to be the most dramatic, if not the most important, day of the Battle of Gettysburg, it was one of relative inactivity for the regiment. Placed in front of Little Round Top, where it provided infantry support for an artillery battery positioned there, the New Yorkers were far away from Cemetery Ridge, Pickett's Charge, and the so-called high-water mark of the Confederacy. Only one of the regiment's soldiers was wounded during the battle, that by artillery fire on July 3.[46]

Upton's return to regimental command was brief. On July 4, after the Second Brigade had participated in a foray toward the Confederate lines on Seminary Ridge, General Bartlett again assumed command of the Third Division, and Upton once again took command of the Second Brigade.[47] This promotion precipitated a change in the colonel's attitude toward his role in the war. Previously he had been willing to accept his fate, be it life or death, promotion or toiling in obscurity. This no longer was true. "The com'd of a brigade is a halfway step between Col & Brig Gen," he wrote his sister from Gettysburg the day he took command, "and I shall try to take the full step in the next battle." One reason he was certain of promotion was that he had seen few generals who met his standards for combat command. As early as 1862, in the aftermath of the disaster at Fredericksburg, Upton had expressed grave doubts about the quality of the leadership in the Army of the Potomac. "Never as yet," he wrote to his sister Louisa, "have I seen evidence of great generalship displayed on our side. It is astounding & depresses one's spirits to know & feel this." He did not entirely blame the generals, however, for he had a vague sense that Washington politicians were somehow responsible for the army's recurring defeats.[48]

Upton's opinion of his superiors was even more critical one year later. "I think our generals betray in some instances total ignorance of human nature," he wrote one of his brothers in November 1863.

They fail to appeal to the emotions or the passions of their men. You know not the good a single word does a soldier when he is under fire. He feels that his commanding officer is directing him & looking at his actions. . . . Our generals I have never heard utter a word of encouragement, either before or after entering a battle. I have never seen them ride along the lines & tell each regiment that they held an important position, & that they were expected to hold to the last. I have never heard them appeal to the love every soldier has for his colors or to his patriotism. Neither have I ever seen a general thank his troops after the action for the gallantry they have displayed.[49]

Compared to these inept generals, the soldiers Upton had commanded, all of whom except Battery D, Second U.S. Artillery, had been volunteers, had very much impressed him. "No soldier in the world," he declared, "can equal the American, *if properly commanded*. He possesses all the enthusiasm of the French, and the bulldog tenacity which has always characterized the English." Upton believed that the 121st New York's actions at Salem Church and its marching 109 miles in six days to get to Gettysburg were examples of what soldiers could do if properly motivated and led.[50]

The young colonel's frustration with the generalship displayed in the Army of the Potomac went much further than the question of tactical leadership. He believed that a vigorous pursuit in the aftermath of Gettysburg would have destroyed Lee's army north of the Potomac River. He approved, however, of the army's inactivity *after* Lee had successfully withdrawn across the Potomac, concluding that the summer in Virginia was far too hot for campaigning. "Both armies seem to have taken a defensive position," he wrote, "and are gathering themselves for the storm that will burst upon them probably in November. I think it decidedly good policy on our part to wait." His personal health, no doubt, influenced this assessment, as he was ill at the time, so much so that in late-August he took twenty days' sick leave for an acute case of dysentery.[51]

By the fall of 1863, the lack of significant action had tried Upton's patience. Referring to the conduct of the recent Mine Run Campaign by Maj. Gen. George Meade, commander of the Army of the Potomac following Chancellorsville, he wrote, "I can, but I ought not to criticise." Yet by implication Upton *was* critical of Meade's failure to meet and defeat Lee's army that fall, claiming that the Army of the Potomac had "followed up leisurely" the Army of Northern Virginia's withdrawal behind the Rappahannock River in early November. Where in July it had appeared to Upton that Gettysburg had been "the decisive battle of the war," by November it seemed to him as if the conflict would drag on for many more months. Indeed, he predicted the course the war would take during the coming year as well as the escalation in casualties that would occur. "Our armies at all points should be reinforced so as to far outnumber the enemy," he wrote one of his sisters. "In the next struggle there ought not to be the possibility of defeat. We have got men enough, and we have only to bring them out. In future, the hardest fighting will be in the East." The colonel also believed that the war would come to a successful conclusion if Mobile, Alabama, and Charleston, South Carolina, were captured and if the Union's Army of the Tennessee were to drive to Atlanta. All told, this was a rather remarkable reading of future events for so junior an officer, especially given the inability of many higher-ranking officers to articulate a strategic vision for the war's prosecution.[52]

Upton's troops had not been completely idle after Gettysburg. In particular, he appears to have been engaged in a grudge match with Lt. Col. John Mosby. "Mosby the guerilla infests this this locality, " he wrote a sister, "& if he gets impertinent he may get chastised but I do not think there will be much trouble." Yet the very day Upton wrote this letter, Dr. Holt reported to his wife that Mosby had bamboozled the young colonel. Near Warrenton, Virginia, a young woman had entered the brigade's camp and asked Upton to provide a guard to protect her property from destruction by Union soldiers. He agreed to the proposal and sent one of his aides and one other soldier to safeguard the woman's house, barely one-half mile away. When the two soldiers arrived, members of Mosby's band seized both, after which the young woman returned to Upton and asked that two more soldiers be sent to her property! Needless to say, he denied this request. Eventually Upton became disgusted with the "bushwhackers'" audacity and in late-August undertook an expedition to capture the partisan leader. This was a total failure as Mosby, whom sympathetic civilians had warned of Upton's excursion, had disappeared into the mountains.[53]

The lack of combat action in the East had one other, very personal effect on Upton: it delayed what he thought was his rightful promotion to brigadier general, for without heroic success in battle, he believed, he would remain a lowly colonel. Upton, according to Peter Michie, was not "blind to his own fitness for the desired promotion," and the "restiveness" that is apparent in his letters of this period was the result "of the delay in the only recognition which the Government could bestow." Despairing of being promoted anytime in the near future, the colonel began a concerted campaign to move that process along. He sought support from officers under whom he had served as well as from his existing chain of command. He must have found the results gratifying, for among those who enthusiastically supported his promotion were Brig. Gens. Joseph Bartlett, Horatio Wright (Upton's division commander), and Frank Wheaton (a brigade commander in the Sixth Corps); Maj. Gens. Daniel Butterfield, John Sedgwick, and Henry Slocum; and the commander of the Army of the Potomac, Major General Meade. "He possesses skill energy and devotion," Butterfield wrote to Maj. Gen. Henry Halleck, the commanding general of the army. "His presence has been felt in whatever position he has served. He has been noticed for gallantry on every field where he has been engaged." General Wheaton wrote directly to President Lincoln, lauding Upton's accomplishments as the commander of an artillery battery as well as that of an infantry regiment and brigade. In writing to Secretary of War Edwin Stanton, General Slocum stated that Upton was "a brave and skillful officer on the field of battle and an excellent manager of troops while in camp."[54]

Before this campaign for promotion could come to fruition, Upton was involved in a spectacular tactical coup, an episode that identified him as one of the more competent and daring brigade commanders in the Army of the Potomac. The Army of Northern Virginia had withdrawn behind the Rappahannock River near Kelly's Ford in mid-October 1863 after Lee had failed to entice Meade into battle near Centreville. The Rebel commander had left two brigades of infantry on the river's north bank so they might be used to threaten the Union army's flank if it attempted a crossing at Kelly's Ford. The Confederate position, where an Orange and Alexandria Railroad bridge had been destroyed and replaced by a pontoon span, had been "fortified with much care and labor," according to Brigadier General Wright. It consisted of one large redoubt occupied by infantry and several pieces of artillery situated on a bluff above the pontoon bridge; a smaller redoubt two hundred yards to the west, also with infantry and artillery; rifle pits that extended from each fortification and circled back to the river, thus forming a semicircular defensive position; and a heavy line of skirmishers in front of these works.[55]

On November 7 Meade ordered the Sixth Corps, temporarily under the command of Wright, and the Fifth Corps to assault and eliminate this bridgehead. The Fifth Corps, which had formed to the left of the railroad, was to conduct a supporting attack, and Wright, whose corps had formed in two lines of battle that extended from the railroad to the banks of the Rappahannock, had the mission of seizing the larger of the two Rebel redoubts. He planned to do this by capturing a ridge one mile in front of the Confederate position from which he could bombard the redoubts with artillery. This, Wright hoped, would drive the defenders out of their fortifications. The Third Division, Sixth Corps captured the ridge in the late afternoon of November 7, but the subsequent artillery bombardment neither panicked nor substantially harmed the Confederates in the redoubts.

At this point Wright considered calling off the attack, but several factors convinced him to press forward. First, the line of rifle pits to the south and west of the redoubts had been pierced rather easily at several locations. Second, he believed that the bluff on which the fortifications were situated would screen any assaulting column from Confederate artillery fire that might come from the far side of the river. Third, he thought that the time of day was in the Union's favor. "The darkness," Wright wrote later, "which was fast approaching, was favourable to the attack. The remaining daylight enabled the troops to see what they had to do before reaching the works, while the succeeding darkness would prevent the enemy on the opposite bank from firing where they could not distinguish friend from foe." Finally, he believed that he had under his command some of the finest soldiers in the army who were more than capable of conducting a complex, nighttime attack.

Wright therefore ordered Brig. Gen. David Russell's First Division to assault the larger of the two fortifications. Earlier that afternoon the division had advanced to and occupied the rifle pits at the foot of the bluff. As dusk fell, the division's Third Brigade stormed the larger redoubt and captured it. This exposed the brigade to a severe enfilading fire from the rifle pits to its right. Russell ordered Upton to bring up two of his regiments, the 121st New York and the Fifth Maine, to "dislodge" the Rebels who were there. The colonel quickly moved his soldiers forward, ordering them to load as they moved in order to avoid any delay. On his arrival at the redoubt, Russell pointed out the rifle pits to be taken. "Under cover of darkness," Upton wrote, "the two regiments formed within 100 yards of the enemy (who still continued his fire), unslung knapsacks and fixed bayonets. Strict orders were given not to fire. Everything being ready the line advanced at quick time to within 30 yards of the works, when the order to charge was given. The work was carried at the point of the bayonet, and without firing a shot. The enemy fought stubbornly over their colors, but being overpowered soon surrendered." Before the final assault Upton gave a stirring speech within earshot of the Confederate trenches. "Men of the 121st New York," he said, "your friends at home and your country expect every man to do his duty on this occasion. Some of us have got to die, but remember you are going to heaven. When I give the command to charge you move forward. If they fire upon you, I will move six lines of battle over you and bayonet every one of them." Not only did the speech inspire his own soldiers, but its reference to "six lines of battle" apparently frightened the Confederates into believing that the assaulting force was much larger than it was.[56]

As Upton reorganized his command in the captured rifle pits, he discovered that Rebels to his immediate right were in complete confusion and hastily moving to the rear. Taking advantage of the situation, he ordered portions of both regiments to charge at the double quick so as to cut off the their line of retreat. The Federals reached the pontoon bridge ahead of the bulk of the retreating Confederates and forced their surrender. Almost simultaneously, heavy musket fire from Upton's soldiers prevented Rebels on the far bank from burning the pontoon bridge, resulting in its capture.[57]

The attack on the Confederate position at Rappahannock Station had been a stunning success. Not only was the enemy bridgehead gone but also, thanks to Upton's bold action, the Army of the Potomac had an intact bridge across the Rappahannock River, thus making Lee's position on its south bank untenable and compelling him to abandon it. More impressively, there had been few Union casualties, Upton's brigade having sustained but eleven dead and fifty-two wounded. The Confederates, on the other hand, had suffered a humiliating setback. Not only had they lost a formidable and operationally important bridgehead on the Rappahannock's north bank but also lost to Upton's brigade alone four cannon, eight colors, and sixteen hundred prisoners. This tactical coup was, to this point in time, unprecedented for the Army of the Potomac. No less an admirer of Confederate leadership than Douglas Southall Freeman conceded, "The real explanation of the reverse was . . . [a] sound Federal plan of attack had been executed admirably by courageous men"; he was particularly laudatory of Sedgwick's, Russell's, and Upton's actions.[58]

Upton's performance at Rappahannock Station impressed his superiors, and afterward they undertook a renewed effort to secure his promotion to brigadier general. Generals Wright, Sedgwick, and Meade wrote the army's adjutant general and argued vigorously that Upton should be promoted, all three insisting his actions at Rappahannock Station alone were proof he deserved the rank of brigadier general. These efforts proved fruitless, and Upton knew why. In a private meeting Meade had told him he would never receive his much-desired and well-deserved promotion without the intervention of a prominent politician. This judgment reinforced the New Yorker's already pronounced distrust of the role political influence played in the commissioning and promotion processes. "The recommendation of those officers whose lives have been periled in every battle of the war have been outweighed by the baneful influence of the paltry politicians," Upton lamented to his sister. "Although the rank of a general may never be conferred on me, yet I hope to leave my friends abundant proof that I merited the honor, but that it was unjustly withheld. Had there been but one friend in Washington my services would have been rewarded but I have not had one."[59]

Despite his disdain for the role of politics in the army's promotions, Upton was more than willing to use political influence to secure his advancement. In April 1864 he wrote his sister: "I have not fully despaired of receiving promotion, *but I have despaired of receiving it in the manner honorable to a soldier.* It is now solely the reward of political influence, and not of merit, and this when a government is fighting for its own existence." It appears Upton had come to this conclusion sometime earlier, for in February 1864 he arranged for Major General Sedgwick to provide the colonel's brother John, who had become prominent in Michigan politics, with a letter of introduction to President Lincoln. "His [John's] brother," the general wrote to Lincoln, "is one of the most promising young officers in the service. His recommendations are of the highest character and he has on several occasions deserved promotion by gallant conduct on the field. I earnestly ask your favorable consideration of his case. I consider his claims to this appointment superior to those of any other officer in my command."[60]

Meade's April 1864 conversation with Upton appears to have prompted him to take an even more direct approach. Simultaneous to complaining to his sister about the politics involved in securing promotion, the colonel wrote to Sen. Edwin D. Morgan of New York inquiring about the status of the commission of Brig. Gen. Kenner Garrard. Having heard that Garrard's commission had been revoked and believing him to be from New York, Upton asked about the resulting vacancy. "I only ask that the recommendations of my superior officers may be compared with those of the other applicants," he wrote Morgan.

> [W]hen, if it be found that other officers have done more for the honor and reputation of the State, the welfare of her troops, or have rendered the Country more valuable and important service, let them be promoted before me. I ask no further favor than for merit to be the test.
>
> Gen. Meade has assured me that I will never be promoted unless the State becomes interested in my behalf, and he specially recommended me to submit my case to Your Excellency, as no one could have the interest of the service and the welfare of the state more at heart.

Upton closed his letter by telling Morgan he was confident that he could "expect justice at your hands."[61] This is a very revealing piece of correspondence, for it shows Upton was willing to resort to seeking political patronage to achieve the rank he felt he had earned. In it he appealed to the vanity of a New York politician by stressing the honor he had brought to the state and the manner in which the colonel had cared for his soldiers. He nevertheless asked Morgan to judge his request strictly on its merit. Upton was at once playing the political game he despised while doing so by his "rules" so that he might, in his mind, maintain his honor and integrity.

The letter had its desired result. In May Senator Morgan wrote Secretary of War Stanton recommending Upton's promotion. "Although young," Morgan told Stanton that Upton "has few superiors for military capacity and courage." Asking that he not be forgotten "when you have occasion to appoint an officer of that rank [brigadier general]," the senator recounted that Upton had "the confidence fully of his superior officers and especially of Maj. Gen. Meade."[62] This letter, written on May 13, 1864, might have aided Upton in his search for promotion, but events on the battlefields of Virginia had overtaken his efforts in political circles: three days earlier he had led an astoundingly successful assault during the Battle of Spotsylvania.

Stephen Ambrose argues that Upton had learned an important lesson at the Battle of Salem Church. "Never again," he states, "did Upton attempt a frontal, daytime assault until careful preparations had been made." With the exception of the meeting engagement at Cold Harbor the following June, Ambrose is correct in this assertion. He also contends that the young colonel had learned that modern weapons' firepower militated against the use of linear tactics and instead placed a premium on skirmishers and attacking in short rushes.[63] This too is factually correct. Upton, however, had learned more than tactical lessons in the nearly eight years between his admission to West Point in 1856 and the eve of the 1864 Overland Campaign.

Over the course of his five years at the U.S. Military Academy, Upton had developed a distrust of politicians. The large number of cadets whom he believed not fit to attend the academy fed this distrust, as did his belief that many had been appointed due to their political connections, not because they might make good officers. President Buchanan's apparent willingness to allow the South to secede in late 1860 and early 1861 reinforced these suspicions. Upton carried these convictions forward into the Civil War, and they can be seen in his resistance to political pressure regarding the appointment of officers in his regiment. By the time of the Battle of Fredericksburg, he had come to the conclusion that political meddling had caused the appointment of incompetent generals to high command. Battlefield defeats and the wasted deaths of Union soldiers were, he concluded, the fault of politicians who had intruded into strictly military affairs. "I can hardly bear to think of it," he told his sister Louisa. "We have been defeated so often when it was not the fault of the brave soldiers, that I am losing all patience. There is imbecility somewhere, but it does not do to breathe it. Our defeats emanate from Washington, for with poor generals the courage of our troops would surmount the obstacles the rebels oppose to our march. How I would like to describe one decisive victory. How I would like to see that general rise who would lead us to great deeds."[64] This distrust of politicians only grew after the Civil War and manifested itself in the pages of *The Military Policy of the United States*.

Other life lessons played out during the first two years of the Civil War. Upton's self-discipline, apparent as a child in Batavia and nurtured at West Point, had become an important organizational trait of the 121st New York. The emphasis he placed on drill and discipline played a key part in the regiment's success at Salem Church, where in the face of withering fire, it had moved farther forward than any other unit in Bartlett's brigade and had succeeded in forcing the Confederates out of their position, the unit breaking off its attack only after having suffered fearful losses. At Salem Church "Upton's Regulars" had proven to their colonel the value, indeed the necessity, of discipline.

Salem Church taught the young commander one other lesson: volunteers, if properly trained and led, could be successful in battle. In this regard Upton's experience reflected the teachings and convictions of Dennis Hart Mahan. It was untrained, undisciplined volunteers, such as those Upton had observed prior to and after First Bull Run, who were unreliable in battle; they were particularly undependable if led by officers who had been elected or who were political appointees. Regular officers, schooled in the science of war and knowledgeable of its intricacies, needed to prepare volunteers for combat.

All of these lessons, learned early in life and reinforced by two years of combat, became hardened truths for Upton in 1864 and 1865. They very much would influence his professional life after the war's end.

CHAPTER 3

UPTON'S CIVIL WAR, 1864–1865

The period between the Battle of Rappahannock Station and the end of the Civil War was an important phase in Emory Upton's military career. At Rappahannock Station he had established his credentials as one of the U.S. Army's best tacticians. He cemented that reputation at Spotsylvania in May 1864, at Opequon Creek that September, and as a cavalry division commander in the western theater during the war's closing months. During this period, the conflict took a bitter turn for Upton and for the nation. By 1864 the Civil War had become a remorseless struggle in which the North could be victorious, it appeared, only by hammering the South's major armies into submission while also destroying the industries, railroads, crops, and other resources the Confederacy required to conduct hostilities. The war had taken on a tenor few could have predicted in 1861, certainly not Upton, and its ferocity and destruction outraged him. His experiences during the conflict's final year and his belief that its costs could have been averted greatly influenced his later approach to the reform of the American military.

Upton's brigade spent the winter of 1863–64 resting and preparing for the upcoming campaign. The brigade had relatively comfortable quarters because, unlike most of the Army of the Potomac, the Sixth Corps's encampment was on high ground. "Here we are in the midst of a fine grove which we leave standing," Dr. Daniel Holt wrote his wife,

> and get our supply from timber adjacent to camp. Water is handy and every-thing perfect for first rate winter quarters. Log huts, good as any I ever saw, grace our well laid out streets, and now the men are engaged in constructing *side walks* running from head Quarters to Captain's quarters, and thence to Hospital, Sutler's tent, &c. The grounds are thoroughly policed. Every man keeps his house in order while the company cooks, in houses erected for that purpose, prepare food for the regiment. Evergreens grace the hospital enclo-sure, as also a walk from thence to my own house.

Holt noted that the regiment had undertaken the construction of a "*gothic structure*" that he thought would be "the pride of the Army" when finished.[1]

Another regiment built a wood-frame structure that served as a chapel, and yet another constructed an amusement hall where soldiers played cards and performed amateur entertainments. Mail came to the camp on an almost daily basis, sutlers provided the soldiers with "luxuries" such as canned food and new socks, and many men found time to fish local streams. Occasional small-scale encounters sometimes disturbed this tranquil lifestyle. One such action occurred in February 1864, when the brigade supported Brig. Gen. George Custer's cavalry in a reconnaissance toward Charlottesville. Returning four days later, the soldiers were perturbed to discover that an "innumerable mass of crows" that was "literally covering the ground" had taken over their camp. Drill occurred frequently during fair weather. The 121st New York's maneuvers favorably impressed Capt. Oliver Wendell Holmes, a member of the First Division's staff, as did Upton's "handsome camp." "So the winter passed away in pleasurable employment and amusement," Isaac Best wrote.[2]

This inactivity did not please Upton as much as it did his men. "I think that officers and soldiers are anxious for marching orders," he wrote his sister in mid-April 1864. "Camp-life has become very irksome, and we welcome any change that will break up its monotony. Excitement is the spice of a soldier's life, and all old troops hunger for it after having rested for a long time." Upton had confidence that newly arrived Lt. Gen. Ulysses S. Grant would defeat Lee, capture Richmond, and end the war. He thought the army was in fine shape, and though he had "no doubt that the bloodiest battle of the war will be fought in a few days," he also believed that the Army of the Potomac was ready for any challenge and would soon disprove its poor reputation.[3]

Upton's prediction about the nature of the coming campaign proved correct. His brigade broke camp on May 4, 1864, crossed the Rapidan River at Germanna Ford, and spent the night two miles south of the ford along the Germanna Plank Road. The following day elements of Lt. Gen. Richard Ewell's Second Corps of the Army of Northern Virginia, moving east up the Orange Turnpike toward Fredericksburg, encountered Maj. Gen. Gouverneur K. Warren's Fifth Corps near Wilderness Tavern. The ensuing battle was one neither Lee nor Meade had intended. Meade's army moved slowly through the Wilderness, but both he and Grant desperately wanted to avoid a battle there. Dr. Holt described the area as "the raggedest hole I about ever saw. No wonder we cannot find or see a reb until we get right upon them. Swampy, hilly, bushes thick as dog's hair, grape vines, rotten logs and fallen trees, make up this pretty picture. A fine place to fight in surely: a perfect quag mire [sic]" Such terrain negated the Union army's superiority in numbers and in firepower. Lee, on the other hand, was unprepared for a general engagement because Lt. Gen. James Longstreet's First Corps was many miles to the west and could not be in the area for another day.[4]

The battle, however, took on a life of its own. Late in the morning of May 5, Upton's brigade moved to support Warren's efforts along the Orange Turnpike two miles west of its intersection with the Germanna Plank Road. The colonel found it impossible to march in line of battle "on account of the dense pine and nearly impenetrable thickets which met us on every hand." The brigade occupied a position north of the turnpike on the Fifth Corps's right flank, and the remainder of the Sixth Corps, minus its Third Division, eventually occupied the line to Upton's right. Almost immediately, Confederates hidden in the dense undergrowth killed Lt. Col. Edward Carroll, the commander of the Ninety-Fifth Pennsylvania. Several of that regiment's companies promptly charged forward, capturing thirty prisoners and seizing a small hill two hundred yards to the brigade's front, where Upton reestablished his line, believing that the hill "was important to hold." There Upton and his soldiers made a grisly discovery. "The woods in front and around our position had been set on fire by the enemy to prevent our advance," he later reported. "The ground had previously been fought over and was strewn with wounded of both sides, many of whom must have perished in the flames, as corpses were found partly consumed." Before the end of the day, the Fifteenth New Jersey had reinforced the Second Brigade, remaining under Upton's command for the remainder of the fighting in the Wilderness.

On May 6, Upton later reported, "There was constant skirmishing during the day but not serious." At 7:00 P.M. the division's inspector general brought him orders to move two of his regiments to counter Confederate efforts to turn the Sixth Corps's right flank. Upton sent the 121st New York and the Ninety-Fifth Pennsylvania to the threatened position. The movement was nearly a disaster as "the dense undergrowth necessarily lengthened out the column" and Confederate attacks at several locations "threw both regiments into unavoidable confusion." Those elements of the regiments that remained cohesive fighting units moved into rifle pits at the corps's extreme right flank, but there another Confederate attack broke their line, resulting in what Dr. Holt termed "a promiscuous skedaddle." In the meantime Upton, who had stayed with the remainder of the brigade, left to direct these two regiments' efforts. In desperate fighting the colonel rallied and formed them to the right of a brigade that had just come up to help repel the Rebels. When the fighting died down and darkness fell, Upton collected the remnants of other regiments that had broken under the Rebel assault and added them to his line. The Confederate attack, successful as it was, had not achieved its objective of rolling up the corps's flank. Later that night Upton's brigade withdrew from its forward position to the vicinity of Wilderness Tavern. The colonel reported twenty-five dead, sixty wounded, and twenty-six missing in action. As was true of the rest of the Army of the Potomac, the two-day battle in the Wilderness had bloodied the Second Brigade but had not beaten it.[5]

The opposing armies remained inactive on May 7 in their hastily dug entrenchments, the woods between them smoldering from the previous days' fires, each side waiting for the other to make the next move. Earlier battles such as that in the Wilderness had led to the withdrawal of the Army of the Potomac and, usually, to the relief of its commander. Grant, however, was determined to pressure Lee continuously. Rather than retreat, he and Meade pushed the army south toward Richmond. They issued orders aimed at the capture of the vital crossroads at Spotsylvania Court House, which if successful would place their force between Richmond and Lee's army. Unfortunately, dilatory action on the part of numerous Union commanders as well as quick thinking by Lee and his subordinates permitted the Confederates to beat the Army of the Potomac to that strategically important piece of terrain. If Grant wanted the road junction, he now would have to fight for it.[6]

At 9:30 P.M. on May 7, Upton's brigade, at the head of the Sixth Corps, left its bivouac near Wilderness Tavern and began marching toward Spotsylvania. The troops spent the night on the road, moving first to Chancellorsville and from there to Piney Branch Church, where there was a brief halt for breakfast. Upton's command arrived at Spotsylvania late in the afternoon of May 8. The brigade moved to the west side of the Brock Road so that it could support an attack by the Fifth Corps, but Confederate demonstrations on Upton's right forced him to face his unit to its right and rear, preventing it from taking part in the assault. The Second Brigade remained west of the Brock Road that night, but the next day it moved to the east and, with the rest of the Sixth Corps, formed on Warren's left, where it passed the remainder of the day digging entrenchments while enduring sporadic artillery fire. It proved to be a sad day for the Sixth Corps, though, as a Confederate sharpshooter killed its commander, Major General Sedgwick. Upton's division commander, Brig. Gen. Horatio Wright, assumed command of the corps, and Brigadier General Russell became the division commander.[7]

On May 10 Wright ordered Russell to inspect the Confederate lines to his front and look for potential weaknesses that an assault might exploit. Russell discovered just such a weakness in the vicinity of the Shelton House. There he found a trail through a woods that led to within two hundred yards of the left side of a salient in the Rebel line that later came to be known as the "Mule Shoe." Infantry that used this trail would be concealed from observation. Furthermore, when attacking soldiers emerged from those woods, they would be almost completely shielded from enemy fire because the Rebels had sited their fortifications poorly. The entrenchments at the Mule Shoe were on the

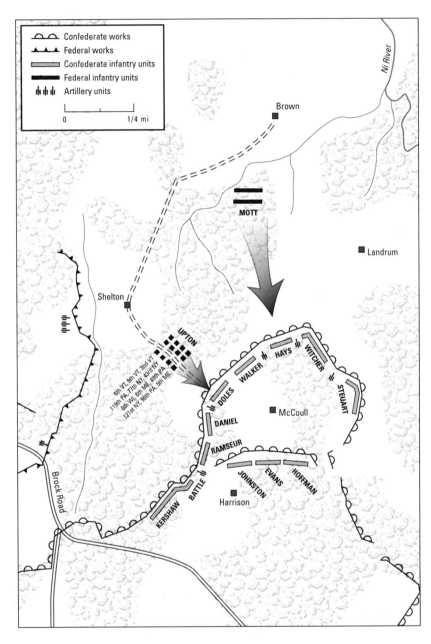

Upton's Charge, Battle of Spotsylvania, May 10, 1864. Map by Erin Greb. Copyright © 2017 by the University of Oklahoma Press.

topographic crest of a small swale rather than on its military crest, thus creating dead space through which an attacker might advance. This meant a sizable force that approached the Confederate position through the woods and across the low ground to its front would be under fire for only the last few yards of its assault. Though the Rebels had built some formidable fortifications—entrenchments reinforced by logs with firing ports cut in them, abatis to their front, traverses that prevented enfilading fire, artillery batteries with traverses between the guns, and a second line of trenches one hundred yards to the rear—it was vulnerable to attack.[8]

Russell assigned the assault to Upton's brigade and reinforced it with nine additional regiments: the Fifth Wisconsin, Sixth Maine, and Forty-Ninth and 119th Pennsylvania from the First Division's Third Brigade; and the Forty-Third and Seventy-Seventh New York and the Second, Fifth, and Sixth Vermont from the Second Division—a total of twelve regiments (between four and five thousand soldiers). Upton's assaulting force therefore had nearly the strength of a full division.[9] After inspecting the ground with his regimental commanders, the colonel formed his units into four lines of battle. The unique aspect of this assault was not its tactics, but that Upton had thought through his actions on the objective. After the war he observed that "most of our assaults had failed for want of minute instructions, and particularly at the moment of success." He was determined this would not happen with his command at Spotsylvania and therefore ensured that all of his officers were fully briefed regarding his plan of attack. "All the men knew what to do," he later recalled.[10]

Each line in Upton's assaulting force—and in the instance of the first line, each regiment in that line—had a specific mission to accomplish once the position had been taken. The first line of battle, consisting from left to right of the Fifth Maine, the Ninety-Sixth Pennsylvania, and the 121st New York, was to seize the entrenchments. The New Yorkers and Pennsylvanians were then to wheel to the right and capture an artillery battery, while the Maine regiment was to wheel left and pour enfilading fire into the trenches there. The second line (the Forty-Ninth Pennsylvania, Sixth Maine, and Fifth Wisconsin) was to halt in the seized trenches and provide covering fire to the front of the assaulting force. The third line (the Forty-Third and Seventy-Seventh New York and the 119th Pennsylvania) was to fall in behind the second and await orders. The last line, consisting of the three Vermont regiments, was to advance to the edge of the woods and await orders—this was Upton's reserve and would be used to meet any Confederate counterattack. Another unique aspect of the colonel's plan was that soldiers in the last three lines were to carry weapons that were loaded but not capped—he did not want them to expose themselves unnecessarily by stopping to fire—and all lines were to charge with bayonets fixed.

Speed was the key. If his command could cross the open ground quickly and suffer few casualties, Upton thought, the assault would succeed.[11]

The attack was to commence at 5:00 P.M., but coordination problems delayed it until 6:00 P.M. Apparently not receiving word of the postponement, one of the three supporting batteries opened fire at 5:00 and continued firing for an hour, after which the other two joined the bombardment. All three ceased firing at 6:10, and Upton's twelve regiments began moving forward ten minutes later.[12] On his command

> the lines rose, moved noiselessly to the edge of the wood, and then, with a wild cheer and faces averted, rushed for the works. Through a terrible front and flank fire the column advanced, quickly gaining the parapet. Here occurred a deadly hand-to-hand conflict. The enemy sitting in their pits with pieces upright, loaded, and with bayonets fixed ready to impale the first who should leap over, absolutely refused to yield the ground. The first of our men who tried to surmount the works fell pierced through the head by musket-balls. Others, seeing the fate of their comrades, held their pieces at arms [sic] length and fired downward, while others, poising their pieces vertically, hurled them down on the enemy, pinning them to the ground.

This struggle, although fierce, was also brief. "Numbers prevailed," according to Upton, "and, like a restless wave, the column poured over the works." Upton personally led the charge that captured a Confederate battery firing canister into its assailants. As the force pushed forward as well as to its left and right, the Yankees captured hundreds of prisoners and numerous fieldpieces, then entered the Confederates' second line.[13]

The Rebels reacted quickly to the threat Upton's success posed and began forming for a counterattack. The colonel ordered forward his fourth line, the Vermonters, only to discover that they had mingled with the assaulting force and therefore were no longer an available reserve. Even more disconcerting was the fact that Upton had not received the planned support on his left. Brig. Gen. Gershom Mott's division, detached from Maj. Gen. Winfield Scott Hancock's Second Corps, was placed at the extreme left of the Sixth Corps line. Earlier that day Meade had ordered Mott to establish a connection with Ambrose Burnside's Ninth Corps, which was farther to the Sixth's left. He also ordered Mott to move to Burnside's aid without orders should the Ninth Corps become engaged. But in midafternoon Meade changed these instructions. Concerned about Upton's impending attack, he told Mott to support the Ninth only if Burnside requested it and then only with part of his division; the remaining brigades would support Upton's attack. Later that afternoon Mott advised Wright that he could not connect with Burnside *and* attack the Confederates with any sizable force. "I regret that your skirmish line is so extended," Wright replied, "but if you cannot withdraw a part of the left in full time, you will not attempt to do so, but advance the whole at 5 P.M., as previously ordered, following it at the proper moment by your column of attack, made as strong as your numbers will permit." It therefore is not clear now, nor was it likely any clearer then, what Mott's division was supposed to do—Meade and Wright clearly expected it to support Upton in some unspecified way. In any event, Mott attacked at 5:00 P.M., as had the artillery battery that had opened fire early, and he did so with only four or five regiments numbering at most fifteen hundred soldiers total. Encountering severe fire as his troops emerged from the woods nearly six hundred yards from the Confederate position, Mott called off the attack.[14]

Though Meade's and Wright's intentions remain unclear, it is absolutely certain that Upton expected someone to support his attack. Almost ten years later, in a letter that outlined his thoughts regarding a draft of Adam Badeau's *Military History of General U. S. Grant*, Upton claimed that his attack would have succeeded had it been "properly supported" and that "the golden opportunity, which would have been given to fresh troops, was lost." He accused Wright of mishandling the Sixth Corps during the May 10 assault. "[Y]ou will see," he told Badeau, "that if before the assault the remaining troops of the Sixth Corps had been pushed up to musket range all along the enemy works, and I had received orders after entering the works to leave therein four regiments to look out for my rear, and with the rest to turn to the right, I might have cleared the front of several brigades of the corps which coming in behind me would have been able to penetrate [?] the work no one can say how far." Upton thus criticized his corps commander for failing to do what he himself had done—thinking through the conduct of the assault beyond sending the soldiers forward and outlining what might happen if the assault succeeded. In doing so he blamed the failure on Wright, a West Point graduate, rather than on Mott, a New Jersey politician. But this would not be the last time during Overland Campaign that Upton would be critical of a high-ranking academy graduate.[15]

Because neither Mott nor Wright came to Upton's aid, the assaulting force remained exposed on both flanks while three-quarters of a mile in front of Union lines. Grant ordered Upton to withdraw when it became apparent that his troops were not going to be adequately supported. But the colonel protested the order, and Grant therefore directed Hancock to lead an assault consisting of units from his Second Corps as well as from Warren's Fifth Corps and Wright's Sixth Corps. Despite a "furious cannonade" and some local successes in piercing the Confederate line, this attack failed, and Upton's command withdrew as darkness fell.[16]

Defined very narrowly, Upton's assault had been a dramatic success. Not only had his brigade captured Rebel entrenchments, thereby giving the Army of the Potomac an opportunity to force Lee's army out of its position, but the Yankees returned to their lines with between one thousand and twelve hundred prisoners and several stands of colors. This success and its squandered opportunity, however, had come at enormous cost, with Upton reporting that his command had sustained more than one thousand casualties. "Our officers and men accomplished all that could be expected of brave men," the colonel concluded in his account of the assault. "They went forward with perfect confidence, fought with unflinching courage, and retired only upon the receipt of a written order, after having expended the ammunition of their dead and wounded comrades."[17]

May 11 was a relatively quiet day for Upton's brigade, but on May 12 it was part of the Second Corps's assault against the apex of the Mule Shoe salient, the so-called "Bloody Angle." The Rebel position there was situated on top of the same roll in the ground Upton had assaulted two days previously but one-quarter of a mile farther east. Hancock's corps began its attack early in the morning of May 12 and reached the Confederate trenches at several locations. At midmorning Russell ordered Upton to support Hancock, whose right flank was vulnerable to a Confederate counterattack. The colonel rode forward to reconnoiter his brigade's movement, and from the crest of a slight ridge nearby he could see Union soldiers occupying the front of the Rebel works from the Bloody Angle west to the location of his May 10 assault. He returned to his brigade and brought the Ninety-Fifth Pennsylvania forward, intending to place it on the right of Hancock's line. When he reached the ridge again, Upton discovered that Hancock's right had collapsed. He ordered the Pennsylvanians to occupy the ridge, which inclined away from the Confederates to a nearby woods. He later wrote that "had the regiment given way, there can be little doubt that the gallant charge of the Second Corps in the morning would have been lost." Upton positioned the regiment while under heavy fire and then brought up the remainder of his brigade, extending it to the right of the Pennsylvanians. Then the colonel, "in a huff," according to Gordon C. Rhea, "commanded his regiments to charge the works. It was a foolhardy act, rendered in a spirit very unlike that which animated him on May 10." Several assaults having failed, Upton eventually permitted his regiments to move to less dangerous ground. In the afternoon he brought up an artillery section consisting of two brass howitzers and placed it within "literal whites-of-their-eyes range" of the entrenched Confederates. From there the section fired canister with terrible effect until all of its horses had been killed and most of its men lay dead or wounded. Over the course of the day, Upton's brigade repulsed numerous Rebel efforts to dislodge it, yet the colonel seldom climbed off his horse—"the only mounted man in sight, going unhurt by some miracle," according to Bruce Catton. Nevertheless, during the day's fighting, his horse was shot out from under him. Still, the focus of that day's combat was farther east in the Second Corps area at the Bloody Angle, which Upton termed "the most sanguinary conflict of the war." Finally, at 5:30 in the afternoon, his brigade, barely eight hundred men strong, departed the line, a brigade from the Second Corps taking its place.[18]

After the fight at the Bloody Angle subsided, the Army of the Potomac began sliding to its the left in an effort to gain Lee's right flank. Warren's Fifth Corps moved around the Mule Shoe and occupied a position to the left of Burnside's Ninth Corps, while Wright's Sixth Corps followed and took up a position to the left of Warren. Moving with Wright, Upton's brigade spent the night of May 13 in the rear of the Ninth Corps. Early the following morning it occupied Myer's Hill, a small knoll to the left front of Warren's position that provided an excellent view of the Confederate defenses and held by two regiments of regular infantry.

Because of the hill's importance as an observation post, the degree to which he was forward of the Union lines, and his brigade's depleted strength, Upton requested that Wright send another brigade to help hold the position. The general replied that he did not have one available and instead sent two badly understrength regiments, the Second and Tenth New Jersey. As the day progressed, Upton's soldiers tried to improve their defenses as much as they could, using wooden rails to erect breastworks, "there being no other means of fortifying at hand." About 4:00 P.M., lookouts discovered enemy skirmishers on a hill roughly one-half mile to the west. Upton, concerned that these Confederates were preparing to move into a wooded area only 250 yards away from his position, sent the Ninety-Sixth Pennsylvania to occupy it. Upon entering the woods the Pennsylvanians discovered two brigades of Rebel infantry hidden there. The Ninety-Sixth pulled back quickly. Upton sent the Ninety-Fifth Pennsylvania and the Tenth New Jersey forward to aid its withdrawal, but fire from Confederate cavalry and from a battery of horse artillery quickly enfiladed the units. In danger of having his command chewed up, Upton abandoned Myer's Hill. Dr. Holt described the retreat as "the wildest imaginable disorder. Never did I make better time in digging to the rear than then. Our entire line gave way. . . . They chased us, firing into our ranks and hastening a retreat which *I* thought plenty fast and disgraceful enough without any such persuaders." Meade and Wright, who were inspecting Myer's Hill at the time of the Confederate attack, were caught up in the confusion.[19]

Though the Battle of Spotsylvania continued until May 19, the action at Myer's Hill on the fourteenth was the last in which Upton's brigade played a significant role. The unit had suffered grievously in the twelve-day battle. Upton had come to Spotsylvania with almost 1,300 soldiers under his command; of those, 599 had become casualties. Because the brigade now was no larger than a good-sized regiment, the Second Connecticut Heavy Artillery joined its ranks on May 21. The Second Connecticut had started the war as an infantry regiment before being assigned to the fortifications outside Washington. Subsequently it was redesignated as heavy artillery, and its strength increased to two thousand men. As the 1864 campaign wore on and casualties mounted in the Army of the Potomac, Grant ordered Washington's defenses stripped and its units sent forward to serve as infantry replacements. Nearly eighteen hundred soldiers strong at this time, the Second Connecticut more than doubled the size of Upton's command.[20]

After Spotsylvania the Army of the Potomac continued to search for Lee's right flank while moving closer and closer to Richmond. After a brief encounter at the North Anna River, one in which Upton's brigade played no substantial role, the army resumed its southward movement. On the afternoon of May 31, Union cavalry attacked advance elements of the Army of Northern Virginia near Old Cold Harbor, barely ten miles east of Richmond. Fighting raged there from midafternoon until nearly sunset, and as night fell, the Union troopers occupied the intersection. Lee, sensing a threat to his right flank, sent Brig. Gen. Richard Anderson's First Corps to dislodge the cavalry and retake the vital crossroads. After moving all evening and into the early hours of the next morning, nearly twelve thousand Confederate infantry attacked Sheridan's sixty-five hundred cavalry and infantry at about 5:00 A.M. on June 1. Sheridan's men fought desperately to hold their position before, at 10:00 A.M., the Sixth Corps arrived and relieved the beleaguered force.[21]

At noon Meade ordered Maj. Gen. William "Baldy" Smith's Eighteenth Corps to move to Cold Harbor and join the Sixth Corps in an advance up the Richmond Pike. As part of this attack, Upton's brigade formed into four lines, the first three consisting of battalions of the Second Connecticut, while the four depleted veteran regiments made up the rear line. At 6:00 P.M. the brigade moved forward, advancing through an open field before entering a pine wood and crossing a small ravine. As it emerged from the ravine, the Yankees' advance came to a halt. Rebel infantry had entrenched roughly seventy feet to its front, and large trees they had felled covered the intervening terrain, making an organized advance almost impossible. "Two paths," according to Upton, "several yards apart and wide enough for 4 men to march abreast, led through the obstructions. Up these to the foot of the works the brave men rushed, but were swept away by converging fire." Realizing he had no hope of seizing the enemy position, Upton ordered his men to lie down but not to return fire. In the meantime, the brigade on his right succeeded in gaining the Rebels' entrenchments. Seeing an opportunity, the colonel moved a portion of the Second Connecticut to the right and through a gap that had been opened in the Confederate line, then moved it back to the left, rolling up the Rebels' position. The entire regiment then moved into the captured entrenchments and remained there despite both its flanks being exposed to fire. Finally, at 3:00 A.M. the next morning, the Rebels retreated to a second defensive line. Upton's assault had cost his command dearly. The brigade sustained 364 casualties during the two weeks it spent at Cold Harbor, the vast majority coming in the first day's combat. The Second Connecticut took more casualties than the other four regiments combined, with nearly 20 percent of its soldiers falling on June 1, one of whom was its commander, Col. Elisha Kellogg.[22]

Upton's brigade was to take part in the general assault Grant and Meade ordered for June 3, but while the men waited in their trenches, "Generals Wright and Russell, and some staff and engineer officers passed along the line of works," noted Isaac Best. "They spent considerable time in the trenches to the left of us talking to General Upton. Shortly after they went away word was passed along that the order to charge had been countermanded at this place, Generals Russell and Upton deeming the position too strong to be taken." The brigade then spent the next ten days in the Cold Harbor trenches, occasionally exchanging musket fire with the Rebels. The break in active campaigning gave Dr. Holt a chance to wash his uniform for the first time since the brigade had crossed the Rapidan; it also gave him a chance to catch up on his sleep.[23]

The respite provided Upton his first opportunity to write home in nearly a month and occasion to reflect on what had transpired during that period. He had reason to be proud of the role he and his soldiers had played in the campaign thus far. At the Wilderness his brigade had helped stem a determined Confederate effort to turn the flank of the Sixth Corps; at Spotsylvania it had distinguished itself in its attack at the Mule Shoe and in support of Hancock's assault at the Bloody Angle; at Cold Harbor it had conducted a spirited if costly attack against entrenched Confederates. These exploits had succeeded in securing for Upton the personal and professional recognition he had sought since assuming brigade command in July 1863. Prior to the start of the 1864 campaign, Grant had received authority "to promote officers on the field for special acts of gallantry." Believing Upton's leadership of the May 10 assault merited such a reward, the commanding general promoted him "on the spot" to brigadier general, an action President Lincoln later confirmed.[24]

Upton was pleased to have secured promotion through his actions on the battlefield rather than through political machinations. "The reasons for my promotion are gratifying to any soldier," he later reported to his sister. "It will be entered upon the records of the War Department that I was promoted for 'gallant and distinguished services'—a record which will help me through life, and one of which you will be far more proud than had it been conferred simply for political reasons. It is contrary to the instincts of all regular officers to seek promotion through the latter influence." This achievement, however, did not quench his thirst for glory and recognition. "I feel quite happy," he confided, "& have not yet ceased to aspire. I shall not be content till I get a division, & time will bring that about."[25] Upton had experienced a remarkable metamorphosis between 1861 and the summer of 1864. At the start of the war he had been willing to serve his nation in any manner required; by 1864 he was in search of personal glory. These two desires were not mutually exclusive. Indeed, Upton believed himself to be one of the Union army's best combat leaders, and it therefore was in the nation's best interest that he be promoted. He had seen far too many examples of poor generalship during the Overland Campaign and believed that his continued advancement would mean that fewer mistakes might happen.

Upton had been critical of the army's leadership since the prior summer. Typical of his feelings was his judgment upon hearing that three corps commanders (George Sykes, William French, and William Newton) had been relieved as the result of the Army of the Potomac's reorganization in early 1864. These officers, he believed, "were anything but able generals, so the Army suffers no loss through their absence." His criticisms became even more pointed as the campaign wore on. On June 4, the day after the unsuccessful general assault at Cold Harbor, Upton wrote his sister: "I am disgusted with the generalship displayed. Our men have, in many cases, been foolishly & wantonly sacrificed. They order assault after assault upon the enemy's entrenchments, when they knew nothing about their strength or position. Thousands of lives might have been spared by the exercise of a little skill but as it is the courage of the poor men is expected to obviate all difficulties. I must confess that, so long as I see such incompetency, there is no grade in the Army to which I do not aspire."[26] His anger had not yet abated the following day. "We are now at Cold Harbor," he wrote,

> where we have been since June 1st. On that day we had a murderous engagement. I say *murderous*, because we were recklessly ordered to assault the enemy's intrenchments, knowing neither their strength nor position. Our loss was very heavy and to no purpose. Our men are brave, but can not accomplish impossibilities.
>
> I am very sorry to say I have seen but little generalship during the campaign. Some of our corps commanders are not fit to be corporals. Lazy and indolent, they will not even ride along the lines; yet, without hesitancy, they will order us to attack the enemy, no matter what their position or numbers.[27]

Upton continued to censure the army's leadership after departing Cold Harbor. Reporting to his family about his brigade's activities near Bermuda Hundred, he wrote:

> This morning a[t] 1 A.M. we were marched outside of the works to support & participate in an assault of the enemy's works. The order was countermanded in time to prevent a deliberate surrender of our troops. The line we were to assault was evacuated by the enemy on the 16th, and was occupied by our troops, who fell back from them without firing a shot. It was not till the enemy had reoccupied them in stronger force than before that it was discovered that their possession was of great importance to us. Brilliant generalship, that, which would abandon voluntarily a line of works, allow the enemy to take possession, & then drive them from it by a *glorious charge!* This kind of stupidity has cost us already twenty thousand men. It is time that it should be stopped.[28]

Even after leaving the Army of the Potomac to serve in the Shenandoah Valley, Upton continued to criticize the actions of its leaders. Referring to the debacle at "The Crater," he wrote, "How humiliating was the reverse at Petersburg, & how disgraceful on the part of the Division Commander to abandon their troops."[29]

Clearly the casualties the army had suffered since early May appalled Upton, and his brigade had endured more than most. "Dead and dying men by scores and hundreds lie piled upon each other in promiscuous disorder," Dr. Holt wrote to his wife from Spotsylvania. "Heaven knows how much longer this battle will last. . . . No doubt we shall at last be victims." The brigade's losses from the beginning of the campaign in May until its departure for the Shenandoah Valley in early July came to 329 killed, 713 wounded, and 263 missing, or 41 percent of the men who served under Upton's command during this time. Few brigades in the Army of the Potomac had incurred more casualties. Though Upton never seemed as fatalistic in his letters home as Dr. Holt, the carnage clearly had affected him. After the June 1 encounter at Cold Harbor, Dr. Holt noted that Upton was "*very* wolfish" for some unknown reason, a characterization that could be applied to the attitude displayed in the letters the general had written in the days subsequent to the battle.[30]

This "wolfish" attitude almost certainly can be attributed to Upton's belief that incompetent generals had wasted men's lives. His description of "indolent" corps commanders at Cold Harbor clearly implies that General Wright was responsible for the losses incurred on June 1, just as he believed Wright had wasted an opportunity at Spotsylvania. Upton did not limit his criticisms to the army's leadership, for he felt that Lincoln too had "made many gross blunders" during the course of the war, though to the president's credit, he had remained, to Upton's mind, "true to his purpose." Still, he reserved his most biting strictures for officers in the Army of the Potomac, especially George Meade and Ambrose Burnside, whom he called "stumbling-blocks of too great magnitude to permit a brilliant execution of any movement in which they may be implicated. I heartily wish they might be relieved."[31]

The encounter at Cold Harbor on June 1 was the last major action for Upton's brigade as a part of the Army of the Potomac. It departed that location on the evening of June 12, moving farther south. Two days later it occupied a position at Bermuda Hundred in support of Maj. Gen. Benjamin Butler's efforts there. Upton's command then marched to the lines south of Petersburg, arriving on June 19. Over the next two weeks it participated in several small-scale actions, including an operation on June 29–30 in support of Brig. Gen. James H. Wilson's cavalry division, during which Upton's soldiers tore up several miles of railroad track.[32]

Perhaps one of the most disconcerting events of this period was the brigade's loss of one of its veteran regiments. The term of service of the Fifth Maine, a three-year regiment that had enlisted prior to the First Battle of Bull Run in the summer of 1861, expired in June 1864, and its men departed for home during the early stages of the Siege of Petersburg.[33] Though nothing in Upton's correspondence suggests that this concerned him, it must have served as an example to him of the bankrupt policy of enlisting soldiers for a period less than the duration of the war.[34] Otherwise, the brigade's relative inactivity at Petersburg was another welcome respite for the weary soldiers, though proximity to Confederate lines made life in the trenches dangerous. On June 20 Dr. Holt observed: "this morning is one of the most severe ones we have had, so far as *shelling* is concerned. I believe I was more exposed than ever before." The next day he noted, "It is pretty quiet to-day, except *sharpshooting*, which *both* sides indulge in."[35]

Lt. Gen. Jubal Early's raid into the North in June 1864, which Lee hoped might force the Army of the Potomac's withdrawal from the Richmond–Petersburg area, ended this relatively inactive period for Upton's brigade. On July 10 the command marched to City Point, Virginia, at the confluence of the James and Appomattox Rivers, where it boarded transports destined for Washington, D.C. Arriving there the next day, the troops were present at but did not participate in the action at Fort Stevens on June 12 that ended Early's threat to the capital. "The timely arrival of our corps saved Washington from capture," Upton wrote his sister one week later from Snicker's Gap in Virginia's Blue Ridge Mountains. "The enemy withdrew from the City shortly after our appearance and made a hasty retreat across the Potomac. We have followed very leisurely & without opposition until achieving this point."[36]

With Early remaining relatively unmolested in the Shenandoah Valley, the prosecution of the war there proved too leisurely for President Lincoln and General Grant. They therefore relieved Maj. Gen. David Hunter of his command and replaced him with Maj. Gen. Phil Sheridan on August 6. Sheridan was one of the few Union commanders Upton admired, but the force he inherited, now designated the Army of the Shenandoah, was badly disorganized and understrength. Made up of the Eighth Corps (Hunter's old command, now led by Brig. Gen. George Crook), Brig. Gen. William Emory's Nineteenth Corps, and Wright's Sixth Corps, the Union force remained relatively static as it prepared for the coming campaign against Early. This continued inactivity led Upton to hope he might have a chance to visit his family in Batavia, though he understood such a possibility was contingent on developments in the Valley. "Our movements depend on Early," he warned his sister, "who is a contrary fellow & may give us much trouble about that time."[37]

Sheridan, not Early, ruined Upton's plans by moving his army up the Valley in mid-August in an effort to find and engage the Rebels. Grant previously had ordered Hunter to push up the Shenandoah, advising him:

> it is desirable that nothing should be left to invite the enemy to return. Take all provisions, forage, and stock wanted for the use of your command; such as cannot be consumed, destroy. It is not desirable that the buildings should be destroyed; they should rather be protected; but the people should be informed that so long as an army can subsist among them recurrences of these raids must be expected, and we are determined to stop them at all hazards. Bear in mind the object is to drive the enemy south, and to do this you want to keep him always in sight.[38]

Sheridan intended to do exactly that. He moved his army as far as Cedar Creek in the Valley's west arm before deciding the situation there was not conducive to success, after which he withdrew to the vicinity of Harpers Ferry. This first phase of the campaign testified to the fact that the war was being waged against soldiers and civilians alike. Partly in response to the depredations of Mosby's Raiders, but mostly in response to Grant's orders, Sheridan ordered farms and crops burned, farm animals killed, and railroads torn up.[39] For the first time, Upton participated in the large-scale, wanton destruction of civilian property, not because that property happened to be in the middle of a contested battlefield, but because it was thought that its destruction might hasten the end of the war.

The Army of the Shenandoah once again moved up the Valley in early September. The Sixth Corps arrived at Clifton, about seven miles east of Winchester, on September 3 and remained there until the morning of

September 19. Breaking camp early that day, Wright moved the corps westward on the Berryville Pike toward Winchester. Sheridan hoped that these veterans, coming from the east and supported by Emory's Nineteenth Corps, would move behind the bulk of Early's force, which he understood was north of Winchester and moving farther north toward Martinsburg. If this were true, it gave Sheridan the opportunity to defeat the Rebels in detail. Early, however, had other ideas. After the Sixth and Eighteenth Corps had driven in their outposts east of Winchester, the Confederates delivered a crushing counterattack north of the Berryville Pike, taking advantage of a gap that had opened between the two corps. The assault succeeded in folding back the right flank of the Sixth Corps and the left flank of the Eighteenth Corps, widening a hole in the Union line that, if fully exploited, might result in a Union defeat.[40]

With disaster near at hand, Sheridan directed Russell to send a brigade to stem the Rebel attack. Russell selected Upton's brigade, which was in the rear of the Sixth Corps and, with the rest of the First Division, was serving as Wright's reserve. At that moment the unit was on the south side of the Berryville Pike roughly two miles west of Opequon Creek. Upton formed his command into two lines, the Second Connecticut followed by the 121st and Sixty-Fifth New York, and then moved the brigade forward another half-mile to the west before facing it to the right and moving to the north side of the pike. Then he placed the two New York regiments' lines parallel to the Confederate direction of attack while sending the Second Connecticut to the brigade's right, inclining its line forward from left to right and creating a crossfire if Early's men attacked there. "Bayonets were fixed and instructions given not to fire until within close range," Upton wrote in his report of the battle. "The enemy's left, extending far beyond our right, advanced till within 200 yards of our line, when a brisk flank fire was opened by the One hundred and twenty-first New York and Sixty-fifth New York, causing him to retire in great disorder. The Second Connecticut immediately moved forward and opened fire. The whole line then advanced, driving the enemy and inflicting heavy loss in killed and wounded." Ten months after the war's end, Sheridan wrote that, at the moment of the Confederate counterattack, the outcome of the Battle of Opequon Creek was "uncertain" until the "gallant attack of General Upton's brigade . . . restored the line of battle."[41] For the third time in less than a year, Upton had proven that he had few equals in the entire Union army in the realm of tactical leadership.

As the brigade regrouped following its repulse of the Confederate attack, the division's assistant adjutant general informed Upton that General Russell had been killed and that he was now the division commander. He inherited a serious command-and-control problem as soldiers from his brigade had become intermixed with regiments of the First and Third Brigades, "making

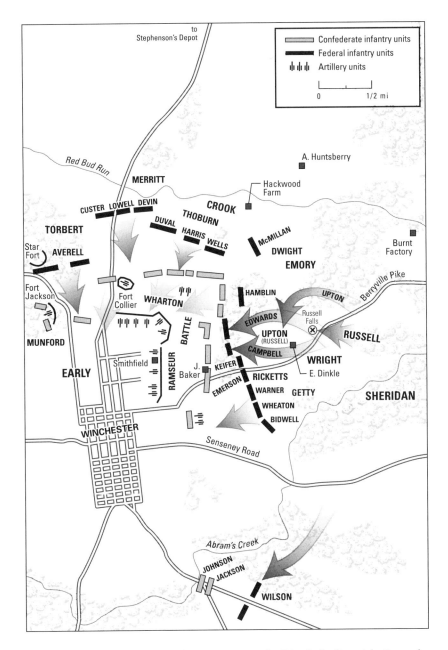

Battle of Opequon Creek, September 19, 1864. Map by Erin Greb. Copyright © 2017 by the University of Oklahoma Press.

it extremely hazardous, if not impossible, to restore order while under fire." Despite this complication, Upton brought the division on a line north of the Berryville Pike facing westward, the division's line, from left to right, consisting of the Third, First, and Second Brigades. He then refused his right flank with the Sixty-Fifth New York and the Second Connecticut so the division might link up with elements of Emory's Nineteenth Corps.

In the meantime Sheridan had ordered Crook to counterattack into the gap between Upton's right flank and the Nineteenth Corps's left flank. To support Crook, Upton ordered his two right-flank regiments to move forward and force the Confederates out of a patch of woods to their front. This attack, which elements of Crook's command assisted, caused the Rebels to "give way" with "great confusion." The Confederates north of the Berryville Pike fell back and reformed their line on the crest of a small hill with a tiny brick farmhouse, re-fusing their left behind a stone wall. Upton sought support for an assault against this position from one of Emory's reserve brigades, but its commander was unwilling to move without orders. Determined to force the Confederates off the hill, the general ordered the Second Connecticut to move to a location "at right angles to the wall," from which its musket fire drove the Confederates from their strongpoint. The Connecticut soldiers and the Sixty-Fifth New York then opened fire on the position. The division's Third Brigade, "which emerged from the woods," reported Upton, "in a beautiful order and giving great confidence to the troops engaged," supported the attack. The assault evicted the Rebels from the hill in the late afternoon.[42]

As Upton urged his soldiers forward in the assault on the Rebel position, a shell exploded near him, a fragment from which ripped into his right thigh, exposing the femoral artery. Hearing that Upton had been grievously wounded, Sheridan rode to the First Division's area and ordered him to the rear to seek medical attention. After the commanding general had departed, according to James Wilson, Upton ordered a surgeon to place a tourniquet on the leg to help stop the bleeding, after which he had himself carried around the battlefield on a stretcher so he could direct the division's efforts. "This was the most heroic action that came under my observation during the war," Wilson wrote in his memoirs. Upton eventually was evacuated from the battlefield, and command of the division devolved to the Third Brigade's commander, Col. Oliver Edwards.[43]

The Battle of Opequon Creek, better known as the Third Battle of Winchester, was an important victory for the Army of the Shenandoah, the first of several that led to Early's expulsion from the Valley. For Upton, it was the end of his war in the eastern theater. Badly wounded, he traveled first to Washington, then to Batavia. He convalesced there until December, when he traveled to the western theater. Brigadier General Wilson, who had taken command of all cavalry serving in the Military Division of the Mississippi in September 1864 shortly after Opequon Creek, had requested Upton's transfer so he could command one of the cavalry divisions there. Upton, now a brevet major general of volunteers (he had been breveted for his actions at Opequon Creek), once again faced new challenges.[44]

James Harrison Wilson, an 1860 graduate of West Point, confronted a daunting task in the autumn of 1864 as the newly appointed commander of all cavalry in the Military Division of the Mississippi. His command was spread from the Mississippi River to Atlanta and from Kentucky to northern Mississippi and Alabama. Though ostensibly organized into divisions, many small cavalry detachments operated semi-independently, and two of its division commanders, Brig. Gen. Ben Grierson and Maj. Gen. George Stoneman, promised to be trouble for Wilson because they were more experienced than their new commander and both outranked him. Moreover, many of Wilson's troopers were dismounted due to a shortage of horses; some were unarmed and most were not carrying the Spencer carbine, the standard weapon for cavalry in the Army of the Potomac. The greatest challenge facing Wilson was his opponent—Lt. Gen. Nathan Bedford Forrest—perhaps the Confederacy's boldest commander.[45]

Wilson had managed to pull together his command—four divisions of thirteen thousand mounted and armed troopers—in time to play an important role in the Battle of Nashville in December 1864. Still, he thought the Cavalry Corps could do more. Wilson had become convinced that both armies had improperly employed their cavalry during the conflict. "He . . . abhorred the idea that cavalry units were good only as messengers, escorts, foragers, scouts, or guards for supply trains," according to James Jones. The general hoped to restore cavalry to a role of prominence, but he understood this could not be done through the traditional cavalry charge. Rather, armed with carbines, Wilson's troopers would act as mounted infantry. In his conception, cavalry should use its speed to strike deeply and quickly, but once engaged it should fight dismounted. The virtual annihilation of General Hood's army at Nashville, which left Forrest's cavalry as the only substantial Confederate force in Alabama and Tennessee, provided an opportunity to test this concept. It was late February 1865, however, before Maj. Gen. George H. Thomas, commander of the Department of the Cumberland, agreed to let Wilson undertake a raid deep into the heart of the Confederacy.[46]

Even as the Nashville Campaign came to its climax, Wilson continued his efforts to gather the dispersed elements of his corps while ensuring it was properly equipped and commanded. One of his first moves was to relieve Stoneman and Grierson and to replace them with men he knew and trusted, one of whom was Emory Upton. Wilson, who had commanded a cavalry division in the Army of the Shenandoah, had been impressed by Upton's actions at Opequon Creek and believed that he would perform well as a cavalry commander. In mid-November 1864 Upton received orders to report to General Thomas "as soon as sufficiently recovered from his wounds." He arrived in Nashville in mid-December, his wound having reopened during his journey.[47] There he found that his command, the Fourth Division of the Cavalry Corps, was scattered between Louisville, St. Louis, and Memphis. Wilson ordered Upton to collect "the men, horses, and transportation of his division," bring them to Nashville, and "take measure[s] to furnish his troops with new arms and equipments."[48]

Upton's task of gathering his division and preparing it for combat was no less daunting than that Wilson had faced, his regiments being scattered across the western theater. It was not until early February 1865 that he was able to assemble the Fourth Division in one place, and even then it lacked enough horses for all of its soldiers. Despite this shortcoming, Upton moved his command to Gravelly Springs, Alabama, on the Tennessee River, arriving there on the twelfth. There his division joined the rest of the Cavalry Corps while receiving the horses it required.[49]

That problem resolved, Upton focused his energies on the division's apparent inability to drill "by the book." His solution was typically Uptonian: a combination of strict discipline, the replacement of incompetent officers, and seemingly endless hours on the instruction field. "Infractions of discipline were promptly, and sometimes conspicuously punished," a soldier in the Fourth Iowa Cavalry later noted. Referring to the hours spent on the drill field, the same soldier wrote, "It was hard work, and so much more strictly required than before that many found it very irksome." As had been true of his commands in the East, Upton's soldiers came to understand the importance of the time they spent training. "It would have been far better for the regiment," the cavalryman concluded, "if it had had such schooling during the earlier periods of its service." Despite these efforts, neither Upton nor his orderly, Pvt. E. N. Gilpin, were completely satisfied with the results. After observing a review of the Second Division, Gilpin wrote, "It beat our Review all to pieces, and the Gen'l [Upton] thinks we'll have to get up another one some day." Notwithstanding his displeasure with the division's performance on the parade field, Upton expressed to Gilpin confidence that "our Division will carry any place the second undertakes."[50] The general's men reciprocated his faith in them. Gilpin noted that Upton was "quite popular among the boys of ours and other Divisions." A soldier in the Fourth Iowa Cavalry wrote, "every one [sic] who met him felt the influence of his zealous spirit and shared his desire."[51]

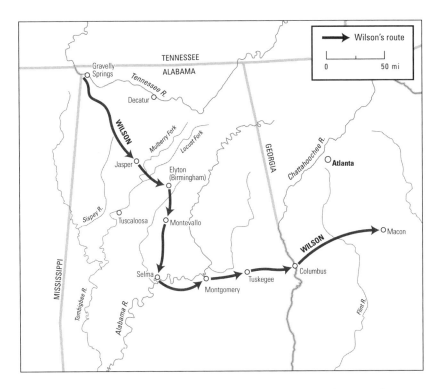

Route of Wilson's Cavalry Raid, March–April 1865. Map by Erin Greb. Copyright © 2017 by the University of Oklahoma Press.

By early March Wilson's corps was prepared to undertake its thrust into Alabama, the objective being to find and defeat Forrest and to destroy the state's industries, especially those in and around Selma. The weather, however, was not cooperative. It had rained often that winter, and the Tennessee River was several feet above flood stage, making it unfordable. Not until March 11 had the water receded enough to enable the corps to begin crossing. Upton's division began doing so on March 16 on what was a cold, gusty morning punctuated by snow flurries. The crossing was not an easy one, if Gilpin's experience was any measure. "Charley [his horse] and I nearly went under," he recorded in his diary. "My boots full of water." Both food and forage were in short supply that night as the division camped at Chickasaw Bluffs. "I managed to confiscate a good feed of oats tonight," Gilpin wrote, "and I can wait till tomorrow."[52]

All of Wilson's command was across the Tennessee by March 18 and began moving south on the twenty-first. To facilitate foraging and rapid movement, and in an effort to deceive Forrest as to his intentions, Wilson ordered his three divisions to move into Alabama along separate routes of march. On the corps's far right was the First Division, under the command of Brig. Gen. Edward McCook; in its center was Brig. Gen. Eli Long's Second Division; and Upton's Fourth Division was on the left. The Fourth Division moved quickly through the barren countryside, traveling 71 miles in three days and, much to everyone's surprise, finding corn and other provisions in Newburg.[53] As he moved farther south, Upton found the terrain "exceedingly mountainous and forage scarce." On March 26, as the division entered Jasper, it encountered a small Rebel force that it quickly drove out. Afterward, according to Gilpin, the town was "plundered and most of it burned." That evening the division's First Brigade, commanded by Brig. Gen. Edward F. Winslow, arrived at the north bank of the Black Warrior River, having marched 125 miles in five days.[54]

Crossing the Black Warrior the next day proved to be one of the more dangerous events of the entire campaign. In typical understatement Upton simply reported that he crossed the river, which was rising rapidly due to recent heavy rains, "over an extremely dangerous ford." Gilpin provided a more detailed description. "Our pontoon train too far to the rear to be of use," he recorded.

> Gen'l Wilson ordered Gen'l Upton to contrive a way of crossing. The river here is about 150 yards wide, rough bottom of shelving rock, slippery and uncertain. The river runs very swiftly and it was with some hesitation that our Gen'l decided fording it. . . . One our Pioneers was mounted on a good horse, and his release was offered him if he would cross and return. It was a queer arrangement and many interested spectators collected on the bank to watch the fun. The brave fellow pitched in all alone, carefully moving, occasionally slipping, sometimes almost falling, but at last across safely and back. Troops crossing nearly all day. . . . Some men were swimming, others clinging to rocks and ledges, and some plunging compulsively far down where the channel ran between high precipitous banks, washing swiftly at the mercy of the foaming waters. . . . It was a dangerous fording, and I felt quite glad I'd got out safely as I stood on the bank & looked back.[55]

The other two divisions followed Upton's across the river, and the entire command pushed on toward Elyton (present-day Birmingham).[56]

Upton's division entered Elyton on March 28 after his Second Brigade, commanded by Brig. Gen. Andrew Alexander, had mounted a saber charge that sent the town's defenders scurrying. The following morning the division moved farther south after setting numerous iron and rolling mills afire. "It did me good to see the flames curling over and around them," Gilpin recorded gleefully in his diary. Wilson feared that Forrest might try to delay the corps at the Cahaba River and therefore urged Upton to cross that obstacle quickly. The

Fourth Division arrived there at 3:00 P.M. on the twenty-ninth only to find that the ford was too deep, had quicksand at both approaches, and choked with obstacles placed by retreating Confederates. Only after Winslow's First Brigade had converted a railroad bridge to a foot bridge by covering it with planking was the division able to cross and move toward Montevello on March 30. Upton's command met scattered resistance during this movement, stopping just long enough to disperse the Rebels and to destroy numerous iron mills in the area.[57]

The next day the Second Brigade encountered advance elements of Forrest's command, led by Brig. Gen. Phillip Roddey, just south of Montevello. Immediately dismounting, Alexander's skirmishers returned fire while the remainder of the brigade prepared for a mounted charge. The charge, supported by an artillery battery, drove the Rebels back in confusion, pursued by elements of Winslow's brigade. On April 1 Long's Second Division moved south along the main road from Montevello to Selma, while Upton moved parallel to Long's column on the Maplesville Station Road farther east. The general had hoped to arrive at Ebenezer Church on the Selma Road before Forrest, thereby turning the Confederate right flank and threatening his rear. On arriving there he found that Forrest already occupied a strong position, his right anchored on a creek and his left resting on a wooded ridge line, and that Long had begun an attack on that position. Upton dismounted the Second Brigade and pushed it forward as skirmishers. Alexander, according to Upton, "threw his brigade into action . . . with great celerity, and after a stubborn fight of an hour's duration routed the enemy and captured his guns." Winslow's brigade, by his own account, arrived "just as the engagement was being decided." Seeing Alexander's troopers moving forward against the enemy entrenchments, Winslow sent two of his regiments, still mounted, around the left so as to roll up the Confederate flank. The result, according to Col. John Noble, commander the Third Iowa Cavalry, was "a complete rout." Winslow's brigade pursued the fleeing Confederates, capturing three hundred men and driving the remainder of Forrest's command south through Plantersville. "The road was strewn with guns' belts, cartridge boxes, and clothing," Gilpin reported. "Too fast for their *goods!* the boys would say as they found their coats, hats, &c."[58]

The following day Upton's and Long's divisions moved from Plantersville to Selma, intent on capturing the South's last remaining industrial center, with its numerous iron mills, rolling mills, collieries, and a naval arsenal. Though it was well fortified, Wilson and his corps had an advantage. On March 30 a soldier in Winslow's brigade had arrested an Englishman who claimed that he was a civil engineer and had helped construct Selma's fortifications. Winslow sent the engineer to Upton, to whom the prisoner provided detailed plans of the city's defenses. Those plans showed Selma was "surrounded by a well constructed, bastioned line of earthworks and stockades, extending in a semicircle of about three miles, from the river bank above to the river bank below the town, with an inner but incomplete line covering the principle roads from the city to the surrounding country." The defenses also included "thirty-two guns in position behind heavy parapets completely covered by well constructed stockades five and a half feet high, the stakes, from six to eight inches thick." These formidable fortifications appeared to have one weakness: they were incomplete near the Alabama River and wherever they crossed creeks or swampland, the Confederates apparently thinking those areas impassable. Both Wilson and Upton sought to take advantage of this oversight.[59]

Arriving outside Selma at 4:00 P.M., the two generals conducted a reconnaissance that took them to within a few hundred yards of the Rebels' first line before artillery fire drove them back. Prior to arriving, Wilson had decided that Long's division would mount the main attack against Selma, using the Summerfield Road as a guide, while Upton's division, coming down Range Line Road, would cross a swamp east of the road and attack a portion of the line that was, according to the Englishman's sketch, lightly held; Wilson and Upton's brief reconnaissance had confirmed this was a workable plan. They decided to mount a night attack in order to negate the Confederates' significant advantage in artillery. Even so, Wilson expected the effort to succeed only if done in a "direct and dashing" manner.[60]

Upton and two soldiers from Winslow's brigade went forward prior to the attack to find a route through the swamp. At one point they came to within two hundred yards of the Confederate position, crawling on hands and knees so as not to be observed. He instructed the soldiers who were with him to note carefully the route they had taken since they would be the guides for the three hundred handpicked cavalrymen who would lead the division's attack. This force, Upton hoped, would move into a lightly held portion of the defenses and then roll up the Rebel line at the moment the remainder of the Fourth Division conducted a frontal assault. But much to the general's surprise, Long's division attacked before dusk and succeeded in carrying the Confederates' first line. "Upton," Wilson later recalled, "hearing the noise of battle to his right . . . waited for neither signal nor orders" before ordering his men forward.[61] Crossing the marsh, Upton's men "charged over the fields and swamps, over rifle pits and embankments, up to the palisades, over the ditches, up to the very mouths of nearly a hundred cannon, through the iron hail and smoke up in the parapets, in among the affrighted rebs, yelling like the devil." Once elements of Upton's division were inside Selma's defenses, Winslow brought up one of his regiments "at a gallop, and, charging into the city in various directions, captured several pieces of artillery and several hundred prisoners." Still, Long's division deserved the lion's share of the credit for the success, a fact Upton acknowledged in a letter home. "Selma was carried gallantly by Long's division," he wrote, "mine but partly participating."[62]

After the Confederate line broke, most of the Rebels fled through the city. Some jumped into the Alabama River to elude capture. But others chose to stand their ground, the result being, according to Wilson, "desultory street fighting."[63] Private Gilpin painted a more vivid picture. "As the Rebels ran," he recorded in his diary,

> they set fire to a large cotton store house [*sic*] near the arsenal and an immense quantity of cotton was burned. Night had set in before we had fairly taken the city and we rode in it by the light of the burning buildings. The fire spread from the store house to barracks and ammunition houses—shell[s] exploding and flying in every direction, fire raging all night, soldiers, many of them drunk and plundering the city. Citizens scared nearly to death, women and children screaming, soldiers yelling screaming. Excitement high everywhere. Of all of the nights of my experience, this is the most like the horrors of war I used to read of—a sacked city, burning at night, shrieking women, helpless children, a victorious and a demoralized, retreating army. Hundreds of frightened Rebs running for their life jumped their horses over bluffs into the Alabama River, falling fifty feet, trying to escape. Our Cavalrymen after them to the brink of cutting them and slashing them with their sabres. From the outside works to the river, truly a "gallop of death."[64]

Union soldiers who had seized and ingested much of the town's supply of liquor, and who later wandered drunk through the streets, made the situation even worse. The horrors did not end that evening, however, as fires from the barracks and ammunition shacks spread to other sections of the city and continued into the next day. "'Two squares burning,' Gilpin reported, "soldiers running with the engines, more for amusement than to put out the fire, splashing the fire and unlucky 'cits' at the same time." Finally, on April 4, the destruction of Selma's war-making potential began, with the burning of its foundries, workshops, powder mills, railroad depot, and rolling stock. Fires burned late into the night, creating a strange, almost festive atmosphere.[65]

Not wishing to allow Forrest to regroup from the disaster at Selma, Upton led Winslow's brigade out of town on the morning of April 3 in search of Confederate cavalry while undertaking the secondary mission of finding and escorting the division's trains to Selma. In a long journey that took him back to the Cahaba River, Upton was unable to find Forrest. He did, however, discover in a barn the bodies of Union soldiers whom he presumed Confederates had murdered while the men slept. After linking up with the division's supply train

and the corps's pontoon train, Upton returned to Selma on April 8, having journeyed one hundred miles in five days.[66]

With Forrest's command defeated and scattered, and Selma captured and its
industries destroyed, Wilson had a number of options open to him. He considered moving to Mobile to support Maj. Gen. Edward R. Canby's efforts to capture
that city, but the cavalryman correctly surmised that it would fall in any event. He
therefore struck east toward Montgomery and Columbus, Georgia, in an effort
to do even greater damage to what little industrial capacity remained in Alabama
and Georgia. Two days after returning to Selma, Upton's command was again on
the move. Crossing a recently erected pontoon bridge across the Alabama River,
the Fourth Division set out for Montgomery at 4:30 A.M. on the morning of April
10. Meeting little resistance, the troopers moved swiftly and entered the first capital of the Confederate States of America late in the afternoon of April 12.[67]

Montgomery was undefended, and the Cavalry Corps moved through its
streets unhindered. It was a testament to the total collapse of Confederate military power that Wilson was able to march his corps through the city as if on
parade. "It was an example of discipline, order, and power lasting nearly all day
and constituting a far more impressive spectacle than a bloody battle would
have been," Wilson wrote in his memoirs. "Five brigades, not far from twelve
thousand troopers, were in that column passing in review, as it were, before the
ladies and gentlemen of the city." Quite obviously, Wilson was engaged in psychological warfare with the citizens of Montgomery, the parade through the
city's streets being an unmistakable statement that the war was lost. The subsequent destruction of the city's niter mills, arsenals, and other industries drove
home that message.[68]

The Fourth Division's movement east continued on April 14, again meeting only scattered resistance. During this advance toward the Alabama-Georgia
border, the Second Brigade of the First Division, commanded by Col. Oscar La
Grange, reinforced Upton. Rebels along the column's route, unable to mount
organized resistance, were reduced to blocking the roads with piles of railroad ties. When the cavalrymen stopped to clear the obstacles, a few well-
hidden Confederates would open fire. Such a scene was repeated frequently
after departing Montgomery.[69]

Upton next moved to secure crossings of the Chattahoochee River at West
Point and Columbus, Georgia. He sent to the former location La Grange's brigade, which captured the bridge there rather easily during the day of April 16.
Columbus, however, was a different story. There three bridges spanned the
Chattahoochee: a foot bridge crossed the river just below the city, another led
directly to the center of the town, and there was a railroad bridge north of
town. The Rebels had prepared all three to be "fired," and the bridges' defenses

consisted of a series of forts, redoubts, abatis, and rifle pits. Arriving at Girard, Alabama, immediately across the river from Columbus, early in the afternoon of April 16, Upton hoped a quick dash might overwhelm some disorganized Confederates and succeed in capturing one of the spans. He therefore sent his advance guard forward in an effort to secure the lower foot bridge. This endeavor ran into a hail of cannon and musket fire that turned back the attack and forced his entire command to take cover behind a ridge, after which the Rebels burned that bridge as well as the railroad bridge.[70]

Upton concluded that capture of the remaining bridge required a well-prepared attack. For this he deployed Alexander's brigade south of Girard on the crest of a low-lying ridge and in plain sight of the Rebels. Meanwhile he sent Winslow's brigade on a wide sweep north of town, where it took cover behind a ridgeline that concealed its location from the Confederates. Upton intended Winslow to conduct the division's main attack by sending dismounted troopers into the Confederate trenchline, thereby opening a breach through which mounted cavalry could ride to capture the bridge. By early evening the general had made his dispositions for the battle, but returning to the north side of Girard, he was unable to find Winslow's brigade. At this moment Wilson rode up and found Upton in a near panic. "Everything is ready for the assault," he reported to Wilson, "but I cannot find Winslow and must delay the attack until he is in position." Wilson, who had just passed Winslow's brigade, pointed out its position, to which Upton replied: "But it is now too late. It will be dark before I can get him into position."[71] Seeing his two superiors nearby, Winslow rode up only to discover that he was the subject of an intense discussion. "The serious loss of time," he recounted later,

> had evidently made Upton nervous and he began to upbraid me in no gentle terms for not obeying his verbal instructions. Of course I stated my understanding of these and stated emphatically my command was located just where he had ordered me to place it and that I had been anxiously awaiting his further orders. He said he had been unable to find me or my brigade. As this appeared almost absurd when there were more than sixteen hundred horsemen for duty I could say little more. He then said we had lost the opportunity for fighting, whereupon I remarked that if he wished we could attack immediately and have every chance of success.

Listening to this exchange, Wilson interjected, "If Winslow wants to fight in the dark, let him do it." Encouraged by his corps commander's enjoinder, Upton proceeded to execute his plan.[72]

The attack began at 9:30 P.M. Winslow had dismounted two of his three regiments and put them into line, one behind the other, leaving the third regiment in the saddle. The two lines of dismounted troopers went forward "yelling and shooting," and the Rebels, apparently caught completely by surprise, were easily driven from their fortifications. At this point Winslow committed the mounted regiment—the Tenth Missouri—which "charged over the slashing and aba-tis, up to the guns, and charged the forts, driving the whole army into a rout. . . . The Rebs were panic stricken, and where our lines came down among them charging and yelling, they fled into a wild rout in all directions." Pushed on by cries of "Selma! Selma! Go for the bridge! Waste no time on prisoners," a detachment of the Fourth Iowa succeeded in crossing the bridge and seizing the defensive works on the river's far bank. With the bridge in Union hands, the town fell rather easily. Once again, Upton's division had performed well, seizing not only Columbus but also fifteen hundred prisoners, twenty-four pieces of artillery, and an ironclad ram that was prepared to go to sea. His troopers also captured fifteen locomotives, two hundred railroad cars, and nearly 100,000 bales of cotton. That night General Wilson declared in his diary that Upton's capture of the town was "a magnificent achievement." Private Gilpin agreed. "A mild exultation seized hold of the soldiery," he recorded in his diary, "and I believe our brigade could have whipped *anything* that night."[73]

After destroying the factories and warehouses of Columbus as well as the ram, the division moved north to the Macon and Western Railroad, then proceeded on to Macon, tearing up the railroad as it moved. As the troopers approached that city, a rumor reached its ranks that Sherman and Joe Johnston had agreed to an armistice. Thinking "the report is a strange one," Gilpin disbe-lieved it. General Wilson, however, confirmed it the next day, and word of the Confederate surrender reached Upton just as his command was preparing to enter Macon.[74] His Civil War was over.

The American Civil War was the greatest bloodletting in the nation's history, with roughly 620,000 soldiers having died; there exists no reasonable estimate of civilian casualties. The economic price was perhaps even more staggering. For the Union, the cost of prosecuting the war's military operations came to over $3 billion, a figure that represents merely the war's direct financial costs and overlooks many long-term and ancillary expenditures.[75]

The conflict's expense, both human and financial, would preoccupy Upton many years later as he wrote *The Military Policy of the United States.* Of more immediate concern were his personal wartime experiences. He had seen inept generals, career officers and politicians alike, waste soldiers' lives through inad-equate planning and incompetent leadership. Spotsylvania and Cold Harbor were, to Upton, very personal reminders of this crime. He had seen a war he had presumed the North would win quickly grow into a paroxysm of death and destruction, and he had participated in some of the war's most devastating campaigns—in the Shenandoah Valley in 1864 and through Alabama and Georgia in 1865. Unlike Charles Royster, who argues that the war's destructiveness and violence were the inevitable outcome of developments in mid-nineteenth-century American society, Upton had come to believe that politicians, some of whom were traitors, and inept generals were responsible for the length of the war and its attendant death and devastation.[76]

There is no question that Upton had conflicting emotions regarding the war. At the end of Wilson's Raid, he wrote to a sister that it had been "the most pleasant and exciting campaign I ever participated in." And yet prior to departing on the operation, he had written, "Hobbes was not a soldier, or he never would have advanced the idea that 'war is the natural condition of man.'" The "horrors of war," in the words of Upton's orderly—the murder of sleeping Union soldiers by renegade Confederates, the burning of Selma and other towns in the Deep South, the destruction of the South's ability to produce and transport not only weapons but also food for its people—certainly did nothing to move Upton away from his conclusion that war was an absolutely unnatural phenomenon. On the sixth anniversary of the Battle of Fredericksburg, in an otherwise romantic letter to his wife that evinced his near-constant concern for her health, he recalled "the bloody battle" and its "flashes of musketry and the roar of artillery, with ten-thousand killed and wounded stretched cold upon the plain, & writhing in their agony."[77] This odd reference communicates well his abhorrence of the conflict's carnage. What Upton had experienced by war's end had truly horrified him. Indeed, his very odd behavior regarding Winslow's brigade prior to the nighttime assault at Columbus suggests that he may have been physically and psychologically exhausted after four years of combat. These were experiences and lessons Upton never forgot, and they soon consumed him.

CHAPTER 4

PROFESSIONAL STAGNATION AND PERSONAL SORROW

D uring the immediate postwar period, Emory Upton experienced the displacement associated with rapid demobilization. A brevet major general of volunteers at war's end, he reverted to his permanent rank of captain in April 1866. Though the army almost immediately promoted him to lieutenant colonel, it was a period of professional dissatisfaction for Upton, a time during which he complained of being a "fifth wheel" and an "idle looker on." The only professional bright spot during these years was the service's adoption of his tactics manual, which secured his reputation as one of its more advanced tactical thinkers. The period was also one of personal trial. In 1866 he met and fell in love with Emily Martin. Emily, however, was in very poor health, and barely two years after their 1868 wedding, she died. These years were thus a time of professional stagnation and personal sorrow for the young officer.

The end of the Civil War did not bring an end to military operations in Georgia. Still in command of the Fourth Division of James Wilson's Cavalry Corps, Upton's immediate mission was to bring stability to the state. It was not an easy task. Private Gilpin noted in his diary that "Rebs" had set fire to the Union commissary established in Macon and that many badly needed supplies had gone up in flames. "The Rebs still cherish antipathy," he wrote, "though meet them on the street they appear to be friendly. The town is full of Rebs." News of Lincoln's assassination and of the horrors of the prison camp at Andersonville caused Gilpin to reconsider his earlier ecstasy over the war's conclusion. "I'd sooner remain in the army for two years yet, than to have the war half-ended," he declared. "It makes me mad to think of a 4 years war for nothing. I'm for making them to suffer."[1]

General Upton's immediate concerns were not so different from Gilpin's. Wilson had sent Winslow's brigade to Atlanta and Alexander's to Augusta, ordering both to accept the surrender of Confederate garrisons in those cities. On May 5 Upton arrived in Augusta, where he found yet another town "full of Rebs." One of the division's staff officers believed the situation so dangerous that he ordered soldiers to sleep with their carbines loaded.[2] Upton conducted a flag-raising ceremony at the U.S. arsenal in the city on May 8 in an effort to cow the populace into submission without bloodshed. He made a brief speech before the ceremony:

> Soldiers! Four years ago the Governor of Georgia, at the head of an armed force, hauled down the American flag at this arsenal. The President of the United States called the nation to arms to repossess the forts and arsenals which had been seized. After four years of sanguinary war and conflict we execute the order of the great preserver of union and liberty, and to-day we again hoist the stars and stripes over the United States Arsenal at Augusta. Majestically, triumphantly she rises![3]

Gilpin observed that many townspeople were present for the ceremony and appeared impressed by its symbolic significance.[4]

The Fourth Division faced a multitude of challenges in its occupation duties. Wilson directed Upton to apprehend "all prominent agitators and rebels"; to parole and disperse all former Confederate soldiers; to "compel all editors of newspapers to publish their papers in the interests of peace, good order, and national unity under the Constitution and the laws"; to discourage any public meetings that might incite trouble; and to encourage "civil officers . . . to enforce good order." Upton split his division into small detachments and dispersed them throughout Georgia and Alabama to accomplish these missions. The situation in the region was one of near-total chaos. When Winslow arrived in Atlanta, he found that "mob law" ruled the city's streets, requiring a strenuous effort to establish a semblance of order. Fire had destroyed most of that city's business district, and few of its homes remained undamaged. Food was particularly scarce, as it was throughout much of Georgia, and the poor, both white and black, were near starvation. Augusta suffered similarly. One of Upton's first actions there was to oversee the efforts of "torpedo operators" to remove mines from the Savannah River, thereby opening it to navigation and providing a means of receiving much-needed supplies.[5]

The thousands of prisoners the Cavalry Corps had captured and the large number of Rebel soldiers making their way home, whom Upton termed "stragglers," presented a potentially dangerous problem as there were far more former Confederates than Union soldiers to watch them. Wilson ordered Upton to pursue a liberal parole policy, yet there was a sticking point over formalities. Confederate officers were chagrined that their terms of parole required them to "solemnly swear" that they would not again take up arms against the federal government. They thought this arrangement "contrary to the custom of war" and believed that they should have been allowed to "pledge their honor." Wilson accepted Upton's recommendation that this wording be substituted.[6]

Upton's command also undertook efforts to seize Confederate assets and to capture escaping Confederate officials. In Augusta soldiers of the Fourth Division "liberated" the gold belonging to the Central Banking and Railroad Company, the specie and books of the Georgia Central Railroad, and the assets of the Bank of Tennessee. Wilson ordered the general to find the archives of the State of Tennessee and to arrest the three officers safeguarding them. Though Upton's soldiers were unable to locate the archives, they found and arrested two of the three men thought to have been guarding them. The Fourth Division also participated in the search for the South's most prominent politicians, Alexander Stephens and Jefferson Davis. Its soldiers captured Stephens, the Confederacy's vice president, in Columbus on May 13 while Upton was visiting the town. Yet the general was not completely satisfied because his men had been unable to find Robert Toombs.[7]

Because Davis was rumored to be traveling through northeastern Georgia, both Alexander's and Winslow's brigades scoured the countryside searching for his party. Upton suggested that the easiest way to ferret out the Confederate president would be to offer a large reward payable in specie, believing the prospect of hard currency in a region that had little might produce a flood of tips. Wilson agreed to this plan, though he stipulated that any poster must be worded so as to imply that the reward money would come from the "booty" Davis was rumored to have in his possession. Not happy with this reply, Upton wired his commander that "a *ruse de guerre* is now justifiable" and suggested that a reward of $500,000 was "a cheap way to end the war." He later requested that Wilson "stand by me in using the name of the Secretary of War," thereby lending a certain credibility, he thought, to the reward offer. Wilson replied that he should "put no price on his head; offer simply for his apprehension and delivery and on the condition that the reward shall be paid out of the treasure to be captured with the fugitive." He also directed, "Don't use the Secretary's name at all, but yours or mine, and we will take the consequences together." None of this aided in Davis's capture, and it was not until May 10 that a detachment of cavalry from the corps's Second Division apprehended the fugitive president near Irwinville, Georgia.[8]

Upton's experiences in Augusta and those of Winslow in Atlanta paralleled those of the entire Cavalry Corps. Wilson, as de facto commander of most of the state of Georgia, had to deal with the consequences of the unparalleled death and destruction the war had brought to the region. Many former battlefields still had unburied remains of Confederate soldiers scattered across them. So many farms had been destroyed and so much livestock "appropriated" that large-scale starvation was a very real threat. A relatively severe drought exacerbated the problem, and nearly all of the state's railroads, the only means of moving food into the interior, had been destroyed during the war. Wilson therefore directed that Confederate stores not needed by the Union army as well as any excess army provisions be distributed to the civilian population. He also disregarded the contrary orders of Quartermaster General Montgomery Meigs and put Winslow's brigade to work repairing the railroad between Atlanta and Chattanooga, hoping it would enable provisions to reach northwest Georgia. It was a demanding task as almost all of the bridges along that stretch had been destroyed and the individual rails rendered unusable. "I never thought rails could be so twisted, twirled, and turned and turned around in such shapes as Ive [*sic*] seen them today," Private Gilpin noted. Wilson's corps was the only viable police force in the area, and as such it faced numerous challenges. Marauders from both the Union and Confederate armies posed a significant threat to the civil peace, one that so concerned Upton that he ordered all of his soldiers be searched for plunder they might have acquired during the campaign from Selma to Macon. Relations between ex-slaves and their former masters presented Wilson and Upton with one of their biggest dilemmas as they feared the potential both for retribution on the part of blacks as well as for brutality directed toward people most white Georgians still thought of as property.[9]

Wilson understood that the war's end meant demobilization of the Cavalry Corps, so he anxiously sought to justify its continued existence. Observing the deterioration of relations between the United States and France over Archduke Maximilian's continued presence in Mexico, he proposed to Major General Thomas that the entire corps be moved to the Rio Grande frontier, where it would be in a position to lead an expedition against Napoleon III's puppet. Thomas rejected the proposal, however, and the corps headquarters mustered out of service in July 1865. This process had begun for Upton's command in late May with the release from duty of Lt. Col. Frederick Benteen's 10th Missouri Cavalry of Winslow's brigade. Wilson subsequently ordered Upton to proceed to Chattanooga to supervise the mustering out of the corps's remaining volunteer regiments. Alexander's brigade was the first unit for which he performed this duty, its regiments departing for home in early June.[10] After his own division left the service, Upton took charge of all of the cavalry in the District of East Tennessee, his mission being to dismantle the command. Having done this chore with typical efficiency, the young officer was out of a job on August 15.

"Our Division breaking up," Gilpin recorded in his diary, "and going into a conglomerated mess." These sentiments mirrored Upton's, for he did not relish the dismemberment of his division. The cavalrymen he had commanded, he thought, had been capable of accomplishing any mission given them, and he believed its officers among the best in the Union army. "Had all of the commands in our armies been animated with the zeal which characterized our Division," he wrote Winslow that summer, "the war would have been terminated long ago." As he watched this fine fighting force reduced to nothing, another event jolted the young officer back to the reality of a postwar army. A brevet major general during the closing stages of the Civil War, Upton was reminded that this rank was only temporary when he received his *promotion* to captain in the regular army in late May.[11]

Upton took a brief leave in June, during which he visited Illinois and Wisconsin, explored Mammoth Cave in Kentucky, and attended the wedding of another of Wilson's division commanders, Edward McCook. Upton reflected that the general had been called "the 'Hero of the South-Western Cavalry,' *of course deservedly*." That McCook, who was not a West Point graduate, would receive such high praise from Upton is noteworthy. While traveling on a train on his return trip to Tennessee, he encountered William T. Sherman and had a lengthy conversation with him. Sherman, Upton reported, was "very bitter toward the Secy of War" because of the manner by which Stanton had rejected the surrender terms he had granted General Johnston's army. Sherman, according to his biographer, "could not forgive Stanton, another in a series of individuals in his life who disagreed with him and thus represented a malevolent force."[12] This first encounter since First Bull Run between Upton and the fiery Ohioan was propitious. Upton had railed against political influence in the army during the course of the Civil War, but seldom had there been an individual attached to those complaints. Now thanks to Sherman, he had a scapegoat in the person of Edwin Stanton and in the office of the secretary of war.

With the conclusion of his duties in East Tennessee, Upton, like many other officers, was unsure of his future. He hoped that he might secure a position in Georgia, but he thought there would be little or no cavalry there for him to command. This uncertainty came to an end on August 15, when he received orders to report to Maj. Gen. John Pope, commander of the Department of the Missouri, who sent him to Denver to take command of the District of Colorado.[13] Upton's trip west took him across the Great Plains for the first time, and the region's beauty enchanted him. Its steep hills, buttes, and ravines caught his eye (he thought it good cavalry country), and he noted that the few cottonwood trees on the banks of its rivers provided welcome shade in the late-summer heat. The wildlife Upton observed fascinated him. Wolves and coyotes, prairie dogs, owls, rattlesnakes, jack rabbits, "polecats," antelopes ("the most delicate [meat] I ever tasted"), and tarantulas all caught his attention, and he carefully recorded the habits and appearance of each. One of his great adventures was a hunt for buffalo, and though he was unsuccessful in his first two attempts, the third proved to be the charm. Afterward, Upton recounted the hunt in a letter to a sister. "You can scarcely imagine the excitement of a buffalo chase," he wrote.

> Mounted on a fleet horse, and armed with two or three revolvers, you sin-
> gle out a large herd and gallop toward it. They soon see you, and, taking the
> alarm from some old bull, follow him, generally running toward the wind. It
> is a beautiful sight to see them as they take the alarm and gallop away. With a
> large mane which gives them a terribly ferocious look, they seem to run as if
> on three legs, and you doubt not that a few seconds more will see you in their
> midst. But not so! After a sharp run you begin to approach them, your horse
> then takes the excitement, and, increasing his speed, closes upon them.

As was true of many first-time travelers across the "great American desert," the number of buffalo there amazed him. "[O]ften you find yourself among herds which extend for miles farther than the eye can reach," he told her.[14]

Upton arrived in Denver on September 29, 1865. There he found a bustling frontier town that had grown to a population of four thousand since its found-ing in 1859. The community's inhabitants, he observed, "are, of course, not so polished as Eastern people, but I have met many nice gentlemen." He thought the cost of living there to be "enormously high." Board at a local hotel was $135 per month, he reported, "and other things in proportion." General Pope had ordered Upton to cut the district's expenses to the bone, and to do so he visited the territory's towns and outposts to evaluate the region's needs. The report he sent to Pope was not at all positive. Upton proclaimed that he had been "edu-cated to believe that a public dollar was as sacred as a private one, and, to the extent that I am, or may be, its custodian, I will be ever faithful to my trust." He lamented that he found himself "surrounded by a set of unscrupulous con-tractors and speculators, who regard the public money as their legitimate plun-der. I will defeat their villainous schemes to the utmost, be the consequences to me what they may. I expect, in fearless discharge of my official duties, to call down on my head the venom of the entire class; and as they have heretofore been all-powerful through the money they have stolen from the Government, I would not at any time be surprised were they to secure my removal." Upton concluded, "All that I ask is to be supported by my superior officers, and if, by the faithful discharge of my duties, I secure their commendation, I shall care nothing for the abuse or vituperation of a horde of defeated speculators." In April 1864 he had complained about "paltry politicians" whose control of promotions had corrupted the system and overrode the recommendations of professional officers. In Colorado he had found the source of that political corruption—money that bought favors and abused the public trust.[15] Upton's report also reveals a fatalism that was creeping into his personality, a belief that he was fated to suffer the slings and arrows of his enemies while in service to his nation. This quality to some degree had long been present in Upton, as his willingness as a teenager to die for the cause of abolition suggests, but it became more pronounced as he became more involved in reform issues, whether tactics, army policy, or civil service. This temperament, in many ways, came to dominate his remaining years.

His duties did not deter Upton from pursuing other interests. The Civil War's carnage and the lethality of its weapons had convinced him that Hardee's tactics manual, which emphasized the importance of the bayonet as a weapon of shock, needed revision, and he undertook that task. Upton's experiences as a commander of infantry in the Army of the Potomac informed his ideas, but those with the Cavalry Corps were particularly important in shaping them, having convinced him that the magazine-fed carbine would dominate future battlefields. General Sherman also had a significant influence on his ideas. During the train ride the two had shared in the summer of 1865, Sherman had related to the young officer that most of the fighting between his army and that of Johnston and Hood in 1864 had been conducted by skirmishers. Remembering this conversation, Upton worked very carefully on that section of his tactics.[16] Based on his experiences and on Sherman's advice, he concluded that Hardee's two lines of infantry should be replaced by a single line that was more dispersed than previous practice and preceded by skirmishers. Though this would diffuse the weight of any single volley, the large volume of fire made possible by a single line would more than compensate, while extending the line by increasing the distance between individual soldiers would make the battlefield far less lethal to attackers than it had been during the Civil War.

Upton had begun to experiment in the summer of 1864, when just prior to the Battle of Opequon Creek, he had employed a battalion of the Second Connecticut to exhibit some of his concepts to Brigadier General Russell and other officers. By early 1866 he had developed these ideas into a coherent manual he believed the army ought to adopt. In January Upton wrote to the adjutant general that he wished to travel to Washington to submit his tactics manual to the secretary of war or to a board of officers in the hope that they might approve its use by the entire army. He told his sister that he had "no misgiving" that his tactics would be adopted. "Were my tactics but a revision of the present system with a few unimportant movements added," he wrote, "I would not be sanguine, but as they aim at a complete revolution, and are far more simple, my confidence increases with every comparison I make." His certainty also stemmed from the fact that he had "military men to deal with, who will adopt the system of tactics that is best for the army." Still, he told her that he would have the manual published at his own expense if it were rejected.[17] Aside from showing Upton's extreme confidence in his system, this letter illustrates his continued, almost blind faith in the ability of the army's officer corps (as opposed to "paltry politicians") to make proper decisions regarding military policy. At the same time, the letter demonstrates Upton's tenaciousness once he had set an objective for himself. He had the right answer for the army's tactical problems, and nothing would stop him from promoting it as a solution, not even its rejection by the officer corps he revered.

In June 1866 the army convened a board of officers chaired by Col. Henry B. Clitz that met at West Point to consider the adoption of a new system of infantry tactics. The most important part of the board's inquiry consisted of testimony given by Upton as well as a demonstration of his tactics by the Corps of Cadets. The *Army and Navy Journal* reported that even though the captain had had only one hour to instruct the cadets, the resultant drill was still a resounding success, thus testifying to the system's adaptability. The Clitz Board considered just one other set of proposed changes, but Upton did not think it posed a substantial challenge to his tactics. "I . . . am confident that my system will be accepted for the Army," he reported to his West Point classmate, Henry du Pont. "[William] Morris is my only competition, and his system is based upon facings. I do not fear him." The board unanimously endorsed Upton's tactics, and General Grant recommended in January 1867 that "Upton's Infantry Tactics, Double and Single Rank" be used as a text at the military academy and be adopted as the army's standard tactics manual.[18]

Upton's *Infantry Tactics, Double and Single Rank, Adapted to American Topography and Improved Firearms*, though not truly revolutionary, was a sharp departure from its predecessor. Hardee's manual had made some effort to account for the development of rifled weapons, but it still placed great reliance on massed infantry formations moving in two ranks across open ground and, upon reaching their objective, driving the defenders out of their positions through force of the bayonet. Upton rejected these practices. In their place he made groups of four soldiers the basic unit of infantry and simplified the commands by which those soldiers would be maneuvered on the battlefield. He emphasized the role played by skirmishers, believing any attack ought to be preceded by a heavy skirmish line, and simplified the manner by which soldiers could be added to the skirmish line by pushing "fours" forward. His single-rank formation, Upton hoped, would make a less inviting target for the enemy while putting more firepower forward. He emphasized the need for individual initiative on the part of junior officers and noncommissioned officers, believing that spacing out the infantry formation, the widespread use of skirmishers, and the confusion attendant to any battle meant that large numbers of soldiers would be beyond the direct control of regimental, brigade, and division commanders.

His system thus represented a significant step forward toward the squad-based tactics of the twentieth century. Still, Upton's tactics are best understood as a drill book rather than a true tactics manual. His system, according to Perry Jamieson, "defined the formations and movements for the various types and size of units, but he did not advise officers . . . 'How to fight.'" In this regard it was little different from previous tactics manuals.[19]

Upton believed that his tactical system had one other substantial benefit—it was, as its title implied, a truly American system. Many of its rudimentary movements and commands, especially the manual of arms, came directly from Silas Casey's *Infantry Tactics*, which itself had been based on Winfield Scott's earlier works as well as on French tactical manuals.[20] Yet Upton offered the army something that was, in many ways, distinctly different. Scott's, Casey's, and Hardee's manuals had adopted French practices with little thought as to how they might apply to the U.S. Army, given its amorphous makeup, and with little concern regarding the demands North American terrain placed on tactical formations as compared to that of northwestern Europe. Upton hoped that his tactics would compensate for future soldiers' lack of experience through the simplification of commands and battlefield maneuvers, and he thought breaking down his infantry formations into groups of four men would make formations more adaptable to the North American continent's broken ground. He had emphasized the latter point when requesting that the army convene a board to consider his system, and Grant, in endorsing the manual, noted one of its strengths was that it was "a purely American work."[21]

Still, Upton's tactics had their detractors, and to satisfy those critics, Grant convened another board at West Point in the summer of 1867. The general in chief presided over this one himself, with Major Generals Meade and Canby serving as board members. After barely one week's work, during which the board heard testimony from several officers who disapproved of Upton's tactics, the Grant Board recommended their adoption by the army. Its members noted the ease by which the tactics could be taught to new soldiers, that their column movements were adaptable to both open and obstructed terrain, and that their movements from column into line as well as their facing movements were done much more quickly than under any previous system—an "advantage of vital importance in the presence and under the fire of the enemy."[22]

William Conant Church's *Army and Navy Journal* quickly endorsed Upton's tactics. "We consider Upton's system far in advance of any other we have seen," it had editorialized at the conclusion of the Clitz Board in 1866. The following February it provided another favorable review. "The great simplification of the tactics is thus apparent," it proclaimed. "It is far more easy to be comprehended by officers and men, than any they have yet seen." The *Journal* lauded their adaptability in broken country, their "marked improvement in skirmish drill," and the degree to which they were "assimilated" to the tactics of cavalry and artillery.[23] After the Grant Board published its findings, the *Journal* again endorsed Upton's manual and noted "the importance of promulgating the decision of the Board at the earliest day possible, and the immediate introduction thereafter of the tactics into use." Once the tactics were ordered to be the army's standard, the *Journal* yet again voiced its approval. Indeed, the new system so impressed Church that he made Upton the publication's tactics editor.[24]

Neither the prestige conferred by the Grant Board's approval nor Church's vigorous endorsement shielded Upton and his manual from criticism by the *Journal*'s readers. Most comments were very minor in nature. One letter writer sought to "point out some inconsistencies and imperfections," while another hoped to suggest "improvements" in the manual. Yet another believed the book was not clearly written, and still another, though acknowledging "that the new system of drill is, as a whole, better adapted to practical use than any previous one," stated, "there is no reason why it should be considered as a finality."[25] These critics did not quarrel with the thrust of Upton's tactics, they merely sought to further simplify its commands or to clear up inconstancies in its manual of arms.

Others were less willing to accept the manual's basic assumptions, and in some instances their analyses were vitriolic. An author whose pen name was "Gettysburg" questioned whether or not Upton's system of fours would work under combat conditions. "Theoretically, the tactics have already been tried," he wrote,

> but the question that presents itself here is, are they adapted to the exigencies of the field of battle? I have no reference to those bloody fields described by some historians on which *one* man was killed, and for which Upton appears to have provided by prescribing that vacancies in the front rank should be filled by those in the rear rank; but I refer to battles like that of Gettysburg in which *fifty per cent* of the regular division were placed *hors de combat*. . . . What will then be the difficulty under a severe fire, when your sets are *all incomplete?*

This analysis brought "Gettysburg" to his verdict. "If the basis—the unit of four men—fails," he wrote, "the superstruction [*sic*], however beautiful and symmetrical it may be, will fall to the ground." A more sarcastic critic came to a similar conclusion, noting that casualties would force a unit to renumber its soldiers time and again. "Keno-callers would make good captains in this sort of business," he concluded, "but even with the assistance of such experts mistakes would probably occur." The same author belittled Upton's efforts to assimilate tactics, complaining that the cavalry's horse and the infantry's soldier were different animals and needed different commands. Acknowledging the letter's tone, the editors of the *Army and Navy Journal* entitled it "A Biped's Whinny."[26]

Another author who called himself "A Lover of Truth" claimed that Upton had copied most of his work from Casey, charging that 1,428 of the 2,147 paragraphs in Upton's manual had been taken from the latter's book. He also believed the ability of the new tactics to conform to broken terrain was a liability, not an asset. Upton, he thought, "had in view some particular section of the country, full of woods and other obstacles. In my opinion it is not proper that a national system of tactics intended for all parts, should be subordinated to one particular section." "Atlanta" disputed the ease with which the tactics could be learned, and he too noted that many of Upton's maneuvers were the same as Casey's. He also believed "Upton's system of skirmishing is so defective that it will have to be completed by additions from the old if we ever again engage in war." "No one will venture to say," "Atlanta" concluded, "that the old system was perfect; but I think that, with all its defects, it was far superior to the new. . . . [I]n exchanging the old tactics for the new we have substituted a certain slowness for precise celerity, slovenly complexity for neat simplicity, and principles that are but partially applicable for those that have been tried by fire and found not wanting." "Atlanta" later penned what he surely thought was his most damning censure. "Our old tactics were, I believe, almost literally translated from the French," he wrote. "It remains to be seen whether the French will translate *our* tactics and adopt them in place of those which we discarded."[27]

Upton did not lack for supporters in the *Army and Navy Journal*. Several objected to "Atlanta's" suggestion that the tactics ought to be thrown out. "Eugarps" admitted that Upton's manual had problems but suggested that they could be worked out. "While I wish the tactics to be revised," he concluded, "I do not wish to see them discarded." "Delta" took "Atlanta" to task over the latter's criticisms of Upton's skirmish drill, stating: "There is not a single movement laid down in this drill that would not come into practice in actual battle. . . . I do not claim that Upton's tactics are perfect, but I do claim that they are so great an improvement on any former system, that the Army and country are under great obligation to the author for his successful labors."[28] Perhaps the most compelling testimony regarding the controversy surrounding Upton's tactics can be found in a letter that his wife, Emily, wrote to him in early 1869. Visiting Havana while convalescing from one of her near-constant illnesses, she reported that one of the army wives she met there "was quite interested last night on hearing that I belonged to 'Upton's Tactics.' She says her husband swears at you every drill night for having changed the Tactics."[29]

As debate over the new tactics raged in the pages of the *Army and Navy Journal*, Upton was strangely silent. Peter Michie noted that he "took no part in the public discussion" of the tactics, though he was "exceedingly interested in all that was said." He suggested that the reason for Upton's reticence was that he was "unshaken" in his belief in his system. This was, in all probability, quite true, but other factors also distracted him. Believing the curriculum at West Point did not adequately address the campaigns and lessons of the Civil War, Upton suggested to James Wilson that he undertake writing a history of that conflict that showed "the combined and simultaneous movements in all the theaters of war." "It is a work needed very much," he insisted, "and I know no one person capable of dissecting the strategy of the war, and placing it clearly before the military eye than yourself."[30]

Upton's ideas about the military academy did not end there. West Point itself, he thought, was badly in need of reform. Wilson had once suggested that he ought return to the school as its superintendent, but Upton demurred, stating that he "would be equally satisfied with the Commandantcy of Cadets." He thought there was much to do at the academy, and he was particularly concerned that the "old professors . . . allow cadets to pass examinations knowing little of their course."[31] This situation had to be corrected if West Point was to remain the primary, if not exclusive, source of the nation's army officers.

The larger issue of the shortcomings of American military policy also received Upton's attention. "When I see changes that ought to be instituted for the great benefit of the service," he told Wilson, "it is difficult for me to remain quiet." The inequities he perceived in the army's promotion system, one he believed rewarded political connections and longevity of service rather than the quality of the service rendered, rankled him. In April 1866 Upton had been mustered out of the volunteer service and reverted to the rank of captain in the Fifth Artillery. Two months later the army offered him the rank of lieutenant colonel in the Twenty-Fifth Infantry, a position he gladly accepted, and he served with the regiment in Paducah, Kentucky, between the summer of 1866 and the fall of 1867.[32] Despite this rise in rank and responsibility, Upton was unhappy with what appeared to be his professional stagnation and thoroughly frustrated with the promotion system. In a letter to Wilson he complained that Romeyn Ayres had "the inside track for a brigadiership" despite being "thoroughly weak and inefficient, a man who never gives an emphatic opinion or assumes the slightest responsibility," and who throughout his command was known sarcastically as "the man who parts his hair in the middle." Upton believed that Ayres's "services are less conspicuous than those of any other officer who served in the field" and that his promotion to brigadier general would "discount the service of every officer who fought successfully during the war." He concluded that Ayres "should be kept out of harm's way by being left a colonel."[33]

Upton also believed that the army's officer corps was poorly prepared for the demands of modern war. It had not kept up with advances in tactics or in weaponry, and to him there appeared to be little interest among officers regarding strategy and long-range planning. Upton thought the obvious solution was that the army ought develop a school of instruction. He outlined a suggested curriculum in a letter to Sherman. It would be, he wrote, "a short course of study; say Tactics, Regulations, Art of War, &c, practical instruction & drill." This program, he told the soon-to-be commanding general, "would be of incalculable benefit to the Army, as insuring uniformity of drill and discipline through-out."[34]

Upton's study of Roman military history confirmed his belief in the importance of discipline. After the Civil War he had read Edward Gibbon's *Rise and Fall of the Roman Empire* and found striking the lessons that could be derived from that ancient state's experiences and applied to the contemporary U.S. Army.[35] Upton discovered that every successful Roman general had "laid the foundation of his greatness in the improved discipline of the legions. Luxurious indolence was superseded by severe drills, and sumptuous living by plain soldiers fare." He also thought Roman military heroes had been "men of nervous temperament" who, when given a mission, "carried into its execution every energy of their soul." Not only does this description of his "successful" Roman general outline what he believed was the antithesis of the untrained, politically connected volunteer and militia officer, but it also describes exactly the kind of officer Upton believed himself to be, a point he acknowledged. He thought the Roman example so applicable to the United States that the original manuscript of *Military Policy of the United States* included a chapter on the Roman Empire in which he took great pains to show what he believed were the numerous parallels between the Roman military system and that of the United States.[36]

In an October 1869 letter to Wilson, Upton elaborated these concerns, again urging his friend and former commander to undertake a significant writing project. This time he urged Wilson to focus his energies on the failures of American military policy in the Civil War. Upton noted that during the conflict,

men fell into ranks like leaves from the forest; and by discipline acquired the steadiness and strength of veterans. But if you look beneath the surface, which success has guilded[,] the material will be found wood instead of gold. Our men were initially pathetic, and they fought to secure their freedom, not for love of fighting, and when the work was done, the last rebel disarmed, the love of conquest so strong in barbaric times was as latent in their bosoms as when the first gun was fired. . . . Hence it is that today you find practically speaking no Americans in the ranks.

This analysis led Upton to what he believed was the crux of the problem. "Ever so slight is the passion for military glory," he continued, "that states attempt to maintain a militia organization when the freedom of election [of its officers] abolishes restraint; and makes discipline a mockery." He concluded that Wilson could "render a national service" if he were to "make the glaring defects of the volunteer system, its cost in treasure and blood, apparent through the medium of a Military History of the War."

Upton was not satisfied to suggest what he thought ought be the thrust of his friend's work and concluded by offering specific reforms Wilson ought advocate. He thought a company ought be the largest organization a state could raise in time of war, that the federal government should reserve to itself the appointment of all field officers, and that West Point should educate "a surplus of officers, who in time of war should be appointed to the grade of field and general officers." These ideas mirror those that appear in Upton's later works. He also made clear that he had not given up on the individual volunteers or on members of the militia, for they had "acquired the steadiness and strength of veterans."[37] Rather, it was a system that had sent them to war unprepared for its exigencies he deplored. By October 1869, then, Upton already had determined in rough form what he believed were the problems with the American military system, their attendant costs, and their solutions.

In addition to his increasing anxiety regarding U.S. military policy, one other factor almost certainly served to distract Upton from the ongoing debate over his tactics: in the summer of 1866, he had met and fallen in love with Emily Martin of Auburn, New York.

Upton and Andrew Alexander, who had commanded a brigade in the Second Cavalry Division, had remained close friends after the Civil War ended. In late 1865 Upton met Alexander's wife, Elvina "Evy" Martin Alexander, when she moved to Knoxville to be with her husband. He was a frequent visitor in the Alexander household, and Evy invited him to call upon her parents whenever he might be near their home in Auburn, New York. Evy's father, Enos Throop Martin, was prominent in New York state politics, and among his friends was William Seward, who also was from Auburn and whose children frequently visited Willowbrook, the Martin estate.[38] Roscoe Conkling, senator from New York, and Francis Blair Jr., chairman of the House Committee on the Military and Defense in the early days of the Civil War and Horatio Seymour's running mate on the Democratic presidential ticket in 1868, also were among Martin's close friends.[39]

While at West Point during the summer of 1866 to testify before the Clitz Board, Upton had traveled to Auburn, arriving there late one afternoon in the middle of July. After dinner with the Martins, he enjoyed the company of their daughter, Emily, in a sunset walk around Willowbrook. He remained with the family for three more days and spent most of his time talking with her. After attending church one Sunday, they sat together in a downstairs room while Emily read to Upton. Later that afternoon they took a walk along Lake Owasco, which the Willowbrook estate overlooked. The next day followed a similar pattern, with the couple taking in a carriage ride to the other side of lake as well as a long walk that evening.[40]

The interests that brought these two together are not entirely apparent. It is clear Emily had fallen deeply in love, but it is equally clear that she was attracted by the possibility of redeeming Upton's soul.[41] He had, she believed, wandered from the path of righteousness, and she was determined to set him straight. This probably was a correct assessment on her part, as references to religion had all but disappeared from Upton's correspondence between 1863 and 1866. The war's prosecution and his search for promotion had consumed him, neither of which were connected to any effort to improve the world in preparation for the millennium. Emily recorded in her diary that she "felt a constant anxiety about the salvation of his soul, and prayed earnestly day and night, *that he might be brought back to God.*"[42]

Emily was aggressive in her assault on what she believed was Upton's agnosticism. "I have been frequently led to think of what you told me last spring about your spiritual state," she wrote him,

> and I have deeply mourned over it. Having once known the blessedness of being a child of God and coming to his table, I truly believe that you can not be willing to give him up, and once more cast your lot with the world, the enemies of Christ our Saviour. . . .
>
> A great responsibility rests on you; you are believed to be a professor of religion. I have heard this from several sources; also of the dedicated stand you took on the Lord's side while at West Point, and in the influence of your example there.
>
> Never was I more astonished than when I heard from your own lips the admission that your faith in God's justice had been shaken and that you no longer felt that you were a Christian. One of the strongest bonds in my friendship for you was the feeling that you could sympathize with me on the subject nearest my heart, and that I could therefore trust you as I would not men of the world.

"For many months," she concluded, "I have seldom closed my eyes without praying for you my friend, and I feel that I can not bear to see you shutting yourself out from God's favor without making this last effort to assure you that someone cares and prays for your soul." Emily's concern continued even after their marriage. "You, I hope my darling, are roaming as a good soldier of Jesus Christ for the right," she wrote in December 1868, "striving each day to put down wrong and uphold the truth as you know it."[43]

It is even more difficult to gauge Upton's feelings toward Emily while they were courting because none of his correspondence with her prior to their marriage survives. Still, his letters during their separation in the winter of 1868–69 makes apparent that he loved her deeply and had a great physical passion for her. While on a brief separation during their honeymoon in Europe, he wrote, "How is it that away from you I feel again like love making?" Almost all of the more than sixty letters he wrote that winter express clearly his love and devotion. At one point he declared: "Writing, reading, or whatever I may be doing, you interrupt me whenever you please, may sit on my lap, or present your sweet face to be kissed as often as you please. I am going to love you and make up for all lost time. In you darling centers all my future and anticipating the bliss you can afford me, I am willing to suppress all ambition."[44]

Whatever might have ignited the romance, it moved quickly. The two met in Washington in early 1867, when Upton was there promoting his tactics. "I saw him constantly and long," Emily recorded in her diary, and upon her return to Willowbrook, she heard from him "quite frequently." In May 1867 Upton asked Emily to marry him, and she agreed. Shortly afterward, however, she felt it necessary to break the engagement. Visiting Willowbrook in August, he again proposed, but this time Emily "could not . . . feel willing; after all that had occurred; to commit to his care my life happiness." Her chronic poor health may have played a role in this decision, yet it is clear that it was also due to the fact that both she and Upton had had other romantic dalliances. "I send you darling a piece of Nettie Haines wedding cake," he wrote his wife in December 1868. "I think you ought to reciprocate by sending me some of Marcus Harris, and then we could bury the memory of flirtations we both struck up in the 'winter of our discontent made glorious summers' when I took you in the 'back car' Nov. 17th 1867."[45]

That was a significant date in the couple's relationship, for on that day Upton returned to Willowbrook and again asked Emily to marry him. Her diary entry conveys the seriousness with which she took this step. "On that day," she wrote, "I promised Gen'l Upton that I would be to him forever a loving wife, that nothing but death should ever part us in spirit, and when we had kneeled and asked God's blessing on the solemn step we had taken, I felt the peace I had so longed for take possession of my heart." Upton took a much less sober tack in his description of their engagement, describing it to James Wilson as if he had secured a military objective. "I have the honor to report that the

troops of my command broke camp at Paducah Ky Nov 11, and in light marching order commenced a decisive campaign, of which Auburn was the objective
point," he wrote. Reporting that he advanced "till my skirmishers reached the
foot of Owasco Lake," Upton complained that his "efficient staff . . . could gain
no reliable information of the enemy" and that he "was therefore compelled at
great personal risk to reconnoiter the lines myself." Resolving to make a "direct
attack," he placed himself "at the head of [his] troops, colors in [his] hands
. . . [and] led them in the assault." "The struggle was short, sharp, and decisive,"
he concluded. "[W]hen the smoke lifted from this miserable battlefield I found
myself engaged to the lovely Miss Emily Martin. The campaign which opened
under doubtful auspices was brought to a successful close. The troops are now
quietly in camp enjoying that repose to which their . . . service and glorious victory entitles them."[46]

Just prior to the couple's wedding, Upton reported to General Sherman
that Emily was "equally fitted for the Army with Mrs. Alexander," but in fact
she was in very poor health. Only one week before the ceremony, Emily found
herself so weak that she could not walk about her room. The attack had come
on quickly, and her doctor, who diagnosed the illness as neuralgia, assured her
that it could disappear just as abruptly.[47] Barely two days before the wedding,
Emily was so feeble that she could barely talk to Upton, and that conversation
so exhausted her that he had to help her up the stairs to her room.[48] Despite this
attack, she was well enough to go on with the ceremony on February 19, 1868.
Many of Upton's wartime comrades attended, including Wilson, Alexander,
and du Pont. Afterward the couple departed for Europe, the relatively expen-
sive journey funded by Upton's earnings from the sales of his *Tactics*. Not only
was this trip meant to be a honeymoon, but the couple hoped that Italy's climate
and that of southern France might be beneficial to Emily's health. Her mother,
however, believed that it would be restored by other means. Mrs. Martin sent
Emily on her way by advising that she was "in the hands of the Great Physician"
whose "healing touch can restore you to perfect health."[49] Upton, on the other
hand, had more secular concerns on his mind. "While in Europe" he wrote
Sherman, "I shall pay special attention to the description and organization of
all large continental armies, and hope to derive much profit therefrom." It was a
promise he fulfilled when, while visiting France, he left his ailing wife for a few
days to observe French army maneuvers.[50]

Unfortunately, neither God nor the European climate served to improve
Emily's constitution. After departing New York in March, the couple traveled to
Brest and from there to Lyon, Marseilles, Sorrento, and Florence. Upton at one
point believed that Emily's health had so improved that the couple would be
able to journey to Russia, but she never was well. In August they cut short their

trip and returned to Willowbrook, where they remained until October, when Upton took his wife to Key West, hoping the climate there might aid her recovery. Because his leave of absence had expired (having taken a one year's leave in the fall of 1867), Upton left Emily in Key West under the care of her sister Nelly while he traveled to Memphis, Tennessee, to assume his duties as lieutenant colonel of the Twenty-Ninth U.S. Infantry Regiment.[51]

There Upton immersed himself in the regiment's day-to-day functions, duties he found less than rewarding. "The command is aggravating when I recall the days of the 4th Div. C.[avalry] C.[orps] M.[ilitary] D.[ivision of] M.[ississippi]," he wrote Wilson, "yet I do my duty toward it with as much zeal as though it numbered ten thousand." He nevertheless allowed that his return to duty had brought him great contentment. He was quite satisfied with the officers under his command. "I am happy to say there are no hard drinkers," he told Emily. "They all too are very glad that I have joined." His obligations kept him "busy as a bee, the battalion having my constant attention." Still, those duties seem not to have been too demanding. By his own account his first obligation on a typical day was guard mount at 9:00 A.M., followed by "office hours" from 9:00 to 10:00 A.M., and "battalion drill" from 3:00 to 4:30 P.M. How he spent the rest of the day Upton left unstated.[52]

Not surprisingly, the lieutenant colonel felt that his first responsibility was to ensure that his command drilled properly. "The post has suffered much from frequent change of commanders. There has been no one to take deep interest in affairs, and while the discipline has been very fair, the drill has been entirely neglected," he wrote Emily. Upton quickly instituted daily instruction in battalion drill. "There is much room for improvement," he continued, "and I am certain when you report for *duty* from sick leave you will learn much has been made." Indeed, less than a week later, he reported to Emily that it would please her "to see already the improvement made in drill and discipline."[53]

Upton invested some of his time into yet again revising his tactics. He began the project in early 1869, likely while in Louisville, Kentucky, for nearly three weeks on court-martial duty. He told Emily that he hoped the revision would be finished by June so he could travel to Washington and present the changes to the secretary of war. Upton expected that he might then receive orders placing him on "special duty" so he could "superintend the printing" of the manual, which would give him "authority to make Willowbrook my HdQuarters." Initially he told her that his revision "progresses favorably," but his evaluation of his progress changed quickly. "I have been trying to complete the revision of my Tactics," he wrote Emily in March, "but so numerous have been my interruptions, so unexpected many demands for my time that I have made little progress."[54]

Upton was far from a social hermit while a geographic bachelor in Memphis. He kept his wife apprised of his activities, which were numerous. He attended the opera during a brief sojourn in New Orleans, the theater and the opera in Memphis, and the theater and a minstrel show while in Louisville. On New Years' Day 1869, accompanied by one of his officers, Upton made calls upon other officers and their families. On one of those visits a captain and his wife "proposed that the officers & ladies of the garrison should assemble in my quarters in the evening and have a Happy New Year." He was unprepared for the event, but "it being incumbent on a commanding officer to promote the happiness of his Post, I could not object to the program." He had the "Post String band" come to his quarters, and there was, he hesitated to tell her, "dancing in your house." On the eve of Lent the lieutenant colonel attended a "masked ball" in Memphis that kept him out until 3:00 A.M.[55]

Despite these social interactions, Upton told Emily that she could not imagine the "unsatisfactory life" he led in her absence, his quarters being turned into a "den of bachelors" by officers who were staying with him.[56] "I feel your absence every moment," he declared,

> and want more and more to enjoy your *presence*. What a comfort it will be during another winter to look up at any time in the evening and find my cherished Pet sitting peacefully and happily beside me. No word need be spoken. It will be enough that you are there, and then how many times I shall come up noiselessly and plant a kiss on your lovely neck or sweet lips. I am sure I shall be prodigal with kisses. And then my dear I shall feel again your soft hand. How many times when you have slipped it into mine at Church. When lonely or fearful I have felt proud, grateful, and happy that it was mine and I was its protector. How I want it again this paper cannot describe.[57]

He noted frequently that Emily's personality compensated for the shortcomings of his own. "How beautiful is our relationship, each the complement of the other," he wrote on Christmas Day 1868. "One harsh, the other gentle; one ugly, the other beautiful; one worldly, the other spiritual." On New Year's Day he admitted, "I need your sweet influence." Six weeks later he told her: "I want again to experience my darling Pet's love and tenderness. I want her to stimulate again into life the better part of my nature now dormant." "As my heart approaches yours in purity, I feel a better, nobler man," he wrote barely one month before they were to be reunited. "In peace with God," he told her, "*true* happiness does not exist outside the family circle, and I bless Him daily for having given me a companion so suited to my temperament."[58]

Religion remained important to their relationship even as the couple was apart. Upton seems to have realized that Emily had married him, at least in part, to bring him back to godliness. "I feel now more and more," he declared, "that each time the sacrament [of communion] is partaken, my sense of duty to God and my neighbor, grows stronger and stronger, and I hope ever long to have that clear faith which possesses true Christians." Shortly after leaving Emily in Key West and returning to the mainland, Upton told her that he had started to read one chapter of the New Testament every day, expecting to be finished by early summer. He asked of her, "won't you do the same, catching up with me when you receive this," a request that likely pleased her. Less pleasing might have been his praise of two Christian sects, Swedenborgianism, and Mormonism. He told Emily that he had gone, "for the first time in my life, to hear a Swedenborgian and found in general terms that I agreed very well with him. They reject the Trinity, [worship] a Christ-God, believe in a spiritual resurrection, and many other things through Gods mercy. I think my desire to submit to these, and to do His Will grows stronger every day." Upton's comments about Mormonism grew out of events in his quarters while it was a "den of bachelors." He told his wife that one guests, an officer by the name of Dodge, "is already urging upon us to break up and go to Salt Lake, where wives are so numerous that a husband can never be left solitary. I must avow that this is the sole advantage I have ever seen in Mormonism, but I can never become a convert so long as I have a darling with all of her sex besides."[59] Though he likely meant this in jest, it is clear that Upton was struggling with his religious beliefs and was using Emily as a sounding board. He seldom attended the same church two Sundays in a row, and his criticisms of the Episcopal faith strongly suggest that he was sorting out his own religious convictions. Yet during these religious tribulations, one aspect of his faith remained unchanged, and that was his disdain for Catholicism.[60]

Upton was certain that his faith required him to evangelize among his soldiers. In February 1869 he received a box of Bibles from the American Bible Society, a shipment he presumed to have originated with his mother-in-law. "I hardly know whether to open it before you come or not," he told Emily. "I suppose I ought as in doing good one cannot commence too soon." He apparently made little progress on this project, for one month later he reported, "Your mother wrote me a letter, half in love and half in fits, so I immediately called the sergeants and requested all the enlisted men who had no bibles [sic] to come to me for them, and already I have distributed quite a number." Upton hinted that he expected Emily to help him with these efforts. "Should you regain your strength," he noted, "you will not be at a loss for doings and to the command I am certain that the visit of a lady to the hospital to read tracts, and to show some Christian sympathy . . . would do much to cheer and comfort the patients."[61]

The Uptons also communicated about more worldly concerns, one of which was finances. When he mentioned that he was revising his tactics manual, Upton also told Emily that by the fall of 1869, he expected his "finances to be in a splendid condition, and we shall set out in life in earnest. Your father has done so much for you that my self respect will soon be involved if I allow him to do more." How much had Mr. Martin done? In their first year of marriage, Emily's father had given her $5,000, and it appears that he gave her another $2,000 sometime in the spring of 1869. To say Upton was distraught over this is no exaggeration. "You may not be able to appreciate it," he wrote Emily, "but I can tell you that all husbands worth having prefer a wife to be dependent upon them, rather than independent of them. The latter condition has ruined the happiness and usefulness of many an officer, and while I think under no circumstances could my usefulness be destroyed, I am sure you would sturdy my happiness by ultimately looking upon me for everything." In late February he reported that he was debt free and, thanks to royalties from his tactics manual, had "on hand" $1,200. "My dear we are *rich*," he told her, "and we will never have to tax your Parents again."[62]

Emily's absence left to Upton the task of establishing a household in Memphis, the prospect of which seems to have unsettled him. The day before he moved into his new quarters he wrote his wife that he would do little to furnish the house until she arrived. It appears, however, that he had second thoughts as that day approached. "You must write me," Upton told her, "whether you want me to have everything in absolute readiness for you to go to housekeeping or whether you would like me to let you exercise your own taste in some of the purchases." He had exercised some of his own tastes, having purchased a few pieces of furniture shortly before taking possession of the quarters. Even then, however, he deferred to Emily's judgment as to what style carpet he ought purchase. "I want to know your ideas," he wrote her, "so that the house may be quite ready for your occupancy." He sketched out its floor plan for her and added that, by the time she arrived, there would be a kitchen built "outside the house, just in view of the dining room."[63]

Friends and family often were the subject of their correspondence. Emily's sister Nelly accompanied her that winter, and Upton almost always sent his regards, conveying to his wife how much he enjoyed receiving Nelly's letters. Once in a while Upton mentioned his sisters Maria and Sara. Both remained single, and at one point he told Emily that he would like to see them "suitably married, for so long as they are single, I feel responsibility on that account. Married life is the only true life for women while a man can live single without so much inconvenience." But a surprising amount of the couple's correspondence centered on one of Upton's West Point classmates, Jacob Rawles, who was stationed at Key West.[64] One of Upton's letters strongly implies that Emily and Nelly, while in Florida, had stayed with the Rawles family. During his brief time in Key West that November, Upton had observed much about his classmate that disgusted him. "You may remember," he wrote Emily, "I called Rawles aside, where he gave me this pledge that he would not drink any whiskey or intoxicating liquor excepting in the officers quarters of his garrison, or on board naval vessels. My aim was to get him away from the rum shops down town where he was spending most of his time and which could only terminate sooner or later in making him a confirmed drunkard." These efforts had little effect, and he later heard of Rawles's "particularly bad treatment of his wife and family," of his "harsh treatment of his children," and that "he was becoming more and more brutalized." "Your disgust with R is no stronger than mine," he assured Emily.[65]

Politics seldom found its way into the couple's correspondence. When visiting New Orleans in the fall on 1868 while en route from Key West to Memphis, Upton noted that the city "is quieter since the election. The people are getting tired of politics, and will soon devote most of their time and attention to filling their pockets, a very sensible resolution." After attending Grant's inauguration in March 1869, he reported to her that the ceremony was "very short and to the point." He applauded Grant's appointment of Alexander Stewart as secretary of the Treasury. "Give us economy and honesty," Upton opined, "in the administration of the . . . laws, and we shall be all right."[66] The only other political reference in their correspondence that winter Upton surely wrote with a glint in his eye. Emily had moved from Key West to Nassau by that time. "I suppose it [Nassau] is full of Rebels," he teased, "but you can turn up your nose at them, and tell them that Reconstruction is a success."[67]

This is not to say that Upton was uninterested in national politics. He most certainly was, as his attendance at Grant's inaugural attests. If anything, national politics had become more important to him, believing as he did that Democrats' return to power not only would mean a reduction in the size of the army but also would signal the ultimate victory of the Confederacy. By contrast he thought Republican success in 1868 would bring a "profound peace." He likened Republican victories in that year's early congressional elections to the political "Vicksburg" of the "rebel *Democracy*" and considered Grant's election its "Appomattox." "What a glorious era is now before us," he proclaimed to Wilson. "The results of the war secured; the national credit established, and peace restored." The success of the Republican Party in these elections so elated Upton that he ruined a good dress hat "by protruding my toe through it in an effort to elevate it into the air." After the election he told his sister Maria that he expected Grant to "continue those functions that brought peace to our land" and thought the country was about "to enter a [period] of prosperity without example."[68]

Upton was optimistic that Grant's election might have a positive effect on the army. John A. Rawlins, a friend of the new president, had been appointed chief of staff of the Army at the end of the Civil War. Rawlins, who suffered from tuberculosis, had been ill most of the time he served in that position. Upton hoped that Grant's election might lead to Rawlins's retirement. "We want a live man in his place," he wrote to Wilson, "and I wish you might get it [the appointment]. It is, or might be made, one of the most important positions in the U.S. Army. The office has at all times the Ear of the General in Chief, and through him the discipline of the Army might be carried to any pitch."[69]

Despite his positive assessments of the nation's future under the leadership of Grant and the Republicans, Upton feared that the wealth the nation was accruing likely would become a source of national corruption. "Wealth will beget arrogance, and develop a spirit of aggression," he thought, a sentiment that had been fueled, no doubt, by his brief experience in Colorado. He believed that "the U.S. have a destiny no other nation ever had" but also thought that many of its political leaders were "so corrupt as even now to jeopardize the liberties we possess." In January 1869 he wrote Rep. Thomas Jenckes of Rhode Island, a prominent Republican who had been an outspoken advocate of civil-service reform, suggesting that civilian government workers should serve under rules similar to those that bound army and navy officers. "If convicted of embezzling or misapplying public funds committed to their care," he advised, "let them be fired, imprisoned, and, as in some cases in the Army, be dismissed [from] the service, and be forever disqualified to hold any office of profit, emolument, or trust with the United States." Upton also thought that life tenure in the civil service would solve many problems, again suggesting that the army officer provided an apt comparison. "Whether from professional pride, life tenure in office, or fear of summary punishment," he wrote, "it is conceded that Army officers in a remarkable degree are faithful to their pecuniary trusts."[70]

Yet Emily's poor health trumped Upton's interests in other areas. Despite her sojourns, first in Key West and then Nassau, her health improved only haltingly. She suffered frequently from severe bouts of coughing and at least once was diagnosed with neuralgia. Upton was terribly concerned about her condition. "Let me know darling just how you are. Are your pains diminishing or increasing," he wrote soon after he had left her in Key West.[71] When it quickly became apparent that cooler-than-expected weather and Rawles's drunkenness were detrimental to his wife's health and state of mind, Upton urged in very strong terms that she go to Nassau. After her arrival there he made clear that, though he missed her badly, Emily ought not come to Memphis until she was well, particularly if Nassau was contributing significantly to better health.[72] At times he could be something of a scold. "Take good care of the cough," he wrote her in December 1868. "Are you not careless in dressing? Do you keep your winter clothing the same? Remember that it is your duty to watch yourself, and not to rely on others to do it for you."[73] Still, most of the time he expressed his concerns in loving terms.

In January 1869, already anticipating that another separation might be necessary during the winter of 1869–70, Upton told Emily, "I am quite sure I will not let you go next winter and if it be necessary I will sooner apply for a year or two in New Mexico." Briefly it appeared the army might cooperate with his willingness to be assigned to the Desert Southwest. Word reached Memphis in late February that the officers of the Twenty-Ninth Infantry would trade places with those of the Thirty-Second Infantry, stationed in Tucson, Arizona. Upton speculated that it would nice for Emily to live near her sister and brother-in-law, Evy and Andrew Alexander. "I would prefer New Mexico or California," he told her but averred, "To go to Arizona even will benefit you." Upton clearly was concerned that his wife would be distraught with such a move. To assuage her fears he told her, "To go there and remain four years would just prepare us to appreciate West Point."[74] He took a somewhat different approach in his next letter. "It will do everything for your health," he declared, "and another satisfaction we shall on the outset of our military life, encounter the worst hardships the Army can offer. But I think they are very few & so must Evy. You have my lovely one a [sic] great advantage over many ladies: . . . we can never be at a less than three [officer] Company Post, so you must have more or less society." As time wore on Upton heard little more about the transfer, yet he continued to try to convince his wife that Arizona would be good for her health. "Granger says that people never get a cold in Arizona, so that would be especially nice for you," he assured her. "Were you in good health we might get out of this arrangement by going to West Point but I do not want to go there till you are strong for I know you look to West Point as an Army heaven. If you are willing to go with me I care not if they send me to a desert, for wherever we are I think with your disposition I can make you happy and I know you will do so by me."[75]

All of these western rumors proved false, however, as the Twenty-Ninth Infantry moved to McPherson Barracks in Atlanta in the spring of 1869. By that time Emily's health had improved to the point that she felt capable of rejoining her husband and setting up a household in Georgia. In late March she departed Nassau for New Orleans, where Upton met her and, after a brief stop in Mobile, took her to their new home. He found a fair degree of professional satisfaction in Atlanta. There were four infantry regiments at McPherson Barracks when he arrived, though two later merged and moved to Alabama. The other two, the Eighteenth and Twenty-Ninth Infantry, remained, and Upton took command of the former and became the post commander as well. Because most of the regiment's men were new recruits and few of the officers had any substantial experience, he immediately undertook an aggressive training program consisting of two drills a day. "I do a great deal in drill and discipline, which are inseparable," he wrote Wilson, "and have always been at a loss to explain the indifference of our celebrated generals during the war to these essential elements of success." This period of professional satisfaction was short lived, however, for in June Col. Thomas Ruger arrived to take command of the Eighteenth Infantry, causing Upton to think of himself as a "fifth wheel" and "an idle looker on."[76]

Politics, both national and local, captured Upton's attention during his stay in Atlanta, and two incidents provide insight into his political beliefs as well as into his personal values. In June he reported to Wilson that John Croxton, who had been a brigade commander in the Cavalry Corps, had passed through Atlanta but had spent some time there. Croxton, according to Upton, was upset because "the only thing he had asked of the new Administration was the appointment of a one armed soldier as assessor of Internal Revenue." President Grant, Upton reported, had instead "appointed a dirty politician who staid at home all the war." Still, he thought newspaper accounts of problems within the new administration, which he attributed to Charles Dana, were slanderous and should be dealt with severely.[77] These conflicting opinions demonstrate a certain tension in Upton's opinion of Grant. He was becoming critical of the president, in particular of his giving in to "dirty politicians" regarding civil-service appointments, yet his overall opinion of Grant had not changed. Within a decade, however, he would come to see the hero of the Civil War as a threat to the Republic.[78]

A second incident likely showed Upton that the South in many ways had not been defeated and was returning to its antebellum ways. In April 1869, soldiers in Alabama had found and released a woman who had been locked in a jail for nearly two years "on account of her Union sentiments" and because she allegedly had been "running off negroes." Her brother, Brig. Gen. Joseph Anderson, who had run the Tredegar Iron Works in Richmond during the war, had visited her in her cell and had promised to secure her release if she would "behave herself," which she refused to do. Anderson then replied that she could rot in jail before he helped her. Upton, when informed of the woman's liberation, gave permission for the jail to be burned, believing that "she had suffered much" and hoping that watching her prison go up in flames would give her much pleasure.[79] Though he did not express his judgment of this incident's significance, the tone of his description of the incident leaves no doubt that it appalled him. For four years he fought to free the slaves and to reunite the nation, yet four years after the war's end, an innocent woman had been jailed for favoring the latter and for taking positive action to achieve the former.

Upton continued work on his tactics while in Atlanta. In 1869 the War Department had convened yet another board, this one chaired by Maj. Gen. John Schofield, to consider another revision of the army's manuals, charging this panel to investigate the full assimilation of cavalry, infantry, and artillery tactics. Upton eyed its proceedings warily. Describing himself as "a little exercised" over the board's "probable action," he laid out his concerns to Wilson. "The work of assimilating the Tactics of the three arms," he wrote, "will not, I apprehend, involve any but the slightest changes in my tactics, yet I fear the purpose in Washington is to avail themselves of this opportunity to seize my copyright, which would rob me eventually of thirty or forty thousand dollars." To prevent this from happening, Upton submitted an amended version of his 1867 manual to the Schofield Board in September, believing it dealt more fully with the question of assimilation.[80] He also applied for permission to travel to Washington at army expense in order to present a copy of his revision to the board. Despite the fact that Colonel Ruger had recommended the request be approved, Sherman, now the commanding general of the army, rejected it. "The presence of all field officers with their regiments is of so much importance," he wrote, "that it is preferable that Gen'l Upton should submit in writing any changes he may want in the system of Tactics. . . . If he wants leave, he must apply for it in the usual form."[81] Sherman's closing remark hit the nail on the head, and no doubt he knew it, for the Society of the Army of the Potomac was scheduled to meet in Washington in late June, the same time period during which Upton proposed to visit the city. Not deterred by this rebuff, the lieutenant colonel took leave and attended the reunion anyway, bringing Emily with him despite the fact that once again she was not well. While in the capital he gave a copy of his revision to Sherman. "I think the revision will be adopted," he informed Wilson.[82]

When the reunion was over, the Uptons proceeded to Willowbrook, where they hoped that the cooler summer climate might help Emily's health, though she thought it had been the housework involved in running the couple's home, not Atlanta's climate, that had set her back. Upton expected his wife to recover sufficiently to allow her to return with him to Atlanta in September. The couple soon realized, however, that she again needed to winter in a more healthful climate. After a brief stay in New York, he left Emily in her mother's care and returned to his duties at McPherson Barracks. In October he traveled to Willowbrook, after which he escorted Emily and Nelly to Nassau. Concerned that he had taken too much leave over the previous eighteen months, Upton applied to the War Department for leave without pay for the period of the journey. Emily thought such a move was silly, though she understood his motives. "I see that you have taken your leave without pay," she wrote her husband. "It may be better, and at least is a sort of comfort to your conscience. I am sure, dearie, that your reputation will not suffer when you are in the line of your duty, as I think all will believe you are in seeing me settled." The War Department concluded that "the pay of an officer cannot be stopped, except by General Court Martial, unless he is absent without leave"; it therefore put Upton on leave *with* pay.[83]

Upton began to contemplate his future in the army after returning to Atlanta. Remaining "an idle looker on" in a regiment held little attraction to him, and other possibilities beckoned. In early 1869 Secretary of State Seward had suggested that Upton go to China to help that nation develop a more modern army, an idea he had briefly considered but dismissed. Now he took the proposition more seriously. Upton admitted to Wilson that "he would like to grapple with the problem of reorganizing, rearming and instructing the Chinese Army," but was unwilling to endanger his financial stability to do so. He therefore returned yet again to the idea of becoming the commandant of cadets at West Point, with Wilson, he hoped, serving as the academy's superintendent. "What my dear Wilson could not we do for the dear old Academy if sent there together," he wrote in April 1870. "I have an idea for many reforms that the two together might institute which it would be difficult for me to accomplish." He confided that he hoped they might rid West Point of the "super-annuated" professors who, Upton believed, controlled the academy. He also believed that the course of instruction needed to be reorganized and "all means of discipline need tightening." Upton promised Wilson he would recommend his former commander to Secretary of War William Belknap as well as to others who might be able to influence either the president or the secretary of war. He fulfilled this promise barely days before reporting to the military academy as its new commandant. While attending the graduation of the West Point Class of 1870, Upton spoke to Belknap, who was there to deliver the commencement address, and inquired about the possibility of Wilson being appointed superintendent. "You are decidedly his choice," Upton later reported to his friend, "and I don't doubt that he will bring it about next year, but I want it this year." Yet his efforts ultimately failed, and Wilson left the service in late 1870.[84]

Emily also had been looking forward to the prospect of her husband's being assigned to the academy, at least partly because she saw West Point as needing her evangelistic fervor. "I hope dearest," she wrote him in the fall of 1869, "if we go to West Point we may be able to exert a good influence. I see many trials ahead, religiously, if we do go, but I feel determined to do what I think right." Unfortunately, she was never to see the academy. Emily's health declined unexpectedly in early 1870, so much so that Upton made plans to visit her in Nassau, but she died on March 29 before he could depart.[85] Those with Emily at the time of her death were concerned that he might be inconsolable over not being at her bedside, and they did their best to comfort him. "The main thing in the matter of your absence is in this," her doctor wrote to Upton, "that she really suffered less, I believe, in dying, than she would have done if you had been present; for the pain of parting would have been increased tenfold, and she expressed herself very decidedly to that effect the day before she died, when she was suffering very much. . . . [T]herefore I think you should consider the matter in the same light as she did, and believe that 'whatever *is* is best.'" Her sister Nelly expressed similar sentiments but also told Upton, "when she was first taken so ill, she had a great longing for you, and she often said, 'If Emory were here he could hold me.'"[86]

Upton appeared truly crushed by his wife's death. He mourned at her casket before the funeral service and placed his handkerchief over her heart before it was sealed. His correspondence also struck a mournful tone. "I strive to bow to this affliction," he wrote his parents, "and to acknowledge in it the goodness of God; yet I selfishly long for my darling. I know this feeling to be wrong, since Emily, having finished her labors, has simply been called to her heavenly rest." Yet professional concerns never were far from the surface with Upton, a fact demonstrated by a letter he wrote to Wilson shortly after Emily's funeral. In it he told him how stricken he was over his wife's death, then quickly shifted his focus to a discussion of schemes concerning future assignments and what the two might do as a team at West Point.[87]

Emily had influenced profoundly her husband's religious beliefs. "I know that in her death I have been drawn nearer to Christ, and that I can now lay hold of the plan of salvation as I never could before," he wrote his parents. "Surely the resurrection of the body, the promise of a blessed immortality, rob death of its sting, and if prepared I can now see that, with St. Paul, we all ought to be able to say that 'for me to live is Christ, and to die is gain.'" He expressed similar sentiments to a sister. Complaining of the desolation he felt upon entering their home in Atlanta, he said that he knew that "God can help me to bear this sorrow."[88] His brief marriage to Emily and her unexpected death had brought God back into his life. Judged by his correspondence, it had been absent from his day-to-day activities since sometime in 1863, but by 1870 he had rejoined the fold.

Aside from religion, one other element of Upton's life promised to help him forget his sorrow. "I know that when again in active duty," he told one of his sisters, "employed in instilling in the minds of the nation's future defenders ideas of devotion to duty and discipline, I shall experience consolation in the thought that I am again useful in the world." In May Emily's mother traveled to Atlanta to help Upton with his move to West Point; he departed McPherson Barracks later that month. After journeying to Charleston, South Carolina, and to Washington, D.C., Upton arrived at his alma mater in June, where he assumed the post of commandant of cadets.[89]

By the summer of 1870, Emory Upton's personal life had fallen apart. Expecting that his wife would join him at West Point, she instead had died, leaving him with memories that would haunt him for the remainder of his short life. Emily had made one very important contribution to Upton's life—she brought him back to God, and once again Upton was His servant. But his military career was similarly empty. Despite his tactics having been adopted by the army, something that identified him as one of the service's advanced tactical thinkers, Upton's career appeared to be stuck in neutral. Serving at backwater posts in Paducah, Memphis, and Atlanta, he was a lost soul in the postwar army. Assignment as commandant of cadets at West Point might rescue him from this anonymity, but the army's promotion system condemned him to remaining a lieutenant colonel until officers senior to him died, resigned, retired, or were promoted. This was anathema to Upton. A conviction that the army suffered from an archaic promotion system, an abiding belief that the unpreparedness of the militia and volunteers had prolonged the Civil War, and a growing disdain for the role played by "dirty politicians" in the development of U.S. military policy had begun to take shape in Upton's writings. He continued to develop these ideas over the next decade, and they found expression in the late 1870s in his proposals for the reform of the American military.

Maj. Gen. Emory Upton. Courtesy National Archives, Brady Photographs of Civil War–Era Personalities and Scenes, RG 111, file B-5877 (529964).

Mess Hall at the U.S. Military Academy in the 1860s, West Point, New York. Courtesy National Archives, Brady Photographs of Civil War–Era Personalities and Scenes, RG 111, file B-2036 (526233).

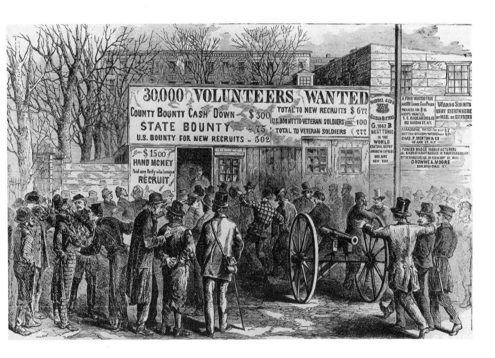

Recruiting in City Hall Park, New York City, 1864, as illustrated in *Frank Leslie's Illustrated Newspaper,* March 19, 1864. Practices such as that illustrated here were anathema to Upton, and their elimination was one of the objectives of his proposed reforms. Courtesy National Archives, Brady Photographs of Civil War–Era Personalities and Scenes, RG 111, file BA2175 (535914).

Maj. Gen. Henry W. Slocum. Upton served in the artillery of Slocum's division during the Peninsular and Antietam Campaigns. Courtesy National Archives, Brady Photographs of Civil War–Era Personalities and Scenes, RG 111, file B-2800 (526985).

Maj. Gen. John Sedgwick. Sedgwick commanded the Army
of the Potomac's VI Corps from the spring of 1863 until his
death at the Battle of Spotsylvania on May 9, 1864. Courtesy
National Archives, Brady Photographs of Civil War–Era
Personalities and Scenes, RG 111, file B-4199 (528343).

Alfred R. Waud, *Upton at the Salient.* 1864. Courtesy Library of Congress, Prints and Photographs Division (LC-DIG-ppmsca-20105).

Lt. Gen. Ulysses S. Grant, March 15, 1865. Grant promoted
Upton to brigadier general after the charge at Spotsylvania.
Courtesy National Archives, Brady Photographs of Civil
War–Era Personalities and Scenes, RG 111, file BA-1663.

B-4462

Maj. Gen. James H. Wilson. Upton commanded a division in Wilson's cavalry corps in the spring of 1865, and the men remained close friends and confidants until Upton's death in 1881. Wilson wrote the introduction to Peter Michie, *The Life and Letters of Emory Upton.* Courtesy National Archives, Brady Photographs of Civil War–Era Personalities and Scenes, RG 111, file B-4462 (528590).

Edwin M. Stanton, secretary of war, 1862 67. Upton had grave concerns about Stanton's role in the events that led to the impeachment of Pres. Andrew Johnson. These concerns had a substantial role in shaping his reform agenda. Courtesy National Archives, Brady Photographs of Civil War–Era Personalities and Scenes, RG 111, file B-4559 (528682).

Maj. Gen. William Tecumseh Sherman. Sherman, when
he was commanding general of the U.S. Army, was Upton's
mentor and benefactor. Courtesy National Archives, Brady
Photographs of Civil War–Era Personalities and Scenes, RG
111, file III-BA-1674.

William H. Seward, secretary of state, 1861–69. Through his wife, Emily Martin Upton, and her family, Upton had connections to Seward. Courtesy National Archives, Brady Photographs of Civil War–Era Personalities and Scenes, RG 111, file B-4305 (528448).

Brig. Gen. George W. Getty. Getty commanded Fortress Monroe, Virginia, when Upton served there in the late 1870s. Courtesy National Archives, Brady Photographs of Civil War–Era Personalities and Scenes, RG 111, file BA-226.

HARPER'S WEEKLY.

A JOURNAL OF CIVILIZATION

Vol. XXI.—No. 1076.]   NEW YORK, SATURDAY, AUGUST 11, 1877.   [WITH A SUPPLEMENT. PRICE TEN CENTS.

Entered according to Act of Congress, in the Year 1877, by Harper & Brothers, in the Office of the Librarian of Congress, at Washington.

THE GREAT STRIKE—THE SIXTH MARYLAND REGIMENT FIGHTING ITS WAY THROUGH BALTIMORE.—From a Sketch by D. Bendann.—[See Page 626.]

The Great Strike of 1877, with the Sixth Maryland Regiment fighting its way through Baltimore, as illustrated in *Harper's Weekly*, August 11, 1877. The strike and other events convinced Upton that "communists were getting control." Courtesy Library of Congress, Prints and Photographs Division (LC-USZ62-99137).

Maj. Gen. James A. Garfield. Garfield. Upton and Garfield
corresponded often in the late 1870s on the subject of army
reform when the latter was a member of the U.S. House
of Representatives. Courtesy National Archives, Brady
Photographs of Civil War–Era Personalities and Scenes, RG
111, file B-4130 (528276).

Sen. Ambrose E. Burnside. A former commander of the Army of the Potomac, Burnside in the late 1870s sponsored an army-reform bill in the U.S. Senate that incorporated many of Upton's ideas. Courtesy National Archives, Brady Photographs of Civil War–Era Personalities and Scenes, RG 111, file B-4594 (528717).

CHAPTER 5

COMMANDANT OF CADETS

From June 1870 until July 1875, Lt. Col. Emory Upton served as commandant of cadets at the U.S. Military Academy. It was a tumultuous yet listless period for the academy. A case of vigilante justice, in which the school's senior class ran three freshmen off the grounds for allegedly violating the Honor Code, and the admission of the first black cadets and their subsequent mistreatment brought unwanted notoriety to the school. Upton, who found himself at the center of both incidents, concluded that these controversies were products of politicians seeking personal gain at the expense of President Grant, the army, and the academy, confirming his low opinion of elected officials.

The turmoil surrounding these events notwithstanding, the academy was in the midst of a period of stagnation. Though it had been a pioneering school for technical education before the Civil War, West Point had not kept pace with national trends and had become an educational backwater. Upton arrived believing that the school's academic program was reflective neither of the army's needs nor those of the nation. He also had concluded that discipline and a sense of honor were lacking within the Corps of Cadets. As commandant, he implemented disciplinary reforms and introduced the cadets to the army's most recent tactical innovations. Reorganization of the course of study was not his responsibility, though he expected to influence the direction of academic reform if his wartime comrade, James Wilson, were appointed superintendent; Wilson's resignation from the army in 1870 dimmed Upton's hopes for meaningful academic reform. The continued presence on the Academic Board of septuagenarian professors who refused to change the program Sylvanus Thayer had established in the early nineteenth century and the resistance of politicians who feared that candidates from their districts would not survive a more rigorous course of instruction dashed those hopes altogether. Upton therefore never saw the academic reforms he thought important to both the academy's and the army's future.

Stymied in these efforts, Upton once again turned his attention to tactical reform. At the urging of Commanding General of the Army William T. Sherman, he chaired a board of officers whose mission it was to assimilate the tactics of the artillery and cavalry to that of the infantry. Armed with what he believed were the lessons of the American Civil War and of the Franco-Prussian War (1870–71), Upton sought an answer to the tactical impasse breech-loading weapons and flexible infantry formations had brought to the modern battlefield. His solution to this problem and his reaction to criticisms of it reveal much about his vision of the nature of future combat.

"Tomorrow I take hold of the Cadets as Commandant, and to discharge the duties of the position acceptably is my biggest ambition," Upton wrote to Henry du Pont on June 30, 1870. "Could I turn out in each class ten or twelve soldiers like yourself I should be quite satisfied, but good soldiers I find are very rare." Upton was concerned about a general want of discipline within the corps, and the cadets' apparent lack of a sense of honor particularly disturbed him. He wrote Wilson that he would attack this problem and hoped "to bring the cadets to a high sense of honor." Discipline and honor were important attributes because without them, Upton believed, academy graduates would not be good officers. He was not the only person who harbored these concerns. Nine months prior to Upton's arrival at West Point, Dennis Hart Mahan had written Sherman expressing concern that fights among members of the corps had become all too frequent, and he that feared they would become more prevalent as southern cadets returned to the academy. "These men," he concluded, "will bring with them even more than the arrogant dictatorial tone that the Southerner formerly displayed here, and it is to meet just such acts, as a pseudo-chivalry of this character takes pride in, that I think your hand will be required to curb." Mahan attributed the atmosphere that condoned fights among cadets to William Hardee, a southerner who, he charged, had "winked" at the practice during his tenure as commandant between 1856 and 1860, and who, he maintained, "did a great deal of mischief here."[1]

The Board of Visitors cited other reasons for the almost-endemic lack of discipline. It noted discipline within the corps had not been a problem when West Point had been relatively isolated from the outside world and cadets' non-military activities had been severely limited. "But all of this has changed," its members noted.

> West Point is now or fast becoming a place of fashionable resort. Hotels have been erected in near proximity to the post, and hundreds of visitors now repair thither where [perhaps] one did in former years. This influx of fashionable life has caused a relaxation of the rules in regard to cadet visiting. The great distance between officers and cadets has been gradually diminished. Cadets of the first class may now visit officers every day of the week, and officers and cadets associate together with a freedom of intercourse not formerly known.

In what Upton must have found to be an embarrassing indictment, the board concluded that the cadets' "standard of discipline has been lowered, until the Academy has less than formerly the character of the Regular Army, and more the features of a militia establishment."[2]

The new commandant intended to remedy this situation by enforcing rigidly the academy's rules of behavior. "Send away every trifler who does not approach his advantages, and meet the requirements of the profession, is the policy," he reported to Wilson. One of Upton's first actions was to direct that cadets submit all communications to him in person. In doing so, they were to "halt ten paces in front of the Commandant's tent and upon invitation will uncover, advance within the tent, halt three paces from the Commandant, assume the position of the soldier, salute, make their communication and having received a reply, will about face and retire." The purpose of this exercise was to "impress upon Cadets the importance of cultivating on all occasions, whether on or off duty, a military appearance and soldierly bearing." Upton issued a similarly detailed order outlining saluting procedures. "The Commandant would remind the Cadets," it concluded, "that the salute is simply an act of courtesy due from the inferior to the superior and that to be appreciated it must be rendered willingly. They should therefore when they see an officer approach or about to pass them at a distance offer the salute as soon as observed preferring to salute at too great a distance rather than be considered deficient in politeness." He soon published other regulations that he believed would restore discipline to the corps, including those detailing the saluting of officers "when in the company of ladies," the proper method of saluting the colors, and procedures cadets were to be use when corresponding with the commandant.[3]

Other practices Upton thought dishonorable quickly came under his scrutiny. He reported to Wilson that he had "made quite a stir" by removing two seniors from the color guard for not marching on the parade field with their own weapons. "It was an unfair advantage they had taken of other cadets who had labored faithfully for this honor," he explained. Another custom he attempted to eradicate was that of the upper classes securing pledges from new cadets that they would not harass the next year's incoming class. A cadet who made such a pledge and then subsequently broke it would lose their furlough privileges. Upton objected to this ritual because he thought a cadet's sense of honor, not coercion, ought to dictate his adherence to regulations.[4]

Efforts to instill upon the corps the importance of honor and discipline were not limited to these martinet-like endeavors. "After I get fully established," Upton wrote Wilson, "I intend to invite members of the 1st Class [senior class] to dine with me and in coming into contact with them socially I hope to impart many valuable ideas in regard to discipline." He also attempted to influence the cadets' behavior through religion. The prayer meetings in which Upton himself had participated had continued since his graduation, with up to seventy-five cadets attending at times, yet they had no official sanction. Upton changed this, not only permitting the group to meet in the academy's "dialectic" hall every Sunday evening (its gatherings previously had been held in cadet rooms) but also allowing its meetings to be extended from one-half hour in length to the period between dinner and tattoo on Sunday evenings.[5] He was, moreover, an active member of the group. According to Peter Michie, Upton "gave his strong support to this organization, frequently met with them, encouraged the timid, and supported all by his words and countenance." He was always present at the academy's nondenominational Protestant church services, and "his practical religious life and humble Christian profession were potent influences to the young men who knew of his marked military success."[6]

Emily's professed desire to bring religion back to West Point no doubt influenced Upton's efforts to encourage cadets' religious activities. "Of all the earthly blessings with which my life has been crowned," he wrote Emily's mother,

> association with Emily's pure spirit is the one for which I cannot express to our heavenly Father the gratitude I feel for the unspeakable gift. Through it he has led me to the foot of the cross, and to the knowledge that the blood of Christ cleanseth from all sin. And I feel again that he has sent me the spirit of truth, and that he comforts me daily and hourly by the presence of the Holy Spirit, which bids me wait patiently for the perfect love which soon will be revealed.[7]

As he had before the Civil War, Upton believed that good deeds prepared a man's soul for the world to come. "The seed which we must all sow is the life which we have spent here on earth," he told his parents. "If our lives are spent in glorifying God, in humbly doing his will, and walking in his ways, it will in death be quickened, and again blossom in eternal loveliness, and ripen in the continual sunshine of God's love." Glorifying God and doing his work brought an individual honor as well as redemption. "With his everlasting arms to support us," Upton believed, "we ought always to press forward for the mark of the high prize of the calling of God, realizing that no yoke is imposed upon us, but that in obeying his will and commandments we are walking in the perfect law of liberty."[8] He hoped to inculcate these values in the Corps of Cadets.

Events during Upton's first winter as commandant overtook his earnest if shallow efforts in this regard. On Monday evening, January 2, 1871, a cadet departed the academy grounds without permission. During room inspection later that night, his roommate, knowing the cadet had left the post, covered for him by stating "all right." Through this action he was giving his word of honor that all cadets in the room were within their prescribed limits and that any who might be absent, to the best knowledge of those present, was also "on limits." As that inspection was being conducted, a third cadet entered the room and stated "all right" even though by entering another cadet's room, he himself was beyond his limits. Later that night Upton, when he learned of the incident, placed the three cadets, all of them plebes (first-year cadets), under arrest, bringing charges against the trio the following day. The academy's senior class, however, took matters into its own hands. After a meeting on the night of January 3–4, thirty-seven of the class's forty-one cadets, including President Grant's son, ran the three out of the academy, giving them fifty dollars "to support them until they could get assistance from their friends." The seniors reported their actions to Upton the following morning.[9]

Walter Dillard's judgment that "the rest of the affair was handled poorly by the authorities" seems an understatement. Upton took no immediate action because, according to Michie, he wanted to act in "a very deliberate manner." An officer the commandant sent to Highland Falls was unable to find the "expelled" cadets. When it was discovered that the three were in Poughkeepsie, Upton ordered them brought back to West Point. The academy quickly dismissed one of the three for academic deficiency, and the other two quit after Upton told them that "under the circumstances it was best for them to resign." Neither cadet's resignation could be accepted, however, without their parents' approval, yet Upton processed the paperwork and sent the young men home on January 9 without receiving that consent. He took this action, according to Michie, because he feared the "useless mortification it [waiting for parental permission] would occasion." The matter seemed concluded on January 10, when Col. Thomas Pitcher, the academy's superintendent, assigned "punishment" to the senior class after a brief investigation. That punishment, which restricted the senior class to the immediate area of the cadet barracks for a short period of time, seemed singularly inappropriate given the seriousness of the offense.[10]

By this time, however, events had moved beyond the control of Upton and Pitcher. Word had reached Washington, D.C., of what had transpired, and on January 8 the House of Representatives approved a resolution that directed the Committee on Military Affairs to investigate the incident. The subsequent report was a scathing censure of the academy's leadership. In a preface to its findings, the committee noted that Upton and other officers had testified that discipline at West Point had improved over the previous six months. "[I]f this be true," the report judged, "its former condition must have been deplorable." It then proceeded to criticize almost every facet of the academy's handling of the incident. "[T]he committee believe," the report continued, that the superintendent of the academy and the commandant of the corps of cadets failed to properly appreciate the gravity of the offense committed by the first class, and showed a disposition to avoid proper investigation and punishment of the gross breach of discipline and violation of regulations committed by the class.

Their conduct in advising these cadets to resign before any notice had been taken of, or investigation ordered into, the outrage of which they had been victims, is censurable. Their failure to take prompt action for the punishment of the offending class, . . . their official expression of a belief that the class were actuated by "good motives" in their unlawful action; and their continuance of the first class on duty as cadet officers to enforce the discipline of the academy, amount . . . to a virtual sanction of the riotous proceedings of the class, and an encouragement of the repetition of the offense. *The position thus assumed by the officers is subversive of the discipline of the academy. . . . The conduct of the officers shows a lack of comprehension of the principles of military discipline surprising in officers of long and honorable service in the Army.*[11]

Both Pitcher and Upton thought the committee's report impugned their honor. In a letter Upton wrote and that Pitcher approved, the two claimed they had been "censured without a trial, deprived of all liberty of judgment in their official action, charged with the grave military offense of sanctioning riotous proceedings, their reputation as officers wantonly assailed, they feel aggrieved by the unjust treatment they have received from the Military Committee." The two requested "a court of inquiry be ordered to investigate their conduct in the matter, with a view to being brought to trial by a general court-martial should there be any facts to sustain the charges made against them by the Military Committee." Upton carried the letter personally to Washington and gave it to the secretary of war. Belknap attempted to calm the lieutenant colonel, telling him, "I want you to understand that I am your friend, *your friend*, and that means a great deal." "I was never so pleased with a man in my life," Upton told Wilson, "and it is my judgment that we have never had a better Secy of War." Not surprisingly, Belknap ignored the officers' request for a court of inquiry, much as he had disregarded a similar recommendation the Committee on Military Affairs had made.[12]

Upton believed that he had not done anything wrong regarding the scandal, but Michie thought otherwise. Had the commandant of cadets acted promptly and arrested the members of the senior class who had participated in running the cadets out of West Point, Michie later wrote, "he would by this act at once have put his seal of condemnation upon this greatest of military crimes." Instead, in his testimony before the committee, Upton implied that politicians were to blame for the events of that January evening and suggested that the superintendent be given authority to court-martial cadets who had violated regulations. This, he claimed, "would stop that political pressure which is always brought to bring a man back who is discharged." The return of discharged cadets, according to Upton, had fostered the climate within the corps that resulted in this incidence of vigilante justice.[13]

In an apparent effort to counter Upton's charge, the committee's final report included a table that gave the name of every cadet dismissed from the academy between January 1, 1861, and January 1, 1871; the date of dismissal; the cadet's offense; and the case's final disposition. The table showed that of the twenty-seven cadets who had been dismissed during this period, twenty-one subsequently had been readmitted, fifteen of whom returned due to the intervention of the secretary of war (the reasons for the other six cadets were not given). The table's clear implication was that it was the secretary of war, not individual congressmen, who had permitted dismissed cadets to return to the academy. Yet this really did not address Upton's allegations, for when dealing with political appointees (which is exactly what cadets were then and remain today), the secretary of war was not operating in a political vacuum. Almost certainly some, if not all, of these cadets had been reinstated due to pressure from members of Congress who had given them their appointments. Moreover, the table actually appeared to support Upton's larger contention that the return of expelled cadets had undermined discipline at the academy. Five whose names appeared in the table, all of them seniors, had been expelled in February 1866 for attempting to force a cadet to leave the academy who they thought had stolen jewelry and money from another cadet. Like the 1871 incident, the senior class had sanctioned this act of vigilante justice at a class meeting. The five seniors were tried by court-martial, found guilty of "conduct prejudicial to good order and military discipline," and expelled. Secretary of War Stanton intervened, however, and allowed all of them to remain at West Point.[14] Thus Stanton, who to Upton was beginning to symbolize the very essence of the corrupt politician, had ordered five cadets returned to the corps who had been found guilty of dishonorable actions.

Upton presumed that he and Pitcher were two pawns caught in a gigantic political chess game. "The false reports calculated against the Academy are abominable," he told Wilson, "and the Military Committee has given them its sanction. Partisan hatred is at the bottom of the whole thing. To strike the President no matter how many molecules like Pitcher and myself might be crushed . . . was the sole object of the Majority of the Sub committee."[15] Upton thus believed that he had been dragged into the crucible of politics and had come out the worse for it. His integrity had been attacked and his professionalism questioned, he was sure, because "paltry" politicians wanted to score points against President Grant. This incident was yet more evidence of the nation's willingness to tolerate corruption in its public officials, or in this instance, in cadets who should have been expelled from West Point. Much as he had seen dishonesty in Civil War promotion practices and in the territorial government of Colorado, Upton now was experiencing what he believed was corruption within the federal government.

In fact, the problems in this and other instances were more the product of West Point's failure to systematize the Honor Code than it was politicians' actions. At this time the Honor Code was not a code at all. Nowhere was it written down, and no formal proceedings took place when a cadet was accused of an honor violation. Rather, peer action enforced the code, a practice that mirrored the situation in the army where officers often refused to serve under or with someone they considered dishonorable. "Honor" thus fell into a shadowy zone where command authority and peer sanctions were not easily untangled. That cadets enforced the code with almost no supervision by the staff and faculty exacerbated this situation. "There appeared to be little if any awareness of West Point authorities that cadets were young men," George Pappas concluded in writing about a similar incident, "and that young men often permit emotion to overcome common sense. . . . That the Academy administration supported cadet honor supervision was admirable; that nothing was done to systematize the use of the honor system was inexcusable." Indeed, as Peter Michie has suggested, such a situation was conducive to a lynch-mob mentality, which is exactly what had happened in the January 1871 incident.[16]

Congress might have acted quickly in this instance because the academy already was under substantial scrutiny for the manner in which its first black cadet, James Smith, had been treated. Smith had gained admission in the summer of 1870, the same summer that Upton became commandant, and had encountered harassment from the day he arrived, though one historian has concluded that he may have gone out of his way to look for trouble. After the entrance examinations, which more than half of the candidates failed, Smith, who had passed, wrote a letter to his congressional sponsor charging that the exams had been rigged in an effort to prevent his admission. Instead, he wrote, "it proved most disastrous to the whites." After several newspapers published the letter, Colonel Pitcher initiated a court of inquiry to investigate the charges. During the investigation, Smith claimed that the newspapers had not published an accurate version of the letter. The court found that the cadet had been harassed, perhaps unduly so, but it also found that he had exaggerated many of his claims and had lied about the letter's content.[17]

Numerous similar incidents marked Smith's first year at West Point, the last of which occurred in the summer of 1871 during the annual encampment.

Serving as a guard, the cadet allegedly had failed to close the flaps on tents as quickly as the corporal of the guard would have liked. Smith then became the object of harassment, to which he responded in an insubordinate manner. For this offense Upton placed him under arrest until he could complete a full investigation. Ultimately, Smith was not punished for the incident, in part out of concern that doing so might lead to another congressional investigation. Although this was his last major brush with the academy's disciplinary system, the controversy surrounding his cadet career remained a public matter as the *New York Tribune*, a newspaper that supported liberal Republicans, and the *New York Times,* which supported the Grant administration, continued to trade barbs over his treatment. The saga came to an end in 1874 when Smith failed the course in natural and experimental philosophy and was dismissed from the academy.[18]

The second and more famous black cadet to attend West Point, Henry Flipper, entered the academy in June 1873. Compared to Smith, he had relatively few problems, though many cadets tormented him. Flipper reported that some behaved with "gentlemanly propriety" toward him and that it was the "rougher elements of the corps" who gave him trouble. He attributed their actions to "prejudices of caste." Still, most white cadets shunned him, and when Smith finally left the academy in the summer of 1874, Flipper found himself in the very lonely position of being the sole African American cadet remaining at West Point. Shortly afterward, when a rumor reached Upton that Flipper was about to resign, he asked the young man to come to his quarters so that he might convince him to "stick it out." This, it appears, was unnecessary, for Flipper had no intention of quitting.[19]

Upton's concern about Flipper's situation impressed the young man, as did the professionalism of the entire staff and faculty. Flipper later wrote that the academy's officials had been fair-minded toward him and treated him "with uniform courtesy and impartiality." "I have not a word to say against any of the professors or instructors who were at West Point during the period of my cadetship," he wrote in his autobiography. "I have every thing [*sic*] to say in their praise, and many things to be thankful for. I have felt perfectly free to go to any officer for assistance, whenever I have wanted it, because their conduct toward me made me feel that I would not be sent away without having received whatever help I may have wanted. All I could say of the professors and officers at the Academy would be unqualifiedly in their favor."[20] Such praise certainly would have included Upton, for he was the only officer Flipper mentions as having shown him special concern.

The exact role Upton played in the Smith and Flipper cases is not clear, though his willingness to intervene regarding Flipper suggests that he empathized with the cadet's plight and undertook a sincere effort to keep him in school. Smith's and Flipper's experiences likely played an important role in the hardening of Upton's attitude toward politicians. That Flipper succeeded in negotiating the academy's course of instruction, and did so without causing a public spectacle, almost certainly convinced him that the Smith controversy, like the furor that had surrounded the vigilante-justice incident of January 1871, had been a product of politics rather than anything improper the academy had done.[21]

In March 1873 the Corps of Cadets traveled to Washington, D.C., to participate in President Grant's second inauguration. The trip provided a counterpoint to Upton's unpleasant experiences with Congress, though he could not forget how Washington politicians had berated him previously. "The Cadets did behave magnificently," Upton reported to du Pont afterward. "Not one subjecting myself to official censure." It appears, in fact, that Secretary of War Belknap had invited the cadets to Washington to showcase the improved discipline within the corps, displaying to people from around the nation who had gathered in the capital "a body of young military men which he believed in discipline, drill and orderly appearance and the qualities that make a military cadet could not be surpassed."[22]

Leaving West Point on March 2, the corps traveled by train, arriving in Washington the next day. The young men favorably impressed *New York Times* reporters when they changed trains in New York City. The paper reported that the cadets "have been making careful preparations for days past and their uniforms and equipments are remarkably neat, bright, and fresh looking." The three days in Washington were busy ones for Upton and for the corps. On March 4 the cadets participated in the inauguration parade in the morning, put on a display of precision drill in front of General Sherman's quarters that afternoon, and attended the inaugural banquet and ball in the evening. The *Times* was effusive in its praise. It reported that during the inaugural parade, the cadets had moved "with precision and high soldierly bearing. They drew cheers and hearty applause from people all along the avenue. Their step was perfection, and as one man they marched without a break in the full company front. . . . Gen. Upton was in immediate command of the corps. The cadets have been under his strict discipline, and have favorably impressed by their manly and soldierlike deportment." The review at Sherman's quarters, which Phil Sheridan, O. O. Howard, Samuel Heintzelman, and a host of politicians and foreign dignitaries witnessed, went just as well. "The drill in the manual of arms was absolutely perfect," the newspaper reported, "and received [the] greatest praise from officers . . . who witnessed the display."[23]

The following day the cadets put on another display of marching and drill on Pennsylvania Avenue for the benefit of the secretary of war. One Washington newspaper commented: "The drill of the West Point Cadets on Pennsylvania avenue [*sic*] was certainly splendid. The whole battalion went through their various and intricate maneuvers with such precision that they even surprised some of the military officers who . . . reviewed them." Afterward the corps marched through the streets of the capital to the train station, from which it departed for New York that evening. Arriving in the city the following morning, the cadets had breakfast at a hotel and then participated in a grand parade up Broadway before they boarded a train for West Point.[24]

Belknap's purpose had been well served by the visit of the Corps of Cadets to the nation's capital. The young men had impressed politicians, soldiers, diplomats, and civilians. Their performance also pleased one of its most severe critics—Emory Upton. Twice he wrote du Pont to tell his friend that the corps had done well in Washington, though a more significant indication of his satisfaction with its performance was his subsequent proclamation to the cadets.[25] "The Commandant," he declared,

> desires to express to the *Gentlemen* of the *Corps* of *Cadets* his grateful appreciation of their good conduct while absent from West Point in attendance upon the second *Inauguration* of *President Grant.* The military deportment and proficiency of the Corps were the subject of universal comment in Washington.
> The *Review* before the *Secretary of War* was far superior to any the *Commandant* has witnessed since his official connection with the *Corps of Cadets.* The *Drill* was commended by the *Secretary of War,* the *Vice President,* the *Speaker* of the *House of Representatives,* and by *foreign ministers,* who in admiration of the movements in double time, conceded to the *Corps of Cadets* a superiority over the best drilled troops in Europe.[26]

Upton was so pleased with the conduct of *his* cadets that he requested that the superintendent suspend all punishment tours between February 1 and 8.[27]

Over the preceding two years, the corps's behavior and discipline had improved substantially. In June 1872 the Board of Visitors noted that there had been a high level of discipline the previous year and that there were no serious incidents to report. "While the discipline is strict and severe," the board concluded, "it is also, in the main, judiciously adapted to the ends in view." There were numerous reasons for this improvement, one of which likely was Upton's efforts in this area. Another was the infusion of new blood into the academy's staff and faculty. Col. Thomas Ruger had replaced Pitcher as superintendent in the summer of 1871 largely because of the previous winter's incident of vigilante justice.[28] Upton applauded the change. As the commander of the Eighteenth Infantry at McPherson Barracks in Atlanta, Ruger had impressed him as "a thoroughly efficient soldier," and what Upton saw of the colonel at West Point reinforced that opinion. "The Academy is now on a splendid footing," Upton reported to du Pont in January 1872. "Ruger is a model soldier and possesses every qualification to make a good Superintendent." He believed that Ruger represented some much needed *"young blood"* at the academy. The corps's lack of discipline concerned Ruger even more than it did Upton, and the commandant surely agreed with the new superintendent's request that Congress pass legislation that would authorize him to court-martial any cadet found to have violated regulations.[29]

A number of the old professors whom Upton had blamed for the academy's problems also had been replaced. It particularly pleased him that William Bartlett, who had been professor of natural and experimental philosophy since 1836, retired in March 1871. Upton told Wilson that, with Bartlett's departure, "we have got rid of our worst impediment." Peter Michie's appointment to take Bartlett's place met with the commandant's approval. "He is a grand man and will fill the place admirably," he reported. "Our men like him on the [Academic] Board and the young blood, Superintendent or no Superintendent, will control the Board and raise the standard of education." Yet these changes were not enough to please him. "The Academy is in a critical period of its history," he observed. "If we get a good corps of young professors, even with an indifferent Supt [Superintendent] the Academy will enter upon another career of glory and prosperity." One more young professor on the Academic Board, Upton believed, would allow the younger officers to "wake up the cadets from their lethargy and teach them that if they would have a commission, they will have to work for it." By the fall of 1871 West Point, Upton reported to Sherman, was back "on its legs, and with Ruger . . . it cannot sink back into the mire of the past few years."[30]

Upton's duties as commandant of cadets did not distract him from his interest in tactical reform. The army's continued efforts to assimilate tactics, and especially that of the Schofield Board, had infuriated him. "They [the Schofield Board] have taken a very short period to elaborate these system of Tactics," he wrote du Pont in June 1870, "and I fear this work will be full of errors. . . . My belief is, judging by the changes I have seen proposed with Infantry Tactics that assimilation will prove detrimental." This might have been a genuine concern, yet it is clear that he also feared that the army's adoption of a new system would endanger the royalty income he was receiving from the sale of his own manual.[31] Moreover, he was convinced that the older generation of officers was incapable of developing a tactical system that addressed the complexity of the modern battlefield. "We must carry the necessary improvements in our power through," he wrote du Pont. "We are young and if anything is to be done giving blood must accomplish it."[32]

Nevertheless, when du Pont suggested in early 1871 that Upton might serve on a tactics board, he had replied that his duties at West Point precluded his participation since his "time is almost wholly occupied in official duties." He noted, however, that one of his primary obligations as commandant, that of instructing the Corps of Cadets in tactics, enabled him "to discover many absurdities [in the army's tactics] which could be done away with." This no doubt played a role in Upton's ultimate decision to undertake tactics revision, as the corps could serve as a guinea pig for his innovations while receiving the instruction for which he was responsible.[33]

In March 1871, though still complaining about the findings of the Schofield Board, Upton wrote du Pont that he had "no objection to assimilation" but also stated that no single arm should have the ability to "inflict" a maneuver on the other two in order to achieve that end. To ensure that this did not happen, Upton proposed that he and du Pont work together to rewrite the artillery tactics in a manner that would bring them more nearly into line with those of the infantry. Less than one month later, he told du Pont that a new board would produce a manual "which could bear the test of years," but he also mentioned, "I am really too busy to have the additional labor of a board imposed upon me." It was not until after Sherman had placed substantial pressure on him that Upton, in December 1872, agreed to chair a board that would attempt to assimilate the tactics of all three arms. The other members of the panel were du Pont, who served as its artillery expert; Capt. Alfred Bates, one of West Point's instructors of cavalry tactics; and Col. John Tourtellotte, who had volunteered for service during the Civil War, had remained in the army afterward, and was now serving as Sherman's personal aide. Upton believed that it would not require a great deal of work to accomplish the task assigned to his group, and he told du Pont that they could "devote from six to nine hours daily and finish the work I hope inside of three weeks."[34] This prediction, as it turned out, was far too optimistic.

Work on the assimilated tactics moved quickly at first. During his visit to Washington with the Corps of Cadets in March 1873, Upton reported to Sherman and Secretary of War Belknap regarding the board's progress, and both responded favorably. Even Tourtellotte, who was the most pessimistic of the board's members regarding the efficacy of assimilation, began to believe that it could work. Yet six months into the project, the manuals were not near completion. Though the infantry volume was almost done (it contained only minor changes from Upton's 1867 work), the cavalry and artillery tactics required significant effort. Compounding this problem was the fact that Captain Bates had left West Point in the summer of 1873 for another assignment. "All the work will be left in our hands," Upton lamented to du Pont. Still, Sherman and Belknap supported his efforts, and they appeared willing to wait for a much-improved, if somewhat delayed, final product.[35]

By late summer Upton and the other members of his panel feared that Sherman's patience had expired. In August Upton reported to du Pont, "Tourtellotte is getting very much interested in Cavalry and if we can overcome his fear of Gen. Sherman's impatience we shall get on finely." Like Tourtellotte, Upton apparently felt pressure from an anxious commanding general. "I am resolved not to be stampeded," he continued. "It is our reputation that is at stake, and the only safe course is to make haste slowly, being satisfied at each step that we are right."[36] Factors other than the loss of Captain Bates also had intervened to impede progress. The Appleton Company, which had been given the contract to publish the manuals, was having problems producing the plates depicting the manual of arms. Du Pont, moreover, had become engaged that summer to a young woman in New York City, and he took every opportunity to visit her, which delayed work on the artillery manual.[37]

Despite the pressure Upton and his fellow officers felt, Sherman seems to have been willing to let the board proceed at its own pace, and in August 1873 he told Upton that he would be happy if the tactics manuals were completed by December. It was early 1874, however, before any of them were published. The first to appear was Upton's *Infantry Tactics*, which was followed quickly by the board's *Cavalry Tactics*, but it was October 1874 before *Artillery Tactics* was published. Upton believed that the three books were substantial improvements over their predecessors. "All in all I think we ought to be proud of the result," he told du Pont. "We have at least given our successors a basis upon which to work."[38]

Upton's committee gave officers much to consider. Members of the earlier Schofield Board (to which Upton and others often referred as "the St. Louis Board") were upset that so much of the new artillery manual resembled the work they had compiled in 1869. Henry Hunt was particularly vociferous in his criticism of the new manual. In a letter to Sherman Hunt, according to Upton, "began with the color of the cover of the book, and then went through it with a savage spirit." He believed that Hunt's principal objection was to the assimilation of artillery tactics to that of infantry, "as if any change in that direction would be an injury both to Cavalry and Artillery Tactics." "Time will certainly eradicate this objection," he told Sherman, "and will indicate your wisdom in insisting upon the result that has been attained." A biting letter from the commanding general "squelched" Hunt's objections. Indeed, Sherman believed that the tactics were "sufficient for my day and generation."[39]

The *Army and Navy Journal* welcomed the effort at assimilation, but it was skeptical of the results regarding the cavalry. "As the new tactics stand," the *Journal* editorialized, our cavalry are really deprived of the right to be called "cavalry." Mounted rifles, dragoons, mounted infantry they may be called, but the fact remains that the new tactics deliberately consign them to a future in which their main dependence must be only on their firearms, and in which the sabre will be a nearly useless encumbrance. As the tactics now stand it would save the Government a good many dollars, and our so-called "cavalry" much needless trouble, to have every sabre used by an enlisted man turned in to the arsenals.

Though the *Journal* recognized that the new tactics were a reflection of the manner in which cavalry had been employed during the Civil War, it lamented that "this state of things is unsatisfactory." "While we cannot deny," it concluded, "that a certain advantage has been gained for manœuvring purposes by the assimilation of the tactics of the two arms, it is equally clear to us that the cavalry service has suffered by the change in its essential qualities, rapidity and dash."[40]

Upton was quick to reply to this criticism. In a letter to William Conant Church, he informed the *Journal's* publisher that the commands for deploying and maneuvering cavalry on the battlefield "are far ahead of anything ever produced." Responding to the criticisms leveled at the concepts that lay behind the new tactics, he declared, "The whole spirit of the book was to increase the offensive firepower of Cavalry as Cavalry and also give ample development to fighting on foot, which with the breech loader will bring the cavalry in all future wars into close relations with the infantry." The Civil War and the Franco-Prussian War, Upton explained, had shown that the enemy's flank had to be gained in order for an attack to succeed, but that the firepower of new weaponry combined with flexible infantry formations meant that it was all but impossible for attacking infantry to achieve that goal. Cavalry, he continued, could solve this problem. Placing several thousand men with carbines on horseback, riding them to an enemy's flank, and dismounting them, he argued, "will turn the scale of victory in favor of the Army which knows this method of using cavalry." Rather than ignoring its "rapidity and dash," Upton hoped to take advantage of those qualities. He believed his cavalry tactics were well advanced of those of European armies, where "they are just beginning to see the future role of Cavalry, which was so amply illustrative in our war." Church apparently did not accept this argument, for three months later the *Journal* repeated its concerns, this time joining cavalrymen who were critical of many of the manual's commands. Despite these criticisms, opposition to Upton's new tactics, if judged by the volume of letters published in the *Army and Navy Journal*, was far less than that of his 1867 manual.[41]

To his friend James Wilson, Upton elaborated more fully his ideas regarding the cavalry. In response to a letter from the Russian government soliciting essays on military topics, he suggested that Wilson write a paper on the role of cavalry in modern war. "There is no duty which cavalry can be called upon to perform in the present day," he noted, "which our war did not exemplify every day of its continuance." He urged Wilson to

> show that Cavalry has become with the breech loader a great aggressive arm, capable of producing dismounted the demoralization within the Enemy's ranks which is indispensable to success, and which must always precede a charge when mounted. You can easily show the close relation as a turning force which cavalry must hold to infantry in all general battles. You can also when a general battle is going show the danger of distancing the Cavalry as in Stoneman's raid at Chancellorsville, and Stuart's raid at Gettysburg.

Upton discounted European writers' efforts on the subject, charging that their thoughts "will be largely theoretical" unless they took into account the lessons of the American Civil War.[42]

These letters to Church and Wilson are exemplary of Upton's belief in the high quality of his tactics and of the American conduct of war relative to those of European powers. At the time of the publication of Sherman's memoirs in the spring of 1875, Upton wrote the commanding general that he hoped the book would "attract the attention of Europe to the achievements of our arms, and open up a fertile field of illustration to the future structure of Strategy and Grand Tactics." He expressed similar sentiments to Wilson.[43] Clearly, he had concluded that the conduct of recent European conflicts offered little for the United States in terms of operational or strategic lessons.

Upton was similarly scornful of European tactical thought. In March 1874 he told Church that his procedure for feeding skirmishers into the skirmish line was far superior to that of any European army. "I would much sooner trust this formation when combating ground troops," he wrote, "than the Prussian Company Column, which everybody is now idolizing." One year later he was almost contemptuous of the Prussian tactical system. "The French have very secretly adopted the 4 company organization for each battalion, in servile imitation of the Germans," he told Sherman, "but I believe it will operate to their injury." To Church again he wrote similarly, concluding, "Nothing but the German mania can account for it."[44]

A paper he wrote for presentation to West Point's Thayer Club in October 1874 more fully developed his objections to the Prussian company column. This essay, which the *International Review* subsequently published, noted numerous strengths of the Prussian tactical system, among them its flexibility, the small target it presented to enemy artillery, and its enabling "the commander to keep his forces well in hand." He nevertheless found the company column to have so many deficiencies as to recommend that the U.S. Army reject it. He was especially critical of its three-rank formation, believing that the Civil War and the Franco-Prussian War had shown the importance of increasing fire-power through the use of a single-rank and that "retention of the three-rank formation encumbers the German tactics with many tedious and complicated movements." Upton also objected to the small number of officers assigned to Prussian infantry companies. Recent conflicts, he concluded, had revealed that officer ranks had suffered a disproportionate number of casualties, and too few officers in an organization therefore risked having a dearth of leadership once in combat. He further argued that the Prussian method of skirmishing all but assured the loss of control of large numbers of soldiers on the battle-field. Finally, he contended that their new tactical system showed that they "but slightly appreciate the value of field entrenchments, which played so conspicu-ous a part on all the battle fields of our civil war."[45]

If the Prussian system was so inferior, how did Upton explain the outcome of the Franco-Prussian War? "The Germans," he explained,

> were matched against troops inferior in discipline, vastly outnumbered them, always attacked in front, and rarely gained the victory until they had envel-oped one or both flanks. . . . The French, demoralized by the first reverses, always maintained a passive defense. . . . The German system was not there-fore put to a crucial test. Had they been matched against disciplined troops like those of England, or of Russia, how many times might not their center have been pierced, the movement converted by the enemy into flank attacks from the center, and their armies have been driven in confusion and disorder from the field?[46]

Upton's analysis of the outcome of the Franco-Prussian War was not new—he had written similarly to Wilson in 1870. At that time he had criticized French timidity and had blamed it on that country's "superannuated generals," whose ignorance had destroyed "a magnificent Army." "The stupidity of the French generals has no parallel in History," he had declared.[47] Now he went one step further, attributing the Prussian victory to French incompetence while also challenging the efficacy of the entire Prussian tactical system.

Upton's critique of the Franco-Prussian War echoed that of Phil Sheridan. Having accompanied the Prussian army on its successful campaigns at Metz and Sedan, Sheridan returned to the United States and wrote in his memoirs that he "saw no new military principles developed, whether of strategy or grand tactics, the movements of the different armies and corps being dictated and gov-erned by the same general laws that have so long obtained, simplicity and com-bination of manœuvre, and the concentration of a numerically superior force

at the vital point." Upton agreed with this very Jominian analysis of the confl[...]
Indeed, his new infantry-tactics manual opened by stating that "the breach-
loader has changed none of the principles of grand tactics." Upton's writings,
both in his manuals and in his correspondence, however, suggest that his conception of warfare was changing, for the new manual also noted, "The rapidity
and ease with which a line of battle can be extended by means of skirmishers will render the movements for turning a flank more difficult." He observed
that thinning out one's line in an effort to turn an enemy's flank risked weakness in its center and recommended the maintenance of a viable reserve that
could be used both to meet any enemy threat and to exploit battlefield success.
Though he incorrectly assumed mass attacks would be abandoned in future
conflicts, he asserted that "a preponderance of men and fire, in the future, as in
the past, will have to be relied upon to carry positions."[48] Upton believed it crucial that the three arms fight as one on the battlefield. Cavalry would be used in
an effort to gain an enemy's flank while forcing him to extend his line; infantry
would tie down the enemy's front and, if the opportunity presented itself, would
assault, pierce, and destroy it; and artillery would provide supporting fires to
cover these maneuvers. Despite the fact that the bulk of the new tactics manuals
addressed mundane issues such as manual of arms, deployments, and maneuvers, Upton's writings demonstrate that his tactical thinking had advanced far
beyond that displayed in his 1867 manual. By 1873 he conceived of battle as a
combined-arms encounter that required flexibility of mind and of tactics. If in
attempting to "assimilate" the tactics of cavalry, infantry, and artillery, these
three manuals had numerous shortcomings, the concepts that continued to
evolve in his mind regarding the branches' employment were far advanced of
those of most contemporary tactical thinkers.

Even if one accepts Upton's claim that he worked on tactics revision twelve
hours per day every day of the week, it is apparent that he had little else to do
but that and supervise the Corps of Cadets. His only social activity consisted of
entertaining occasional guests such as du Pont and Wilson as well as the cadets
he would invite to his quarters. His youngest sister Sara, who lived with him
from time to time, often assisted by serving as his hostess.[49] He frequently was
alone, however, and it is clear that he was desperately lonely. In many letters he
pleaded for du Pont and Wilson to visit him; these are the plaintive cries of a
solitary, isolated man. Without close friends who were nearby and apparently
aloof in his social relationships with his subordinates, Upton spent his waking
hours immersed in his work.

Some authors have charged that Upton and other reform-minded com-
mandants who served at West Point in the late nineteenth century confined
their efforts to tactical developments rather than the pursuit of substantive

reforms such as the elimination of hazing.[50] This may have been true of some who served as commandant during this period, and Upton's deep involvement in tactical reform while in that position makes him particularly susceptible to the charge. It is difficult, however, to criticize Upton's focus on tactics given the pressure Sherman had placed on him. Moreover, at the time of his appointment, Upton was convinced that "great changes [were] impending" and believed he was an agent of those changes. He had hoped to reorganize the academy's course of study, tighten discipline, and turn out better officers who would be a credit to West Point and would serve the nation with honor. That he was unable to accomplish all that he had hoped was due more to the academy's internal struggles than it was to any single failure on his part.[51] It would take congressional intervention in 1900, after a number of plebes, among them Douglas MacArthur, had been physically abused, before the academy put an end to the practice of hazing. And not until MacArthur became superintendent in 1920 did West Point have a visionary leader in the mold of Sylvanus Thayer, one who would shake up the institution and drag it into the twentieth century. Given the system within which he worked, the personalities at the academy, the byzantine nature of academy and army politics, and the public's antipathy toward the military, Upton probably did as well as could be expected during his tenure as commandant of cadets. Certainly he had no regrets and did not doubt he had done his best. "I shall always look back to my time spent there with satisfaction," he wrote to his sister Maria in August 1875 as he voyaged across the Pacific Ocean.[52]

As the assimilated tactics neared completion in the summer of 1874, it became apparent to Upton that his time at West Point was nearly over. June 1875 would be the end of his fifth year there, and he understood that he was unlikely to remain any longer. It was not at all clear, however, where he might be assigned. Still too junior to take command of an artillery regiment, he had little stomach for serving as second in command. When Sherman inspected West Point in August 1874, Upton proposed to him a third alternative: that he be sent to Europe in order to observe its armies so that he could scrutinize recent developments in military science for possible adoption by the U.S. Army. In the course of this conversation, Sherman recounted that he himself and another officer had considered a similar trip in 1849. They then had hoped to visit Japan, Persia, Tabris, Tiflis, and the Caucasus, but "circumstances beyond . . . [their] control prevented its accomplishment." Seizing upon Upton's suggestion, he expanded the idea into one that would combine Upton's proposal with Sherman's own long-ago rejected trip to Asia, and in late September 1874 the commanding general approved this amended plan.[53] Beginning with Japan, Upton was to visit the great nations of Asia and Europe during a one-year journey around the world.

Questions regarding the trip's funding plagued Upton and Sherman throughout late 1874 and into 1875. At one point Sherman told him that it might be necessary to seek funding from the State Department's contingency fund. Upton replied that he thought the idea worthwhile and advised the general that Secretary of State Hamilton Fish, a fellow New Yorker, had "always been very kind toward me, and I think a suggestion from you to him would have great effect." Sherman eventually secured War Department funds for Upton, but the question remained as to whether other officers would accompany him, and if so, how their expenses might be paid. Barely two months before his scheduled departure, Upton informed Sherman that Lt. Col. Joseph Audenried, the commanding general's aide, would gladly accompany him if his expenses were paid. "This the Secretary [of War] will hardly do," Upton concluded. He also told Sherman that Capt. Joseph Sanger, an artilleryman, would agree to participate in the expedition if he could receive full pay and have "commutation of quarters." Upton volunteered to "forgo expenses, taking instead full pay and commutation," if doing so would allow Sanger's proposal to be accepted.[54]

In June 1875 Lieutenant Colonel Upton finally received orders from the War Department to undertake his tour of Asia and Europe. Secretary of War Belknap directed him to visit China, Japan, India, Russia, and various European nations to "examine and report upon the organization, tactics, discipline, and the manœuvres" of their armies, and while in Germany he was to conduct a "special examination of the schools for the instruction of officers in strategy, grand tactics, applied tactics, and the higher duties of the art of war." Not at all surprisingly, given the commanding general's contentious relationship with the secretary of war, Upton received completely contrary guidance from Sherman. Just prior to his departure in July 1875, Sherman wrote to his protégé that "the armies, forts, garrisons, and camps of Europe seem to me to have been studied by American officers and authors, until we know all that seems applicable to our system of government and people; but Asia, especially India, Afghanistan, Persia, Khokand, Bokhara, Toorkistan, etc.—the lands whence came our civilization, whence came the armies of Xerxes, Genghis Khan, etc.—remain to us, in America, almost a sealed book." He directed Upton to pay particularly close attention to the Russian and British armies in Central Asia, hoping that in the latter instance he could "cultivate the acquaintance of the officers, civil and military; ascertain how a small force of British troops, govern 200,000,000 people; ... [and] notice how they quarter, feed, and maintain their men, and transport them in peace and war." Though Upton was skeptical regarding what might be learned from these nations, he saw value in closely observing developments in the region due to Russia's growing influence there and because of "the interest the whole world is taking in the solution of the Asiatic problem."[55] Upton's interest in the armies of Asia would grow by leaps and bounds, however, as his trip progressed.

The War Department assigned two officers to accompany Upton during the trip. Maj. George Forsyth was to be the group's authority on cavalry, and Captain Sanger was to provide expertise in artillery. Both were distinguished officers who had served the nation during the Civil War and afterward. Forsyth had entered the service as a twenty-four-year-old volunteer in the Chicago Dragoons in April 1861 and had risen to the rank of brigadier general of volunteers by the war's end. His service record included recognition for meritorious service at the Battle of Opequon Creek and for gallantry and conspicuous bravery at Dinwiddie Court House and Five Forks. After the war he served on the western frontier, where his most notable achievement was defeating a band of Cheyenne Indians in a battle along the Arickaree Fork of the Republican River near the junction of the borders of Kansas, Colorado, and Nebraska.[56] Sanger's career was similarly distinguished. A twenty-one-year-old student at the University of Michigan when the Civil War broke out, he joined the service as a member of the First Michigan Infantry and was breveted twice for bravery during the conflict. After the war he was ordered to Fort Niagara, New York, where in 1866 he participated in an expedition against the Fenians, who had raided Canada. He subsequently served as professor of military science at Bowdoin College in Maine and while there was admitted to the Maine bar. Though Upton too was an artilleryman, he had had far more experience in the infantry and was the group's expert on that branch.[57]

Upton, Forsyth, and Sanger reached San Francisco on July 26 and departed that city on August 3 on a journey that would take nearly seventeen months.[58] The product of this trip would be a study whose recommendations would consume the remainder of Emory Upton's short life.

CHAPTER 6

ASIAN AND EUROPEAN ARMIES AND AMERICAN MILITARY POLICY

The journey Lieutenant Colonel Upton, Major Forsyth, and Captain Sanger undertook in 1875 was something Jules Verne might have envisioned for Phileas Fogg. Departing San Francisco, they planned first to visit Japan, China, and India. The three officers then hoped to cross into Russia by way of Afghanistan and, after inspecting the tsar's army, to continue on to western Europe to observe the armies of Germany, Austria, France, and Britain. Upton had little in his possession that might open doors when his party arrived in those countries. Commanding General Sherman had prepared letters of introduction to the governor general of Calcutta, to the commander in chief of the British Army in India, and to the Imperial Grand Duke of Russia, and Secretary of State Fish had provided a letter of introduction that was to be presented to American ministers in the various capitals the three officers might visit.[1] Upton was otherwise on his own, carrying only a letter from Sherman addressed "To whom it may concern" that described the three travelers as "officers of merit, experience, and distinction" and asked for them "the courteous attention of all my friends in Foreign Lands."[2] These letters served Upton and his party well everywhere they visited save Germany, and the controversy there due to the party's lack of proper credentials embroiled not only Upton and the American minister and chargé d'affaires in Berlin but Sherman, Secretary of State Fish, and President Grant as well.

The voyage across the Pacific was uneventful. Upton likened the ship on which he traveled, the *Great Republic*, to a "Fifth Avenue Hotel launched on a tour around the world" and found its meals among the best he had ever enjoyed. The crossing's only excitement came when a ship in distress signaled the vessel. Investigation revealed that it was out of provisions but not "in danger of immediate starvation" because it carried a cargo of oranges and coconuts. Upton was not bored, for he used the three-week voyage to study French and to read about the history and culture of the countries he expected to visit. His preparation for the trip had begun nearly a year before. In September 1874 he had written Sherman, "Much can be learned in history before this journey is commenced," and he told the commanding general that he intended to read as much as he could about the nations he would visit. Later that fall he informed du Pont that he was "now spending my time agreeably in reading of India, Afghanistan, and Persia, in anticipation of a trip through those countries."[3]

During the voyage, he enjoyed the company of two American women, one the wife of a naval officer, the other married to a gentleman who, he presumed, had business in the Far East. The latter captivated Upton. "Not the loveliest of her sex," he commented, she seemed "to be an impulsive, warm-hearted creature, one moment all smiles, and even boisterous in her mirth, the next pouting and humbling her husband, who bears her freaks with patient resignation, knowing that in a moment the cloud will be dissipated, and that regardless of company, she will smother him with ill-timed caresses." Each couple had a young son, and Upton was amazed at the attention the parents paid to the boys. "They live on condensed milk and laugh and crow lustily from morning till night," he observed. The "belle of the vessel" was the ten-year-old daughter of the American consul at Canton. Gentlemen on board would "pay her attention and promenade with her with as much apparent pleasure as with a young lady of twenty years."[4]

Upton's party arrived at Yokohama on August 26, 1875. They traveled extensively throughout Japan, visiting Kobe, Osaka, the former imperial capital of Kyoto, and Edo (Tokyo). Upton found life in Japan to be very fast paced, and Kyoto especially fascinated him. "We met carts, horses, and bulls, laden with heavy burden, and vast numbers of men and women walking under large umbrellas," he wrote. "The women are particularly graceful and attractive. Their costume is a single garment, a loose, flowing robe, open in the front, yet so secured by a broad sash as to conceal the person. . . . Sometimes they wear an underskirt of bright scarlet, the overskirt being looped up so as to reveal a brilliant combination of colors." The industriousness of Japanese farmers impressed him, particularly the manner in which they terraced their fields on mountainsides, "making every inch available for cultivation." Upton admired the manner in which this nation was emerging from its self-imposed isolation. Japan, he believed, was "steadily progressing toward a stable and well-regulated government," and Tokyo was developing into a Western-style city. "She has gone too far forward to recede," he proclaimed. "The railroad, telegraph, and steamboat, are uniting her people, while on every hand there is a manifestation of increasing knowledge and power, which gives an earnest of what she will do in the immediate future."[5]

John Bingham, the U.S. minister to Japan, arranged for the visiting officers to confer with the nation's minister of war. Inadvertently, however, he had scheduled the meeting for a Sunday, and Upton was unhappy about devoting the Sabbath to duty. Still, with the aid of an interpreter, he "had a very agreeable interview." The following Tuesday the war minister sent an army general to answer any technical questions the Americans might have. "The poor man came this morning," Upton reported, "and . . . we kept him six hours and tortured him with questions which would have puzzled a 'Herald' interviewer." The officers subsequently visited several military installations as well as the nation's military academy, inspected the drill and discipline of various army units, and met the former Japanese ambassador to the United States, numerous flag officers, and the ministers of several European nations.[6]

Upton reported that modern "military institutions have been established, and many buildings erected, within the space of three years, and that the same period has sufficed to inaugurate a uniform system of instruction in all corps and arms of the service." He lauded Japan's fledgling naval and military academies, "the former embodied in West Point," as well as its endeavors to develop an industrial base capable of producing advanced weaponry.[7] The Japanese also had learned much regarding modern methods of warfare. Upton's party observed rifle pits, redoubts, batteries, and entrenchments that rivaled any they saw on their journey, and they also looked with favor upon the manner in which Japanese cavalry and infantry drilled according to the French tactical manual.[8]

Yet Upton was critical of Japan's military establishment and of its society. Though he praised Japanese efforts to imitate French military organization, he found that they had adopted practices he thought had caused French defeat in the Franco-Prussian War. He observed that Japanese soldiers displayed the "slovenliness of march" he thought characteristic of the French and "so utterly in contrast with the precision and steadiness of the English and German soldiers." Upton found the Japanese people to be "sunk in the vices of heathenism" and practicing "idolatry." "One needs only to visit a heathen land," he wrote, "to admit the necessity of Christ's mission of peace and good-will toward men." Still, he found the Japanese to "have . . . some of the nobler traits of Christian character," and his overall impression of the nation was quite favorable. Japan, he concluded, was destined to become "the England of the East."[9]

The Americans left Nagasaki on September 21 aboard the steamer *Costa Rica*. They arrived in Shanghai several days later, where the city's bustle impressed the officers. Upton's party then traveled by coastal steamer to Tientsin, and from there rode "ponies" for the eighty-mile journey to Peking, reaching that ancient city on October 4. There the Prince Regent, accompanied by the nation's cabinet ministers, received the Americans. The following day Upton met with Li Hung Chang, the generalissimo of the Chinese military, who impressed him as "a man of fine stature and personal appearance, and [who] strode into the legation like a king." Though Li was majestic in his mannerisms, he was not so proud that he was unwilling to discuss China's military weaknesses. During their meeting, Li acknowledged "the feeble condition of China, the necessity of a military academy, and the . . . [need for] a large army." After an obligatory trek to see the Great Wall, Upton, Sanger, and Forsyth left Peking and returned to Tientsin. There they inspected the city's arsenal, which was "the only object of military interest." Afterward they dined with the "quartermaster-general of the viceroy," enjoying a *fourteen course* dinner. From Tientsin they traveled by steamer down the Chinese coast to Shanghai. On this leg of their journey, the Americans inspected numerous fortifications, none of which Upton found particularly impressive.[10]

Upton was far less complimentary of China than he had been of Japan. Where Japan's cities were rapidly modernizing, Upton observed that Shanghai and Tientsin were immersed in squalor and poverty. "The houses are mostly of mud," he reported, "the streets are unpaved, narrow, filthy, and redolent of bad odors. To one who has seen the worst streets of New York, a comparison herewith would convey but a slight idea of Tien-tsin. Squalid men and women, half-famished dogs gnawing offal from the butcher-shops and the kitchen, hogs wallowing in the gutters, and rooting up their malarious contents, carts, wheelbarrows, mules and donkeys—*voilà* Tien-tsin!" Upton found the imperial infantry to be "dirty and ragged, armed with the old smooth bore muskets," and the cavalry armed with bow and arrow. The Chinese artillery was in even worse condition, with no apparent organization and little discipline.[11] The imperial army's training, he reported, was "a mere burlesque of infantry-drill. . . . There was no order nor step; the men marched . . . laughing, talking and firing their pieces in the air." China's problems, however, ran far deeper than the quality of its soldiers and weapons. Because the central government maintained only a small national army and navy, every province provided naval and military forces in time of war. "The result of this policy," Upton believed, "is that, as a measure of economy, each province, in time of peace, seeks to reduce its military forces to a minimum, relying in time of war both on regulars and volunteers to supply its deficiency." When hostilities came, "Men are called from the field and the workshop, arms are thrust into their hands, and, without knowledge or training, they are exposed to the dangers and fatigues of campaigns."[12]

The root of China's military shortcomings, Upton contended, was the power the provincial governors general wielded. Responsible for promotions, reports, inspections, and the discipline of their troops, they were, according to Upton, "practically the heads of the regular army in their respective provinces, having the power to arm and equip, to increase and reduce, both the regular and irregular forces." Yet he did not believe that they could be held completely responsible for the "inefficiency, lack of discipline, and disorder, that everywhere prevail," because some had attempted to implement reforms along

European lines. "Their plans had been opposed or disapproved at the capital," Upton reported, "where conservatism, like a barrier, resists all progress." Still, he argued that "the wide discretion given to the governors inevitably tends to destroy uniformity in the army," thus no two provincial armies were equipped or trained similarly.[13]

Upton thought that other problems plagued China that limited severely its military capabilities. He believed its civilization to be "essentially pacific," due in part to the "absence of formidable neighbors." This had lulled the Chinese into "a false sense of security," which in turn led to "a state of political and military decadence" that imperiled the nation. He believed that recent rebellions had proven the cost of such a culture as they were put down "only . . . after years of devastation, cruelty, and carnage." The Chinese government's inability to make quick work of these rebellions encouraged others to revolt, and the slaughter of innocent civilians that invariably accompanied government triumphs was a deliberate effort to discourage any further uprisings. These costs, he concluded, were attributable to the lack of a strong, centrally controlled army that might have ended these rebellions quickly, if not deterred them in the first place.[14]

China needed to revolutionize its political and social structures, according to Upton, in order to develop a modern military. "Nothing but a war," he wrote James Wilson, "and the overthrow of the present Tartar [sic] dynasty can awaken the Chinese from their lethargy."[15] The Chinese population's "blind adherence" to Confucianism was, he believed, at the root of this conservatism. Confucianism, he wrote, " has killed all progress by teaching the people to regard the sages of his day as superior in wisdom to all those of succeeding years. . . . Confucius would weep could he see what a deplorable state the perversion of his doctrines has reduced his people." Upton saw but two alternatives for China: it could either adopt Western social and religious manners, with their possibilities of eternal peace and expansion of its empire; or it could continue its debased Eastern customs and its discredited Confucianism and thereby be "delivered over to weakness, cruelty, ignorance, and superstition." If the latter remained the case, Upton thought it likely that China would, "like India, become a vassal of a nobler people."[16]

What then was China to do? First, Upton believed that it had to adopt "Christian civilization" and "encourage purity, justice, truth, and integrity, by recognizing as the basis of human action responsibility to divine power." Next, "the government at Peking . . . [needed to assume] full control of the organization, discipline, and support of the army." Finally, China must imitate the example of Japan, which was itself emulating Western nations' models in developing a modern military. It needed to procure modern weapons, modernize its transportation and communications establishments, initiate civil-service reform

within the government bureaucracy, and establish modern schools for the education of the army's officers.[17]

Upton had a personal stake regarding this last point. After initially broach-
ing the subject in 1869, former secretary of state William Seward had again
approached him in 1872 concerning the possible establishment of a military
academy in China with Upton serving as its superintendent, for which he
would receive an "indemnity" of $150,000 for five years' service. He responded
favorably to the plan, and Seward wrote the American minister in China suggesting that negotiations begin concerning such an arrangement. The minister
crushed Seward and Upton's designs when he replied that the provincial chiefs,
not the central government, controlled the nation's armies and were not likely
to assent to the creation of such an institution.[18]

This setback did not entirely discourage Upton. In the months prior to
departure on his around-the-world trip, he continued to work on a plan for a
Chinese military academy, one modeled, not surprisingly, on West Point. En
route to Asia he wrote:

> I am still open to propositions from the Celestials, but shall not accept any
> which do not promise a fortune. The fact is, I have been very anxious to have
> Mr. [Alexander ?] Stewart endow a national university, on the principle of
> West Point, with the magnificent sum of ten millions, but I have now con-
> cluded that I would like to make that sum, and then establish the institu-
> tion myself. There are, it is true, some difficulties in the way, but, after having
> organized a large imperial army, I may be able to convince Prince Kung that
> railroads will be necessary to transport troops, suggest to him that my large
> experience riding on railroads will enable me to build them, and thus find
> myself a railroad king as well as a military mandarin of high rank. If success-
> ful in this part of my programme, I feel we shall have a national university.[19]

Upton clearly expected to profit handsomely if he undertook such a venture.
"In China I may seek employment," he wrote his sister Maria, "but my terms
may prove too extravagant—$100,000 in gold and $10,000 per year for five or
ten years would be a consideration not to be resisted." While there he spoke to
the viceroy of Tientsin, the U.S. minister in Peking, and to the U.S. consul in
Shanghai about the establishment of a military academy. He also arranged for
numerous technical and tactical manuals to be sent to the viceroy of Tientsin.
American diplomats nevertheless dashed Upton's hopes yet again, telling him
that "the conservatism of China is so absolute that nothing is to be hoped in
that direction for a long time."[20]

The parallels Upton found in Chinese and American military policies are
striking. He believed that the United States, much like China, had forgone an

adequate military in the name of economy. As a consequence the United States, again like China, had never had an adequate army when it went to war, which led to lengthening those conflicts and to unnecessary expenditure and loss of life.[21] He also found a parallel between the power of provincial governors general of China and that of state governors in the United States. Much as he believed that China could reform its military system only if the power of the central government was increased, Upton held that a system that gave the states virtual sovereignty in raising, training, and equipping militia and volunteer regiments meant that the United States was doomed to a dangerously ineffi-cient military system. "Our military policy is essentially Chinese in its character and would be identical with that of the Chinese," he wrote Wilson after return-ing to the States, "were it not for the fact that corruption has not yet seized, or captured, the civil administration of our government."[22]

Upton and his party left China in late October and traveled to Hong Kong, where the American counsel arranged for the lieutenant colonel to meet the colony's governor and Gen. Francis Colborne, commander of British forces. The governor subsequently became ill and was unable to receive the American, but Upton had "a pleasant interview" with Colborne and later met with officers assigned to a regiment stationed in the colony. From Hong Kong the Americans traveled to Singapore, Penang, and Ceylon, finally arriving at Bombay in late November. After a brief stay, during which Upton dined with Sir Philip Woodhouse, the "Governor of the Bombay Presidency," the Americans boarded a train for Delhi on December 3. En route they disembarked several times—at Allahabad, Cawnpore, and Agra, among other places—to inspect the colony's military facilities.[23]

In Delhi the officers had dinner with Lord Napier, the commander of British forces in India, who invited them to attend infantry, cavalry, and artillery reviews being conducted in preparation for the impending visit of the Prince of Wales. The Americans also undertook an excursion to the foothills of the Himalayas. "Clad in white, reposing in solitude and grandeur," Upton wrote, "they stood before us the mighty witness of Him whose power is infinite and whose ways are past finding out." Upton's party left Delhi on December 18 and two days later arrived in Calcutta, where the American consul had arranged for them to have lunch with Lord Northbrook, the viceroy of Calcutta. Northbrook told Upton that the "unsettled condition of Afghanistan" made travel in that country exceedingly dangerous and convinced the Americans to travel to Russia through Persia. He also informed Upton that his party would be invited to all ceremonies honoring the Prince of Wales. The Americans therefore remained in Calcutta and attended several receptions for the prince. Returning to Delhi in early January 1876, Upton's party attended further festivities celebrating the prince's visit and viewed maneuvers the Indian army conducted for him. At their conclusion, Prince Edward asked all three officers to dine with him in his tent. "During the evening he was very affable," Upton reported, and "spoke with gratification of his visit to America, and of the friendly relations between the two countries." Afterward the Americans left Delhi for Lahore and then, traveling by carriage, skirted the Himalayas en route to the Punjab. Following an expedition to the Khyber Pass, Upton's party returned to Bombay. Having spent nearly three months crisscrossing India, they left the British colony on February 11, 1876, on a steamship destined for Persia.[24]

Upton found India's culture to be similar to and as repulsive as that of China. "From China to India," he wrote Wilson, "is a total change, *not in population for in that respect all Asia is one*, but in gov't." He reported that Calcutta, "the sacred city of the Hindoos [*sic*] is wholly given to idolatry," and though he thought "the view of the city from the Ganges . . . imposing," he found nothing but "dilapidation and squalor" there. "We were glad to leave the city," he wrote. "In fact, when we shall have once seen the Asiatics of different countries, we shall all hope never to see them again, except it be the Japanese." While visiting Allahabad, Upton condescendingly observed a "religious festival" in which "immense crowds of men, women, and children, lined the shores; while going to the city were streams of people, some believing they had washed away their sins, others hurrying to seek absolution. Those who had bathed had to walk back in the blazing sun amid clouds of dust, yet to their ignorant minds they were free from pollution, and returned on their way rejoicing." "I wish you could see the native villages," he wrote Maria. "Nothing but mud huts so small and dark as to be unfit for pig sties. Yet those people will not forsake them. . . . and certainly do not care to learn from their English masters."[25]

Though India's people and culture had failed to impress Upton, the British Empire's accomplishments there astonished him. "Here at every stop," he wrote Wilson, "you witness the mighty power of England. Education, railways, telegraphs, works of civilization proclaim a new era. . . . Before her arms anarchy . . . [has] gradually disappeared. Her system of common law already understood by the peasant-native has taught him self-respect, and that he has rights that cannot be disregarded." Methodist missionaries' achievements captivated him, but he was concerned that the sheer enormity of their task was discouraging them. "Though it may be years before Christianity may prevail," he thought, "eventually at no distant day it will illustrate in India the parable of the mustard seed. It took seven hundred years to convert Germany; the missionaries therefore need not despair if their work appears to be slow."[26] The spread of modern means of communication and transportation, along with the continued effort of missionaries to convert the masses, he concluded, were "sure pledges of a bright future for India, and we cannot leave without hoping that England may preserve her sway till, in the order of Providence, she shall have accomplished the mission she was called to perform."[27]

Much as Upton thought British administration had had a positive effect on Indian society, he concluded that it also had had a constructive influence on the Indian army. Examination of India's military history led him to conclude that "native" soldiers performed well when led by British officers. At the Battle of Plassey in 1757, according to Upton, "the great Clive, with a force numbering 3,000 men, of whom less than 1,000 were English, defeated an army of 60,000. . . . The stupendous results of this battle . . . can only be attributed to the wisdom of distributing military talent among the native troops, and to their subsequent perfection in drill and discipline." The Sepoy Mutiny suggested similar lessons. "Natives" led by European officers performed well during that turbulent period, he argued, but "left to the management of their own officers, . . . the utmost disorder and confusion prevailed."[28]

Inspection of the contemporary Indian army confirmed this conclusion. He found British and "native" infantry to be equally competent on the drill field, both capable of executing tactics "according to the Prussian system." Upton credited the performance of "native" infantry to the successful inculcation of British-style discipline. "Whatever may be the external appearance of the native troops," he judged, "whether infantry or cavalry, their value almost wholly depends on the European officers who lead them."[29] An incident Upton witnessed while observing maneuvers drove this point home. "An exploit which was regarded as particularly brilliant on the part of the offensive," he later wrote,

> was to mount eighty infantry on the caissons of the artillery, and to send them at a fast trot to the bridge over the canal eight miles in advance of the camp of the army. In the same situation we would have sent a company [sic] of cavalry, which, in the event of opposition, would have dismounted and fought on foot, and would have thought no more of it. In India, however, *few officers appreciate the true use of cavalry*, so infantry had to be mounted on artillery-carriages for an exploit which legitimately belonged to the cavalry.[30]

Thus it was not the soldiers' fault they had participated in a relatively useless exercise, but that of the officers who had led them. For Upton, the lessons of the Battle of Plassey, the Sepoy Mutiny, and the Indian army's maneuvers were clear. First, even unreliable "natives" could be turned into first-rate soldiers if regular officers trained and led them. Second, officers must be well versed in the rudiments of their profession. Finally, officer talent must be distributed across the breadth of the army.

Because Upton considered "Asiatics" to be "cowardly wretches" compared to Europeans, there can be little doubt that racism tainted his judgment of the quality of "native" soldiers under "native leadership." In this context, however, his racism is instructive, for in describing the relationship between "native" soldiers and British officers, he outlined exactly what he believed ought to have been the relationship between American citizen-soldiers and the officers of the regular army. Upton contended that the Union army's refusal to adopt a "cadre" system in 1861, through which officers and noncommissioned officers of the regular army would have been assigned to volunteer regiments to train and lead them into battle, had resulted in "prolongation of the war and a useless sacrifice of life and treasure."[31] Just as in India, where "natives" led by "their own" had proven unreliable, state-appointed officers with little or no military training or experience had led volunteer regiments during the Civil War with disastrous results. In Upton's mind the Indian army's "natives" were analogous to the undisciplined militia and volunteers of the American Civil War, while its British regular officers represented West Point–trained regular officers.

Upton also praised the Indian army's system for the assignment of staff officers. At the time of India's transfer to British administration from that of the East India Company, so many officers served on indefinite detached service with the staff "that companies in time of peace were frequently left in the hands of boys fresh from England, who were without the slightest military experience. Even when this did not occur, those who stayed with their regiments during the intervals of peace, and were ambitious of distinction, found themselves superseded at the opening of each campaign by officers hastily ordered back, who years of detached service had unfitted for command." The result of this scheme, Upton declared, was "the most dangerous, if not the most criminal, of all experiments, the sending of men into action under incompetent leaders." The system's ensuing reform, he believed, was exemplary, for it presented "a spectacle of nearly 200,000 men conquering and keeping an empire in subjection, without a single permanent staff corps." Contrary to staff assignments in the United States, which were permanent and for which there existed no means "to weed out the inefficient or to encourage the aspiring," line officers served on the Indian army's staff for but five years. Moreover, any staff officer could be relieved of his position if found to be incompetent. This policy, Upton found, "has unquestionably produced a beneficial effect in India upon the corps of officers, and has imparted to them a variety of military knowledge and experience not possessed by any other army." These officers, as a result, "showed a capacity and self-confidence far above their rank" because they "had been acting in spheres of responsibility far greater than those occupied by officers of other armies."[32]

This account of the Indian army's staff system sheds light on Upton's concerns regarding that of the U.S. Army. He believed that reforms similar to those undertaken in India would ensure "the highest professional training, and the widest experience" possible. He also contended that the rotation of officers between line and staff would keep the staff "in sympathy with the troops, know their wants and fighting qualities, and, furthermore, know how to manœuver them in nearly every emergency that may arise."[33] To Upton, such a system was only common sense.

Upton also admired the relationship between India's military and its civil government. Though regulation placed military officers under civil authority, he found government officials subordinated to the military "whenever, as in military construction, economy can be promoted." This arrangement, he argued, was far superior to that under which the U.S. Army labored. "Could our 'regulations' prescribe with equal clearness the relations of our officers to the civil authorities, and relieve them from responsibility for the use of troops in civil affairs," Upton wrote, "it would place this duty before the country in a proper light, and would tend to disarm personal and partisan criticism." He despised the fact that the commander of a U.S. Army post did not have control of the installation's various expenditures. "As matters are now conducted," he complained, "we may have, as at Fort Monroe, three separate jurisdictions at the same post, where staff officers have disbursed, and may continue to disburse, large sums of public money—and yet the commanding officer cannot offer a suggestion; nor can he apprise the Government of a useless expenditure without placing himself in the light of an informer." By comparison, commanders in the Indian army exercised "limited control over all disbursements for military purposes within, or in connection with, their commands."[34] Upton believed that American politicians, like their counterparts in India, ought to yield to the military concerning issues that were of a purely military nature. Not only would such a practice save "large sums of public money" in time of peace, but it also would save lives in time of war. One only needed to look at the meddling of Secretary of War Stanton in the campaigns of 1862 to know that the latter was true—or so Upton later would argue.[35]

Upton's assessment of the Indian army certainly overstated the harmony that existed between civil and military officials on the subcontinent.[36] Nevertheless, much that he wrote about that army appears to have been accurate. British-led Indian troops were well disciplined and had distinguished themselves in battle. His conclusion that the military reliability of the army was directly proportional to the number and quality of British officers who served with it also was well founded. He was correct in blaming the mutiny on Indian units that were "left to the management of their own officers," and it is also apparent that those units in the Bengal army not part of the revolt reacted to it slowly largely due to the lethargic leadership of their British officers. Yet there were deeper reasons for the mutiny Upton failed to recognize, one being that the "natives" were unhappy about the support British officers had given Christian missionaries. He also failed to note that Indian soldiers were treated as second-class citizens in their own country.[37] His evaluation of the army thus was a product of his personal prejudices, the agenda he was pursuing, some sound observations, and most certainly the manner in which the British had conducted his tour.

After departing India, Upton's party stopped at Kurrachee (Karachi, Pakistan); Muscat, Oman; and Bunder Abbas, Persia (Bandar 'Abbas, Iran); before finally landing at Bushire (Bushehr), Persia, on February 20. From there the journey to Teheran was a long and arduous one, with the American officers traveling the entire distance, more than five hundred miles, on horseback. Because they were to continue on horseback from Teheran until they reached the Russian border, the officers carried only necessities with them, having sent the remainder of their baggage ahead to Naples. Upon departing Bushire on February 28, Upton's party consisted of the three officers, three horses, six mules, and a small escort that stayed with them only a few miles. They spent their nights in villages along the route, and each morning local inhabitants might accompany them briefly before returning to their homes. Upton, Sanger, and Forsyth otherwise were on their own. During the journey, they visited the ruins of Persepolis as well as the tomb of the ancient Persian emperor Cyrus. Exhausted and filthy, they reached Teheran on March 16. "Our party look as brown as the Indians of the plains," Upton wrote. "My nose has peeled, and my ears have been as badly swollen by heat as they could have been by cold. In addition to this, an incipient beard, which I shall cut off at Naples, does not add to my personal appearance."[38]

The Americans had intended to remain in Teheran only three or four days, but their host, the British minister to Persia, had organized two dinners in their honor and also had arranged for a meeting between him and the shah. At the conclusion of that meeting, the Persian prime minister told Upton that the shah desired he delay his departure an additional week in order to observe maneuvers scheduled to take place. Fearing it would constitute a breach of etiquette to refuse the invitation, Upton agreed to remain, which also gave him the opportunity to meet with the shah once more.[39]

Upton found Persia to be the most backward of the Asian nations he visited. There he discovered what he presumed was the archetypal "Asian" civilization. Completely unaffected by advances in technology or tactics, the Persian army was poorly armed, equipped, and organized. Many infantrymen still carried muzzle-loaders, and most of the artillery consisted of smoothbore rather than rifled pieces. The cavalry, though maintaining a paper strength of sixty to seventy thousand soldiers, was capable of mustering fewer than twenty thousand; though most were fine horsemen, there was little evidence of training or organization. Upton was aghast at the corruption in the Persian army. "The soldier who is too poor to escape the draft," he wrote, "buys his time from his officers, and frequently remains at home, when he is supposed to be in the ranks on the distant frontier. Even when following the colors of his regiment, by relinquishing his pay he may ply his trade, or freely engage in commercial pursuits." Officers encouraged these activities because only through such "corrupt practices" could they augment their low salaries and "eke out means of support."[40]

The lieutenant colonel believed that the military's shortcomings were endemic to Persian society and to Asia as a whole. He found the country's government, in which "monarchy and absolutism culminate" in the person of the shah, to be as corrupt as any on earth. "Even the Shah takes bribes," Upton reported, "and when he wishes to extort money he announces a visit to some distant province, in order that the governors and officials may buy him off, rather than incur the expense of entertaining him." Such practice at the highest levels of government naturally encouraged local imitation, and when money was "not forthcoming, the people are squeezed till they yield the last farthing." He found Persian civilization backward and cruel. As opposed to God-fearing Christians or even Muslims, Upton was appalled to find "fire-worshipers" in Teheran whose religion, he believed, dated back to the days of Cyrus. "All is poverty and wretchedness," he wrote. The people lived in mud huts that, he observed, "wash away in heavy rains giv[ing] the entire country the appearance of being in ruins." Persians, he reported, "do not know the use of the knife and the fork, and instead eat with the thumb and first two fingers." The country, its people, and its ways depressed Upton. "I am glad to have seen Persia," he wrote, "but, were I now permitted to leave it, I would go off as the crow flies."[41]

At least one person disagreed with this assessment. After reading a condensation of *The Armies of Asia and Europe* published in the Italian newspaper *Gazzetta d'Italia*, the paper's correspondent in Teheran charged that Upton had badly misjudged the shah's army. In a letter published in the *Army and Navy Journal*, the correspondent acknowledged that the Persian army was "certainly not at the altitude of the foremost European armies, nor is its mechanism such as to leave nothing to be desired." If the poor of that country were disproportionately represented in the shah's army, he continued, the same was true of all the armies of the major European powers. He also felt that Upton had failed to observe that Persia had adapted modern, open-order infantry tactics. "I do not fear," the correspondent concluded, "that I shall be deceived in predicting a happy future for the Persian army. This people has all the stuff to furnish excellent soldiers—they are courageous, strong, sober, docile, and of a patience that never fails them."[42]

Not surprisingly, Upton quarreled with the letter's substance. He admitted to William Conant Church that the section on Persia "was the one weak part in my report" but blamed this on the fact that he had been unable to secure any orders or publications that would give a more detailed picture of its army. Left unsaid was the fact that Persia had not been on the trip's original itinerary, meaning that Upton had done little if any preparation for his visit. He continued by stating that his facts were "derived . . . from a person, who had an exact knowledge of the Persian Army." "As to the observation on discipline and drill," the lieutenant colonel declared, "I needed only a gallop along the line to satisfy any military critic." Upton told Church that he had sent his report to a scholar who had lived in Persia for over twenty years and "who perceived it correct," assuring the publisher that his "picture of the Persian Army . . . conveys the truth." He concluded by charging that the Italian correspondent had "slander[ed] . . . a book he has not seen" and that the attack was "inspired" by General Andrini, the Italian officer who was in charge of the foreign military instructors in Persia.[43]

By identifying government corruption as the largest cause of Persian military ineptitude, Upton yet again was addressing a similar problem in the United States. He had seen similar practices during the Civil War and after, and it must have galled him that corruption in the United States paralleled that of a nation of backward "fire-worshippers." Ironically, this point was driven home during his stay in Teheran. While there he received a telegram detailing the scandal surrounding Secretary of War Belknap's sale of sutler contracts to his cronies. Upton initially blamed Belknap's plight on the spoils system of American politics. "[I]f it be true," he wrote home, "that the one of our Cabinet ministers whom we supposed to possess the most integrity has been guilty of corruption, it is time for the American people to take the subject of civil-service reform in hand."[44] His attitude toward Belknap later hardened. Though understanding of his plight, Upton insisted to one correspondent that the secretary of war "can not construe sympathy with approval of his conduct." "He has sinned and sinned deeply," he concluded.[45] Corruption in high places could not be tolerated, Upton thought, for the Persian example showed that corruption led to anarchy. Moreover, venality in its public officials would cause the United States to lose what he believed was its position of moral superiority. "It is not enough for us to be no more corrupt than other governments," he wrote Wilson. "We ought to be the purest on earth."[46]

The Asian phase of Upton's tour ended in early April 1876 after he had spent almost nine months visiting four countries. What then is its importance in helping understand Upton and his ideas? Historians have asserted that he was unimpressed with what he found in Asia and ignored the lessons of that continent.[47] Yet in *The Armies of Asia and Europe* Upton wrote, "The military institutions of India present more features for our imitation than those of any army or country in Europe." General Sherman agreed. In a letter to then representative James A. Garfield, with which he enclosed a portion of the manuscript of *The Armies of Asia and Europe*, Sherman wrote, "probably no military establishment affords us so near a parallel as that maintained in India."[48] The fact is that Upton's observations in India, as well as elsewhere in Asia, are important, for in them it is possible to see what he believed were the weaknesses of the American military system and, in some cases, their solutions. To ignore or to dismiss Upton's Asian experience as insignificant is to overlook much about how his mind worked.

Mounted on horseback, Upton's party left Teheran on March 29, 1876. They traveled to Tabriz and then across the Caucasus Mountains. Their route took them near Mount Ararat, which the Americans tried to climb, but inclement weather ended their effort. From there they crossed into Russia and, before boarding a train for Tiflis, had the opportunity to observe Cossack horsemen firsthand. Upton was not disappointed with what he saw. "They are certainly wonderful riders," he reported, "far excelling anything we saw in India or Persia." After arriving in Tiflis on April 11, they met Grand Duke Michael, "who received us very cordially"; visited a school for officers; and attended Easter services in an Orthodox cathedral. "We had enjoyed our ride through Persia," Upton wrote. "We had seen its misery and decay, and were glad once more to be under the protection of a progressive nation."[49] From Tiflis the three officers journeyed to Rostov, Simferopol, and Sevastopol. En route from Russia to Italy they, stopped briefly in Constantinople before arriving in Rome in the summer of 1876.[50]

Two issues consumed Upton's attention in Italy. The first was the declining power of the Roman Catholic Church in that nation, or so he believed. During his honeymoon there in 1868, Upton had perceived what he thought was the beginning of this process. "Saw the Pope on his throne," he had written his brother John, "borne on the shoulders of men; saw him sniff incense, saw cardinals, priests, and the whole multitude kneel before him, and . . . around the altar were stationed sentinels who would not let you approach unless you were dressed as for an evening party. Long lines of troops were drawn up within the vast edifice to form part of the pageant. The sight was magnificent, but to call it religion one must be beside himself." Such decadence, Upton had thought, was the target of King Victor Emmanuel, who had "struck several blows to the

Church." He had predicted the eventual expulsion from Rome of the French troops there to protect the pope's interests, both political and military, from Italian government attacks, which would mark the end of Roman Catholic influence in Italy. That nation would "then rise up and demand Rome for her Capitol, will expel the Pope, and St. Peters like the Coliseum, may at one distant day be one of the grandest ruins of the World." Eight years later it was apparent to Upton that the movement against the Roman Catholic Church had gained strength. Not only did the French no longer occupy the Vatican, but Italian army officers "are all bitter against the Pope and priesthood. One told me there was no religion in Rome, only superstition, and quoted an old proverb, 'If you want to become a heretic, go to Rome.'" Another informed him that Protestantism was on the rise. "There is too much intelligence," Upton concluded, "to permit religion to be made a mockery of much longer."[51]

The other development of interest in Italy was its army's "Prussianization." Upton found its recruitment policies, organization, tactics and training, officer appointments, promotion policies, and education system all resembled those of Germany. In particular he thought that the Italian general staff held valuable lessons for the United States. As had been true in India, the Italian army's staff consisted largely of officers of the line who served short tours of duty with the staff and a small number of permanent staff officers. "This constant interchange from the staff to the line, and from the line to the staff," Upton believed,

> draws to the staff the highest talent and skill in the army; prevents the staff officers from becoming slaves to routine; enlightens them as to the wants of the troops; gives them a thorough knowledge of the instruction, drill, and discipline of the troops; and, by holding command of companies, battalions, and regiments, qualifies them for all the higher grades of the army. The army, too, in its turn profits by all the talent of the staff, whose officers. returning periodically to the command of troops, become instructors in the grades where their influence will most surely be felt.[52]

Upton's positive assessment of the Italian army's staff system, like that of the Indian army, spoke to what he believed were the weaknesses of the U.S. system.

After a brief stay in Italy, Upton's party traveled by train to St. Petersburg via Geneva and Warsaw, reaching the Russian capital in late June or early July. There the American chargé d'affaires, Hoffman Atkinson, had undertaken significant efforts to prepare the way for the three officers, the result of which was an invitation to attend the Russian army's maneuvers at Tzarskoye-Selo.[53] They were personal guests of the tsar and therefore were "given apartments [in the tsar's field palace]; provided with horses and . . . a Colonel of the Staff was detailed to accompany us; we took our meals with the Emperors Suite, and we received the courtesies extended to officers of other foreign armies who were accredited by their governments." "The Emperor has been very kind to us," Upton reported afterward.[54]

Upton's correspondence from Russia suggests that he was more interested in the tsar's people and the conditions in which they lived than in that monarch's army. "Today it is the peasant," he wrote Wilson, "who pays all the taxes and while he shares his abode with his pigs, his sheep, and cattle, exceeding them in filthiness, the noble sits in luxury." The Russian people would soon demand reform, Upton predicted, and if those demands were not met, the result would be "as frightful as those of the French Revolution." Despite his belief that the people would eventually rise up against the aristocracy, the American deemed that "in stolidity and stupidity I have never seen anything approaching the Russian peasant."[55]

These observations contrast starkly with Upton's fascination with the tsar's field palace. "Foreign officers visiting the camp are treated in such a manner as to shame our government," he reported enviously. Visiting royalty received even better treatment, and among the tsar's guests during the Americans' visit were the crown prince of Italy, the kings of Denmark and Greece and their consorts, and the tsarina of Russia. The meals served to foreign visitors were unrivaled; Upton was told that they cost five hundred pounds per person. "If so," he wrote, "there is need of reform in Russia." The field palace was so large and consisted of so much equipment and tentage that it required more than seven hundred horses to move it, its retinue, and foreign guests during the army's maneuvers. "You can imagine what must be the expense of maintaining a movable hotel, with guests, horses and carriages, and other impedimenta in proportion," he reported.[56]

Upton's contempt for European aristocracy and their military traditions became apparent during a dinner the tsar held for foreign dignitaries. Near the end of the evening's festivities, a Russian officer told the American that Tsar Alexander desired to bestow a decoration upon each of his visitors. "I informed the officer," Upton wrote, "that our Constitution forbade us to receive a foreign decoration, and that, with thanks, we would have to decline." Later in the evening he noted that while European generals were adorned with "crimson scarfs [sic] and crosses of Ste. Anne or Stanislaus," Forsyth and he "sat modestly and contented in our plain but not ugly uniforms." At the end of the affair the tsar and his brother, Grand Duke Nicholas, came to the Americans' table "in order to show that no slight had been intended." Upton reported that after a long conversation he "felt rather proud . . . to be able to decline a favor from the Autocrat of all the Russians, which has no more significance than our own much-abused brevets."[57]

Aside from the expense of maintaining a palace in the field, little about the Russian army seems to have impressed Upton. His account in *The Armies of Asia and Europe* is a brief, matter-of-fact description of its various components, and only Russia's professional education system merited special comment. Upton believed that the tsar had taken special care to educate his officers and noncommissioned officers. This fact, "in connection with the long term of service and stolid temperament of its soldiers," he thought, "has enabled the army, despite the introduction of breech-loaders, to preserve the steadiness in battle which made it so famous in the days of Napoleon."[58]

Upton's brief portrait of the Russian army is disappointing; only Japan and Persia received less attention in *The Armies of Asia and Europe*.[59] Its most apparent shortcoming is its failure to address the reforms the Russian army had implemented after the Crimean War. That disastrous conflict combined with domestic discontent to force Alexander to abolish hereditary serfdom and to institute universal military conscription.[60] That Upton was either unaware of or uninterested in these developments is rather curious. Almost certainly he would have seen several of the so-called Miliutin Reforms in a positive light. There are three likely reasons he did not address them, none that are mutually exclusive: first, despite his preparations for his journey, Upton was woefully ignorant of the nations and the armies he inspected; second, where there was a significant language barrier, his reports declined in their quality; and third, Upton's proposed reforms, if already implemented in an autocracy like Russia, would encounter significant opposition in the United States.

Upton had planned to travel from Russia to Germany to observe that army's fall maneuvers, but because he had not yet received the requisite invitation from the Ministry of War, he remained in Berlin only briefly, then went to Vienna to inspect the Austro-Hungarian army. Arriving there in late August, the American officers observed maneuvers near Nicholsburg the first week of September. Upton later reported that "officers specially assigned to impart information" had accompanied him, and they had been "given every facility for observing the movements of the troops." Afterward the minister of war granted permission for the party to visit various military facilities in the vicinity of Vienna.[61]

The report on the Austro-Hungarian military emphasized its resemblance to that of Germany. Its practice of interchange between line and staff, whereby a staff officer, once promoted, had to serve two years in a line unit before he could return to the staff, appealed to Upton. He also had high regard for its promotion system. There were, he wrote, two means of advancement: by selection and by seniority. "Promotion by selection," Upton reported, was "based entirely upon efficiency and a superior degree of military education." Those promoted on the basis of seniority still required a "certificate of qualification" from a board of officers. This system, combined with the interchange of officers between staff and line, enabled "intelligent and efficient young officers to obtain while young the highest grades in the army, in which, at any moment, they may be called upon to influence the destiny of the nation." And unlike that of the United States, the Austrian promotion system provided for the elevation of officers to high command while still young and vigorous.[62]

Upton also looked favorably upon the Austro-Hungarian army's educational system. Regimental schools and schools for one-year volunteers taught soldiers the rudiments of their vocation. Divisional preparatory schools readied young men and qualified noncommissioned officers for entry into cadet schools, while these trained their students for the rank of "cadet," the attainment of which made them eligible to be appointed lieutenants in the army. Austria also maintained a modern officer-education program. The army operated two preparatory schools that were the equivalent of *gymnasia* and two military academies, one of which provided a broad-based liberal-arts education, the other a rigorous program in the sciences. Later in his career an Austro-Hungarian engineer or artillery officer might attend a "school of application" that taught advanced methods in those two arms, while the Central Infantry School prepared senior infantry captains for promotion to major. Finally, the capstone of the army's education system was its War School, whose purpose was to prepare officers for high command. Though Upton offered few judgments about the quality of this system, the detail he provided suggests that he thought it worthy of emulation.[63]

As was true elsewhere on his journey, Upton's observations of the Austro-Hungarian army were only partially accurate. He was correct that it had adopted a promotion-by-merit system for its officers, and he accurately described its educational system too. Yet he appears to have been unaware of the role patronage continued to play in promotion and failed to report that officers of certain nationalities received preferential treatment regarding school attendance. And some aspects of the army that Upton failed to address are as illuminating of his mindset as those he highlighted. Nowhere, for example, did he mention one of the more significant reforms the Austro-Hungarians had undertaken after the disaster of 1866, that being the development of separate Hungarian and Austrian national guards (the Honvédség and the Landwehr, respectively), and that the former was somewhat independent of its Austrian counterpart. Upton had to have been aware of this, given how recently it had happened, so why not put it in his report? Almost certainly it was because he abhorred the practice. The United States and China maintained state or provincial military organizations that were largely beyond the control of the national government, and he believed that these had adversely affected both nations' effectiveness in war. That Austria-Hungary had only recently adopted a system whereby the "national guard" came under the control of a subnational government did little to support Upton's contention that in the United States, the federal government ought rigidly control the American military system.[64]

Upton also failed to report on the ongoing controversy regarding command of the Austro-Hungarian army. As in the United States, there existed concern as to whether the minister of war was simply an administrator or if he was in fact the army's commander. Upton must have been cognizant of this issue too, for it was far from resolved at the time of his visit and was the subject of a contentious dispute that could not have gone unnoticed.[65] Moreover, given his concern regarding the secretary of war's relationship to the commanding general, it seems unlikely that he would have failed to have inquired about the circumstance in Vienna. But it was advantageous for Upton to ignore this controversy, for to admit there was a question about the relationship that ought to exist between the Austro-Hungarian army and its minister of war would have suggested that the issue was far from settled in Europe.

The Americans quickly concluded their inspection of the Austro-Hungarian army and, still lacking an invitation to attend the German maneuvers, traveled to Serbia to observe the ongoing Serbo-Turkish War. They left Vienna on September 13 and arrived in Belgrade four days later. The next day the officers boarded a stage for the overnight trip to Deligrad, the location of the Serbian field headquarters.[66] After a briefing and a quick examination of nearby Serbian positions, Upton's party returned to Vienna on September 25.[67]

The conflict between the Serbs and the Turks had broken out in the summer of 1876 when, encouraged by a Bosnian revolt against the Ottoman Empire, Serbia and Montenegro had declared war on Turkey and opened offensive operations. Despite initial Montenegrin success, disaster quickly beset Serbia, which began the war with an army of only 130,000 men, lacked any reserves, and was short on hard cash. Upton inspected a portion of this conflict's battlefront during a temporary armistice. After being briefed at Serb army headquarters, the Americans viewed entrenchments the Serbs had occupied near Deligrad after the Ottomans had repulsed their offensive. Upton attributed the defeat to numerous problems. He was dismayed that Serbia had initiated the war with only two squadrons of cavalry, four battalions of infantry, and eighteen batteries of artillery in its regular army, relying on militia to fill out the ranks. Officers of the regular army were supposed to provide rudimentary tactics instruction to the militia, but no such training had taken place in the two years prior to the war's outbreak. "In reality when the troops were called into the field," Upton reported, "the militia was without instruction; none of the battalions was organized; the officers were as ignorant as the men; the militia of the first class was armed with breechloaders of old and abandoned patterns, while the second class was armed with muzzle loaders of every variety." The Serbian army was thus "little better than a mob." Upton found the militiamen "ferocious" but inept, and he blamed them for the initial defeats.[68]

Several factors had aided subsequent Serbian efforts, according to Upton. The militia had occupied entrenchments that had been prepared prior to the start of the war, thereby bringing the retreat to a halt, and artillery from the regular army had given them "the necessary courage to face about and give battle." Most importantly, Russia had sent officers to lead the militia. The foreign-led Serbs, supported by artillery, succeeded in defeating a Turk effort to take Alexinatz despite the fact there were so few Russian officers present "that some of them commanded ten to fifteen battalions." Afterward, however, they had "poured in in such numbers as to transform the Serbian mob into a Russian camp," and the army had begun to resemble "a Serbian trunk with a Russian head." These developments brought Upton to the conclusion that "[h]aving failed to crush the militia when in a state of disorganization and demoralization the prospects for further offensive operations on the part of the Turks is very slight." He was convinced "that the Serbians, led by the Russians would be able to take care of themselves."[69]

Upton was correct that the militia made up the bulk of the Serbian army; that it was poorly equipped, badly led, and lacked adequate training; and that the appearance of Russian officers and noncommissioned officers had bolstered the militia's morale and improved its fighting ability. But as with his observations elsewhere during this journey, he saw what he wanted to see in Serbia and viewed the army and militia through a prism his experiences in the United States had shaped. The battles around Alexinatz, in fact, had been a disaster for the Serbs, and when hostilities resumed at the conclusion of the armistice, only Russian diplomatic intervention prevented a complete Turkish victory. Nevertheless, it was convenient for Upton to see this clash as a Russo-Serbian triumph because it allowed him to argue that the competence of the Serbian army rose in direct relation to the increase of the ratio of Russian (professional) officers to Serbian (militia) soldiers. The force thus fit the model Upton had come to see as appropriate for the United States: a "volunteer" force trained by regular officers performing well in battle. That the fighting around Alexinatz had been a debacle for the Serbs and their Russian-led militia may explain in part why Upton never published an account of his visit, for the campaign's outcome suggested that his conclusions were flawed. Still, his predictions concerning the Turkish-Serbian conflict proved prescient. "Russia I think is causing the Serbian difficulty," he wrote to Wilson, "and in the coming of Spring I believe she will show her hand." He also wrote that Russia "intends to keep Serbia on her legs till next Spring, when, prepared herself, she will step in as the principle actor in the drama."[70] This is exactly what happened.

The Americans finally arrived in Berlin in the last week of September for their long-awaited official visit. Upton's tour of that nation was the high point of his trip to Europe, and he enjoyed it immensely. "If the Germans are not all blondes," he observed, "the freshness and joyousness of their complexion are pleasant to behold." German women were particularly pleasing to him. They, "like Englishwomen[,] seem to enjoy better health than their sisters in America." He was unable to determine why this was so, "unless we ascribe it to the tonic effects of ale or beer," a rather surprising conclusion given his advocacy of temperance. He also enjoyed the amusements Berlin had to offer. "You can take a family of ten to hear the best orchestra in the world," he reported, "and have a private box, for $1.25. If all drank beer at six and a half cents a glass the total will be $1.90." Upton was surprised to discover the degree to which Germans misunderstood American society and its political system. One staff officer even asked him whether the "court language" in the United States was French or English. "There are a great many Europeans," he concluded, "whose minds are cloudy on this subject."[71] It clearly was Upton's fervent hope that the same could not be said about America's knowledge of Germany and its army after he reported on his visit.

Yet the lieutenant colonel's efforts to inspect the German army and to view its fall maneuvers had run into difficulty well before he arrived in Berlin. While still in St. Petersburg, he had written the American minister in Berlin, J. C. Bancroft Davis, to request that an invitation to attend the exercise be secured for himself, Sanger, and Forsyth. Davis first replied that he could not secure an invitation without specific orders from the secretary of state and that he would wire the State Department for instructions. The next day he wrote Upton requesting that he identify the military schools and institutions he wished to visit while in Germany. Before Upton could reply to either of these communications, Davis wrote again, this time to tell him that the secretary of state had cabled that the "President says not advisable to ask invitation."[72]

Upton's surly reply began a downhill slide that ended in an embarrassing controversy. "I have just been to see the Military Attache of the German Legation [in St. Petersburg]," he wrote,

> who tells me that when foreign officers, under instructions from their Governments, desire to witness the manoeuvres before the Emperor, an application has to be made through their Minister to their Department for Foreign Affairs, whence it is forwarded to the Emperor, and that the authority which

is always cheerfully granted involves being the guest of the Emperor. The same
rule obtains here. . . . All we want is to see the manœuvres that will take place
in his presence, and to receive the courtesies that will be extended to officers
of other armies.

Regarding Davis's query about the schools Upton wished to visit, he replied,
"I desire very much to visit the Academy and other schools at Berlin and
Potsdam."[73]

Davis's response was equally quarrelsome. "You ask me to apply for permission for you to visit 'the Academy and other Schools at Berlin and Potsdam,'" he
wrote. "I am sure from previous experience that such an application would be
referred back for [a] more explicit statement. If you cannot ascertain from the
German Military Attache at Petersburg the exact names of all the schools you
wish to visit, perhaps it will answer your purpose if I take the list furnished me
by Genl Andrews at the West Point Academy." He also informed Upton that the
maneuvers "are open . . . for anyone to see who chooses to go there and mount
and take care of himself."[74]

This was not a satisfactory answer. Upton replied that German officers had
informed him that an official invitation from the emperor was not required to
attend the maneuvers and it was necessary only to apply to the War Ministry
for permission to do so. Davis had temporarily left the legation by the time
this letter arrived in Berlin and had turned the issue over to the chargé d'affaires, Nicholas Fish. Fish pursued Upton's proposed course but soon replied
that the war minister had refused to issue an invitation. Despairing that the
matter could be settled in an exchange of letters, Upton left St. Petersburg and
went directly to Berlin, hoping that his personal intervention might help find
a solution to the impasse. Arriving at the American legation on August 25, he
met with Fish and showed him the letter of instruction the secretary of war
had given him. Fish, according to Upton, said he understood that the officers were traveling under orders from the secretary of war, but he "refused to
send any telegram to the State Department that might change the answer to
Mr. Davis' dispatch." Upton left Berlin convinced that the legation there was
unwilling to pursue the issue properly. Upon his arrival in Vienna, he cabled
General Sherman and asked, "Has Berlin legation been instructed to make
application to see German [maneuvers]?" Sherman, in turn, wired President
Grant, who was vacationing at Long Branch, New Jersey, for instructions.
The president informed Sherman that Davis had been instructed not to inter-
cede on Upton's behalf. The general therefore told Upton that the president
was unwilling to intervene in the situation and to "renew your application to
Legation at Berlin."[75]

Citing Sherman's last sentence, Upton made one last effort to secure an invitation to the German maneuvers. "In accordance with the order of the General of the Army," he wrote Fish, "I hereby renew my request that you make application for . . . [my party] to witness the German manœuvres." Upton pointed out that the secretary of war had required him to attend the maneuvers of the armies of the countries he visited and had asked that his observations of the German army be particularly comprehensive. Fish was unimpressed. "The Legation has nothing whatever to do with your obedience to the orders of the Secretary of War," he replied.[76] Clearly, Fish had had his fill of Upton.

The perceived incompetence and laziness of the American diplomats outraged Upton. Rather than aggressively pursuing the question with the German minister of war or foreign minister, neither Davis nor Fish, Upton charged, had even mentioned his name to the Foreign Ministry. Had they done so, he believed, the Germans would not have denied authorization to so distinguished a soldier to see their maneuvers. "I regret to say that our minister is a flunky," he wrote Wilson, "and that his excessive appreciation of the honor conferred upon an American citizen by being the guest of the Emperor prevented us from witnessing the German manœuvres." Thus prevented from observing the largest peacetime military spectacle on the European continent, he concluded, "we have failed [to view the maneuvers] for the same reason that Gen. Sherman failed to see the Emperor in 1871, 'Flunkeyism.'" He told Wilson that he intended to report "dispassionately" on the matter when he returned to the United States.[77]

That report was far from dispassionate. Privately, Upton was willing to admit: "The German Gov't is all red tape. It took two weeks to get permission to see what our War Department would have granted in half an hour." Officially, however, he made no such admission. In a twenty-five-page missive to the adjutant general, Upton recounted every communication he had exchanged with Davis and the chargé d'affaires and accused both of failing to perform their duties properly. In no other country, he recounted, had he had difficulty obtaining permission to see army maneuvers and to inspect installations. The legation, he charged, "was not disposed to assist us, but was rather interposing obstacles." Upton thought Davis had treated him poorly due, in part, to the minister's belief "that officers of our Army are socially unworthy to be the guests of the Emperor." "It was only in Berlin," he concluded, "through the position obsequiously assumed by our Legation that we were prevented from executing our orders, and were deprived of the professional advantages freely accorded by the German Government to officers of other Armies."[78]

The truly fascinating aspect of this affair is that in impugning the integrity of the American minister and chargé d'affaires in Berlin, Upton had taken on two very prominent figures. The minister, Bancroft Davis, was a highly regarded diplomat who had played a key role in the settlement of the *Alabama* claims, while the chargé d'affaires, Nicholas Fish, was the son of the secretary of state. It should not have been surprising, then, that Hamilton Fish wrote a stinging rebuke in reply to an inquiry from the secretary of war that Upton's report had prompted. "I fear that disappointment and failure to occupy a coveted position in a grand military display," the secretary of state wrote, "has led a very meritorious officer of the Army to do great injustice to the Diplomatic officers of whom he complains." The account, he charged, was "the report of General Upton's own personal disappointment and individual griefs, relieved from the egotism of the singular pronoun by the association of them [Sanger and Forsyth] with himself." The secretary of state pointed out that "the rules of certain European Courts are more strict and exacting than others." Sherman and then secretary of war George W. McCrary were at the end of their patience with the receipt of Secretary Fish's letter. In forwarding it to McCrary, Sherman attached a note stating, "My opinion is that this controversy had better cease." "I entirely agree," McCrary replied.[79]

When after several months Upton failed to receive a satisfactory reply to his complaint, he wrote the secretary of war and requested a copy of the secretary of state's response. McCrary told the adjutant general to send a copy of Fish's findings to Upton. "This request is not granted without reluctance," he noted,

> and only if refused Gen'l Upton might have cause to feel that he has been unjustly treated. Any reflections upon Gen'l Upton's personal motives which the letter may seem to contain are not concurred in at all by members of this Department, and I hope that Gen'l Upton's good sense will convince him that no good to the service or to himself will result from carrying this controversy any further. Its continuance in official form will not be sanctioned.[80]

The door thus slammed in his face, Upton dropped the issue, though he continued to brood over it. In July 1877, nine months after the incident and two months after McCrary had brought an official end to the wrangling, he wrote Sherman, "I only regret that there was not sufficient nerve in the War Department to have called both the minister and Mr. [Nicholas] Fish to an account for their conduct."[81]

What could have prompted his impolitic actions? Secretary of State Fish was certainly correct that Upton's inability to observe the German maneuvers had supremely disappointed him. This explanation, however, only scratches the surface, for Upton's conduct in this matter was typical of his refusal to compromise on almost any issue. It is a pattern of conduct that had been evident early in his life (his duel with Wade Hampton Gibbes at West Point), in the publication of his tactics manual (he would have pursued private publication had the army not approved it), and in his writings (especially with *The Military Policy of the United States*). The Berlin affair also demonstrated his disdain for politicians, regardless of party affiliation. This incident, then, was merely a manifestation of personality traits that drove him throughout his life.

Despite this unhappy incident, Upton clearly saw a great deal of the German army. "The soldiers are handsome, cleanly young fellows, from twenty to twenty-three years of age," he reported. "Their bearing denotes a good discipline, while the cheerful face shows an absence of oppression." The officers, Upton continued, "are well dressed, have no swagger, but they walk with the self-consciousness that, in the social scale, they stand next to the Kaiser."[82] Far more than the German army's morale and bearing concerned Upton, and because some have charged him with attempting to "Prussianize" the U.S. Army, his observations deserve a detailed analysis. In the thirty-four pages he allotted to his report on the German army, four areas stand out as having impressed him: its organization for recruitment and mobilization, its officer selection and promotion systems, its educational system, and its general staff.

To rationalize its recruitment process, Germany was divided into seventeen corps districts, each of which consisted of two division and four brigade regions, and which themselves consisted of several *Landwehr* battalion districts. The resultant 275 Landwehr districts were responsible for supplying a set number of recruits to the army. Within each, a commission examined all young men, determined who was fit for service, and gave exemptions from service to those who had "compelling reasons" such as being "morally unqualified" (for example, criminals) or "sole support of indigent families." Those who remained were compelled to serve in the army for a total of twelve years: three in the active force, four with the reserve, and five in the Landwehr. An important part of this machinery was the army's depot system. Each regiment had a depot where reserve troops would report for duty; obtain uniforms, weapons, and other equipment; and receive additional training prior to their deployment to the regiment. It also was where the Landwehr battalions reported prior to their attachment to a regular regiment.[83]

The key to Germany's mobilization process, Upton believed, was its ability to provide men to the army who already had military experience. He lauded the fact that soldiers in the reserve had served previously "with the colors" and that those in the Landwehr had been in both the active army and the reserves. Upton also approved of the practice by which officers in the reserves and the Landwehr had served either as an officer in a line unit, had "distinguished themselves in the field," or had been certified by a board as being qualified for commission. Moreover, during their four years of service with the reserves, soldiers could be called back to duty twice for up to eight weeks of maneuvers; those in the Landwehr could be called back to duty twice in five years for up to fourteen days of training.[84] Upton judged this system for raising manpower as far superior to that employed by the United States during the Civil War.

Officer selection and promotion merited special attention from Upton. He found that the German army's commissioning process differed substantially from those of other European countries, whose "officers of all arms of service are for the most part commissioned directly upon graduating from the various military schools and academies." By comparison, Germany required its officer candidates to serve five to six months in the ranks prior to being commissioned. Those selected to become officers then attended one of two demanding educational programs that emphasized mathematics, military engineering, and tactics. The successful completion of one of these courses of instruction resulted in receipt of an officer's commission. Germany's promotion system considered both competence and seniority, though "the Emperor is free to advance or retard the promotion of an officer according to his pleasure." A system of reports that stated "in detail the character, capacity, and qualifications of the officer" was the basis for company-grade promotion. The chief of each arm's bureau in Berlin received these reports and from them prepared lists showing those officers qualified and unqualified for promotion as well as those capable of serving as an aide-de-camp, performing staff duty, or serving on detached service. Though seniority still dictated promotion to higher ranks, Upton considered the German system superior to that of the United States because it "hasten[ed] the advancement of all capable and deserving officers to the responsible grades in the army." Those passed over for promotion, he reported, usually retired.[85]

The army's education system predictably impressed Upton. "The perfection of the German military system," he thought, "lies less in the military organization than in the exactness with which men in every grade, in every branch of service, are trained for the efficient performance of their duties." Enlisted men received training in the rudiments of soldiering as well as a good "general educational training, such as is required in every other walk of life." Such a program, he believed, was "the only sure basis for success." A series of army schools prepared those who remained in the army and attained the rank of noncommissioned officer for their increased responsibilities. The officer-education system, the capstone of which was the War Academy in Berlin, most interested the former West Point commandant. The War Academy's three-year program prepared outstanding officers for high command and assignment to the General Staff. The course of instruction included classes in tactics, strategy, military history, geography, and military engineering, among other subjects. Its ultimate purpose was "less to acquire positive knowledge than to develop the habit of thinking, so as to insure action from insight rather than impulse." That "every nation in Europe" had adopted a similar program was evidence, Upton concluded, of the school's value.[86]

The General Staff was the last component of the German military system that captivated Upton. He credited the Prussian victory over France in 1870–71, not to a superior army per se, but to the exceptional organization the General Staff had developed.[87] It was responsible for collecting intelligence regarding the armies of potential enemies, preparing "plans of campaign" and mobilization plans, and devising logistical and transportation systems to support large armies in the field. Various bureaus within the staff, each of which focused on a specific area of expertise and reported directly to the chief of staff, performed these functions. Upton reported that the organization served a second function in that it was "specially designed to increase professional knowledge and enable the Government to call the most highly educated officers to the highest posts in the army." Only graduates of the War Academy were eligible to serve on the General Staff, and only those who showed potential for advancement received multiple staff assignments. Officers rotated regularly between line and staff assignments, the purpose of which was "to preserve the habit of command, and to keep them in sympathy with the troops." Unlike the practice in the United States, no German officer could serve with a staff bureau for their entire career. Upton recognized that this system did not eliminate the possibility that bias might play a role in promotions or assignments, but he believed that "it reduces the evils of favoritism, if they exist, to the minimum, by requiring of the officers so advanced a thorough professional training."[88]

Upton's observations regarding the German army were accurate if also somewhat simplified. He was hazy concerning the organization and role of the German reserve and Landwehr. He correctly noted the reserve consisted of the number of men required to bring the army to a war footing, but he failed to explain how those soldiers fit into the military organization. His description of the manner in which the Landwehr would be mobilized is less confused, having noted correctly that its battalions would organize in their districts in wartime and would become a part of a predesignated regiment. Considered as a whole, however, Upton presented a relatively accurate picture of the German system of recruitment and mobilization.

He also failed to observe that the German officer corps was becoming more representative of the population at large. The Junker aristocracy no longer could provide the number of officers needed to man the wartime German army, and the victories in the Austro-Prussian and Franco-Prussian Wars had increased enormously the army's popularity within the bourgeois elements of society. Upton's portrait of the German army's educational system was accurate in its details, but he misunderstood the basic thrust of those schools responsible for producing junior officers. Rather than impressing its students with the importance of discipline, as Upton implied, Germany's cadet schools emphasized "the truly difficult task of initiating young men into the basic principles of war," the object of which was "to produce sound apprentices who will ripen with time and practice into masters." The inculcation of discipline certainly was part of this process, but it is clear that the German army's school system encompassed more than the combination of discipline and academic classes that so fascinated Upton. It was in fact a program that indoctrinated its students in the traditions of the army and of its officer corps, a function that was all the more important given the ongoing democratization of the officers corps. Upton's description of the German General Staff's organization was not entirely accurate, though he was not as interested in its composition as he was in its functions and its relationship to the de facto commander of the army, the chief of the General Staff. In these areas his observations were largely correct.[89]

More importantly, Upton's portrait of the German army showed little understanding of the tension that then existed between the military and the nation's emerging civil government. His only comment concerning that relationship was, "The operations of the general staff are entirely independent of the Minister of War, and are directed by the chief of staff." Though this was a correct statement, it badly oversimplified the army's relationship to the minister of war, the chancellor, the Reichstag, and the emperor as well as between the army's chief of staff and its senior commanders. Upton appears either to have been unaware of or uninterested in the role the military had played in Prussia's constitutional crisis of 1861–62. He also ignored or was ignorant of the serious conflict between the chief of staff, Helmuth von Moltke, and the German chancellor, Otto von Bismarck, both during and after the Franco-Prussian War and between the army and the minister of war.[90]

How could Upton have missed these problems in German civil-military relations? A possible explanation is that their depiction would not play well in the United States, where he wished to institute a somewhat similar command system. Though this may be partly correct, Gordon Craig argues that at the end of the Franco-Prussian War, Bismarck still maintained control over Moltke and the military, thus exhibiting "the principle of the predominance of politics in war-time."[91] If so critical a historian of the German army as Craig, more than eighty years after the fact, could have come to this conclusion, why after but a brief visit in 1876 should Upton have been able to discern a trend toward militarism? Another possible explanation for his ignorance of the growing strain between German politicians and the military is that Upton was an appallingly poor observer when it came to domestic politics in foreign countries. His failure to see China as an essentially feudal country is a good example of this tendency, as was his belief that Roman Catholicism in Italy was doomed. In both instances Upton certainly saw what he desired: a unified China needed *his* military academy, and the devout Methodist in him no doubt rejoiced at the prospect of the decline of Catholicism in its "native" land. Despite having made some insightful assessments of the military situation in Europe and in parts of Asia, Upton appears to have been a poor judge of those countries' domestic political scenes.

Another reason he paid little attention to politics in Germany (or for that matter, to that of most countries he visited) is that he thought that its political system had little application in the United States. The monarchical form of government appalled Upton, for it was the antithesis of a republic. "A republic based on intelligence and propriety," he wrote his sister-in-law Julia, "is the wisest and most beneficent of all forms of government." He in fact blamed the fall of the Roman republic and the subsequent rise of a dictatorship in that country upon the political machinations of Julius Caesar.[92] It therefore is unlikely he found any aspect of the German political system worthy of comment. Finally, because the intent of his report was to provide observations from which lessons might be drawn regarding the American military system, Upton was uninterested in Germany's internal political turmoil. His report on that nation was not unique in this regard, for those about the others he visited paid little if any attention to domestic politics. Upton thus prepared a report on the German army that was concerned with its structure and function, for it was the military's inner workings he thought America ought emulate, not that of the nation's political system.

After leaving Germany, Upton made somewhat perfunctory visits to France and Great Britain.[93] In a short report on the French army, he related that the Franco-Prussian War had resulted in reorganization along German lines, in particular the adoption of a mobilization organization much like that of Germany and the development of a war college similar to that in Berlin. The French army still had weaknesses, he reported, the most glaring of which was its failure to understand the importance of discipline in a modern military. Upton believed that the course of instruction at l'École Polytechnique and l'École Speciale de St. Cyr was "too short to train a cadet in the principles of exact obedience and discipline, and to this defect in the two great military schools of France must be largely attributed the want of respect, obedience, and discipline, which was charged against the army during the Franco-German War." The army's staff organization too remained as it had been prior to 1870, but Upton predicted that it would evolve into a German-style system as the l'École Superieure de Guerre became a more vital part of the army. "With the exception of conservatism in reference to the staff," he concluded, "the [French] army, since its late reverses, has made immense strides in organization, instruction, and discipline, and already gives evidence that in a future struggle it may regain its former prestige."[94]

Upton's report on the British Army was even more terse than that about the French. Though he opened *The Armies of Asia and Europe*'s chapter on the British Army by stating that it "is so nearly like our own that only its main features need be stated," his report emphasized its parallels to European rather than to American practices. He found that the German and British programs of preparing young men for service provided "a course of purely military instruction" as well as a "good general education." As was true in the German army, no British officers, with the exception of engineers, could serve on the staff without having graduated from the staff college. Also like Germany, the United Kingdom had adopted a system that divided the nation into territorial districts that served to rationalize recruiting as well as training of the militia. "The division into sub-districts; the linking of regiments; the establishment of regimental depots; and the association of militia and volunteers in the same brigade with the troops of the line," Upton pointed out, "is an approach [similar] to both the German and Austro-Hungarian systems."[95]

Why then did Upton believe Britain's military system was similar to that of the United States? Certainly, both armies were relatively small, and they also resembled each other in that the primary mission of both was to serve as a constabulary in "uncivilized" portions of their nations' "empires." More importantly, however, Upton believed that the two armies' systems of raising manpower were comparable. The British system of recruitment, he found, was based upon voluntary enlistments into the regular army. Volunteers enticed into service by large bounties augmented the army in time of war. Because of the regular army's small size, these volunteers constituted Britain's "principal bulwark in case of invasion," though the militia could supplement them. Upton found the British militia to be inadequate despite the fact that it could be called out annually for three to four weeks of training, often conducted by officers of the regular army. "The salient defect of . . . [Britain's] system," he argued, "is the non-expansive organization of the regular army." Compared with the major Continental powers, the least of which could quickly place an army of over 500,000 soldiers in the field, Britain, he estimated, could organize an army of barely 100,000 men. "The adherence of England to . . . [this] military system," he thought, "can only be explained by her insular position, and the security from invasion afforded by a powerful navy." If in the future, he continued, Britian should "assail any of her formidable neighbors, we may

safely anticipate that the war will be followed either by the speedy reorganization of her army, or by the total abandonment of the policy of armed intervention in foreign affairs."[96]

Upton's observations concerning the organization, training, and mobilization of Britain's militia and volunteers appear largely correct. Though he badly
overestimated the number of men serving in the reserves, recent historians
agree with his evaluation of the system's inadequacy in the event of a general
European war. Yet Upton completely ignored the recent elimination of "purchase" as a method of acquiring an officer's commission and, in its place, the
requirement that all prospective officers attend either Woolwich or Sandhurst
as well as the implementation of a system of promotion by merit.[97] It seems that
he also overstated the value of the British military academies and of the staff
college. Graduates of the former had a "disappointingly low" standard of professionalism, whereas the latter "trained for everything but war." It would not
be until the early twentieth century that Britain had a staff college that was on a
par with that of Germany. These shortcomings and the reasons for them mirror
those in Upton's observations of other countries' armies. His failure to report
the end of the purchase system underscores the fact that, with the exception of
India, he had little interest in what had preceded the contemporary situation.
And it is doubtful that Upton (or any British observer for that matter) could
have been cognizant of Sandhurst and Woolwich graduates' shortcomings
because, at the time of Upton's visit, those two institutions had been the army's
primary source of commissioned officers for only a few years.[98] The same cannot be said of his appraisal of the staff college, where exaggerating its achievements served to justify his advocacy of an American war college.

Upton's perfunctory report on the British Army belied his admiration
of the United Kingdom and of its empire. This respect went far beyond its
accomplishments in India. "You need only glance at the maps to see the far-
reaching . . . fore-sight of the English Gov't," he wrote his sister Maria.
"Recognizing the vast wealth of the East, and the importance of opening up
all of Asia for her manufactures," he continued, "she has seized every strategic
point commanding the channel of commerce from Western Europe to Eastern
Asia. . . . Where ever there is a strait, she lays her iron clutches upon it. . . . With
all this diplomacy and artful policy, one cannot fail to admire English pluck and
enterprise. In the East her foundations are granite. At every seaport her government or consular buildings loom up as emblems of her mighty power."[99] No
other nation, not even Germany, merited this sort of effusive praise of its non-
military institutions.

Though Upton's report focused almost entirely on the organization, mobilization, recruitment, and officer education of the armies he had inspected, he

did not lack interest in their tactics. In a separate chapter of *The Armies of Asia and Europe* entitled "Infantry Tactics," he focused on the company and battalion column those armies employed. The chapter's first eighteen pages were a rehash of the article on the Prussian company column he had written for the *International Review* in 1875. Its remaining pages dealt with how France, Italy, Austria, Russia, and Britain had made minor modifications to German tactical doctrine but had otherwise adopted it as their means of small-unit combat. Upton noted that trenches "provided with abatis and headlogs, underneath which were horizontal loop-holes for musketry," had succeeded in halting mass attacks during the Civil War, and he predicted similar results for any army that persisted in its emulation of the Prussian tactical system. His observations in Serbia, where a poorly trained and ill-equipped militia, upon occupying hastily built entrenchments, had succeeded in temporarily halting the Turkish counteroffensive, almost certainly reinforced his conclusions regarding the future of massed frontal assaults against fortified defenders.[100]

Upton, Sanger, and Forsyth returned to the United States in December 1876 after a seventeen-month journey. It is difficult to overestimate the importance this trip had in the development of Upton's proposals for reform of the U.S. Army. Much as he thought that China's isolation and Britain's "insularity" would not protect those nations from future aggression, Upton believed that the United States had relied far too long on its geographic isolation as its primary means of national defense. In China he had observed a military that was inordinately weak relative to its potential strength. He believed this largely attributable to the excessive power of provincial governors in relation to that of the central government, a situation he thought paralleled the relationship between state and federal governments in the United States. While visiting India, Upton saw regular officers and "native" soldiers working together in commendable fashion, much as had regular officers and volunteer soldiers during the Civil War. Upton's observations in Serbia reinforced this finding. India, Austria, and Germany all provided examples of staff systems worthy of emulation. In Germany he found the mechanics by which volunteers could be trained quickly and efficiently so as to prepare them for war. The nation's division into recruiting districts, the employment of local depots, and the attachment of reserves to regular regiments all seemed to be much more orderly than the helter-skelter manner in which American volunteer regiments had been raised during the Civil War. All of these played an important role in Upton's formulation of a solution to the "problems" of the American military system.

CHAPTER 7

A PROGRAM OF REFORM

A fter returning to the United States from his around-the-world trip, Emory
Upton reported to his new assignment at the U.S. Army's Artillery School
at Fortress Monroe, Virginia. There he undertook writing a report of the observations he had made during his seventeen-month journey, and he began work
on a companion volume meant to be a critical history of American military
policy. Though they differed vastly in their approaches, both were efforts to
convince the public and politicians that the U.S. Army was in desperate need
of reform. His ideas reflected lessons he had learned during and after the Civil
War, and they represented an effort to adapt the German system to American
realities. This was particularly true of his proposal to expand the army in wartime through an organization he called the "National Volunteers." Though
Upton's National Volunteers looked very "German," he rejected universal military obligation, one of the German system's fundamental components. His reliance on volunteers rather than obligatory service is representative of Upton's
efforts to craft a military that incorporated German ideas yet would serve and
preserve democratic-republican institutions.

Upon his return to the United States in late 1876, Upton took leave and visited his family. After a short stop in Washington, D.C., where he met with
General Sherman, he called on Emily's parents in Auburn, New York, and then
traveled to Batavia to visit his mother and father. He continued his journey
in January 1877, going first to Decatur, Michigan, to visit his brother Henry,
then to Chicago, where he boarded a steamboat that took him to New Orleans.
From there Upton traveled overland to Ringgold Barracks, Texas, to visit
Emily's sister Evelina Martin, her husband and Upton's Civil War comrade
Andrew Alexander, and their newborn son, Upton, whom Emory found to be
"a very promising nephew." He enjoyed his time with the Alexanders but found
Ringgold Barracks to be "a place almost as distant in time as Cain in Egypt" and
was quite happy to depart the dreary outpost and return to the East Coast when
his leave was over.[1]

Upton reported to Fortress Monroe in March 1877. Though still a lieutenant
colonel, he thought President Grant had intended that he would take command

of the artillery regiment stationed there. Sherman demurred, however, believing such a move would be "unjust to the colonels." Instead, Upton assumed the duties of "Superintendent of Theoretical Instruction in Mathematics, Artillery, Engineering, History, Law, and Infantry" at the artillery school, which made him responsible for the instruction of all officers in attendance there. "It is all right for the present," he wrote James Wilson. "I can do more good as Supt. of Instruction in Military History." Upton believed that the lack of any form of advanced military education for officers had accounted for the ignorance of proper staff procedures displayed by Union generals during the Civil War. "Here I think we can correct that defect," he told Henry du Pont, "and form a corps of officers, who, in any future contest may form the chief reliance of the Government." Upton hoped that in this manner he would be able "to repay to the Government all of the expense it accrued in sending me abroad."[2]

Writing the report of his trip consumed Upton, and he admitted to du Pont that it "so engrosses my attention that to go away for a day is impossible." He intended that describing the militaries he had visited would "expose the vices of our system." His conclusions, he continued, would "disappoint many people," but he also believed that they would lead to a much-improved U.S. Army. "*We cannot Germanize, neither is it desirable*," he concluded, "but we can apply the principles of common sense, and by choosing a plan in time of peace save the Gov't in the event of war much of the blood and treasure it had expended in its former contests." Upton intended to drive this point home in the report's last chapter, in which he would trace American military policy through the Civil War in order to "expose its folly and *immorality*."[3]

As he continued work on the report, it became apparent to Upton that concluding it in this manner would be impossible. Though all of the factors that led him to this decision are not discernible, it is clear that the length of the proposed chapter had become a major consideration, for he anticipated the portion of the manuscript addressing American military policy would consist of "at least 500 pages" and would "make a good second volume." Upton clearly was disappointed that he would not be able to include this historical analysis in the account of his journey because he believed it showed the folly and cost of relying on "raw troops" in battle. "But on reflection," he reported to Sherman, "I think it would be more logical to let the report close with the army of England and then on my own responsibility publish a book entitled *The Military Policy of the United States*."[4]

Upton's efforts thus turned to the completion of his report regarding the armies he had inspected in Asia and Europe. He constantly feared that he was too verbose and sent excerpts to du Pont and Wilson hoping they might make suggestions concerning his prose. Originally, he had hoped to complete the project in the early fall of 1877, but it was December before he forwarded a final draft to the secretary of war. His work on the chapter on American military policy had caused much of the delay; otherwise, he told Wilson, he would have been finished in October.[5]

Upton's anxiety about the report's prose and its conclusions proved unfounded. It so impressed Sherman that he forwarded portions of the manuscript to Rep. James Garfield. The commanding general promised his protégé that the War Department would underwrite the report's publication, believing, as did Upton, that politicians might learn from its findings. In this time of budgetary retrenchment, however, Sherman was unable to secure the necessary funds. Upton therefore contracted with D. Appleton, the publisher of his tactics manuals, to produce the book at his own expense, and it came out in April 1878. Though Upton reported that "all the reviews of my report were gratifying," its reception was, at best, tepid. The *Army and Navy Journal* never formally reviewed *The Armies of Asia and Europe*, which must have disappointed Upton deeply. The *Journal's* only recognition of the book came when it published a copy of a letter Upton had sent to Sherman in early 1877 outlining the report's conclusions, after which an editorial recommended that Upton's views were "interesting" and "commend[ed] them to the consideration of our readers." The *Nation's* reviewer noted that little "was gained by the author's personal examination of the localities visited." Upton's major contribution, it continued, was in his "reflections and suggestions which . . . should and doubtless will be attentively considered." His potential audience appeared just as unimpressed with the book, for fewer than six hundred copies were sold; its publication eventually cost Upton one thousand dollars.[6]

The Armies of Asia and Europe concentrated on the contemporary organization of the armies Upton had visited and, with the exception of India, displayed little interest in their history or in the relationship between those forces and the states they served. He concluded his observations with a chapter that summarized his findings and made recommendations concerning the American military system. "The true object to be kept in view in studying European military organization," Upton wrote, "is to present those features which are common to all armies, and to indicate those which we should adopt as indispensable to the vigorous, successful, and humane prosecution of our future wars." He noted that European powers maintained a regular army that constituted "the chief bulwark in case of invasion; and almost the sole instrument for waging wars of aggression" whose manpower in most cases came via universal military service. These forces maintained extensive reserve systems that were critical to their wartime expansion. European regular armies were in time of peace "but a school of training to prepare officers and men for efficient service in time of war." Among the keys to the success of this training was the practice of regular officers instructing the reserves as well as requiring soldiers leaving the active military to serve in the reserves for a period of time. Upton's conclusions highlighted the German reserve and depot systems, which he thought ensured the quick and efficient expansion of the army in time of war. He also observed that most European armies possessed a "War Academy" and had a general staff consisting of officers of "the highest professional training, and the widest experience," whose assignments alternated between the line and the staff. Finally, he observed that European armies promoted officers through a system that emphasized merit rather than seniority.[7]

Upton turned these observations into recommendations for the U.S. Army. He advocated "the assumption by the [federal] Government of the recruitment of its armies," the division of the nation into recruiting districts, the abandonment of bounties, and the construction of depots around the country. He urged the reform of the staff's organization, the assignment of officers to the staff through an evaluative process, and the rotation of officers between the staff and the line. He recommended elimination of regimental promotion, whereby an officer was promoted only within his regiment and only when a vacancy occurred. This system destroyed esprit de corps by "confining an officer from twenty to thirty years to the same regiment," circumscribed his knowledge of the army as whole, and produced great inequalities in promotion. In its place he advocated the adoption of lineal promotion, whereby all officers in a branch of service would be considered for advancement if a vacancy occurred in any of that branch's regiments. Such a system was not only more equitable, Upton believed, but it would provide broader experiences for the army's officers. Moreover, promotion no longer would be based strictly upon seniority. Instead, there would be an examination that determined an officer's fitness for increased responsibility. The result, Upton expected, would be a more competent officer corps and one with a higher level of morale.[8]

An aspect of Europe's armies Upton did not find worthy of emulation was the manner by which they educated young men preparatory to their commissioning as officers. Though he felt that West Point's program still needed reform, Upton believed that the military academy was superior to any similar school he had seen in Europe. He found military schools there committed too little time to military training, had classes that were too large, and lacked any sense of military discipline. He contrasted this with the program of instruction at West Point. "We have been able, at our Academy," he related, "to train officers equally for engineers, for ordnance, for infantry, for artillery and cavalry, and have given the cadets such a competent knowledge of all the arms of service that in the late war they were transferred from one arm to another, frequently serving in all three, with a success and distinction that challenged foreign admiration." Upton was willing, however, to permit civilian colleges to train officers who would assume junior positions in an expansible army so long as the training was "uniform." He thought such a program could be implemented under the provisions of the Morrill Act of 1862.[9]

Though Upton believed West Point superior to any similar institution in Europe, "we have nothing to compare with the War Academies of Europe, except the Artillery School." He therefore called for the establishment of "postgraduate institutions . . . where meritorious officers, from whatever sphere they may enter the army, may study strategy, grand tactics, and all the sciences connected with modern war." Upton thought that the Artillery School at Fortress Monroe ought be the model for these newer institutions. There, practical exercises that emphasized drill and hands-on experience supplemented courses in the employment of artillery and infantry, mathematics and engineering, and law, history, and strategy. The success of this program of instruction led him to conclude that the infantry and cavalry should open similar institutions. He also believed that the army ought to appoint a superintendent of military education who would be responsible for the quality of instruction within army schools.[10]

Regarding the army's size, Upton offered very specific recommendations. History as well as current events suggested its "peace establishment should be capable of expansion to at least 150,000 men." He reached this conclusion by considering the number of men who had fought in the Mexican-American War (100,000 men by his calculations), the War of 1812 (500,000 men, though there were never more than 100,000 in the field at any one time), and that Spain reportedly had deployed to suppress the recent insurrection in Cuba (160,000). An army of 150,000 men, according to Upton, therefore was "prudent." But this was not to be an army of 150,000 regulars. Rather, he believed that a small regular army should be maintained and then expanded upon in the event of war. He proposed a peacetime army consisting of twenty-five regiments of infantry, each consisting of a headquarters, a depot, and two battalions of 233 men each (roughly 25 percent strength), for a total of 12,500 infantrymen. In time of war these units could be expanded, either by filling the existing battalions to full strength or by using the men in the regiment's two existing battalions to serve as the cadre for expansion to four battalions. The infantry could thus expand from 12,500 to 100,075 soldiers in a short period of time. Similarly, Upton proposed that the cavalry maintain a peacetime strength of 6,900 men, expandable to 13,250 in time of war, and the artillery maintain a strength of 3,885 men, expandable to 18,340. This brought the aggregate strength of his proposed army on a war footing to 132,665 men. The remainder of the 150,000-man force would consist of the soldiers assigned to various staff bureaus, headquarters, and the engineers.[11]

How might the army achieve its wartime expansion? Upton proposed two possible methods. The first was to adopt the expansible-army concept and thereby "so organize, localize, and nationalize the regular army that, by the mere process of filling its cadres, it may be expanded to such proportions as to enable it, without other aid, to bring our wars to a speedy conclusion." The other option was "to prosecute our future wars with volunteer infantry, supported by the regular artillery and cavalry, appointing the officers of the regular army among the volunteers in such a manner that all of the staff departments, and, if possible, all of the companies, battalions, brigades, and higher organizations, shall be trained and commanded by officers of military education and experience." Upton embraced the latter concept, believing that "the prepossession in favor of the use of volunteers is so strong in the popular mind as to endanger its [an expansible army] being set aside at the first outbreak [of war]."[12] The difference in these options is not readily apparent. The first entailed the maintenance of a nearly empty skeleton organization within the army into which recruits could be absorbed in time of conflict. In the second, volunteer organizations would be maintained at local depots in peacetime and incorporated into the army as whole units, retaining their local flavor as had the state regiments of the Mexican-American and Civil Wars. The second was skeletal in concept, but rather than being an empty skeleton, it would contain enough soldiers and officers to enable regiments and battalions to undertake minor missions without augmentation.

Upton advocated employing the second method of raising manpower through the formation of what he called the National Volunteers. He proposed that each of the army's twenty-five infantry regiments have a depot where, in time of war, "one or two battalions of *National Volunteers* . . . could unite with the two battalions of the regular regiment." These depots, which regular soldiers would man, would provide the equipment required for the mobilization of the volunteers and also would help supervise training these citizen-soldiers after their mobilization. The National Volunteers not only would be the means for the army to expand in time of war but also would "nationalize and popularize our army," or so Upton hoped. The "impulse of such men as could not find places in the . . . national volunteers," he argued, "would be to enlist in the . . . regular regiment. The whole regiment would thus become volunteers, would go forth with the sympathy of the community, and differ only from the volunteer regiments of the late war in having at the beginning trained officers to lead every company."[13] Upton expected that the National Volunteers, through regularly scheduled training supervised by regular officers and noncommissioned officers, would be ready to go to war quickly if called into duty, thereby avoiding the typical shortcomings of a skeletal military. Thus he did not advocate an army organization that rejected the volunteer experience, but one that built and improved upon it.

Historians have dismissed the National Volunteers as merely Upton's attempt to "satisfy the public's prejudice for volunteers." Russell Weigley has argued: "Even if the general outlines of Upton's expansible army plan should win acceptance, no likely enlargement of the standing army would render it big enough to provide a skeleton for more than a moderately large wartime force. No conceivable change of American opinion would create a standing army large enough to provide, without excessive dilution, the nucleus of a genuine mass army, comparable to the wartime armies of Europe." Thus, because his small cadre army could not undertake a wartime expansion on the magnitude of European armies, Upton had "proposed a military system . . . which even he scarcely expected to work in the American context." Stephen Ambrose echoes these thoughts. He argues that because Upton "never advocated a peacetime conscription or short-term service with the colors" and the National Volunteers "would receive no training in peacetime," that organization "did not constitute a true reserve."[14]

These criticisms overlook much that is in Upton's correspondence and do not take into account his professional and intellectual background. Realizing that Congress would never approve a standing army of 150,000 soldiers, the National Volunteers was an effort to take advantage of a system that Upton *knew* worked. The 121st New York, which he had trained and led, had fought as well as any unit could. It was an experience Upton never forgot. After a regimental reunion in 1880, he wrote to one of his former officers: "When I saw the veterans . . . I had a right to feel proud. They had fought as few men had ever fought before to save their country and liberty."[15]

Yet Upton's belief in the efficacy of well-trained volunteers does not address the contention that the National Volunteers "did not constitute a true reserve" because they were too few in number and would receive no formal training before joining the army. Three points suggest this is an incorrect conclusion. First, Upton's analysis of potential threats facing the United States implies that he believed the army would need to expand to 150,000 soldiers only in the event of a war with a European power. In that circumstance an enemy expedition that could place a large body of soldiers on the North American mainland would be costly to mount, restricted in size, and very difficult to conceal. In the 1880s, when he was commanding general, Phil Sheridan concluded that any attempt to conquer the United States would fail, though he believed it possible an enemy fleet with a small landing force might be able to subdue the defenses of a major port city. Upton's own estimates echoed Sheridan's. "Should we have war with England ten or twenty years hence," he wrote to du Pont, "and begin it as we did the last war, with 50,000 regulars she could lay every one of our larger sea-coast cities under contribution, and it would require two or three years to shake her off." He wrote similarly to Wilson. "At the proper place [in *Military Policy of the United States*]," he told Wilson, "I shall treat our future relations with Canada and show that relatively we are not stronger than when the few British regulars dispersed the 5700 militia at Bladensburg, and burned Washington."[16] This analysis implies that a well-trained army of 150,000 could have dealt with the British then and in the future would be sufficient to deal with any potential foreign threat.

Indeed, he argued forcefully in *The Armies of Asia and Europe* that armies ought be limited in size. In Europe he had found "from 6,000,000 to 8,000,000 of young men taken from the family, the field, and the workshops, to compose armies whose object is less the preservation of internal peace and the present status of their governments, than to contend for new territory and increased power, in the ceaseless struggle for ascendancy which has characterized the history of Europe for the past thousand years." Not only did the apparent triviality of these intramural contests disgust Upton, but their costs appalled him. "To enable these vast armies to accomplish their mission," he wrote, "not only are national resources exhausted, but human ingenuity is taxed to the utmost."[17] But the United States did not require so large a force. A small regular army, supplemented by a modest force of National Volunteers, could defeat any potential threat to the country and would avoid the waste inherent in the maintenance of a military the size of those of Europe. Upton's 150,000-man army therefore was an explicit rejection of European practices and an acknowledgment of the uniqueness of the American circumstance.

Second, it appears that Upton hoped to disseminate his tactics via existing social and fraternal organizations. In 1870 he had authored a book entitled *Tactics for Non-Military Bodies, Adapted to the Instruction of Political Associations, Police Forces, Fire Organizations, Masonic, Odd Fellows, and Other Civic Societies*. Based upon its improbable title, one might expect the contents to consist of drill so basic that civic organizations might maintain some form of order during Fourth of July celebrations. Upton helped foster this impression when he noted that the book provided marching instructions for those organizations that frequently were on parade. He had applied a military structure to these fraternal societies, he wrote, because military-like organizations had "been found . . . most convenient in all countries to control the movements of large bodies."[18]

In fact, *Tactics for Non-Military Bodies* was a simplified version of Upton's 1867 infantry-tactics manual. In it he stressed the value of training and discipline for any organization. "Experience will prove," he wrote, "that the *soldier* who strictly conforms to the instructions for marching, marches with the least labor and fatigue, and acquires an elasticity of step, firmness of carriage, and command of his person, which every individual should imitate."[19] This passage shows not only that Upton cared about the quality of the training given to these "non-military" organizations but also that he thought of their members as soldiers, not as Masons. The heart of the book is a very business-like approach to organizing and training fraternal organizations. It provides detailed instructions for the individual "soldier" concerning elementary actions such as marching and saluting, and it dedicates several chapters to unit drill, each of which contains instructions for intricate maneuvers unlikely to be performed during any parade. Twelve pages outline various drum beats, and army bugle calls consume thirteen additional pages. Altogether, *Tactics for Non-Military Bodies* is a very strange product if it is presumed that the manual was meant to be used on purely ceremonial occasions.

If, however, Upton intended the book to provide already existing organizations some rudimentary instruction in the army's new tactics so that, in time of war, they might form the basis for the army's expansion, *Tactics for Non-Military Bodies* takes on a completely different cast. That the great advocate of the volunteer soldier, John Logan, endorsed the manual and as commander in chief of the Grand Army of the Republic ordered the GAR to adopt it for use in all of its ceremonies suggests that both Upton and Logan saw *Tactics for Non-Military Bodies* as a means by which the army's tactics might be transmitted to volunteer organizations. There can be little doubt this was Upton's intention, for in 1880 he wrote General Sherman and asked that he again be allowed to revise his tactical system, a revision that would include a new chapter on "applied tactics." Publication of "this indispensable knowledge," he wrote, "can be conveyed to the militia in the only book they are familiar with in time of peace."[20] From this it is clear that Upton recognized the need to keep potential citizen-soldiers abreast of changes in tactical developments. *Tactics for Non-Military Bodies* must be seen as an effort in that direction.

Finally, Upton *did* intend that the National Volunteers would receive rudimentary training prior to mobilization. "These volunteers," he wrote Representative Garfield, "organized in connection with the regimental depots, and instructed from time to time by the depot officers, would alternately give us the best possible organization, and ... would enable us to reduce the army to the lowest possible level."[21] This training, combined with the drill he hoped to impart to "fraternal" organizations by means of *Tactics for Non-Military Bodies*, would provide a basis of experience for the volunteers upon which the regulars could capitalize in the event of mobilization. Upton thus had not given up on either the militia or the volunteers as a source of manpower in time of war.

Rather, he had come to the conclusion that the nation's volunteer soldiers must come from a semitrained organization, one that the federal government, not the states, regulated.

Upton's critics also argue that there was no mission that could have justified a larger army. "The disappearance of the frontier and the Indian menace," according to Stephen Ambrose, "was depriving the army of its traditional function," and because he was unable to articulate any threat from a foreign power, Upton "fell back on the menace of labor radicals." Such an argument, Ambrose states, led nowhere because not even Upton believed that strikes posed a threat to the nation's institutions. "By arguing that Congress take the necessary steps to create a professional army in the United States in order to crush striking workers," Ambrose concludes, "Upton was making an almost abject confession of failure."[22]

This critique is badly mistaken. Though it was evident to Upton that "Indian difficulties" would soon "subside," a development that he understood would permit a reduction of the active army, he certainly did not believe that the wars of the Great Plains were over. He wrote *The Armies of Asia and Europe* barely a year after Custer's disaster at the Little Big Horn, a debacle he thought had highlighted the fallacies of the government's Indian policy as well as the need for a stronger army. Custer had been killed, Upton had written Wilson from St. Petersburg, Russia, "by the ill judged [*sic*] economy that has forced the government to send out feeble instead of strong columns." Only many years after the fact did it become apparent that Little Big Horn was a last gasp for the Plains Indians, and even then a desultory conflict continued for another two decades.[23] To Upton, the near-destruction of the Seventh Cavalry was an all-too-recent reminder that the conflict in the West was still being fought in deadly earnest. It is doubtful, then, that he "fell back on the menace of labor radicals" because it was apparent that Indian fighting was at or near an end.

Moreover, Upton *was* deeply concerned about the potential threat the strikes of 1877 represented. Numerous historians have pointed out that his response to that year's labor unrest was an apparently dismissive "I don't fear any danger to our institutions" and have suggested that his professed fears of rebellion therefore were insincere, serving merely as justifications for a larger regular army.[24] This passage, however, is almost always removed from its context. In the letter from which it is extracted, Upton told Wilson that he believed "the 'International' will attempt to get a controling interest in this country, and aspire to run the Gov't solely in the interest of the laboring classes." Its efforts would fail, he predicted, because an "insignificant . . . portion . . . of the laboring classes" supported the strikes. Still, he felt only "reasonably secure" manning Fortress Monroe with just fifteen soldiers.[25] Upton's correspondence during the period is filled with similar references to the strikes and their supporters. In 1878 he asked Wilson, "does it not look as if the communists were getting control of legislation?" Upton believed that a "bunch of foreign tramps" bent on "ultra-democracy" had led the strikes. "Those who love republican institutions should quake," he wrote to his sister-in-law Julia. "We need not fear monarchy for hundreds of years, but we should fear anarchy, which . . . may come upon us at any moment." "The growth of communism," he believed, "will destroy all public and private morality; and end in the distrust of what should always be our precious and beloved institutions. How far we shall move toward anarchy no one can foretell."[26]

Doubtless James Wilson was in part responsible for Upton's view of the threat the strikes represented. As the vice president and receiver of the St. Louis and Southeastern Railway, Wilson had taken a hard line against the strikers, shutting down railway operations despite the insignificant number of workers who had struck the railroad, and through his political connections he had secured the intervention of the Illinois militia at the railway's East St. Louis yard. Some have argued that "institutional provincialism" motivated the officers who took seriously the "fearful predictions" of labor unrest. Yet Upton was not unlike many army officers who perceived the strikes as a threat to the nation's stability; their views largely reflected those of the American public.[27] Such analyses, moreover, overlook Upton's and other officers' experiences prior to and during the Civil War. They did not place that conflict in the same category as the War of 1812 or the Mexican-American War, which had been fought against external enemies. The Civil War had been waged against an internal insurrection and was similar in nature to Shays's Rebellion (1786–87) and the Whiskey Rebellion (1794). The numerous articles published by the *Journal of the Military Service Institution of the United States* whose subject was the army's role in suppressing civil disturbances reflected these concerns. Some simply recounted events in which the army had been involved, some discussed the legal aspects of the army's interventions, and some examined the tactics involved in handling civil disturbances. Given the number of articles and the diversity of their subjects, it seems difficult to conclude that these officers' fears and concerns stemmed solely or even primarily from institutional provincialism.

Upton was typical of these officers. He called the Civil War the "Great Rebellion," and as his correspondence from West Point in the spring of 1861 makes clear, he believed then that the Buchanan administration could have stopped the rebellion before it gained momentum had it acted swiftly to do so. Upton considered the "Railroad Riots of 1877" (as he called them) to have been similar to other "rebellions" in the nation's history, all of which had convinced him that "the military policy of a republic should look more to the dangers of a civil commotion than to the possibility of a foreign invasion." Because these disruptions represented the interests of a small minority of the population, "it should be our policy to suppress every riot and stamp out every insurrection before it swells to rebellion."[28] He saw "communists" and others as a threat to the nation's short-term stability (if not to its "institutions," which after all had survived the Civil War), a threat that required an adequate military response lest there be another "Great Rebellion." If in the future the government failed to respond quickly and with adequate force, thereby allowing an insurrection to become a costly civil war, according to Upton the United States would be guilty of pursuing the same policy he had noted and deplored during his trip to China.

Upton believed that the railroad strikes of 1877 had shown that militia could not be relied upon to deal with rebellion, though he also realized that the regular army was not the answer to problems of internal security.[29] "The Army does not wish to shed blood," he wrote to du Pont, "and would be glad, as you know, never to have to fire a shot at our people." Who, then, would provide internal security? Upton expected the National Volunteers, if properly trained, could do as well as those few militia units that had distinguished themselves during the strikes. So that they might be available for that mission, he proposed that in time of peace state governors should be able to call them out "the same as the militia." Not only would this relieve the active army of a distasteful duty but also "would spare the pride of some Governors, who swear they will not call on [the] General Government for aid to preserve the peace."[30] Upton, then, was not as unconcerned about the strikes as some have suggested and took great pains to find a militarily and politically palatable solution to the threat he believed they raised.

Ironically, some of Upton's critics condemn his ideas both for being too Prussian and for not replicating exactly the Prussian system. His proposals, they argue, could not possibly have produced a mass army on the scale of those of Europe primarily because his system did not rely on universal conscription and the "skeleton" that volunteers were to fill was far too small. Yet it is those very points that argue that Upton was not trying to duplicate the Prussian system. He admired the European practice of universal military obligation, and his regard for it went beyond the question of the number of soldiers the system provided. "Every able-bodied male citizen . . . owes his country military service," Upton thought, a practice he believed as "thoroughly republican in nature as it classifies in the same category, and exposes to the same hardships, the rich and the poor, the professional and non-professional, the skilled and unskilled, the educated and uneducated." Sherman took steps to ensure that Upton's admiration of conscription did not turn into full-scale advocacy. "We must base all our calculation for the near future on 'volunteers' which I construe our Regular Army to be in fact," the commanding general wrote, "and I advise you gradually to direct your argument to the great proposition that war is a science needing education, training, and practice, and that the rank and file must be drilled, instructed, and habituated to the duties of war before being subjected to fire." To underline his point, Sherman directed Upton to the appropriate passages of his own memoirs. The commanding general's concerns were unwarranted. Upton had conceived of the National Volunteers well before he had received his mentor's guidance, and he understood that conscription, however desirable he felt it might have been, had no chance of acceptance in the United States. The reforms he proposed were an effort to combine American military requirements and political realities with the efficiency of the German military system. The problem for Upton, then, was one of justification. He realized that he had to show that the American military system was broken and expected his next project, *The Military Policy of the United States*, to do just that.[31]

Upton's study of American military history had "impressed . . . [him] with the conviction that our military policy is a crime," and he believed that his research showed the "expense of treasure and blood a nation must prosecute war so long as it relies on raw troops." He had no false expectations about the consequences of presenting such an argument. "I do not hope for any immediate results—except unlimited abuse," he told du Pont.[32] He hoped to avert some criticism by sending parts of the manuscript to various friends for their advice, and du Pont proved a particularly valuable editor. Not only did he help Upton with his turgid prose but also succeeded in toning down the argument's tendentious nature. Upton was appreciative of his friend's efforts. "I feel that in submitting the M.S.S. to you I shall escape much criticism not only as to style but to manner," he wrote. "You must caution me more and more freely whenever prejudice comes out." Upton also sought the aid of Wilson and Sherman, both of whom provided valuable advice. Realizing that his argument would upset many members of Congress, he told James Garfield that he wished "to avoid all unnecessary controversy" and hoped the Ohioan would give his "unreserved criticism" of the manuscript. "You know the popular pulse," he continued, "and can place me right whenever I make an intemperate statement, or present a fact in an objectionable light."[33]

The United States had evolved since its inception in 1776, Upton argued, but its military system had not progressed similarly. "The military policy of an agricultural nation of 3,000,000 people just emerging from the forest was no policy for a nation extending from ocean to ocean and now numbering more than fifty millions," he wrote in the manuscript's introduction. Upton believed that the United States had pursued an unsatisfactory military policy for a number of reasons. "Our remoteness from powerful nations," he wrote, led to the belief "that we shall forever be free from foreign invasion." A statesman "would have recalled the Revolution, the War of 1812, and the Mexican War. He would have pointed to the British possession on the north, to Mexico on the west, and Spain on the south; he would not have forgotten the affair of the *Virginius* and the frequent complications on the Rio Grande as proof that at any moment we may be plunged into another foreign war." "Ultimate success in all our wars," he continued, "has steeped the people in the delusion that our policy is correct and that any departure from it would be no less difficult than dangerous." Victory in war "has so blinded the popular mind, as to induce the belief that as a nation we are invincible."[34]

Because of these delusions, Upton continued, American military policy was badly flawed, which led to the prolongation of wars and the expenditure of vast sums of public money. "Our military policy," he wrote scathingly, "is a crime against life, a crime against property, a crime against liberty." Upton recalled the sacrifice of the Civil War. "Every battlefield of the war after 1861," he wrote, "gave proof to the world of the valor of the disciplined American soldier; but in achieving this reputation the nation was nearly overwhelmed with debt from which we are still suffering, while nearly every family in the land was plunged in[to] mourning." He concluded, "Already we are forgetting these costly sacrifices."[35]

But the greatest problem the nation's inadequate military system posed, according to Upton, was that it had jeopardized the Republic's health. "No matter what the form of government," he wrote, "war, at the discretion of the rulers, means absolute despotism, the danger from which increases as the war is prolonged. Armies in time of peace have seldom overthrown their government, but in time of anarchy and war the people have often sought to dictate, and purchase peace at the expense of their liberty. If we would escape this danger, we should make war with a strong arm." This danger had manifested during the Civil War when, "unable to suppress in two years an insurrection which culminated in a great rebellion, the representatives of the people were forced to adopt conscription and to concentrate in the hands of the President all the war powers granted by the Constitution." "In time of rebellion," he concluded, "our own Government grew more despotic as it grew stronger." Because the United States had been unable to suppress quickly the rebellion of the southern states in 1861, "our existence as a nation depended upon the irresolution and supineness of a band of insurgents."[36]

Upton traced this trend to the Revolution when, after the disasters of Long Island and Fort Washington in 1776, the Continental Congress had given George Washington near-dictatorial powers. He believed that such powers, "arbitrary arrests, summary executions without trial, forced impressment of provisions, and other dangerous precedents of the Revolution—were the legitimate fruits of the defective military legislation of our inexperienced statesmen." Lincoln, he continued, had pursued the same course. "Sworn to protect and defend the Constitution," the president "saw but one method to save the Union," the assumption of dictatorial powers. "Viewed in whatever light we may choose," Upton continued, "the fact remains that in default of a judicious system for the national defense the President raised armies, provided navies, and opened the doors of the treasury to irresponsible citizens." The suspension of habeas corpus, the practice of arbitrary arrests, and the government's seizure of the railroads were examples of an emerging despotism in the nation's capital. Upton acknowledged that the nation had had two leaders during the Revolution and the Civil War who were not by nature despotic and who had used their powers wisely, but the country could not depend on this always being the case. "Let us not stultify ourselves," he wrote, "by talking of the danger of an army, but rather reflect that the lack of one may at any time, in the space of two years, bring upon us even graver disasters than Long Island or Brandywine, or the two Bull Runs," which might again result in conferring dictatorial powers on a president. "Our danger lies not in having a regular army," he concluded, "but in the want of one."[37]

Who was responsible for this failure of policy? The majority of the blame, Upton asserted, lay with Congress. The military's organization, he argued, "is wholly within the province of the statesmen. Under our Constitution Congress has the power to raise and support armies." He asserted that "in time of war the civilian as much as the soldier is responsible for defeat and disaster. Battles are not lost alone on the field; they may be lost beneath the Dome of the Capitol, they may be lost in the Cabinet, or they may be lost in the private office of the Secretary of War. Wherever they may be lost, it is the people who suffer and the soldiers who die."[38] This had been particularly true during the Civil War. "In seeking to trace all the great mistakes and blunders committed during the war," he argued,

> it is important to bear in mind the respective duties and responsibilities of soldiers and statesmen. The latter are responsible for the creation and organization of our resources, and, as in the case of the President, may further be responsible for their management or mismanagement. Soldiers, while they should suggest and be consulted on all details of organization under our system, can alone be held responsible for the control and direction of armies in the field.[39]

Such an analysis is characteristic of Upton's approach to all of America's wars. Errors in execution that caused battlefield defeats were the fault of the military;

if poor organization or lack of preparedness were to blame, Congress was at fault. Yet even when a general made a mistake, something Upton seldom was willing to concede, he usually traced that officer's failure to a flaw in the system. For but one example, he contended that Henry Halleck's failures in the western campaign of 1862 were due, in large part, to the army's lack of a unified command.[40]

Upton considered the Militia Act of 1792 the great example of congressional incompetence that had laid the groundwork for many subsequent problems. "A mere glance at the military edifice proposed by this law," he argued, "shows that its foundations were built on the sands." One of its major shortcomings was that it delegated to the states all authority for training and raising the militia yet provided the federal government with no means of enforcement. The law also made it the responsibility of citizens to provide their own arms and, if necessary, horses. Beyond this, the act had a still more serious defect. "Even had the citizen been prepared to furnish at his own cost that which it was the unmistakable duty of the government to provide," Upton noted, "the further execution of the law depended wholly on the voluntary and concurrent action of the States." This deficiency became apparent during the War of 1812, when the governors of Connecticut and Massachusetts had refused to call out their states' militia. Early in the course of the Civil War the same problem resurfaced when, according to Upton, the governors of several border states failed to call out their militia. These incidents, he contended, "reveal[ed] the utter weakness of our military system, based on the theory of confederation."[41]

Upton argued that most military legislation Congress had passed during the nineteenth century had suffered from similar shortcomings. For example, he found the 1846 statute that provided for the calling up of volunteers during the Mexican-American War particularly appalling because it allowed the president "to accept the services of volunteers 'for twelve months' or 'for the war.'" Pres. James K. Polk chose the former, and when the war extended beyond twelve months' duration, the volunteers left the service in the middle of Winfield Scott's campaign against Mexico City. The law also provided too small an allowance for soldiers' clothing and food and allowed the states to appoint officers, "thus placing the fortunes of the country, as well as the lives of the soldiers, in the hands of generals utterly ignorant of the military art." Due to these "errors of statesmanship," according to Upton, "we needlessly exposed our army to the dangers of capture for a period of more than six months."[42]

The legislative history of the Civil War gave Upton like cause for complaint. "The surviving officers and soldiers of our armies," he stated, "many of whom participated in the Battle of Bull Run, will not for a moment deny that through the inexperience of themselves and their commanders the war for the Union was prolonged. But when all of their mistakes are summed up and their deficiencies considered, it will still be found that the underlying causes were inherent in a military system which was the creature of law." The mistakes of the military legislation of 1861 mirrored those of 1846. Enlistments were of short duration—from six months to three years in length. Though most men who enlisted after the First Battle of Bull Run were three-year soldiers, even this term of service proved too short. When their enlistments ran out in 1864, the Union army was in danger of losing almost half of its veteran infantry, cavalry, and artillery units.[43] The statute also authorized states to appoint officers as well as the election of officers by the volunteers themselves. These shortcomings had sown the seeds of subsequent battlefield disasters. "In no monarchy or despotism of the Old World," he concluded, "do the laws give to the ruler such power to do evil."[44]

Such an analysis led Upton to be hypercritical of Congress. "It is a well-known fact," he asserted, "that in all representative governments professional party leaders usually care more for power than for principle." Not without reason, Upton believed, Radical Republicans had engineered the downfall of George McClellan in 1862, fearing his potential as a presidential candidate. Some of that general's most outspoken critics were Republican members of the congressional Joint Committee on the Conduct of the War, and it was for this body that Upton reserved some of his most scathing criticisms. "Of all the persons admitted to the confidence of the President and his Cabinet, the members of the Committee on the Conduct of the War, were the most active and officious." They manipulated strategy, created commands, and "on the least alarm, cause[d] troops to be rushed hurriedly from one state to another." Even worse, Upton accused the committee of treason through its open conduct of investigations that revealed secrets to the enemy.[45]

Abraham Lincoln did not escape criticism. Upton blamed him for much that had happened in the eastern theater in 1862. The president's failure to forward Irvin McDowell's corps to McClellan that spring, he argued, had ensured the collapse of the Peninsula Campaign. He also was very critical of War Order No. 3, which had removed McClellan as commanding general of the army without naming a successor. "By this stroke of the pen," Upton wrote, "the command of our vast armies . . . passed from the hands of an educated soldier, to those of the President and the Secretary of War, neither of whom possessed any knowledge of the military art."[46] He charged that factors other than the purely military had impinged upon Lincoln's decisions. "The President was by no means the master of his own actions," he wrote.

He had assumed all the personal responsibilities of a military commander, with the further disadvantage that, as the Chief Magistrate, he could not, even in matters of detail, turn a deaf ear to the appeals and representations of his political and military advisers.

Whenever a territory was threatened with real or imaginary invasion, the people felt they had the right through their representatives to appeal to him for protection.

Educated in political life, he could not fail to apply the same system of reasoning to the decision of military as to political questions. Troops could not be ordered from one department, district, or place to another without first paying "a due regard to all points."

In this manner strategical principles, involving perhaps the fate of an army, had to give way to political considerations.[47]

"Everything," Upton objected, "was weighed in a political balance."[48]

Yet Upton reserved his harshest criticisms for Lincoln's secretary of war. Edwin Stanton, he charged, "without quoting the authority of the President," issued orders to the army, thereby "usurping" the constitutional power of the president as commander in chief. Upton believed that "there could be no success in military operations while any civil officer other than the constitutional Commander in Chief was permitted to exercise military command." To him, the campaigns of 1862 proved this point. Upton accused Stanton of meddling in the operational plans of army commanders, particularly those of McClellan, and thus creating "chaos" in the field rather than concentrating on his administrative duties—"organizing, recruiting, and supplying our armies." "The only parallel to this system," he declared, "will be found in the history of the Punic Wars, when two Roman consuls—chief magistrates of equal dignity—shared the honors of command on alternate days. The total destruction of their army at Cannae, convinced the Republic of its folly. Fatal as was this feature in the Roman system, it involved less danger than our own."[49]

Upton was sharply critical of Stanton's formation of an informal war council. Sarcastically referring to it as the "Second Aulic Council," he berated the manner in which it had made operational recommendations to the president and the secretary of war without consulting the various commanders concerned.[50] He believed that its members were unqualified for such responsibilities, having served for many years in the bureaus rather than in line units, and therefore had little concept of "the practical duties of a soldier." The council, Upton concluded, was an effort to consolidate the secretary of war's power, and that centralization of authority "was at the bottom of all the disasters of the year 1862."[51]

Upton thus blamed Stanton, and to a lesser degree Lincoln, for the failure of McClellan's Peninsula Campaign, the cost of which went far beyond a simple tally of those who had died or had been wounded during the fighting. The retreat from the gates of Richmond had allowed the Confederacy to mobilize more fully for war. "It was no longer a question of dealing a dissolving army a deathblow," he wrote. "We had permitted a rival government to reorganize its forces, which we were now compelled to destroy by the slow process of attrition." The cost of prosecuting the war after the summer of 1862 thus had been wholly avoidable. Upton argued that this demonstrated "that a nation which goes to war unprepared educates its statesmen at more expense than its soldiers."[52]

But Stanton's meddling alone had not lengthened the war; military unpreparedness also had condemned the nation to a lengthy conflict. The army in 1862, Upton stated, had consisted of "906 regiments of infantry, 126 regiments of cavalry, and 27 regiments of light and heavy artillery," a force larger than "the present Russian Field Army on a war footing by 237 battalions." Raising and maintaining this force had cost the government $389 million in the twelve months following the bombardment of Fort Sumter. By contrast, the army's appropriations totaled less than $72 million in the three fiscal years immediately prior to the conflict's outbreak. It was clear to him that had more been spent on military preparedness during time of peace, the war would have been shorter and less costly. Failure to invest in peacetime, Upton concluded, had led to wartime expenditures that "foreshadowed a national debt from which a century of taxation will scarcely relieve us."[53]

How, then, to reform this broken system? First and most importantly, politicians needed to become statesmen, thereby being more concerned about the welfare of the "state" than about their political fortunes or those of their party.[54] Second, a strong federal government needed to enact legislation that addressed the military's defects, the most glaring of which was its continued reliance on untrained militia and volunteers. As in *The Armies of Asia and Europe*, Upton did not reject the use of volunteers. Rather, it was their lack of preparation for war that he found contemptible. He applauded the volunteers' performance in the Mexican-American War, arguing that they differed from militia employed in prior conflicts because they had undergone eight months' training prior to their first combat. This had led to the army's successes at Monterey and Buena Vista, where "the volunteers fought with a steadiness that earned the applause of their comrades in the regulars." This experience provided a valuable counterpoint to the use of the militia in the War of 1812. "In one war," he argued, "an army of more than 6,000 raw troops, posted in the defense of our own capital, fled with a loss of but 19 killed and wounded; in the other a force of less than 5,000 trained volunteers, supported by a few regular troops, overthrew a Mexican army four times our number." Upton believed that this represented nothing less than a revolution in the way in which the United States could, in the future, expand its army in time of war.[55]

Still, the volunteer system had its defects, not the least of which was its reliance upon the states for recruitment, appointment of officers, and initial training. "In all foreign wars, as well as in civil commotions greater than a riot or insurrection," Upton argued, "the Constitution intended the government should 'raise and support' its own armies, but Congress thought otherwise." He contended that Congress had abrogated its responsibility in 1861 when its legislation had "sanctioned all of the extravagance of the military system under the Confederation, by permitting each State to send, subsist, clothe, supply, arm, equip and transport its troops." This blunder occurred because the law "was based on the theory of confederation: the troops were to be State, not national." He was particularly critical of allowing states to appoint officers to the volunteer regiments they raised, believing this practice "was dictated by mistaken ideas in reference to States rights."[56] The federal government therefore needed to assume responsibility for raising and training volunteers.

Finally, Upton argued that command of the army ought to be unified in the office of the commanding general. "In every country but our own," he complained, "the inability of unprofessional men to command armies would be accepted as a self-evident proposition." Stanton's meddling in the conduct of the Civil War had confirmed this lesson. "Subject to the supervision of the President," Upton concluded, "only professional soldiers should command" armies.[57]

Two of these proposals later became focal points for Upton's critics. His desire to reduce the power of the secretary of war to that of being a "minister" has led some to conclude that he was contemptuous of civilian leadership, a trait that led him, they allege, to distinctly un-American proposals for military reform. There certainly is reason for such an analysis. Clearly, Upton *was* contemptuous of politics and of politicians. He also approved of what he believed was the European practice whereby a general staff drew up and submitted legislation concerning military affairs to the nation's legislative body. The nation's representatives "may refuse to incur the expense of reforms," Upton wrote, "but do not question the wisdom of the details." He realized that this meant a severe diminution in the power of the secretary of war. "Sherman is accused of desiring to dwarf the Secretary till he can, without inconvenience, carry him in his vest pocket," he wrote Wilson. "Confidentially there is just where I would like to see him." But it is an oversimplification to suggest that Upton was simply "sneering at the frocks," for he had genuine concerns about the power of the secretary of war. "Neither by the Constitution nor by the laws," he wrote du Pont, "is the Secretary of War entitled to exercise command, & . . . whenever he departs from the sphere of administration to conduct military operations he is nothing more than a usurper." Upton realized this was strong language, but he believed himself justified making such a statement. "When our President," he continued, "has been impeached by the House for attempting to remove a Secretary who claimed that his orders were the Presidents orders, I think it is time that someone should present his position in a proper light."[58]

In this passage Upton was referring to the events of 1866–68. The army, which had been given the mission of enforcing federal policy in the South, had found itself caught in the middle of the conflict between President Johnson and Congress regarding Reconstruction. The First Reconstruction Law apparently had created a second U.S. Army responsible for the execution of Reconstruction policy that was under the command of Congress rather than the president, and it gave the secretary of war the power to remove any commander he deemed was not executing the law as Congress desired. Stanton and Grant, then the army's commanding general, "concluded neither the President nor any Cabinet members could interpret the reconstruction law. Congress had delegated this power to the military governors alone." By mid-1867, military governors throughout the South were violating orders Johnson had given them. Subsequent legislation removed the command of the army almost entirely from the president. Officers often found themselves in the position of either disobeying Johnson or of failing to execute the law. To address this dilemma, Stanton and Grant assured commanders in the South that they had complete independence from the president. Even more shockingly, in the middle of Johnson's impeachment proceedings, the president proposed to create a new command led by Sherman who would report to Johnson as a counter to that led by Grant and answerable to Stanton and Congress.[59]

It is in this context that one must look at Upton's concerns regarding the powers of the secretary of war. Attorney General Caleb Cushing's finding during the Pierce administration that "the order of a cabinet minister is valid as the order of the President; without any reference to, or consultation with him" greatly troubled him. "So long as this ruling stands," he wrote du Pont, "we shall have Stantons, who will not hesitate to usurp all of the functions of the President and General-in-Chief." Upton saw other dangers in allowing the secretary of war to command the army. "In administration he [the secretary of war] is independent of the President and ought to be," he wrote, "as thereby the purse is separated from the sword. Congress undoubtedly has the right to enable him to make all contracts for supplies &c. This power belongs to it under the Constitutional right to raise and *support* armies. Could it give the right to command, then the Army could pass under the absolute control of Congress. It was to prevent this that the Constitution declares that the President should be Commander-in-Chief of the Army & Navy." In this passage Upton described almost exactly the sequence of events that had transpired in 1868. With congressional sanction and wielding the power of the "purse," Secretary of War Stanton "commanded" an army that had been removed from the control of the president. It was Upton's ultimate nightmare—an appointed official becoming a despot and using the army to enforce his authority. Such an analysis led him to conclude that "politicians, and not a standing army, are dangerous to liberty."[60]

This critique of Stanton presented Upton with a very real intellectual dilemma. On the one hand, he truly believed that the power the secretary of war wielded represented a threat to the Republic. On the other, he understood that congressional Republicans likely viewed favorably his best evidence of that threat, which was Stanton's actions in 1867 and 1868. Upton therefore had to "prove" that Stanton had betrayed his Republican political allies by prolonging the war through his actions in the spring and summer of 1862. To do this he needed to portray George McClellan as the wronged commander, a man who would have won the war had the overzealous, interfering, and intriguing secretary of war left him alone.

Such a view of McClellan's military abilities contrasted sharply with Upton's earlier evaluations of the general. After attending the reunion of the Army of the Potomac in July 1869, he had spoken disdainfully of the "McClellan clique." "McClellan's weakness was never as manifest to me as it was at the reunion," he had told Wilson, an admission that implies those weaknesses had been manifest long before. Now he had to argue that McClellan had few if any weaknesses, apparently understanding that doing so entailed performing some serious intellectual gymnastics. While drafting the chapters that addressed the 1862 campaigns, Upton wrote du Pont, "It may astonish you that I now regard McClellan in his military character as a much abused man." Upton argued that McClellan had been removed, not for his military blunders, but for mistakes in the political realm. "But the difference of opinion between him and the Administration would probably never have arisen but for the interference of Stanton," he continued. "He was at the bottom of all the disasters of the year 1862, and if this fact can be established then the blame can be laid upon a system which still permits the Secy of War to usurp military command." Upton thus linked Stanton to the military failures of 1862, and if he could argue convincingly that the secretary's actions had led to a longer conflict, he would not need to address the more politically contentious issue and the one that truly alarmed him, namely Stanton's role in the events of 1866–68. Trying to prove that the secretary of war had undermined McClellan caused Upton great difficulty. "The campaign of 1862 gives me much trouble," he admitted to du Pont.[61] Ultimately, it proved too great a challenge, for he produced a passionate if badly flawed analysis.[62]

By contrast, nowhere did Upton contest the authority of the president to command armies in the field; he simply questioned the wisdom of doing so. He did not fear the abuse of presidential authority within the constraints imposed by the Constitution, nor did he believe that Lincoln had been a "usurper."[63] He was not happy with many of Lincoln's actions during the Civil War, but he never questioned the president's authority as commander in chief; rather, he questioned the efficacy of his actions.[64] It was not Lincoln but Stanton and his usurpation of the president's power as commander in chief who was the true target of Upton's wrath. Upton, then, was reacting to what he believed were the lessons of the Civil War and, perhaps more importantly, of Reconstruction.

The evaluation of the militia and volunteers in *Military Policy of the United States* also has attracted numerous critics. Though not the first, perhaps the most important of these was John McAuley Palmer.[65] An 1892 graduate of West Point, Palmer played a substantial role in the shaping of U.S. manpower policy during the 1920s and 1930s as well as during the Second World War and was dedicated to the concept of a citizen-soldiery. In an effort to refute Upton, Palmer undertook research into the origins of the military's manpower policies. His research uncovered several documents that Washington had written that Upton had failed to find. The most important of these was "Sentiments on a Peace Establishment," written in 1783, in which Washington advocated an army that consisted of a regular force as well as "a well organized Militia."[66] Palmer argued that the regular army Washington had advocated was really "a special function of the militia like our present National Guard." This force would be activated only in time of national emergency and thus "was not in any sense what we have in mind when we refer to the regular army to-day." Washington's militia was to be a local force of young men who would supplement the so-called regular military and would react to regional threats. In overlooking this important document, according to Palmer, Upton had made a grievous historical error. Rather than portraying Washington as a friend of the militia, he had depicted him as its enemy. As such, Upton "used Washington as his principal expert witness in opposing that institution."[67]

This critique is questionable on two points. First, it is not altogether clear that Upton's and Washington's sentiments concerning the militia differed to any great degree. James Flexner, in his biography of the president concluded that Washington was wary of the nation's dependence on the militia and therefore advocated a "National Militia" that the federal government would equip and regulate. "We must have a permanent force," Flexner quotes Washington as saying, "not a force that is constantly fluctuating and sliding from under us as a pedestal of ice would do from a statue in a summer's day."[68] Such a sentiment rang true for Upton. Palmer's larger mistake was overstating Washington's importance to Upton's argument, which did not rely upon the Founding Father's complaints to prove his case. Rather, he employed Washington's criticisms of the militia to reinforce a point he made by historical example. The Revolution, the Whiskey Rebellion, Shays's Rebellion, the War of 1812, the Indian wars of the 1820s and 1830s, and the Mexican-American War were all preludes to the great crime of the American military system—the Civil War—and it was in his narrative of that conflict that Upton hoped to convince his readers of the folly of the manner in which the United States prepared for its wars.

Some historians have recognized that Upton was more concerned with the Civil War than with Washington and the Revolution and that his "attitudes toward militia and state volunteers were more complex than his critics acknowledged." The National Volunteers, Stephen Ambrose correctly points out, would be "militia operating under federal authority and directed by the army." Still, they argue that Upton's true goal was enlarging the regular army. Implementation of the National Volunteers, they contend, would bring about "public acceptance of the principle that only the regular army—and not civilians in arms—was capable of defending the nation. Once that principle had been accepted, then the regular army would naturally and logically grow. . . . Upton did not need to ask for a larger army—that would be the result of the acceptance . . . of his program."[69]

Upton certainly hoped that the National Volunteers would "nationalize" the army and make it more popular with the public at large, a recurring theme in *Military Policy of the United States* and in much of his correspondence.[70] There is, however, no evidence to support the assertion that Upton hoped to secure a larger regular army as a result of this "nationalization."[71] In fact, in the late 1870s Upton lobbied against enlarging the army, believing that Congress would "increase" its size simply by creating more regiments without approving a commensurate augmentation of manpower. He expressed a similar sentiment to John Schofield, lobbying him to "use your influence to limit . . . [any] increase to filling up companies, instead of adding new organizations. . . . If we can keep our present organization and limit the action of Congress to an increase or decrease of the number of men in one company, it would be a great step toward permanence in the military system."[72]

To make this point, Upton urged Church to publish an editorial in the *Army and Navy Journal* that endorsed "filling up the companies instead of adding new organization." He even argued that the National Volunteers "would enable us to reduce the army to the lowest possible level." Had his true goal been the development of a larger regular army, Upton almost certainly would have accepted a severely skeletonized force in the hope that it eventually would be filled with new soldiers. Because his primary objective was to design a military system that would produce an army that could be made ready for combat quickly, such an organization was anathema to him.[73] Finally, his criticism in *The Armies of Asia and Europe* of European nations' needlessly large and costly armies renders unsustainable any contention that he was seeking a larger military.

The proposals Upton put forward in *The Armies of Asia and Europe* and in *Military Policy of the United States* therefore must be viewed with his personal experience, both during and after the Civil War, clearly in mind. In recommending that the United States adopt a small regular army that could be increased to 150,000 in time of war, Upton proposed a system that he believed would provide a reliable force large enough to meet any potential threat, internal or external, to the United States. That it could not meet the demands that the wars of the twentieth century would place on it is a false criticism. No one in the 1870s could conceive of a situation demanding the United States field a mass army, and even if they could, there existed almost no political support either for conscription or for universal military obligation, the tools by which such an army would have been raised. Upton's proposals for the reform of the means by which the army expanded its organization in time of war, of its bureau system, of the relationship between the secretary of war and the commanding general, and of the officer promotion and education systems all were efforts to apply the lessons of America's previous conflicts as well as what he had learned from his observations of other nations' armies.

Although *Military Policy of the United States* remained unpublished in Upton's lifetime, it nevertheless had important consequences. Many became aware of his critique of American military policy and of his remedies for its "problems," and if some disagreed with these ideas (especially those who served in the staff bureaus), it appears that most officers approved of them. Whether Upton, as the first author to attempt a scholarly, if jaundiced, analysis of the historical roots of the United States military system, thereby defined the parameters of the discussion about the relationship between the army and American society for a generation of officers is a more difficult question—one that will be addressed in the final chapter.

It appeared at the time that Upton's manuscript might have a more immediate effect, for while he was drafting and revising *Military Policy of the United States* in 1878, a joint congressional committee headed by Sen. Ambrose E. Burnside of Rhode Island held hearings regarding reform of the U.S. Army. Sherman hoped that portions of Upton's draft, if provided to members of Congress, might help persuade them that the army was in need of "progressive" legislation. Representative Garfield thought Upton's arguments compelling. "I am exceedingly anxious that he will get his book out before Congress meets in December," he wrote Sherman in June 1878, "for it will be of great value in the next discussion of the army."[74] Though Upton disappointed Garfield by failing to complete the book in time for Congress to consider its content, the legislation the Burnside Committee proposed was unmistakably Uptonian in its outlook. Whether or not Burnside, Garfield, and Sherman could muster the political support necessary to pass such legislation remained in doubt even as Upton continued to labor.

CHAPTER 8

THE POLITICS OF REFORM

I f it was clear to Emory Upton that the army needed to adopt his reforms, others were less certain. Upton's proposals threatened the interests of a diverse set of politicians and soldiers. They were a direct assault upon the War Department's bureau system and upon the staff officers it empowered. His criticisms of the militia and volunteers assailed practices that granted tremendous power to state governments, not only alienating politicians who saw those organizations as valuable sources of political patronage but also those who, in the aftermath of the Civil War, wished to reduce substantially the power of the federal government over the states. Upton's desire to diminish the authority of the secretary of war raised the suspicions of those who thought such a move would endanger civilian control of the military. Many officers who were incompetent or infirm understood that Upton's ideas, if adopted, posed a substantial threat to their careers. Finally, his proposals regarding officer advancement would reduce the immense power of regimental colonels in determining promotions. By attacking such disparate interests, Upton aroused the opposition of many who otherwise might have supported individual changes.

There was, however, significant support for reform. Many line officers favored Upton's designs as did some prominent politicians, among them James Garfield and Ambrose Burnside. Popular, albeit conservative, journals of the day also supported many of his ideas. Still, it remained to be seen whether or not there existed the political will required to change a military system whose legal basis was nearly a century old, with many traditions dating to the beginning of the English settlement of North America. There was a question, moreover, as to whether legislation could be enacted that would give power to the federal government in an era when states were attempting to reassert their authority. Overcoming these obstacles promised to test the political acumen of the ablest of statesman.

In June 1878 E. N. Gilpin, who had been Upton's orderly during Wilson's raid into Alabama and Georgia in the Civil War's closing months, visited his former commander at Fortress Monroe. "He has not changed much. Is taller apparently, and older looking, and wears his honors modestly," Gilpin wrote his brother Tom, who also had served under Upton. He thought his former commander appeared relaxed and discovered that Upton greatly enjoyed talking "of old times." Yet Gilpin, perhaps unknowingly, also noted the loneliness that had pervaded Upton's life since his wife's death. "He ranked me to have you visit Washington, and then both of us call upon him." Gilpin continued. "He was very insistent." This and other evidence suggests that Upton was not, while assigned to Fortress Monroe, the social hermit some have depicted.[1] Siblings visited him frequently, often spending many weeks at Fortress Monroe, as did Emily's mother and at least one of his sisters-in-law. Professional colleagues and Civil War comrades also visited, and he frequently asked others to call on him.[2] If anything, his frequent requests that friends and family visit confirm that he was quite lonely but hardly a recluse.

Upton's duties kept him busy. Col. George Getty, the commander of the post and of the Artillery School, reported to the secretary of war in 1878 that the rapid pace of technological change demanded that artillery officers receive "special instruction" in artillery techniques as well as in "kindred subjects" that would provide them with a broader understanding of that branch's role in the army. As the school's superintendent of instruction, Upton placed as much emphasis on the "kindred subjects" as he did on instruction in technical and tactical developments in the artillery. One of his innovations was to require officers become proficient in infantry tactics because he expected future battle would require close coordination between the two branches. This training went well beyond the parade-field drill that had been the staple of tactical instruction before and after the Civil War. Infantry training, Getty further reported, would involve "its application to ground and the requirements of war." One year later the colonel communicated that this included practical exercises in "applied tactics" in which "the battalion is divided into parts which operate against each other on any ground illustrative of attack and defence."[3] These developments reflected the evolving nature of Upton's tactical thought.

Strategy was another "kindred subject" to which Upton attached great importance. His course on the topic "embrace[d] General history and all military operations connected with handling armies in campaign." Upton and members of the school's staff lectured on the major campaigns of the Revolutionary War, the War of 1812, and the Mexican-American War as well as on selected campaigns of Napoleon, Frederick the Great, and Marlborough. The course also included an analysis of the Franco-Prussian War, but its centerpiece was a detailed examination of the "War of Rebellion" that attempted to explain the outcomes of numerous important battles. Yet this investigation of the Civil War went far beyond battle history as it also attempted to assess the value of joint operations with the navy, the evolution of cavalry organization and tactics, and the role technological developments, especially railroads and the telegraph, played in the war's conduct. These exercises in historical understanding, Upton hoped, might "illustrate . . . the great principles of warfare." His efforts to incorporate instruction in history and infantry tactics into the Artillery School's curriculum forced officers to view themselves as part of a larger whole, thereby helping diminish the provincialism that often characterized their perception of other branches.[4]

The school's day-to-day operation provided Upton with numerous illustrations of the army's lack of efficiency. In October 1878, for but one example, he wrote the adjutant general requesting that he be allowed to utilize the post's ambulance wagon to transport officers for map and tactical exercises because, he explained, the Artillery School did not have enough saddle horses to do so. Neither he nor Getty was able to make this rather unimportant decision, he continued, due to a Civil War–era law that "reserv[ed] ambulances for the exclusive use and benefit of the sick and wounded." The adjutant general forwarded the request to General Sherman. "I understand that the existing orders prohibit the use of ambulances for any . . . [reason] other than the use of the sick," Sherman wrote the adjutant general. "Reconnaissance by wagon is exceptional, and I am not willing to advise a Separation from the Established Rule without the assent of the Hon. Secretary of War, otherwise . . . exceptions will be asked from nearly every post in the Army." The general then forwarded the request to the secretary of war, who rejected it. Upton therefore had to employ horses from field-artillery batteries stationed at Fortress Monroe for the task.[5] That the post commander was unable to employ all of the post's assets as he saw fit, and that only the secretary of war could render a decision in this rather minor matter, must have confirmed for Upton the byzantine nature of the army's lines of authority.

Upton's work at Fortress Monroe, at least initially, did not prevent him from making considerable progress on *The Military Policy of the United States*. He clearly had undertaken an impressive amount of research, and footnotes in the manuscript as well as correspondence with Sherman, Garfield, and Schofield indicate that he consulted a wide range of primary and secondary sources.[6] By June 1878, barely two months after publication of *The Armies of Asia and Europe*, he had completed the section addressing the American Revolution and had sent the manuscript to Garfield for comment. Upton, no doubt, felt himself under some pressure to finish the project before Congress convened in December because he believed that "the book will be more valuable to Members of Congress than other readers." He was even more explicit in a letter he wrote the following month. "I think that the great object of the book," he declared, "should be to bring home to Congress that all important fact; that it is entitled to the credit for all that is good, and equally responsible for all that is bad, in our military system. Until it appreciates this fact improvement will be slow and difficult."[7]

Despite his desire that the manuscript might influence Congress, Upton's work slowed considerably in the summer and early autumn of 1878. By the end of August, he had progressed only to the end of the War of 1812, and mid-October found him working on the Mexican War. "I shall push ahead as rapidly as possible," he wrote Sherman, "but cannot say when I can finish." Sherman had noted Upton's lack of progress and was so concerned about his protégé's lethargy that he asked Garfield to encourage him to finish the project before December. This the congressman did, telling Upton that he was "delighted with the chapters, and feel[s] confident that they will be of great service to Congress and the country." After offering "a few suggestions," he concluded by saying, "I hope you will bring your book out, if possible, before the next meeting of Congress." One month later Garfield offered even more encouragement. "Your plan for a national army . . . is excellent," he told Upton, "and I hope you will work it out so fully in its details that we can embody it in a bill to be introduced before Congress."[8]

Still, Upton's work lagged. He reported to Sherman that his duties at Fortress Monroe had delayed him greatly. Perhaps more importantly, his publishers, the Appletons, had told Upton that there was little interest in the kind of book on which he was working. "I did not debate the point as to when the book should be published," he told the commanding general. "Could it have come out on top of the riots [the Great Strike of 1877] it certainly might have attracted attention."[9] Whatever the reasons for the lack of progress, events in Washington, D.C., overtook his efforts. In the summer of 1878 a joint committee convened to study the question of military reform and to make recommendations to Congress.

Military reform was not a new issue in 1878. There had been numerous attempts to legislate army reorganization between 1867 and 1875, but as often as not, they had been thinly disguised efforts to reduce the size of the military rather than genuine attempts to modernize its organization. Sen. John Logan's 1874 proposal to decrease the regular army without a similar reduction in the number of line regiments was one of the more extreme examples of such thinking. Bitter personal animosities oftentimes motivated these proposals. Both Logan and Rep. Benjamin Butler had recommended reductions in military spending more as a means to strike out at Sherman, against whom both had deep grudges dating back to the war, than out of any real concern about military expenditures. Yet despite apparent widespread support for decreasing the army's size,

Congress could agree neither on the magnitude of the reductions nor on its resulting organizational structure.[10]

Debate in Congress over army reorganization had grown so acrimonious that in the spring of 1878 Garfield wrote a two-part article for the *North American Review* in an effort to garner public support for military reform. He opened the piece by proclaiming that public opinion immediately after the conclusion of the Civil War "was almost unanimous that the army should be larger in proportion to our population and extent of territory, than it was before the war." The military's subsequent decline in popularity, he asserted, had been due to the nature of its postwar duties. "It was a period of transition from war to peace," he wrote, "and the work of reconstruction, as undertaken by Congress, could only be successfully accomplished by the aid of the army. The employment of the army in a service so closely related to political action, produced not a little prejudice against the entire military establishment." In enforcing Reconstruction laws, the army had done the bidding of Congress, and for so doing, Garfield thought, Congress now was punishing the military.[11]

Garfield then laid out reasons for maintaining a regular force. Its purpose would be "to keep alive the knowledge and practice of military science, so that, at any time, in case of foreign or *domestic* war, the nation may know how to defend itself against the most skillful enemy." Such an army would provide the nation "an active, disciplined force sufficient to preserve inviolate the national boundaries; to protect our widely-extended frontier against a savage and treacherous race; to protect the public property and preserve the peace in all places subject to the exclusive jurisdiction of the United States; and to aid the several States in case of invasion or insurrection too powerful to be controlled by their local authorities."[12] Like Upton, Garfield thus sought to justify an army more as a constabulary force than as one that might defend the nation against a foreign threat.

Having emphasized the need for an adequate military, Garfield moved to the question of its strength and organization. Citing letters from Sherman and Winfield Scott Hancock, he laid out two substantially different alternatives. Sherman proposed the acceptance of an expansible army that could increase in size to nearly 250,000 soldiers in time of war, while Hancock argued that such a skeleton organization would leave peacetime infantry companies and cavalry troops so short of enlisted men they would be unable to train effectively. Hancock instead suggested that companies should be manned up to 100 percent of their authorized strength and that the number of companies in a regiment be reduced to eight so that the army's aggregate strength would remain unchanged.[13]

Garfield also referenced a letter by Judge Manning F. Force of Cincinnati. Force had served in the West during the Civil War, and his assignments included duty as a brigade commander during the Vicksburg and Atlanta Campaigns as well as during the March to the Sea. His actions during the Battle of Atlanta had earned him the Medal of Honor, and he subsequently served as a division commander during Sherman's advance into the Carolinas. Force criticized the fact that the army staff and the secretary of war issued orders with neither the consent nor the knowledge of the commanding general. The heart of this problem, he argued, was the army staff's political influence. "The staff and bureau officers in Washington," he wrote scathingly, "pampered by this system, have, from time to time, procured the passage of laws to foster it." Force's brother-in-law, John Pope, concurred with this assessment in another letter Garfield cited, alleging the fraud that had permeated the War Department during Belknap's tenure had been the product of this system. "The concentration of every detail of army administration in Washington," Pope concluded, "has reached a point where every sort of fraud is made possible."[14]

With these letters serving as background, Garfield set forth his proposals for military reform. He argued that the secretary of war's powers and those of the commanding general should be strictly delineated, with the former responsible for administrative matters and the latter for "command." He asserted that the staff was "still an honorable, intelligent, and effective body of public servants" but contended that "its functions have been distorted by the usurpations of the Secretaries of War." Garfield's solution to this problem, one he acknowledged that his reading of *The Armies of Asia and Europe* had influenced, was to end permanent staff assignments and to adopt a staff organization similar to that of the Indian army. Finally, he argued that Sherman's proposal for an expansible army was the logical and economical solution for the organizational dilemma.[15]

Garfield concluded his essay by assailing the intentions and integrity of legislators who wanted to reduce army pay and to decrease its size or disband it entirely. Noting that "there has been in Congress a growing spirit of unfriendliness, if not of positive hostility, toward the army," Garfield criticized those who had advocated closing West Point for their inability to understand the imperatives of defending a nation. "A republic, however free," he argued, "requires the service of a certain number of men whose ambition is higher than mere private gain; whose lives are inseparable from the life of the nation, and whose honors and emoluments depend absolutely upon the honor and prosperity of the Government, and who can advance themselves only by serving their country." He contrasted these public servants with members of Congress who were more concerned about their pay than they were that of soldiers performing unappreciated, often hazardous duties in the service of the country. Lashing out at those who would reduce soldiers' incomes, Garfield concluded, "The friends of good government and fair dealing will not be slow to condemn these repeated assaults upon the honor and usefulness of the army."[16]

Not surprisingly, this essay struck a responsive chord with Upton. "I have read with great pleasure and profit your two articles in the N.A. Review," he wrote Garfield, "which, coming from one who has had such great experience in the field, and on the floor of Congress, cannot fail to urge public opinion toward a reform which all military men know to be of vital importance." Sherman was even more laudatory. "I feel sure," he told Garfield, "you have laid the foundation for the true system of Army administration from which we have sadly departed too much."[17] The degree to which the article might have influenced Congress is not altogether clear, but it makes apparent that Garfield and Upton were thinking along similar lines. Whatever its influence, in June 1878 Congress established a joint committee to scrutinize and propose changes to the army's organization.

Senator Burnside chaired the committee, which consisted of two additional senators and five representatives whose leanings reflected the era's political divisions. Along with Burnside, the Republican members were Sen. Preston Plumb of Kansas and Reps. Horace Straight of Minnesota and Harry White of Indiana, all of whom supported progressive military reform. The Democrats on the committee manifested the interests of those in Congress who wished to reduce the army's size and influence. Two of them, Sen. Matthew C. Butler of South Carolina and Rep. George Dibbrell of Tennessee, were ex-Confederate generals who represented regions that had suffered much under Radical Reconstruction. The third Democratic member, Rep. Henry Banning of Ohio, had served as a general in the Union army, but in the postwar era he had led congressional Democrats' efforts to reduce the army, cut the number of officers, and reduce soldiers' pay. The last appointee to the committee, Rep. Edward Bragg of Wisconsin, like Banning, had served as a general of volunteers during the Civil War, and he too was deeply opposed to strengthening the regular army. Unlike Banning, however, Bragg declined to serve on the committee.[18]

After a brief session in Washington, the committee moved to White Sulphur Springs, Virginia, where in early July it held ten days of hearings behind closed doors. There it heard testimony from numerous officers and civilians, and though Upton did not appear before them, the members received his views by means of a paper he had written that critiqued Sherman's proposed bill. The commanding general also had forwarded copies of *The Armies of Asia and Europe* to the committee, and he specifically referred its members to the section of the book that dealt with the Indian army. The committee then adjourned until December, when it met in New York City to compile its massive final report. This consisted of 516 pages, including letters written by officers and

civilians to the committee, hundreds of pages of historical documents addressing the question of army organization during the previous century, Garfield's
North American Review article, and the bill itself—724 separate sections and
more than 70 pages, including a proposed revision of the Articles of War. For
those who found this to be a daunting read, the committee provided a 4-page
summary of the proposal's major points.[19]

The Burnside Bill, as the measure came to be called, reflected the committee's mixed membership. It reduced the number of generals on active duty from
eleven to five and eliminated the rank of lieutenant general effective with the
retirement of Sherman and Phil Sheridan, both of whom held that rank. The
bill also decreased the number of infantry regiments from twenty-five to eighteen and cavalry regiments from ten to eight. Though it left the number of artillery regiments unchanged, it reduced officer strength in that branch by fifteen
and reduced total officer strength in the army by three hundred. These final
proposals almost certainly indicate Banning's influence.

Other portions of the bill reflected the efforts of reformers such as Burnside
and Garfield to modernize the military service. The measure consolidated
the adjutant general's and inspector general's departments into one organization that would resemble an embryonic version of a modern general staff and
reduced the strength of most other bureaus. It mandated retirement of general
officers at age sixty-five, while all other officers, with some exceptions, would
go on the retired list on their sixty-second birthday; retired officers would
receive pay up to 80 percent of their salary at the time they left the service. The
bill also proposed an end to the system of regimental promotions, replacing
it with a scheme by which the most senior available officer in a branch was to
fill a vacancy in any regiment in that branch. All officers, moreover, would be
required to pass a proficiency examination before they could assume the duties
of a major, lieutenant colonel, or colonel. All of these were substantial gains for
progressive-minded reformers.[20]

The bill also attempted to define more clearly the relationship between the
secretary of war, the army staff, and the commanding general.

> The Secretary of War, under the direction of the President, shall exercise
> supervision and control over all branches of the military service, not only in
> those cases where his supervision and control are specifically required by law,
> but in all cases embraced with the functions of the President as Commander-
> in-Chief of the land forces; and such supervision and control may be exer-
> cised by the Secretary of War as circumstances may require, *either directly or
> through the Commanding General of the Army, and other officers of the Army,
> or through such agents as the Secretary may appoint in accordance with the law.*

The very next section of the proposed law stated, "the General of the Army, or other general officer assigned by the President as Commanding General, under the direction and during the pleasure of the President, *have command of the entire Army, line and staff.*" These provisions made a murky situation even murkier, which likely would alienate both sides in the debate over the role of the two offices.[21]

The bill quickly became the object of criticism. Speaking on the floor of the Senate on the day of its introduction, Burnside noted that its opponents already had assailed the measure for its apparent curtailment of the secretary's powers, and he attempted to dispel any concerns in this regard. He noted that in some instances the proposed law had taken power away from the secretary of war and had given it to the president; in other areas the "Secretary and commanding general of the Army are jointly named"; in still others the secretary received "new authority"; and finally there were parts of the law that transferred "authority . . . from the Secretary to the commanding general." This last category, according to Burnside, provided that all correspondence from the staff to the army's various field commands must pass through the commanding general. "It needs no argument to sustain the propriety of this section," the senator proclaimed. Another aspect of the bill upon which its critics quickly focused was the provision that restricted the president to appointing new officers to the staff from a list of names the commanding general provided to him. That same day Sen. Stanley Matthews, an Ohio Democrat, argued vehemently that this was an unconstitutional limitation on the authority of the commander in chief.[22] Though the point seemed inconsequential at the time, it proved to be the one upon which the Burnside Bill ultimately foundered.

In Upton's eyes, the measure's largest shortcoming was its total neglect of how manpower was to be raised in time of war. Its only references to this question were a number of passages that related to "when volunteers or militia are called into service." The bill Sherman had proposed had left this question unaddressed too, and Upton had been sharply critical of that shortcoming. Its effect, he wrote the Burnside Committee, would be "at the beginning of every war to flood the country with raw troops, volunteers, and militia." Surely he felt similarly about the legislation now before Congress. The measure's failure to address this issue might actually have made its passage more difficult. Upton's proposal for the formation of the National Volunteers had included the development of depots in numerous congressional districts that would support the training and equipping of volunteer battalions. He clearly understood the political implications of such a system. "Could forty representatives [who would have depots in their districts] become personally interested in the army," Upton had written Sherman, "they would wield a powerful conservative influence. It is painful to use such arguments but we know that no member of Congress ever yet refused to vote for an appropriation to be spent in his own district. The construction of forty regimental depots and the disbursements to National Volunteers, if the system could be inaugurated. would be sufficient of itself to make many members favorable to the support of a suitable army." He expressed similar sentiments to James Wilson. "I think if Congressmen could be impressed with the fact that all of the money to be spent on depot building, national volunteers, &c will be spent among their constituents," he wrote, "they might take kindly to the proposed change." Nevertheless, the legislation's failure to provide for an expansible organization did little to dampen Upton's enthusiasm for the bill. Though he told Sherman that the measure "agreeably disappoints me," he also told his mentor: "Congress has never shown so favorable or friendly a disposition before. The provisions for reduction are extremely liberal, while the proposed settlement of many vexed questions is so manifestly for the best interests of the service that I hope the bill may become a law."[23]

Despite the fact that the measure was a compromise between the Burnside Committee's southern contingent led by Representative Banning, who wished to see the size of the army and its expenditures reduced, and Burnside and other members of the committee who advocated modernization of the army's organization, it quickly ran into trouble as it moved through the legislative process. Led by Banning, the House amended the then-pending army appropriation bill by adding most of the Burnside Bill to that measure. The House then strengthened the appropriation bill's posse comitatus clause by repealing an 1865 law that had allowed military force to be used "to keep the peace at the polls." This combined measure passed the House on February 8, 1879, by a vote of 101–91. Upon reaching the Senate, the amended appropriations bill fell afoul of Republican James G. Blaine, chairman of the Senate Appropriations Committee. Blaine delayed the Senate's consideration of the bill because, he claimed, his committee had not had time to give it full and thoughtful consideration. Despite this interference, Burnside was able to get the full Senate to vote on the so-called Banning Amendment to the appropriations measure. The key vote came on February 22, 1879. By a vote of 45–18, the Senate removed the Banning Amendment, effectively killing the army reorganization effort.[24]

The reasons for the demise of the Burnside Bill and its Uptonian reforms have long been fodder for those who have attempted to assess Upton's influence. Russell Weigley contends that Upton's Germanized "system" was anathema to a democratic nation since it threatened to lead to the development of American versions of Helmuth von Moltke and Erich von Ludendorff, a conclusion with which others have concurred. This, however, was not a contemporary concern.

Few politicians and only a small minority of army officers had noted the bill's alleged "Prussian" nature. Of those prominent line officers who wrote letters for the committee's consideration, only Generals Sheridan, Irvin McDowell, and Pope voiced concerns about the measure's "Prussian" nature, though none provided substantive reasons for that judgment.[25] Indeed, Pope had earlier proposed many "German inspired" reforms such as promotion by merit, mandatory retirement, and reorganization of the army's staff. These officers' criticisms thus appear to reflect American chauvinism rather than any real concern about the consequences of adopting a military system modeled to some degree on that of Germany. Moreover, they were the exception among serving line officers, many of whom were at least as admiring of Germany as was Upton.[26]

More importantly, by the 1870s many in the United States had come to have a high regard for Germany and for its institutions. Its university system had become the model for American university reformers, and prestigious institutions such as the University of Michigan and Johns Hopkins University had adopted many German-inspired innovations.[27] Germany was also a haven for many nineteenth-century American writers, among them Edward Everett, Henry Wadsworth Longfellow, and Joseph Cogswell, whose experiences there greatly influenced their works. The influence of German thought was apparent in the work of such ardent nationalists as John Fiske and the Reverend Josiah Strong, both of whom "believed in Aryan race superiority, [and] also accepted the 'Teutonic' theory of democracy."[28]

Much as German ideas had influenced American scholars, educators, and writers, the American public held that nation and its people in relatively high esteem. During the Civil War, Prussia had gone to great lengths not to antagonize the United States, and it had been one of the few European nations to respond favorably to U.S. efforts to sell bonds to finance the war effort. Moreover, almost one man in ten who had enlisted in the Union army had been born in Prussia or was of German descent, and the northern public remembered their contributions to the war effort. As a consequence, many thought favorably of Germany.[29]

The Franco-Prussian War had done little to shake this positive attitude. During that conflict Bismarck had assured the United States that Prussia's sole aim was to protect its borders rather than to destroy French power or to enlarge German territory, recalling the Prussian minister to the United States for making statements to the contrary. The subsequent occupation of Alsace and Lorraine had caused little consternation in the United States. Many Americans believed that Germany represented the future of European democracy, whereas France, under the rule of Napoleon III, as well as Austria, which in concert with France, had attempted to place Maximilian on the throne of Mexico, represented reactionary monarchies. Germany, according to *The Nation*, stood "for a free press, a free parliament, popular education . . . , supremacy of reason over brute force, of the citizen over the soldier." Americans had reacted similarly to German unification, and they had watched with great interest that nation's development, hoping a liberal democracy might emerge. Some reformers even took their lead from this fledgling democracy, hoping to establish a merit system within the civil service modeled on that of Germany.[30] Upton's admiration of certain aspects of the Prussian military system therefore appears to be in concert with the nation's general veneration of things German during the late nineteenth century. Thus it can hardly explain the Burnside Bill's rejection.

Given the South's antipathy toward the army due to the role it had played during Reconstruction, one might presume that Southern Democrats played a key role in the bill's demise. But that was not the case. In the Senate vote of February 22, 1879, ten of the eighteen votes in favor of the measure came from Democratic senators who represented former slave states.[31] Northern Democrats cast three of the remaining eight votes, and a southern Republican holdover from the Reconstruction era cast another. Thus only four northern Republicans voted to support the measure, Ambrose Burnside being one of them. The party alignment is even more surprising when the votes against the bill are considered. Thirty of the forty-five senators who voted in opposition were Republicans, and all but four of these men represented former free states.[32] What, then, accounts for the measure's failure to acquire the support of northern Republicans while garnering a surprising number of southern Democrats?

One explanation for the South's support was the provision that prohibited the army's interference in elections. Another is the role Henry Banning played in shaping the bill and managing it through the legislative process. Neither explain, however, the overwhelming opposition of northern Republicans decisive to the measure's defeat. Although some northern senators undoubtedly opposed the bill due to its restrictions on the use of federal troops in civil matters, in the aftermath of the strikes of 1877, many had concluded that the use of the military in enforcing the law had to be curbed. It also seems likely that business opposition to increased military appropriations swayed some Republican votes.[33]

Another reason for the bill's downfall likely was the tepid support it received from those reasonably expected to have been enthusiastic about it. The *Army and Navy Journal* gave the measure a surprisingly lukewarm reception. William Conant Church opened his December 28, 1878, editorial by commenting, "No one who reads the bill of the Army Committee with care and with candor, can fail to recognize the proofs of industry, intelligence, sound judgment, and general good-will toward the Service which mark it from beginning to end." Yet he went on to condemn numerous of its provisions, being particularly critical of the proposed officer reductions. Church demonstrated a great deal of insight, however, in attributing the cause of this reduction to the internal politics of the Burnside Committee and to the need for the army's advocates to compromise on this and other issues. Immediately following his editorial, the *Journal* published a letter whose author expressed doubt about the measure's efficacy and was especially critical of its provisions for the retirement of officers.[34]

Still, the *Journal* appears to have been supportive of the bill, reprinting Upton's letter to Sherman noting Congress's favorable disposition regarding the army and thereby suggesting that it was unlikely an even more agreeable measure might emerge. Church also published a letter from Major General Schofield, then the superintendent of the U.S. Military Academy, which gave the bill his overwhelming support. The *Journal* then inveighed against the ongoing "War on the Army" it claimed was taking place in Congress and in certain newspapers. "The first requisite for having an opinion on a subject being total ignorance of what it means, the country is, of course, amply provided with opinions on the Army," the *Journal* stated, decrying the "ignorant clamor and pretentious claptrap" that surrounded the debate over army organization.[35]

The Nation expressed similar sentiments. Like the *Army and Navy Journal*, it chided certain members of Congress for their antimilitary proclivities, though it articulated deep concerns about the increased power the Burnside Bill gave the commanding general. The measure, it noted, "will disappoint the ultra-economists who clamor for a material reduction in the Army, as its effect is by no means so marked in that direction as in its radical change of authority, division, and arrangement." This "radical change of authority," the editorial implied, might lead to the establishment of a military dictatorship. *The Nation* expressed apprehension too, arguing that a proportionate reduction of all branches ought accompany any reduction of the staff.[36] Thus two of the more important conservative, promilitary journals of the day were cool in their support of the Burnside Bill.

Just as curious were Sherman's and Garfield's apparent lack of interest in the measure. One historian has characterized the commanding general's actions regarding the bill as "feeble." Moreover, at the height of the debate over the Burnside Bill, Sherman left Washington, ostensibly to inspect military posts in the South, although his real purpose was to visit Civil War battlefields. His absence allowed "staff officers who opposed the bill an even freer hand in their own lobbying efforts." Garfield too did little to help the measure along in Congress, being deeply engaged in the formulation of monetary policy.[37] The bill's two most influential backers thus did little to give wavering politicians cause to support its passage.

The army staff's opposition almost certainly was another reason for its defeat. Burnside believed that Blaine had represented the staff's interests in the Senate, and he vented his frustration at the Maine senator's obstructionism in a speech on the floor of the Senate. "There has been a hue and cry against this bill from the very day it was reported," he declared. "Where has this cry come from? Much of it from the staff bureaus of the Army. . . . I must say that some of these staff officers have gone beyond the line of duty, particularly . . . in Washington." Supported by powerful political allies, the staff, as Burnside charged, *had* conducted an intense lobbying effort against the measure, one that included the publication of a pamphlet that circulated among numerous politicians that justified maintaining the status quo regarding the staff by citing statements made by Washington, Grant, and Sherman.[38]

Key staff members wrote to the Burnside Committee expressing their concern about any changes that might be made in the bureaus. The comments of Edward Townsend, the adjutant general, and Montgomery Meigs, the quartermaster general, were particularly harsh. "It is believed," Townsend told the committee, "a very large number of disinterested officers would concur in the opinion that the present system is good enough." He then went on to argue, much as had Pope, Sheridan, and McDowell, that foreign models were impractical for the United States. "It must be remembered," he continued,

> that the institutions and political economy of the United States differ widely from those of other nations. The system of recruiting in Germany, France, and Great Britain, for instance, could not possibly be carried out in the United States. It is a sort of conscription based on acknowledged obligation to military service, to which the people of this country will never voluntarily submit. The present system of recruiting, of organization, and of military service is the simplest, the most effective, and the farthest removed from undue political bias that can be devised for this country.

Townsend thus linked fear of conscription, about which the bill was silent, to the possibility that such a system might be subject to political corruption and abuse.[39]

Meigs took a different approach, arguing that the staff was not meant to support the army at its existing strength of twenty-five thousand soldiers but instead was designed to be one for a corps d'armée. The size of the army, he continued, ought not to dictate the size of the staff. Rather, the expanse of territory it served as well as requirements for any future conflict ought to drive its size and organization. A reduction in the number of staff officers, he continued, "will end in throwing more and more of the work of making contracts, of providing and issuing supplies, of erecting buildings for shelter for men and materials into the hands of clerks; and the Secretary of War will . . . find himself exposed to the mortifying criticisms which attend some of the departments of the government which have no permanent officers to charge with these delicate and responsible duties."[40] Thus Meigs, as had Townsend, linked the reduction in staff size with the potential for fraud and political abuse.

It was not just the members of the staff branches stationed in Washington who resisted the Burnside Bill. Post traders, merchants, and sutlers opposed the measure as it would have put an end to their lucrative businesses, enterprises that had greased the palms of many politicians.[41] The bureaus also found allies in staff officers serving in the field, for they too believed the measure's terms unacceptable. Lt. Francis H. Parker, an ordnance officer stationed at Fortress Monroe, reflected the concerns of many junior staff officers when he penned a poem entitled "Upton's Lament" after the Burnside Bill had suffered a procedural defeat in the Senate in January 1879.

> We are beaten, oh! we're beaten with disaster,
>   The Congress says our little scheme won't wash,
> That the Secretary still must be our master
>   And that interchangeability is bosh.
>
> Our forces all were ordered to the lobby,
>   Miles, Marrow, Hazen, little Sangree,
> Murkook and Poe and Andenried so nobby,
>   Lieutenant Trowel, Rice and Company.[42]
>
> Burnside did his feeble best in explanation,
>   And our letters have been published far and wide,
> But they answer with sarcastic approbation,
>   That our efforts only help the *other* side.
>
> Poor Banning made a last expiring effort,
>   As reducer and reformer all in one,
> But he says they gave him very little comfort,
>   and he wished to God he never had begun.
>
> We had it all our own way in star chamber,
>   But alas it would'nt bear the light of day,
> For when it was exposed you may remember,
>   That then the very devil was to pay.
>
> For the lawyers hit us with the Constitution,
>   And the Staff so many facts and figures had,
> And the papers by their general distribution,
>   Made our case, I will acknowledge, very sad.

Now after all I'm sadder, but I'm wiser,
  And more circumspect in future I shall be,
I renounce attempt to make a Yankee Kaizer
  And my busted interchangeability.[43]

Like Townsend, Parker thus made vague charges about the German nature of the bill, but his true concerns were evident in the final line of the poem's first and last stanzas. It was not "Germanization" of the army that troubled Parker as much as the the requirement that junior staff officers alternate their assignments ("interchangeability") between the line and the staff.[44]

It seems unlikely, however, that any of these single factors explain the large number of Republicans who voted against the measure. At the height of the preparedness controversy during the First World War, more than thirty-five years after the Burnside Bill's defeat, Francis V. Greene summed up the major problem it had faced. "Congress," he wrote, "represented with substantial accuracy the opinion of the majority of the voters—that this country would never again be engaged in war; and therefore, in the midst of such pressing problems as the building of the Western railroads, the resumption of specie payments, the silver question, and the tariff, there was no time to think about the needs of the army. There was no 'military situation in the United States' worth thinking about."[45]

Greene's analysis rings true. The Burnside Bill ultimately died, not due to its "Prussian" nature, the staff's opposition, or the failure of Sherman or Garfield to adequately support its passage, but due to the convoluted nature of national politics in the 1870s. Not only had the military's role in policing the South during Reconstruction infuriated southern Democrats, but also many Republicans who represented industrial districts in the Northeast and Midwest believed that the use of the military to put down the Great Strike of 1877 had been illegal and evidence of the coercive threat a standing army represented. Issues such as monetary policy, civil-service reform, and the tariff also deeply divided the two parties. The vitriolic debate over these issues, the scandals of the Grant administration, and the machinations that surrounded the election of 1876 has led at least one noted historian to conclude that "by the late seventies there was much to suggest that the vaunted American democratic system was collapsing."[46]

Corruption in government was a principal reason for the perception that democracy appeared to be breaking down, which fostered intense efforts at governmental reform. That the Burnside Bill became caught up in that debate likely was the most important reason for its demise, for it explains many northern Republicans' refusal to support it. One historian has concluded that the bill's effort to curb the president's power to appoint officers to the army staff represented Burnside's efforts to end "a military spoils system, which civilian appointments to the officer corps of the army had verged on becoming." There is much to commend in such an analysis, for the senator had defended the bill's provisions restricting the president's authority to appoint staff officers by stating: "Otherwise they [the staff officers] will be left entirely to the will of the President, and the President can make them from any part of the Army without reference to their service in the department—can make them, in other words, *at the solicitation of friends outside of the Army, and friends who know nothing about the subject.* This section was put in to insure efficiency in the staff departments."[47]

This defense of the measure addressed both strains of thought evident in the era's civil-service-reform movement: the creation of "an efficient, nonpartisan bureaucracy" and "an effort to eliminate the evils inherent in a spoils system." Burnside's incorporation of these themes implies that he saw his bill as the army's equivalent to civil-service reform and tried to sell it as such. Changes to the army's organization thus became entangled in a contentious question that had badly divided the Republican Party in the final years of the Grant administration and continued to do so afterward. Leaders of the "Stalwart" faction of the party in the Senate—like Blaine, Colorado's Edward Teller, James Cameron of Pennsylvania, Angus Cameron of Wisconsin, and New York's Roscoe Conkling—were among the Burnside Bill's strongest opponents, a fact that suggests they feared the measure would reduce their access to the military's spoils system.[48] In pursuing a civil reformer's approach to the measure, Burnside in all likelihood lost the support of many senators who under normal circumstances would have been supportive of army reform.

Upton appears to have believed the Stalwarts were responsible for the bill's defeat, for in the late 1870s he began to exhibit renewed concern about civil-service reform. It was an issue that had interested him for many years, but now it assumed greater importance. Shortly before the bill's rejection in the Senate, he had written his sister-in-law Julia:

> In the general government the object of each party is to possess the spoils. Statesmanship is banned, and in its place a shameful demagoguery has sprung up which makes a merit [?] of yielding to every demand and whim of the ignorant and vicious. . . . No one can now affirm that the leaders of *either* party scorn corruption. They have but one idea—personal and party success, and to accomplish this they will countenance every vanity of dishonesty and fraud. . . . The next conflict will not involve the question of whether or not we are a nation but which set of demagogues shall hold the public purse and deliver the spoils.[49]

"The man who sells his vote is a political assassin," he later wrote Julia. "The leaders who buy them are political brigands. The one cares nothing for anarchy. The other would prefer anarchy to political defeat."[50]

Indeed, the scandals surrounding the Grant administration brought Upton to the rather surprising conclusion that the hero of the Civil War was himself a threat to the nation's republican democracy. In February 1880 he wrote Julia, "Unless Grant is nominated it is probable the next election will pass over peaceably."[51] He was even more suggestive on this point in other letters. "A Caesar could buy the vote of the Roman populace by a distribution of corn," he told her.

> His partisans could plant their tables in the streets and buy the votes that would elevate him to the office of chief magistrate or counsel, carrying with it the command of the armies which afterwards he led against the Republic. The men who would then sell their votes would rush to the polls, and then by threats and bloodshed would drive away all supporters of moral candidates. Do you recognize this practice? And do you think a republic in the 19th Century better able to withstand the influences which led Rome to Monarchy?[52]

Upton elaborated on these fears in an intended chapter of *The Military Policy of the United States* entitled "Civil and Military Policy of Rome."[53] In it he argued that Rome's numerous dictatorships were the result of "the dangerous right conceded to the Senate to invoke personal government whenever the privileges of their class were threatened or invaded." "Demagogues," Upton declared, "fawn[ed] upon the people" of Rome, and the republic's officials were "venal and corrupt." The republic's decline, he continued, was due to the collapse of the moral values of its citizens and to their all-consuming desire to be rich.[54]

This chapter was not a simple historical exercise, for it is apparent that in this passage Upton was thinking of Grant. According to him, the Roman people accepted Julius Caesar's dictatorship as a means to bring peace and stability to their republic after nearly forty years of civil war. Caesar then solidified his position through graft. "The favor of the nobles," according to Upton, "he purchased by promising them the offices of praetors and consuls." Caesar was given power to veto any and all legislation, and "the *imperium* or 'military rule' [was] vested in him for the remainder of his life." All of this brought Upton to a startling conclusion. "The Roman republic," he wrote,

> possesses an interest, civil as well as military. "Forewarned is forearmed." Free people like the Romans admire heroism, and love to reward military achievement.
>
> No monarch in Europe has to day [sic] the power of an American President. With the consent of the Senate, from the Chief Justice down, he has the gift of

more than 90,000 civil offices, any one of which save in the judiciary, he can vacate and fill at pleasure.

Ever since the acceptance of the pernicious maxim "To the victor belong the spoils," these offices, like so much gold have been distributed by senators and representatives to the men who have been, or may be, most loyal to themselves and the party.

With the people thus accustomed to executive corruption let us imagine, as under the Roman System, our President, in uniform, booted and spurred, galloping from the White House to the camp, his military retinue swelled by senators and representatives, fawning for favor and scrambling for spoils, how long it be asked would our liberties survive. . . .

The historian, from the example of Rome, might not fix the exact duration of the Republic, but he could make at least one prophesy of speedy fulfillment: At the first [meeting] held at headquarters the means would be discussed of prolonging the term of the President, if not the more startling proposition to declare him President for life.[55]

These references to a military hero assuming the role of dictator clearly were the product of his anxiety that Grant might again run for president. Other prominent serving and former officers would not seem to merit such concern. Sherman, the only other Union officer who approached Grant in popularity, had earlier renounced any desire to serve as president, and Winfield Scott Hancock, the eventual Democratic Party nominee, was a dark horse until well into 1880. Moreover, even after Hancock had secured the party's presidential nomination, Upton believed that the Democrats had nominated a candidate who would make "a strong run" but likely would lose.[56]

Upton was not alone in worrying about the potential threat another term for Grant might pose to the Republic. In the summer of 1878 *Harper's Weekly* noted the widespread nature of this concern and attempted to discount it. "The absurdity of the talk about General GRANT as an emperor or a dictator is mainly due to the tone of the Republican journals which have suggested his nomination," a *Harper's* editorial argued. This piece went on to urge Grant's nomination because "if he be the one man indispensable to our continued peaceful national and social existence, we must keep him in the position of savior as long as Heaven graciously spares him. We can not afford to take the risk of the dissolution of society at the end of four years."[57] If the editors thought talk of Grant as monarch absurd, it was sentiments such as this that fueled Upton's and other's concern that his continued presidency might lead to dictatorship.

The Nation came to just such a conclusion. Supporters of a third term for Grant, one of its editorials argued, are not concerned about the fortunes of the Republican party as a party. They do not look upon Grant merely as the most available Republican leader. They have no high esteem, many of them have no respect whatsoever, for his civil capacity. Their reliance on him, whether they confess it or not, is a *military* reliance, and their condition of mind, if plainly stated, would be that they think the war between North and South not yet over, or that it is about to recommence.

These third-term supporters, the piece continued, have "so little faith in the stability of the Republic that the abuse of their powers by a parliamentary majority appears to them to involve an appeal to force; so little confidence in the provisions of the Constitution and the temper of the people that they are not easy unless a military President is at hand, ready to exercise the arbitrary powers of a commander-in-chief in the midst of hostilities." *The Nation* berated this "Mexicanization of our politics" and chided those who thought that "a military dictator . . . [is] the only possible saviour of society."[58]

Debate over the implications of a third term for Grant raged in the pages of *The North American Review* between 1878 and mid-1880. Articles entitled "Is the Republican Party in its Death-Struggle," "The Death-Struggle of the Republican Party," "The Third Term," "The Third Term: Reasons for it," and "General Grant and a Third Term" provided its readers with an at-times vitriolic and illogical discussion of the merits of a Grant candidacy. Upton, a frequent reader of the journal, certainly was aware of the turmoil surrounding a potential third term, and he could not have been happy with that prospect. In 1876, upon hearing of Hayes's campaign promise not to seek a second term, Upton had told Wilson, "a one-term President and life secure in the civil service are all that we need to purify our politics, and once established and accepted corrupt men cannot again secure the mastery." He had come to this conclusion due to the scandals that had rocked the Grant administration, and though he found solace in the fact that "the President's integrity has not been questioned," he also understood that many of Grant's appointments had been "controlled by political considerations or . . . family preferences."[59] Under these circumstances a third term for Grant would have been anathema to Upton. His Roman allegory therefore provides great insight regarding his concept of democracy and the army's relationship to a democratically elected government.

Upton had other reasons for distrusting his former commander. His criticisms of Edwin Stanton's role in President Johnson's impeachment by implication applied to Grant as well, for it was his cooperation with the secretary of war that had placed the army at the secretary's disposal. Upton also had seen that Grant could be petty and disloyal toward old friends. He had ostracized Wilson because he had reported to the president that numerous members of the cabinet and presidential staff were involved in scandalous activities. Upton became entangled in the dispute when Wilson had asked him to comment on a letter he had written to Grant. The letter attempted to explain his knowledge of Horace Porter's role in a government construction scheme, and it concluded by asking that the now-former president acknowledge that Wilson had had no part in it. Upton believed that the letter indicated that neither Grant nor Wilson had been involved directly in Porter's activities, but it also gave him a firsthand look at the inner workings of the administration and at Grant's pettiness. If personal loyalty was important to Upton, it apparently had little meaning for Grant where Wilson was concerned.[60]

Upton's ruminations about Grant and the Roman Republic also provide insight regarding his concept of democracy and the army's relationship to a democratic government. There is little doubt Upton was not a "democrat" as that word is understood today. Indeed, he feared "ultra democracy," which he believed meant a turn toward anarchy. He was not alone in this fear. In an article published in the *North American Review* in July 1878 entitled "The Failure of Universal Suffrage," Francis Parkman argued that universal suffrage had led to governmental corruption and the purchase of elections. Upton found Parkman's argument so compelling that he forwarded several copies to his sister-in-law Julia. Democracy to him meant that "foreign tramps," "communists," and "Negroes," all of whose votes were "a commercial commodity," could undermine the republican system of government, though Upton had "no fear as to the ultimate triumph of republicanism." "To my mind," he wrote, "there is but little choice between the cruelty of despotism and the ferocity of a democracy. Between the two lies republicanism which is the only safeguard of liberty."[61]

In this regard Upton was participating in the long-running debate regarding the desirability of democracy versus that of republicanism. In "Federalist No. 10" James Madison had lauded the republican nature of contemporary American constitutions, though they had not yet, he thought, eliminated the dangers of democracy.[62] The political debates of the 1830s through the early 1850s, a period that included Upton's formative years, often focused on the dangers "The Democracy" posed to the nation; Upton's parents almost certainly participated in the Whig side of that debate.[63] His "anti-democratic" tone thus represented political beliefs likely learned in childhood, and it was not a dangerous departure from then-acceptable political discourse. Moreover, his concerns about the threat that "foreign tramps," the uneducated, and non–property owners posed to republicanism reflected many Americans' worries in the late nineteenth century.

Upton's anxiety regarding a possible military dictatorship under Grant demonstrates that it is impossible to argue that he sought to place the military in a position much like that the German army had assumed by 1917. He had no desire for the army and its commander to become the nation's dominant political power or one that operated even semi-independently of elected officials. Such a prospect frightened him. Upton, rather, saw himself as a defender of the virtues of republicanism and his proposals as a means to maintain a republican military.

The Burnside Bill's defeat did not lead Upton to withdraw from the political arena nor did it lead him to the conclusion that the cause of reform was hopeless.[64] Sherman, at the time of the measure's introduction in Congress, had been concerned that the proposal's length and the number of changes it envisioned gave its enemies numerous vulnerable points that could be exploited. "The bill is so infernal long that it offers a vast surface for attack," he had written Sheridan. Upton appears to have come to just such a conclusion in the aftermath of its defeat, thereafter concentrating his efforts on securing legislation to implement a program of mandatory retirement. "It is young men who ought to lead every army," he had written Greene. "If man has not good judgment at 30 he will never have it."[65]

In late 1879 Upton started lobbying William Conant Church to publish editorials in the *Army and Navy Journal* that advocated such a system. He insisted that line officers should be forcibly retired before their age incapacitated them and thought the reasons for such a system were self-evident. "On the staff," he wrote, "where sitting around is the chief occupation, age does not matter so much . . . , but in the line there is scarcely an officer above 50 who shows the slightest interest in his command. The war was fought by young men, and in peace their opportunity is equally manifest." He believed that the experience of the Fourth Artillery, to which he recently had transferred, provided an excellent example of such a situation.[66] "In the last three campaigns on the Pacific Coast," he told Church, "the 4th Arty was required to take the field each time without a single field officer." Upton understood that his advocacy of mandatory retirement would bring charges that favored his own career ambitions. To counter this argument, he pledged to Church, "after my promotion [to colonel and command of a regiment] I shall be a persistent advocate of compulsory retirement—not at the Age of 94, 85, or 65, but at 62."[67]

The issue of mandatory retirement appears not to have concerned Church as much as it did Upton, for the *Army and Navy Journal* said nothing about it in 1879. As of February 1880 Church had still not taken a public stand, thus prompting Upton to ask if he had "decided to take up the subject of mandatory retirement? Everybody in the army wants it, except those who are over, or are hovering around the age of sixty-two." He charged that officers over sixty-two years of age who were unable to perform field duty were "manifestly pensioners of the Gov't." Upton attributed Congress's failure to act to the influence wielded by "about twenty" officers serving on the staff. Again he acknowledged that opponents of his proposals would charge that mandatory retirement meant almost immediate advancement for himself. Upton therefore concluded, "You know I am very young . . . and I can wait for promotion; but how does that case stand with first-lieutenants and captains who are grandfathers?" In another letter he told Church: "Time must . . . give me my promotion. Thus according to self interest I *ought* to oppose retirement."[68]

Despite these protestations, there can be little doubt that Upton's career aspirations at least partially motivated his advocacy of mandatory retirement. "There is no prospect of my promotion," he had told Henry du Pont in February 1880, "till we get a law of compulsory retirement. Sherman does not like to put anyone on the retired list except for cause."[69] Still, it is clear that his professional concerns transcended his personal interests. His rejection of a large yet empty skeleton as a "solution" to the army's organization problem also argues that he was more concerned with the welfare of the service than he was with his own professional advancement. Had the latter been the case, he would have accepted an army with numerous poorly manned organizations because it would have offered more opportunities for promotion.

With the *Army and Navy Journal* having failed to publish a favorable editorial on the subject of mandatory retirement, Upton presented his case to the public, writing a three-part article for *United Service*. In it he used history to prove that war was a young man's duty and that with age came sedentary habits that led older men to miss fleeting chances for battlefield victory. Starting with Rome and Greece, he sought to show that history "leaves no doubt that the greatest commanders . . . in all armies and countries have been below the age of forty-five." Upton also tried to appeal to common sense. "An officer who has passed the climax of his physical powers," he argued,

> if in command of a brigade or a division, may still issue excellent orders for the instruction of his troops. But take two officers, one twenty-five, the other sixty, and place them at the head of raw regiments, which will have the most drills and recitations? Which will visit his guards the more frequently at night? Which will be first in the assault? Which will have the most endurance? Which, through sympathy, cheerfulness, and earnestness of temperament, will urge his men to the greatest endurance and achievements?[70]

To Upton, the answers to these questions were obvious.

Church rejected this logic, though. Taking note of the first of Upton's articles in *United Service*, the *Army and Navy Journal* lauded it as "the most convincing yet made on the question," but the *Journal* also argued that "the zeal of the acknowledged advocate has been pushed just a little beyond the dispassionate consideration of the judge." Speaking of Helmuth von Moltke, the *Journal* pointed out, "the greatest soldier of Europe is a living refutation of the compulsory retirement doctrine." Such a soldier, however, was an exception, the editorial went on to say, and it concluded that "when the wisest plan of compulsory retirement is framed, it will be found to reap the advantages not only of the rule but of any really remarkable advantage in the exception." Neither the *Journal*'s unenthusiastic endorsement of Upton's proposal nor the realization that Congress was in no mood to pass such legislation dampened his enthusiasm. Not only did he continue his work on the second and third parts of the article for *United Service* but also was thinking ahead to his next project. He told Church that he would work for compulsory retirement "as long as I live unless it becomes law" and that "lineal promotion is the next step."[71]

As of mid-1880, then, Upton had not given up on his program of reform. Though Congress had rejected the Burnside Bill, he continued to advocate the adoption of changes he thought critical to the army's welfare. Upton's professional star, moreover, was on the rise. In the summer of 1880 the army promoted him to colonel and assigned him to command the Fourth U.S. Artillery Regiment stationed at the Presidio of San Francisco.[72]

CHAPTER 9

DEATH AND RESURRECTION

In July 1880 Emory Upton's long-awaited promotion to colonel (he had been a lieutenant colonel since 1866) finally came through and with it an appointment to command the Fourth U.S. Field Artillery Regiment stationed at the Presidio of San Francisco. This ought to have been an event of unqualified joy for him, but it actually caused a great deal of concern. Anticipating his imminent promotion, in June Upton had requested two months' leave of absence before taking command. Stating that the leave was for "personal reasons," he indicated that "should the regiment be ordered to the field, I would hold myself in readiness to join it." In an apparent effort to placate Upton, General Sherman ordered him to Washington to serve as a member of a board that was to meet in August and September to review and propose changes to army regulations. The time in the capital apparently did not provide Upton with enough opportunity to settle his affairs, and at the conclusion of the board's sessions, he again asked permission to take leave, this time for three months. Sherman recommended approving the request, though he doubted such a long leave was legal. The commanding general eventually circumvented this problem by assigning Upton as the presiding officer of a board that was to meet at Fort Hamilton, New York, to examine light artillery equipment and procedures, thereby allowing him to remain on the East Coast.[1]

Nowhere in his correspondence with the War Department did Upton mention his reasons for attempting to delay his assignment to San Francisco, but subsequent events make clear it was due to his failing health and to his desire to find a cure before he assumed the physically demanding duties of a regimental commander. The illness, which manifested itself in the form of severe headaches, had troubled him since shortly after his assignment to West Point in 1870. An examination by the academy's dentist revealed "a distinct and regular throbbing in his head . . . and not in unison with the temporal artery." The dentist feared that this symptom signaled a possible aneurysm, but he did not confide this concern to his patient. In the meantime Upton had sought other opinions, but he received no special medical treatment before departing on his 1875–76 journey to inspect Asian and European armies. Still, "as time passed . . . the annoyance from it increased to such an extent that the general could not sleep unless greatly fatigued."[2]

In early 1879 a doctor diagnosed the problem as a recurring case of malaria and recommended that Upton take thirty grains of quinine every time his head began to pulsate. This provided him with some relief, but by the summer of 1880 the throbbing was near incessant. Plagued by an illness that was causing him intense pain and for which there appeared to be no explanation or cure, Upton sought the aid of a Philadelphia doctor, Harrison Allen. He was not happy having to delay his assumption of command to undertake treatment for the ailment, but he told Henry du Pont, "there is too much at stake to delay longer." Doctor Allen specialized in treating "nasal catarrh," a term the medical profession no longer employs but that in the 1880s meant "an acute inflammation of the mucous membrane." To relieve this affliction, Allen proposed to use electrical probes to cauterize Upton's nasal passages, promising that such treatment would cure him within six weeks. Almost unbelievably, Upton told du Pont the procedure caused little or no pain but that his illness made him "feel uncomfortable to myself, and therefore I have not as yet disclosed myself to any of my friends." He reported to his sister Maria that the treatment was "by no means severe" and "the actual cautering [*sic*] gives only a little pain."[3] Despite Doctor Allen's promises, however, Upton's condition did not improve significantly.

Through this period of physical trial, Upton sought relief in the institution to which he had often turned in times of trouble: the church. While attending Bible class at Fortress Monroe in the winter of 1880, he told other members of the gathering

> that religion is to be enjoyed now. "Blessed are the poor in spirit, for theirs *is* the kingdom of heaven." This great gift is ours to enjoy now. "Blessed are they that mourn, for they shall be comforted." What a precious promise this is! God does not willingly afflict or grieve his children. We may sorrow over the ills or trials of those we love, we may sorrow over our own frailties and short-comings, yet above all is the assurance that we shall be comforted.[4]

Yet religion did not give Upton the comfort, physical or mental, that he was seeking, and by late summer his letters had become decidedly morose in their tone. Writing his mother on his forty-first birthday, August 27, 1880, Upton stated:

> A day like this should make one look forward to the end of life. We are all hastening to the Border-Lands, and beyond them by faith we can see those who have been near and dear to us in life.
>
> Rachel, Le Roy, and Emily, are all awaiting that reunion which shall know no separation.[5] They have received the crown of life, and to us it is promised if we remain faithful unto the end. It may be our heavenly Father's will to afflict

us with pain in this world, but we have the assurance that eye hath not seen nor ear heard the things which he hath prepared for those that love him.[6]

Upton had come to the conclusion that God might desire to inflict pain on people during their brief stay on earth rather than attempt to alleviate their suffering. Under these conditions, true peace could be found only in heaven. It seems very likely that Upton was slipping into the throes of depression, which made a life in the hereafter appear more desirable than his existing, painful, tortured existence and that eventually caused him to end his own life.

Despite his melancholy mood, Upton took an active interest in the 1880 presidential election, which pitted Republican James Garfield against Democrat Winfield Scott Hancock. These candidates presented northern veterans of the Civil War with a difficult choice since both had been Union generals with distinguished war records. One of Upton's former soldiers in the 121st New York found himself in just such a quandary and asked his ex-commander's advice on how to vote. "You ask me about the candidates of the two great parties," Upton replied.

> I say to you personally did I have but little choice as to the two men. They would either of them honor the Presidential office. But I have a decided choice as to the parties. We know that the party that stood by us in 1863–4 was true to the country then and has been ever since. Never was a country so blessed by Providence as ours is now. Why then should we change? You exposed your life because you believed we were a nation. This is the creed of the Republican Party and I will believe it will triumph again.[7]

But Upton was not entirely sanguine about Garfield. It appears that he, along with many other proponents of governmental reform, thought that the candidate, by choosing Chester A. Arthur as his running mate and by hedging on the issue of civil-service reform, had sold out to the Stalwarts.[8] And it seems likely that Upton resented the fact that Garfield had all but abandoned the cause of military reform when it became apparent the Burnside Bill would be defeated.

One other issue appears to have caused Upton to reconsider his evaluation of Garfield, that being the congressman's involvement in the case of Fitz-John Porter. In the late 1870s Porter, a Union general who had been a close friend of George McClellan, had petitioned the army for a review of his 1863 court-martial conviction for disobeying John Pope's orders at the Second Battle of Bull Run. In response to the growing outcry over Porter's case, Pres. Rutherford B. Hayes had appointed a board of officers, chaired by John Schofield, to review the court's findings. After hearing testimony from numerous witnesses, some of whom were former Confederate officers who had been unable to testify at the

1863 trial, the Schofield Board recommended to President Hayes that Porter's sentence be remitted. Rather than acting on the board's recommendations, however, the president forwarded them to Congress, claiming that he was without power to act in the matter. The House of Representatives subsequently took up the case, and by the spring of 1880 it was the subject of almost daily debate.[9]

Two factors sparked Upton's interest in the Porter case. First, one of the members of the Schofield Board was Col. George Getty, the commander of Fortress Monroe, who almost certainly provided Upton with information regarding new developments in the case. Second, as the result of his research on the Second Bull Run Campaign for *The Military Policy of the United States*, he had become convinced that Porter had been wronged. In late 1879, when it became evident that Congress would reconsider the matter, Upton wrote Garfield to ask him to support Porter's cause. Comparing Porter's treatment to that of British admiral John Byng, who had been executed for his failure to defeat the French fleet at the Battle of Minorca in 1756, Upton asked that Porter not be accorded a professionally and morally similar fate. He concluded by telling Garfield that he was "always a Republican" and that he desired "simply to see justice done. The great party has saved the Union, and can well afford to restore to honor a man who has fought so gallantly for his country."[10]

Upton appears not to have understood the degree to which Garfield thought himself bound by the court's verdict. Whether or not Garfield thought overturning Porter's conviction would impugn his own honor, might damage his political aspirations, or both is not clear. For whatever reason, however, he was one of the staunchest opponents of reopening the Porter case. Through February and March 1880, Garfield spent numerous hours preparing his defense of the court's findings should he ever be forced to debate the issue on the floor of the House, a process that caused him to collect and review thousands of pages of legal briefs, testimony, and firsthand accounts relating to Second Bull Run.[11] He even sought the advice of a lawyer regarding the propriety of publicly defending the court's verdict. "No public act with which I have ever been connected," Garfield wrote, "was ever more clear to me than the righteousness of the findings of that court which convicted Fitz John Porter." At one point during the proceedings in the House, he looked up and saw Porter in the gallery. "I pity him for the great misfortune he brought on his own life," Garfield wrote in his diary that night. "Really the political spirit of the McClellan Cabal in the Army of the Potomac is as guilty as Porter and probably was the cause of his crime."[12]

That Garfield responded unfavorably to Upton's request therefore is not surprising. The congressman promised Upton that he would consider new evidence "with the utmost care" but added, "it will require new and striking evidence to unsettle the conclusions of my mind in reference to that case." Garfield was more inclined, he told the colonel, to believe witnesses who had testified during the court-martial than to trust to someone's memory seventeen years after the fact. He understood that he might be subject to charges that the trial had been aimed more at McClellan than at Porter and attempted to convince Upton this was not so. "There was not in my heart," Garfield wrote, "nor could I discover it in the conduct of other members, anything to indicate passion or political bias in the course of the trial." Historians have since judged otherwise, and Upton, who had gone to such great lengths to revise the record concerning McClellan's actions in 1862 and saw backstabbing politicians as the cause for the general's demise, certainly must have believed that Porter had been railroaded and that Garfield had had a hand in it.[13]

After spending August through November 1880 under the periodic care of Doctor Allen, Upton finally departed for San Francisco, and on December 23 he took command of the Fourth Artillery. One of his first actions as commander was to increase the amount of *infantry* drill his *artillery* regiment undertook. This is not to say that infantry training had not been occurring, for in the last quarter of 1880 one battery had had forty-two periods of infantry drill, and the remaining batteries had averaged sixteen such periods. Upton maintained this level of training for his light and heavy batteries, but he now directed his foot batteries to undertake daily instruction in infantry tactics. He was particularly concerned that officers participate in these exercises, ordering them to attend all drill periods unless directed to be elsewhere. The colonel ensured their participation by directing that they serve as infantry squad leaders.[14]

Upton also immersed himself yet again in tactics revision. He had written the adjutant general in August requesting permission to update his infantry-tactics manual. "It was a maxim of Napoleon," he wrote, "that 'the tactics of an army should be changed or modified every ten years.'" Upton justified a revision on numerous grounds. He noted that subsequent to the publication of his assimilated tactics, the army had adopted new methods of target practice, arguing that the manual ought to be revised to reflect those changes. He also thought that the tactical lessons of recent European conflicts must be heeded, believing that Indian fighting, which he called "bushwhacking," had little or no relevance for a modern army. European campaigns, he argued, especially those of the Russo-Turkish War (1877–78), "have demonstrated that troops under fire of the breech-loader cannot move in masses; they must break up into battalions, battalions into companies, and these in turn to skirmishers, supports and reserves." Upton therefore proposed his skirmish system, which was applicable to the regiment, be extended to the company level as well.

The ability of a regimental commander to control ten companies effectively in battle also concerned Upton, and he hinted that any revision of his tactics must therefore address the possibility of a four-company battalion. He understood that existing law did not permit the permanent formation of battalions within regiments but pointed out that this did not "prevent the organization of two battalions of four companies each for tactical purposes if expediency demanded it." Upton also believed that breaking the ten-company regiment into two four-company battalions might decrease the amount of time required to prepare volunteers for war. Finally, he hoped a revision of his tactics might allow him to "settle many points . . . which have been referred to me from time to time." "I would respectfully suggest the importance of making modification in tactics in time of peace," he concluded the letter, "so that nothing will have to be unlearned in time of war."[15]

Upton had expressed these sentiments to Sherman six months earlier, telling the commanding general, "the revision will be quite radical." He also had told the commanding general that a revision of tactics had to do more than teach soldiers how to parade around on the drill field. "You are well aware," he wrote, "that thus far in our history tactics in all arms of the service have been simply a collection of rules for passing from one formation to another. How to fight has been left to the actual experience of war." This "experience," Upton believed, had come at an enormous cost; the lethality of the modern battlefield, with its breach-loading weapons, made it even more critical that soldiers learn how to fight before engaging in battle. He therefore proposed that a new manual ought have a chapter on what he termed "applied tactics." This section, he explained, would include "how to get into line of battle with a company battalion regiment brigade &c, how to turn a flank, how to meet flank attacks, to occupy ground, make or procure shelter, &c &c." Thus, a revision of the army's tactics manual was required in order that this "indispensable knowledge" might be disseminated throughout the army and made available to the militia as well.[16]

Upton's argument did not persuade Sherman, who told his protégé to focus his energies on the completion of *The Military Policy of the United States*. Upton ignored the commanding general's wishes, telling Sherman that he would wait until the fall to finish the book. "It seems to me," he said, "that would be the most favorable time for publication as the facts would thus be available for the new Congress which may look upon the country as one nation instead of as a confederacy." Upton nevertheless sought reasons to cease work on *Military Policy*. "If the Democrats come into power I shall not have my book out for four years," he told du Pont. "There will be too much anti-state sovereignty in it to please them." Garfield's victory that November did little to move Upton toward completion of his manuscript. Before leaving for San Francisco, he met with Sherman to again lobby to revise his tactics. "I told him that I wanted to perfect the system," he wrote Maria, "when he said 'You revise it

[and] bring it to me and I will get it approved." With Sherman having relented, the manuscript for *Military Policy*, which Upton had told Julia was "to be the work of my life," was set aside, never to be finished.[17]

Numerous factors probably contributed to this outcome. Almost certainly, Upton's growing disenchantment with Garfield over the Porter case influenced his feelings about the new president's willingness to work with the military on reform, as did his belief that he had sold out to the Stalwarts. The election, moreover, had not changed substantially the makeup of Congress, with Democrats still in the majority in the House and each party holding thirty-seven seats in the Senate. Upton's efforts to rehabilitate McClellan's reputation also had impeded his progress. "I get discouraged," he confided to du Pont in June 1880. "The McClellan question has run the M.S.S. up by nearly four hundred pages. The campaign of 1862, the most critical of the war, is hardly in shape for your painstaking review."[18] All of these, compounded by a deepening depression, united to convince him that completion of his project would be for naught.

Upton proceeded, then, to revise his tactics. His concept for fighting the four-company battalion stressed what he called "the dispersed order of fighting." In an attack two of the battalion's companies would move forward in skirmish formation, running "from cover to cover" while advancing on the enemy position. At "the critical moment" the battalion's remaining two companies, advancing in column of fours under cover of the skirmishers and taking advantage of whatever protection the terrain offered, would be employed "and by their impetus carry the fighting line forward."[19] This represented an advance beyond his earlier tactics manuals in that it recognized the need for smaller units and an even more dispersed organization when maneuvering against entrenched defenders. There are points, however, where Upton's tactical thought appears to portend the bloody disasters on the Western Front between 1914 and 1918. "When works are to be assaulted," he had written Francis V. Greene in 1878, who at the time was observing the Russo-Turkish War, "it is easy as a rule to form your battalions in line within three to eight hundred yards of the position. From this time till the works are carried there is but one movement, and that is straight to the front. As you say, when the advanced skirmishers have exhausted, or rather are about to exhaust their strength other lines like waves should come up and sweep onward."[20] Still, Upton understood that he was dealing with the capabilities of new weaponry and attempting to find an answer to what he perceived as a tactical stalemate on the battlefield. Élan alone would not be enough to carry an enemy's position. Units had to be prepared to fire and maneuver according to the dictates of the terrain and the enemy's defense, hence the requirement for some form of "applied tactics." An assault

was doomed unless planned with care, led with precision, and remained flexible in its execution. Trained technicians had to lead these complicated maneuvers—amateur officers could no more expect to succeed in this demanding,
highly specialized environment than they could be expected to perform adequately the duties of a doctor.

While Upton toiled with tactics revision through the early months of 1881,
he continued to battle his mysterious affliction. One evening, after accompanying Capt. Henry Hasbrouck, a West Point classmate, to a play one of the regiment's officers had written, the captain asked his commander's opinion of the
show. "He told me he could form none," Hasbrouck recalled later, "as his head
so much pained him that he had no remembrance at all of the first act." Upton
went on to say that "he was frequently unable to sleep, and after lying down for
a while he would be compelled to get up and walk the room for some hours,
and until he became so fatigued that he could get a little sleep before reveille."
Upton later told Hasbrouck that the headaches were becoming longer in duration and increasingly painful.

On Sunday morning, March 13, 1881, Hasbrouck, alone with Upton in the
regimental commander's office, took the opportunity to ask about his friend's
health. Much to the junior officer's surprise, Upton "broke down completely,
laid his head on his desk, and sobbed." Startled to see his commander weeping
uncontrollably, the captain escorted Upton to his quarters. There Upton told
him that he had lost his willpower and believed that the regiment's officers had
little respect for him. He also confessed that his new tactical system was a failure, and if "adopted it would involve the country in disaster in the next war."
This despondent mood so concerned Hasbrouck that he remained with Upton
for the remainder of the day and well into the evening. Because he had to serve
on a court-martial the following day, the captain did not see Upton until later
that night. Visiting the colonel at his quarters, he was disturbed to discover
his friend still deeply depressed. The visit apparently improved Upton's mood,
however, for Hasbrouck thought him relatively cheerful later in the evening.
A promise that he would visit Monterey the next day especially encouraged
Hasbrouck.[21] It was a trip Emory Upton never made.

At 8:30 the next morning Upton's orderly reported to Hasbrouck, whose
quarters were adjacent to that of Upton, that something had happened to the
colonel. The captain rushed next door, where he found "the remains of the
General lying in his bed, his right hand grasping a Colt revolver, Cal. 45. I
also noticed a large pool of blood near and on the bed, also blood on the right
cheek."[22] On a writing desk Hasbrouck discovered three letters Upton apparently had written sometime the previous evening or early that morning. "Since
writing you last Sunday," he told his sister Sara,

I have been in no little distress over the revision. It has seemed to me that I must give up my system and lose my military reputation. God only knows how it will eventually end, but I trust he will lead me to sacrifice myself, rather than to perpetuate a method which might in the future cost a single man his life. Whichever way it may turn, I know I shall have your sympathy, and may our Heavenly Father bless and keep you and our precious father and mother! I need all you[r] prayers, for I would keep my integrity.

After a brief paragraph describing a trip he had made recently to Oakland, he closed the letter: "I don't feel like writing any more. Only let me feel that I have your love and sympathy."[23]

Upton also had started a letter to the adjutant general of the army in which he admitted that his tactical system was a failure. Halfway through the first paragraph, however, he had put down his pen, taken another sheet of paper, and in a two-sentence letter to the adjutant general tendered his resignation.[24] Upton then apparently took his own life with his revolver.

After an autopsy, Upton's body, accompanied by two officers from the Fourth Artillery, journeyed by train from Oakland to Auburn, New York. Andrew Alexander joined the party when the train reached Ogden, Utah, and also escorted the body to Auburn. Upton's funeral services took place on March 29 in Sand Beach Church, where Emily and he had been married, and the burial was at Auburn's Fort Hill Cemetery, his grave next to that of his wife. The funeral attracted many who had served with him during his twenty-year army career—William Sherman, Henry du Pont, James Wilson, Irvin McDowell, and Peter Michie were among the literally hundreds of mourners as was former secretary of state William Seward.[25]

The overwhelming reaction of those in attendance was shock. Wilson could not conceive the circumstances that would have provoked his longtime friend to take his own life. "I was never more astounded in my life than I was today when I read the account of poor Upton's suicide," Wilson told du Pont. "I can hardly imagine anything which even a philosopher would call a justification. The memory of his dead wife could not have induced him after so long a time to do the deed, sustained as he was by a christian [*sic*] hope of Eternal Life. The noise in his head was an inadequate cause for such an act to *such* a man. What could it have been?"[26]

Others were not so sure. John Tidball, one of Sherman's aides and an attendee at the funeral, acknowledged that Upton "in character and temperament . . . was the last person in the army to be suspected of taking such a step," but he also thought that he understood his motivations. Near the time Upton had been promoted to colonel, Tidball recounted in his memoirs, a brigadier general's position had opened up. "He was anxious for this," Tidball recounted, "but was headed off by [Nelson] Miles who was even more ambitious for the place than he." He next applied for the position of chief signal officer but had failed in this effort too. Upton finally appreciated

> that the colonelcy of a regiment amounts to little more in peace than the command of an ordinary post, . . . [and] he evidently felt that it was but a limited sphere for one of high aspirations, and that it might prove to him a winding up of his ambitions, an ending of the rapid promotion heretofore attending his career. He had no thought of being buried alive as a mere post commander. He wanted something in which he could branch out and keep himself from being forgotten.

For this reason, Tidball continued, Upton had expressed interest in serving as commander of Fortress Monroe, superintendent at West Point, or the head of a general-staff school that he proposed be established at Carlisle Barracks, Pennsylvania, but he received no encouragement in any of these ventures. "All of these failures," Tidball concluded, "gave him deep disappointment and he saw nothing in store for him but to join his regiment and bury himself in obscurity at the Presidio. So much had he been favored he felt aggrieved when favors ceased to be showered upon him, and this rankling upon a mind of unquenchable ambition without . . . [doubt] caused him to commit the fatal act."[27]

There were other theories regarding Upton's motives. Irvin McDowell, commander of the Division of the Pacific, reported to the War Department that the board of officers that had investigated the colonel's suicide had concluded the act had been "caused by temporary unsoundness of mind brought on by an over-taxed brain" as well as by disappointment regarding ongoing efforts to revise his infantry tactics. Upton's family reacted vehemently to this conclusion. Alexander cabled McDowell that the Uptons "are satisfied that the cause of his death was not anxiety about his tactics, but serious trouble in his head of long standing originating in malignant catarrh. Please correct newspaper reports." Though McDowell subsequently heeded the family's wishes, Sara wrote to the *Army and Navy Journal* to correct what she believed were the near-slanderous charges that her brother had committed suicide because he was depressed over the perceived failure of his tactical system.[28]

Those who believed that Upton had been depressed about his career prospects, the "failure" of his tactics, the death of his wife, or even Congress's failure to enact the Burnside Bill probably were correct in their assessments. These events certainly played a role in his decision to take his own life, but this conclusion begs the question as to why he had become so deeply depressed in early 1881. Other than his concern regarding his infantry tactics, all of these elements already had been present in his life, some for many years. Indeed, if anything, his recent promotion to colonel ought to have signaled that his career had not reached a dead end. What, then, drove him to suicide?

Upton's family appears to have been correct in attributing his actions to the pain from his "nasal catarrh." Medical historians have concluded that Upton almost certainly suffered from the growth of a benign tumor in his sinus cavity, an affliction known today as frontal sinus mucocele. Tumors such as these have been observed to have been "giant" and "enormous" in size; under such circumstances one might penetrate the sinus wall and cause cerebral compression. In such cases "the mental changes suffered by . . . Upton, including headache, depression, impaired memory, deterioration of handwriting, and other personality changes" are not unusual.[29] The pain from this disease, in all likelihood, was the source of the depression that caused Upton to take his life. Other concerns were manifestations of a psychological problem that had severe physiological roots.

Upton's suicide left *The Military Policy of the United States* unfinished, and it long appeared that it would remain that way and therefore unknown but to a small circle of friends and family. Three months after her brother's death, Sara Upton wrote to du Pont, who was in possession of one copy of the manuscript, to say that her brother "a few months previous to his death" had told a friend "in case anything ever happened to him he wished his 'Military Policy' sent to you as you knew more about finishing it than anyone else." Du Pont, however, had left the army several years before and, as president of the Wilmington and Northern Railroad, had little time to undertake the project, though he occasionally worked on parts of the manuscript. Peter Michie then stepped into the picture. Still professor of natural philosophy at West Point, Michie began work on a biography of Upton. To assist him in this project, numerous of Upton's friends and family members loaned him letters they had received from Emory, and du Pont sent Michie the unfinished manuscript of *Military Policy*. In 1885 Michie published *Life and Letters of Emory Upton*, which provides an incomplete yet invaluable portrait of the man: incomplete due to its hagiographic nature as well as to Michie's editing of Upton's correspondence; invaluable because much of the correspondence reproduced in that volume has disappeared.[30]

Michie had hoped his project might prompt du Pont to work on *The Military Policy of the United States*, but du Pont resisted his pressure and did nothing. Sara Upton corresponded with du Pont regarding the matter, but she too proved unable to convince him to complete the manuscript. In the meantime General Sherman had become angered at du Pont's unwillingness to complete what he believed was an extremely valuable work. Comparing Upton's incomplete manuscript with the works of Shakespeare and Dickens, the commanding general told Michie that *Military Policy* "must be published now, immediately, or it will be lost forever." "The world is more like a kaleidoscope," he continued, "than a mathematical figure, after the turning of the tube the former figures are lost to the vision and soon to the memory." Sherman confided that he feared such would be the fate of Upton's magnum opus if it were left incomplete too long. He asked Michie to urge du Pont to publish the book "without one word of endorsement or comment, and allow them to enter into the general current of public thought for better or worse." Sherman concluded his letter by saying that if du Pont did not finish the manuscript before the next Congress, "I for one will question his fidelity to the friend who trusted him as a brother. . . . Thoughts are ephemeral. Deeds substantial. To unite both requires genius." Michie sent a copy of Sherman's letter to the Appletons, the publishers of *Life and Letters*, and they forwarded a typed copy to du Pont along with a plea that he begin work on the manuscript. Neither Sherman's nor the Appletons' efforts moved du Pont to publish the work, though he did circulate the manuscript among a small number of friends and army officers.[31] This seemingly inconsequential action kept Upton's ideas alive in the consciousness of the officer corps.

Still, it appeared that Sherman was correct in his judgment about the fleeting nature of public memory as it related to Upton's work. As late as 1894 Upton's own family considered his tactics manuals to have been his most important contribution to the military profession. And with the sole exception of the establishment in 1881 of the School of Application for Infantry and Cavalry at Fort Leavenworth, Kansas, no Uptonian reform had been undertaken by the time of the outbreak of the Spanish-American War in 1898. But the organizational and administrative breakdowns that had hindered the American war effort during that conflict gave new life to the cause of army reform and with it, renewed interest in Upton's ideas.[32]

In 1899 Pres. William McKinley appointed Elihu Root to be secretary of war with the understanding Root would undertake to remedy the army's shortcomings. Thanks to the new secretary's efforts as well as to those of influential legislators, between 1901 and 1908 Congress enacted four major pieces of legislation known collectively as the "Root Reforms." The Reorganization Act of 1901 expanded the maximum size of the regular army to 100,000 soldiers; established a system of rotating officers between the staff and the line; and ended the practice of permanent staff appointments. The General Staff Act of 1903 added to this program by creating a "General Staff" and replacing the army's commanding general with a "chief of staff." The Militia Act of 1903 (otherwise known as the Dick Act, named after Rep. Charles Dick, chairman of the House Militia Affairs Committee) preserved the tradition of state and local autonomy in many National Guard activities, including the appointment of officers, but it involved the federal government in areas that heretofore had been the province of the states: it required National Guard units to adhere to federal standards in training and tactics and mandated that the army was responsible for providing instruction to the guard as well as for evaluating its degree of readiness. In return for this federal involvement, the Dick Act required the government to supply the National Guard with equipment and appropriations to support training activities. But the Dick Act had its shortcomings, among them limiting any activation of the National Guard to nine months and retaining the geographic limitations the Constitution imposed on the militia. The Militia Act of 1908 (enacted after Root no longer was the secretary of war) addressed these issues while also making the National Guard the nation's first-line reserve force. Finally, Root began the reorganization of the army's schools system. This process, complete by 1910, resulted in the School of Application at Fort Leavenworth changing its name to the Army School of the Line, thereby becoming the infantry and cavalry's counterpart to the Artillery School. During this period, the army also opened schools for numerous of the support branches and established the Army War College in Washington, D.C.[33]

From an Uptonian point of view, the Root Reforms suffered from numerous weaknesses. Almost certainly Upton would have been appalled that states still were permitted to appoint officers to the National Guard. He also would have looked askance at the Dick Act's failure to differentiate between the constitutional militia and the National Guard, a shortcoming the 1908 act fixed. Upton would have been critical of aspects of the General Staff Act too. Under its provisions, the chief of staff, aided by the forty-five officers of the General Staff, had only informal authority over the bureaus and line units, and the bill did not consolidate bureaus that exercised overlapping authority. Finally and perhaps most disconcertingly, the measure placed the chief of staff between the secretary of war and line units, thereby making it clear that the secretary was in the chain of command.[34]

Other aspects of the Root Reforms would have met with Upton's wholehearted approval. He had long advocated the establishment of a war college as well as the development of schools for each branch. The Militia Reform Acts of 1903 and 1908, taken as a whole, succeeded in addressing most of his concerns regarding citizen-soldiers. Now with a modicum of federal control, the national government could ensure a degree of quality and uniformity in equipment and in training that previously had been lacking in both. Just as important, however, were provisions of the 1908 law that removed the constitutional limitations on the employment of the guard. That act also guaranteed that National Guard units would maintain their organizational integrity, and thereby their local character, when incorporated into the army in time of war. This legislation turned the National Guard into something that resembled Upton's National Volunteers. The Reorganization Act of 1901 also would have pleased Upton with the limitations that it placed on the length of assignments to the staff and for mandating the rotation of officers between the staff and the line.

The degree to which Upton's proposals inspired the Root Reforms is open to debate. The Dodge Commission, which had studied the problems the army had encountered during the Spanish-American War, had provided Root with substantial documentation of the military's shortcomings. Root also had read Spenser Wilkinson's *The Brain of an Army*, a work that marveled at the German General Staff's efficiency. Yet it is clear that Root had devoured Upton's published and unpublished works. Shortly after Root had been appointed secretary of war, Maj. William Carter had given him a copy of *The Armies of Asia and Europe*. Impressed by Upton's point of view and with the help of Upton's family, Root undertook to find a copy of *The Military Policy of the United States*. Henry du Pont, they discovered, had only one chapter buried in his attic. The remainder of the manuscript, as it turned out, was in the hands of the Appletons.[35]

Upton's influence on Root's thinking is apparent not only in the legislation enacted between 1901 and 1908 but also in the secretary's statements regarding army reform. Speaking before the Republican convention in Chicago in 1904, Root recounted the accomplishments of the McKinley and Roosevelt administrations in modernizing the army and concluded, "The teachings of Sherman and Upton have been recalled and respected." He stressed a similar theme at the laying of the cornerstone of the Army War College building in Washington, D.C., in 1903. "Were Upton alive today," he told the assembled crowd, "he would see all of the great reforms for which he contended substantially secured."[36] Upton's use of history to prove the inherent weaknesses of the militia had found a receptive audience in the new secretary of war. "Four years ago," Root told the Republicans assembled in Chicago,

> we were living under an obsolete militia law more than a century old, which Washington and Jefferson and Madison, and almost every President since their time, had declared to be worthless. We presented a curious spectacle of a people depending upon a citizen soldiery for protection against aggression and making practically no provision whatever for the training of those soldiers in the use of warlike weapons or in the elementary duties of the soldier. . . . In default of national provisions, bodies of state troops, created for local purposes and supported at local expense, had grown up throughout the Union. . . . Their arms, equipment, discipline, organization, and methods of obtaining and accounting for supplies were varied and inconsistent. They were unsuited to become a part of any homogenous force, and their relations to the army of the United States were undefined and conjectural.[37]

This analysis is pure Emory Upton. That Root found such logic compelling is further suggested by the fact that in 1904 the War Department published *The Military Policy of the United States* and distributed it throughout the army.[38]

Others clearly had exerted some influence in Root's ideas. For example, it appears that General Schofield more than Upton influenced Root regarding the General Staff and the relationship between the secretary of war and the commanding general. If in the end Root did not undertake all of Upton's prescriptions for the army's ills and tinkered with the details of those he did embrace, it is clear that he acknowledged the logic of Upton's arguments. Upton's ideas, he told Philip Jessup thirty years after enactment of the Root Reforms, "gave me the detail on which I could base recommendations and overcame my ignorance as a civilian."[39]

There can be little doubt, then, that Upton had substantial influence on the Root Reforms. His intellectual legacy to the army, however, stands on more contested ground. Numerous historians have charged him with creating a sense of "Uptonian pessimism" that pervaded the officer corps in the late nineteenth and early twentieth centuries. This pessimism, they argue, led Upton and his followers to reject democratic control over the military. These officers, they declared, desired a large standing army and the adoption of conscription as the means for manning that force. In sum, they charged the Uptonians with being militaristic.[40]

Was Upton a "militarist"? Alfred Vagts, in his *History of Militarism*, argued that a militaristic army's core value is narcissism. "An army that is so built that it serves military men, not war," Vagts contended, "is militaristic; so is everything in an army which is not preparation for fighting, but merely exists for diversion or to satisfy peacetime whims."[41] "Armies may protect society," he continued,

> if they prepare intelligently for defense; they may threaten it if they lose a sense of proportion between their own interests and those of the rest of society. It has happened that armies become so involved in contemplating domestic critics and foes, Liberals in an earlier age, Socialists later and Communists more recently, that they have forgotten to concentrate on the enemy abroad— or they have even sympathized with foreign armies and made common front with them against internal antagonists. In so doing, militarists have sharpened conflicts at home and permitted political views to cloud considerations of military efficiency.[42]

Gerhard Ritter expanded on this theme. "Militarism," he wrote,

> is one of the vaguest and hence most confusing catchwords of our day. The distinction between the military profession proper and militarism is being more and more obscured. It is not appreciated that they differ as much as do

character and truculence, steadfast and enlightened self-assertion and head-long recklessness, loyalty and slavish submission, genuine power and brute force. . . . [Militarism is] military extremism that falsifies policy because it completely misreads the essential and foremost purpose of all social order.

Ritter concluded, "There is a difference between an armed and a militarized state."[43]

Employing these definitions of militarism, it seems clear that Upton was not a "militarist." He had proposed a system he hoped would defend the American democratic republic in time of war and protect its institutions from potential Caesars. He advocated neither a large standing army nor conscription, proposals that clearly would have been "militaristic" in Vagts's terms. Indeed, compared to Upton, the era's true militarists were those who supported a mass army when there was no need for one or those who supported mandatory military instruction in the nation's public schools.[44]

Ritter provides another insight regarding Upton's alleged militarism. Though Upton certainly was a proponent of a more efficient military force and of somewhat drastic restructuring of the American military, he in no way proposed a militarized state. His National Volunteers would have been a military force barely large enough to meet the nation's needs in the event of a rebellion, one that never could have competed on the European battlefields of the period. And though he wished to diminish the power of the secretary of war, Upton saw this as protecting democracy from the threat of militarism, not as promoting the latter at the expense of the former. Indeed, many of those who see him as the epitome of the "professional " officer and as a "militarist" often fall into the intellectual trap Ritter describes as misconstruing an armed state for a militarized one.

But whether or not Upton was a militarist does not address the larger question of his subsequent influence on the officer corps. Russell Weigley argues that Upton's writings inspired a "pessimism" in these officers that manifested itself in antidemocratic tendencies, citing James S. Pettit's work as important evidence of this influence.[45] In 1905 Colonel Pettit submitted an entry to the Military Service Institution's essay competition, the title topic for that year posing the question, "How Far Does Democracy Affect the Organization and Discipline of our Armies, and How Can its Influence be Most Effectively Utilized?" Upton's works as Pettit understood them clearly influenced his article, especially in the deep distrust it exhibited of elected politicians. Early in the essay Pettit observed, "A careful reading of . . . [*The Military Policy of the United States*] will give a complete answer to the title of our essay."[46] Like Upton, he placed little confidence in Congress's abilities to reform the army, submerged as it was in "the slimy oil of political spoils." Presidents, he believed, were too deeply involved in the spoils system to be able to command effectively, and the secretary of war, Pettit argued, was simply a meddler. All of this sounds more or less like something with which Upton would have agreed, but this line of thought took Pettit places Upton never approached. In answer to the essay contest's question, Pettit wrote: "It is a self-evident proposition that a democracy based on the will of millions of people, expressed through devious and changing channels, cannot be as skillful or efficient in the conduct of military affairs as a monarchy headed by a wise and powerful chief. . . . The further we depart from these principles the weaker we become."[47]

To what degree had Upton influenced Pettit? Clearly, Pettit had read *The Military Policy of the United States*, but nowhere in it did Upton come close to recommending the adoption of a monarchy. Indeed, as his musings about the potential consequences of a third term for Grant makes clear, he feared such a development.[48] Pettit clearly had read Upton's complaints about the American military system but had completely overlooked his goal: the preservation of the American democratic republic. Thus, Pettit's Uptonian pessimism appears to have stemmed either from a selective reading of Upton's works, from a complete misunderstanding of them, or from both.

Pettit certainly was not alone in harboring such thoughts, but even those who sympathized with his concerns often found hope for democracy's ability to manifest feasible military policies. Commenting on Pettit's article, Col. Charles Larned wrote, "While many of Colonel Pettit's epigrammatic deliveries are very true and forceful, some, I fear, are forceful without being wholly true; while some few are rather vituperative rather than expedient." Larend specifically took Pettit to task for his opinion that democracies were inherently weak, reminding the *Journal*'s readers: "Rome, as a great democratic republic conquered all of the autocracies of the world about her, and quite literally sat on the heads of the 'one-man powers' whose undisputed wills controlled many times her population and military resources. Later on, republican France effected a somewhat similar achievement."[49]

Capt. Matthew Fourney Steele also found Pettit's analysis compelling but argued that the only way to solve the problem he described was to "get the interest of the people and educate them." Brig. Gen. Theodore Schwan, who also accepted much of Pettit's commentary, rejected his notion that Congress had acted appropriately only when required to do so in time of war, noting that it had passed both the Dick Act and the General Staff Act in peacetime. "Other instances," he concluded, "might be cited when extraordinary army legislation was wrested in peace time [sic] from an unsympathetic Congress by an alert and persistent Secretary of War." Larned's, Steele's, and Swan's sentiments hardly seem to be those of officers who had given up on democracy's ability to pursue an appropriate military policy.[50]

More to the point, Pettit and those who thought like him appear to have been the exception rather than the rule. The vast majority of articles in late-nineteenth-century professional journals that addressed the subject of citizen-soldiers acknowledged either their desirability or the reality that the army could experience a large expansion only through a volunteer system. Moreover, these officers' sentiments often provide important clues relating their commitment to democratic institutions.

In 1888 the institution's prize essay topic was "Organization and Training of a National Reserve for Military Service." First Lt. A. C. Sharpe's winning entry echoed many Uptonian ideas, but in the term's properly understood context. Sharpe delineated what he believed were the constitutional and political problems involved in nationalizing the militia, proposing that "Congress should provide that all regularly-organized, uniformed and equipped active militia or National Guard . . . should be eligible to enrollment in a force to be known as the National Reserve of the United States." Sharpe outlined an organizational structure; logistical necessities; promotion, pay, and retirement policies; and training requirements for this "National Reserve," all of which are reminiscent of Upton's National Volunteers.[51]

Maj. William Cary Sanger of the New York National Guard echoed Sharpe's sentiments in an essay that won honorable mention in the 1888 contest. Sanger pointed out, "The political conditions and military needs of the United States are so totally different from those of European countries, that the sacrifices which foreign nations are forced to make in order to develop their defensive or aggressive strength, are no proper measure of what we should do." But, he continued, "nor should we blind ourselves to the preparations which other countries have made for war, however little we may anticipate that they will be used against us." Sanger argued that for a "National Reserve . . . to be efficient, [it] must be so closely connected in organization and training with the standing force, that the Reserve cannot be organized or even written about as a separate or independent body." To accomplish this he recommended a reserve system not unlike that of Germany, though on a much smaller scale, as well as the nationalization of the militia.[52]

Several points are worth noting about these articles. They were published barely eight years after Upton's death, and it therefore seems likely both Sharpe and Sanger were aware of his criticisms of and recommendations for the American military system. Both anticipated that Congress could and would take appropriate action. Both expressed the desirability of centralizing control of the reserve under the federal government. Finally, and most interestingly, it was Sanger, a serving National Guard officer, who wished to nationalize the militia, while Sharpe, a regular officer, wished to make optional the militia's participation in the National Reserve. Indeed, Sanger in many ways was more Uptonian than was Sharpe.

Numerous essays quickly followed that picked up on these themes.[53] In 1892 the titular subject of the Military Service Institution's essay contest was "The Army Organization, Best Adapted to a Republican Form of Government, Which Will Insure [sic] an Effective Force." The three essays the institution subsequently published offer tremendous insight regarding both the officer corps's commitment to citizen-soldiers and to democratic government. In his prize-winning essay Lt. Sidney Stuart of the Ordnance Department stated that a republican army must be an "army of the people," that it must command "popular approval," and that it must be inexpensive to maintain. He pointed out, "The establishment of a federal national guard has seemed to many to be the only means of escaping from the burdens of a large standing army on the one hand, and on the other, from the lack of thoroughness and uniformity of training and discipline, and the insubordination to federal authority when opposed to State sentiment, which have on more than one occasion in our history proved the cause of national disgrace." The federalizing of the National Guard, he concluded, "seems to be well adapted to the conditions of our subject-title and capable of affording a practicable solution of the problem."[54]

Capt. E. L. Zalinski's essay, which received honorable mention, emphasized the importance of military instruction in public schools and in colleges as well as "short and long courses" as a means by which to solve the chronic weaknesses National Guard officers had exhibited. Referring to the guard's recent strikebreaking activities, he asserted:

> The advantages of effective state troops has been recently shown in widely separated portions of the United States. . . . It is, therefore, the best of policy for the state authorities to support liberally an effective National Guard force, as a reinforcement to the regular civil authorities, in times of unusual excitement and disturbance. The general government derives advantage in having ready an effective force which can be used in the first line whenever the country may be involved in war.[55]

The National Guard thus would have had both state and national responsibilities. Zalinski, a member of the Fifth U.S. Artillery, reminded his readers that National Guard soldiers were not the same as the militiamen who had preceded them. "Recent years," he continued, have shown a marked change in the relations of the Regular Army and the militia forces of the country. These were looked upon with indifference by the army because of the apparent lack of earnestness in their work, the "fuss and feather" element appearing to predominate. With the disappearance of this element and the evidence given of real earnestness and thoroughness of work, the disposition of the army has changed towards the National Guard.[56]

As had Upton, Zalinski sharply criticized Congress. The nation's "deplorable weak condition is directly chargeable to Congress," he concluded. Bills to reform the military had been defeated "usually because of insufficient general interest to push them through the eager crush to pass measures of moment to political parties or for local betterments." Yet Zelinski sounded a hopeful note in this regard. "Prudence dictates," he concluded, "a thorough preparation in every way consistent with and not endangering our republican institutions. What is everybody's business is said to be nobody's business. The methods pointed out for the national defense demand joint legislation on the part of the states and Congress. Action is necessary. If the initiative were taken by Congress, the states would quickly follow in doing their share."[57]

Col. William Sanger's essay also received honorable mention, and in it he differed with Upton as to who was at fault for the nation's lack of military preparedness. Rather than Congress, Sanger blamed the situation on "public indifference to military matters, which has done us so much harm and made it impossible to bring about the wished for changes." But citizens, he believed, were beginning to recognize the importance of the subject, the naval reforms that recently had been implemented being evidence of this.[58] As had Stuart, Sanger recommend a frugal force, one that relied on the National Guard as its source of manpower. He also proposed a territorial plan for organizing the guard reminiscent of Upton's desire to have one depot per congressional district for his National Volunteers.[59] Sanger argued that his system would "give every military formation in the country its proper place in a carefully considered and comprehensive military system, and the Government would be constantly informed of the condition and efficiency of all the various forces, over which it could, in time of need, exercise control." He also believed, as had Upton, that regulars should be responsible for training these citizen-soldiers in a system that "would establish a connection, however slight, between the militia and the army, a connection which I cannot but feel would grow closer and closer, and would be of great value to both forces." Sanger concluded that he had the highest regard for the National Guard, but its "present independent organization has resulted in greatly diminishing . . . [its] usefulness for national defense."[60]

That the *Journal of the Military Service Institution* sponsored an essay contest on this subject suggests that it was a topic of concern to the journal's staff, to the institute's membership, and probably to many officers. But it seems important that it phrased the topic in positive rather than negative terms (instead of something like "Restrictions a Republican Form of Government Places on Army Organization"). And it is even more important that the Military Service Institution published three thoughtful essays on the subject, all of which took a positive approach to the question and have several points of congruence. Each clearly stated or strongly implied that the army needed to be closely connected to the people and that reliance on citizen-soldiers was the best manner by which this might be accomplished. Though disagreeing regarding the magnitude of control to be exercised, each concluded that it was desirable for the federal government to exert some degree of control over the National Guard in each state. Finally, each essay strongly implied that it was possible for a democratic republic to work in a responsible manner toward improving the military. And these officers were not alone in holding such sentiments, for in the years that preceded the war with Spain, numerous others wrote articles that struck a similar chord.[61]

The Philippine Insurrection (1899–1902) put to the test the concept of federally controlled citizen-soldiers, and many regulars judged it a success. The U.S. Volunteers, as they came to be known, closely resembled Upton's National Volunteers. The federal government raised and trained the volunteers, but it organized them so as "to preserve local pride and neighborhood connections." More often than not their field-grade officers came from the regular army and company-grade officers "were chosen from proven State volunteer officers, from recent West Point graduates, and from Regular non-coms." Finally, the U.S. Volunteers received extensive individual and unit training before they went into combat. These regiments performed admirably in the Philippines. Of the U.S. Volunteers, Capt. Charles Rhodes wrote: "As volunteer regiments, it has been the almost unanimous verdict that they have never been surpassed. Certainly never, in such a short space of time, have such excellent troops been organized, trained, and put into the field." Such sentiments have led Brian McAllister Linn to conclude, "The U.S. Volunteers . . . seem to have been outstanding soldiers, if the number of testimonials to them by Regulars is any indication."[62]

There were other signs that regular-army officers accepted the Root Reforms and their consequences. In 1904 Maj. Alfred C. Sharpe, assistant adjutant general of the army, wrote glowingly of the previous year's maneuvers at Fort Riley, Kansas, and near modern-day Fort Knox, Kentucky, in which elements of the National Guard and regular army participated. "The educational value of the Maneuvers," he wrote, can hardly be overstated. They are a realization in large measure of the dreams and hopes which American military students have been cherishing *for the past twenty years.* They constitute a true War College, a post-graduate course of application for all arms of the service. . . . Indeed, this system of instruction, made possible by the wise and liberal provisions of the Dick Bill, has already assumed such proportions, and its bearing upon the future course of military training among our people is so potent and permanent and far-reaching, that it may well arouse the thoughtful interest of statesmen as well as soldiers.[63]

Capt. William H. Johnston, referring to the same maneuvers, told the *Journal's* readers that the term "A Military Chautauqua" far more aptly described events in Kentucky and Kansas than did "army maneuvers." Johnston noted that both regulars and National Guard had been ill prepared for the exercises and that there were too few soldiers from both components for them to be considered "maneuvers." But, he continued, regulars and guardsmen at each camp studied tactical problems, "and their attempted solution admirably explained and criticized by the Chief Umpire, Col. A. L. Wagner." Johnston also noted that qualified officers provided lectures on various subjects. He concluded, "If this year's experience had accomplished nothing more than the initiation of the fraternal feeling which was observed between officers of both services, and the realization by those of each force of the virtues of the other, the money devoted to the experiment would have been well spent. We met as strangers, but parted as brothers. Each force has more friends among the other force than ever before."[64]

Arthur Wagner agreed with these sentiments. "I observed with much satisfaction," he wrote, the National Guard's "almost universal zeal and desire to learn." He criticized the guardsmen's lack of tactical skill but praised their fire discipline. He also noted "with much pleasure" their "marked improvement, from day to day."[65] Wagner concluded that joint U.S. Army–National Guard maneuvers ought to be continued. "We can improve very much upon the European methods of conducting maneuver," he wrote, quoting a letter he had received from an unidentified high-ranking officer. Holding such exercises in the future, the anonymous letter writer continued, would permit the American army to "outstrip the Europeans before many years, even if we have to make up our forces from troops who have had less training." Thus even Wagner, whom Weigley identifies as being "familiarly Uptonian," understood both the importance of citizen-soldiers and the position of the military in a democratic republic.[66] Given the substance of these essays, written both before and after implementation of the Root Reforms, it seems difficult to argue that the officer corps was mired in pessimism, Uptonian or otherwise.

As late as 1904, when the War Department published *The Military Policy of the United States*, Upton's ideas had few well-known competitors. John Logan's *The Volunteer Soldier of America* had been published posthumously in 1887, and its theme was decidedly anti-Uptonian, especially in its insistence that inherent genius, not an understanding of military art and science, was the key requirement for successful military leadership. Logan also disagreed with Upton regarding potential threats to democracy. It is "admitted by all," he proclaimed, "that a standing army is a standing menace to free institutions." Others such as Schofield and Frederic Huidekoper had taken positions somewhere between those of Upton and Logan, but Upton was the benchmark against which all other ideas were measured.[67] At the height of the preparedness debate during the First World War, those who advocated for increased military preparedness dusted off Upton's work. Army chief of staff Hugh Scott ordered the War Department to publish a summary of Upton's ideas as well of their historical background, believing his writings would "bring to the attention of our citizens the facts of our military history as bearing upon the present problem of national preparedness for defense." Entitled *Epitome of Upton's Military Policy of the United States*, Sen. Frank Brandegee placed the pamphlet in the *Congressional Record* while declaring in the Senate that it was "well known" that Upton was "one of the most celebrated American military experts."[68]

The preparedness bill the Wilson administration submitted to Congress in 1915 contained provisions the General Staff had drafted that enlarged the regular army while creating a new force, the Continental Army. Numbering nearly 400,000 soldiers, the Continental Army was to be a federal reserve over which states would wield no influence, one that was to supplant the National Guard as the nation's first-line reserve. This bill, according to Weigley, demonstrated that Secretary of War Lindley Garrison had accepted the "Uptonian" creed about the worthlessness of the citizen-soldier. Congress eventually dropped provisions for the Continental Army from what would become the National Defense Act of 1916 and replaced it with others that placed the National Guard under even more federal control than before. The bill, which President Wilson signed into law in May 1916, represented a defeat for Uptonians, according to Weigley, because it continued to recognize the value of the citizen-soldier and the tradition of universal military obligation.[69]

Such logic misrepresents the nature of the Continental Army as well as the thrust of Upton's argument. The Continental Army was to have consisted of volunteers, and its officer corps was to have incorporated men who had participated in Plattsburg-like camps, in reserve-officer training programs at colleges and universities, or had been members of the officer corps and had resigned their commissions. Rather than rejecting the citizen-soldier, the Continental

Army appeared to be an effort to build upon the Plattsburg movement's efforts to train them.[70] More to the point, it was not the citizen-soldier himself of whom Upton disapproved, but the untrained and poorly disciplined citizen-soldier.

This basic misunderstanding of the value Upton placed on citizen-soldiers permeated John McAuley Palmer's work. After serving on the staff of the American Expeditionary Forces, Gen. John J. Pershing sent him home in 1919 to help shape army manpower policy for the postwar era. In Washington Palmer discovered that the bill the army staff had prepared proposed a skele-tonized force that would be led by regulars and whose ranks volunteers and recruits would fill in time of war. Believing that such an army reflected the military and political traditions of Germany rather than of the United States, Palmer proposed that citizen-soldiers, not regulars, ought be the basis for war-time expansion. Federalizing the citizen-soldier under the control of the army, he felt, risked trading democratic values for military security. To avoid such a fate, Palmer suggested that the United States adopt a system similar to that of Switzerland, which made the regular army responsible for maintaining con-stant vigilance on the nation's frontier, while in time of war the nation would quickly mobilize its reserve formations independently of the standing army.[71]

This was not a new idea. It had, in fact, been discussed in military and political circles since at least the first decade of the twentieth century.[72] The key to such a system, one that Palmer and others believed to be "democratic" rather than "militarist," not only was the acceptance of the concept of universal mil-itary obligation but also that of universal military training. The incongruence of such a proposal had struck at least a few congressmen during the prepared-ness debate of 1915–16. "We are told . . . that what we need in the United States is the Swiss system," Rep. William Gordon declared in a speech on the floor of the House in March 1916,

> but following the remarks of many of the gentlemen advocating the Swiss sys-
> tem we are constrained to believe that they know very little about that system
> because the Swiss constitution, like that of every other nation upon the conti-
> nent of Europe, contains a provision authorizing compulsory military service;
> and because there are some well meaning gentlemen in this country, largely
> Army officers, who want Congress to enact a compulsory military service law,
> we hear these heated advocates of the Swiss system exhibiting their lack of
> knowledge of what that system provides.[73]

It is in this context that Palmer's "argument" with Upton makes little sense. Upton had hoped that his National Volunteers would serve to educate the pub-lic regarding the concept of the citizens' military obligation to their nation, even that they could popularize the army to the extent that its ranks and those of the National Volunteers might be filled with a constant stream of recruits. Still, he never went so far as to propose universal military training. After all, if a volunteer organization such as the National Volunteers could not achieve political acceptance because it was "too militaristic," what chance did universal military training have of becoming a reality? Also, who would enforce this "universal" obligation and training? Palmer is not clear on this point, but the only logical answer was the federal government. If so, how could a system in which the national government forced large numbers of its citizens into service and to undertake mandatory military training be any less militaristic than one that relied on a small number of volunteers who drilled under the guidance of regular officers and noncommissioned officers?

Whether Palmer ever understood that Upton was not suggesting national reliance on a large standing army is questionable, but his juxtaposition of a "citizen army" with an "Uptonian" solution suggests he did not.[74] This misunderstanding has led to a false debate concerning the merits of Palmer's citizen army versus those of Upton's regulars, a debate that has influenced soldiers, politicians, and scholars for at least seventy-five years. In 1981 a serving officer in the U.S. Army argued that Upton was responsible for the development of the "Uptonian premise" in the army's officer corps. This premise, he argued, assumed that the failure of American military policy was the fault of politicians who were either incapable or unwilling to pass proper military legislation and considered a standing army was a threat to liberty. Eliot Cohen has argued that Upton's intellectual legacy to the army was the "Uptonian Hunker," which he defined as "turning inward" and away from society at large. This "hunker," the argument continues, manifested itself in numerous ways: a belief in the "fecklessness of democracies," "a deep mistrust" of politicians, and an "obsession with quantity" that led to empty, skeletal organizations.[75] Upton indeed had doubts about the ability of pure democracy to work, and he believed that many, if not most, politicians were self-serving and interested only in their own fortunes rather than the nation's best interests, but he never questioned the wisdom of a republican form of government. He also believed that a standing army supplemented by well-trained, disciplined volunteers would serve as a protector of that government, not a threat to it. It is also clear that Upton was not an advocate of a large standing army that would replace the citizen-soldiers who had served the nation with varying degrees of success since 1776, nor did he advocate that these volunteers join a skeletal organization.

Why, then, do historians believe the "Uptonian pessimism," the "Uptonian hunker," and the "Uptonian premise" are Upton's most important legacies to the army? Actually, Upton himself is in part responsible for this phenomenon. Because he never completed *The Military Policy of the United States* himself, historians have based their understanding of his ideas on an incomplete and mostly unedited draft of the envisioned work as well as on the heavily edited correspondence available in Michie's *Life and Letters*. Moreover, these historians' evaluations disconnect Upton's ideas from their proper historical context, and they ignore much that suggests he was neither antidemocratic nor the enemy of the citizen-soldier. Considered as a complete body of work, *Military Policy*, *The Armies of Asia and Europe*, and Upton's other ruminations demonstrate that he was an advocate of citizen-soldiers serving their nation, a concept he deemed "thoroughly republican in nature."[76]

Emory Upton is therefore a truly misunderstood reformer. Believed to be the enemy of the citizen-soldier, he was in fact his advocate. Portrayed as antidemocratic and Prussian-like, Upton believed himself to be the defender of republicanism and molded his reforms to accomplish that mission. If in the end he failed to achieve all of the reforms he thought necessary to ensure that the United States could maintain an effective military, his intellectual and substantive influence, albeit misunderstood, remains today.

Notes

Abbreviations

AAE   Emory Upton, *Armies of Asia and Europe*

ANJ   *Army and Navy Journal*

CPLC   William C. Church Papers, Library of Congress, Washington, D.C.

DAB   *The Dictionary of American Biography*

DFP   Dickman Family Papers

DPPHL Henry A. du Pont Papers, Winterthur Manuscripts, Hagley Museum and Library

EMD   Emily Martin-Upton Diary

HLOM   Emory Upton Letters, Holland Land Office Museum

GCHD   Upton Family Papers, Genesee County History Department

GDLC   Gilpin Diary, E. N. Gilpin Papers, Library of Congress, Washington, D.C.

GPLC   James A. Garfield Papers, Library of Congress, Washington, D.C.

GPNYPL Francis V. Greene Papers, New York Public Library

JMSIUS *Journal of the Military Service Institution of the United States*

JSPLC John M. Schofield Papers, Library of Congress, Washington, D.C.

L&L   Peter S. Michie, *Life and Letters of Emory Upton*

MPUS   Emory Upton, *Military Policy of the United States*

NARA   National Archives and Records Administration, Washington, D.C.

OR   U.S. War Department, *War of the Rebellion*. All references are to series 1 unless otherwise noted.

TMFP   Throop and Martin Family Papers, Princeton University

USAMHI U.S. Army Military History Institute

USMA   U.S. Military Academy

WPLC   James H. Wilson Papers, Library of Congress, Washington, D.C.

WPUIL Edward F. Winslow Papers, University of Iowa Library

WSPLC William T. Sherman Papers, Library of Congress, Washington, D.C.

Introduction

1. *L&L*, xxvii–xxviii.
2. Jamieson, *Crossing the Deadly Ground*, 92; Williams, *Americans at War*, 101–2; Skirbunt, "Prologue to Reform," 173–74, 178.
3. Millett and Maslowski, *For the Common Defense*, 271–76; Brown, "General Emory Upton." Millett and Maslowski correctly point out that Sherman and Stephen Luce were, respectively, the mentors of Upton and Mahan, but that it was the latter two who had the long-term influence on their respective services.
4. See J. Pope to W. T. Sherman, Jan. 2, 1879; Phil Sheridan to W. T. Sherman, Jan. 4, 1879; and Irvin McDowell to the House Subcommittee on Military Affairs, May 21, 1878, in U.S. Congress, Senate, *Papers in Relation to the Reorganization of the Army*, 11, 27–29. See also Phil Sheridan's testimony before the House Committee on Military Affairs in U.S. Congress, House, *Reduction of Army Officers' Pay, Reorganization of the Army, and Transfer of the Indian Bureau*, 19, 21.
5. Palmer, *Washington, Lincoln, Wilson*, 3–4, 263–81. For another example, see Cheseldine, "Where Upton Made His Big Mistake."
6. Weigley, *Towards an American Army*, 109–10 (emphasis added).
7. Weigley, "Long Death of the Indian-Fighting Army," 29; Weigley, *Towards an American Army*, 110, 159.
8. Ambrose, *Upton and the Army*, vii–viii, 121, 132 (emphasis in original). This is a nearly unchanged version of his dissertation, "Upton and the Army." Ambrose acknowledges that "Upton's contributions to American military policy were essential to the development of modern armed forces in the United States." Ibid., viii.
9. Lane, *Armed Progressive*, 151–52 (emphasis in original); Cooper, "Army's Search for a Mission," 186; Bacevich, "Emory Upton." See also Walker, "Emory Upton and the Officer's Creed."
10. Linn, *Echo of Battle*, esp. chap. 2; Bruscino, "Naturally Clausewitzian."

Chapter 1

1. *L&L*, 1; [Byrns et al.], *Golden Years*, 7; *Combination Atlas Map of Genesee County*, 66–67. For a discussion of the Upton family's history, see Fitzpatrick, "Emory Upton: The Misunderstood Reformer," 12–14.
2. Cross, *Burned-over District*, 31–32, 138–50, 296–97; P. Johnson, *Shopkeeper's Millennium*, 5, 109–10.
3. P. Johnson, *Shopkeeper's Millennium*, 3–4, 111, 115; Parker, "Philosophy of Charles G. Finney," 143–44.
4. *Combination Atlas Map of Genesee County*, 67; [Byrns et al.], *Golden Years*, 7.
5. M. Starr, "General Emory Upton," 12; E. Upton to "My Dear Little Sister" [Sara?], Oct. 28, 1860, in *L&L*, 24; E. Upton to Mother, Aug. 27, 1879, ibid., 476–77.
6. W. Upton, *Upton Family Records*, 252; Starr, "General Emory Upton," 12; Fairchild, *Oberlin*, 28–29.
7. *L&L*, 3–4; Starr, "General Emory Upton," 12, 14; Ambrose, *Upton and the Army*, 5. Starr contends that Henry and Emory entered Oberlin in 1854, but the college records show that they attended only during the 1855–56 school year. See *Triennial Catalogue of the Officers and Students for the College Year 1854–55*, 15–20; and *Annual Catalogue of the Officers and Students for the College Year 1855–56*, 18–19. Both catalogues can be found in the General College Papers, Oberlin College Archives.

8. Fletcher, *History of Oberlin College*, 2:507–9.

9. Ibid., 507, 524–25, 526 (emphasis in original), 535–36; Fairchild, *Oberlin*, 113–15.

10. Fletcher, *History of Oberlin College*, 2:509, 616–21, 638–46.

11. Ibid., 1:350, 2:750–51.

12. Ibid., 2:595–603, 607.

13. Ibid., 517–18, 711–12.

14. John J. Shipherd to his parents, Aug. 6, 1832, quoted in Fairchild, *Oberlin*, 18 (emphasis in original).

15. Fletcher, *History of Oberlin College*, 1:223–30, 2:574–79, 757–58; Fairchild, *Oberlin*, 53–54, 92–93.

16. Fletcher, *History of Oberlin College*, 2:579–81, 601–2, 669–70, 673–75.

17. Starr, "General Emory Upton," 14; *L&L*, 4–6.

18. *Annual Catalogue of the Officers and Students for the College Year 1855–56*, General College Papers, Oberlin College Archives, 25–26; *L&L*, 4–5.

19. *L&L*, 6–7; E. Upton to "Sister" [Maria], Feb. 13, 1858, HLOM.

20. Rep. Benjamin Pringle to Upton, Mar. 12, 1856, in *L&L*, 7–8 (emphasis added).

21. E. Upton to "My Very Dear Sister," Apr. 8, 1861, ibid., 35; E. Upton to [Rachel Upton], June 24, 1856, GCHD; E. Upton to Sec. of War Jefferson Davis, Mar. 17, 1856, USMA Appointment Papers, RG 94, NARA.

22. *L&L*, 10; Descriptive Lists of New Cadets, 1838–63, USMA Archives; USMA Staff Records, ibid., 6:162–63. Six appointees did not report to West Point, two declined their appointment after arriving there, and one left without being examined. Two prospective cadets are double counted in this tally because they failed both the physical and academic examinations.

23. E. Upton to [Rachel Upton], June 24, 1856, GCHD.

24. Ibid.

25. Regarding the socioeconomic makeup of the Corps of Cadets between 1842 and 1879, see Morrison, *"Best School in the World,"* 61–62.

26. Circumstances of the Parents of Cadets, USMA Archives, vol. 1; Morrison, *"Best School in the World,"* 61–63. Morrison avers that graduates of West Point were "caste conscious" and constituted a "military aristocracy." See ibid., 153–54.

27. Morrison, *"Best School in the World,"* 85–86. Forty-three of the seventy-three cadets admitted in Upton's class were from the North. "Cadets Admitted Book, 1846–1912," USMA Archives. For data on the regional makeup of the cadet population during the antebellum period, see Cunliffe, *Soldiers and Civilians*, 360–73. For but one example of the postwar bias that the antebellum academy was overly "southern" and elite, see Logan, *Volunteer Soldier*, chap. 7.

28. H. A. du Pont to Mother, July 14, 1856, in Ambrose, "West Point in the Fifties," 295.

29. Schaff, *Spirit of Old West Point*, 23; E. Upton to [Rachel Upton], June 24, 1856, GCHD (emphasis in original). Regarding hazing during this period, see Morrison, *"Best School in the World,"* 69.

30. Morrison, *"Best School in the World,"* 71.

31. For a detailed discussion of the five-year program, see Morrison, *"Best School in the World,"* chap. 8. See also Pappas, *To the Point*, 304–9; Ambrose, *Duty, Honor, Country*, 141; and Schaff, *Spirit of Old West Point*, 76–77.

32. Morrison, "Military Education and Strategic Thought," 117; U.S. Congress, Senate, *Report of the Secretary of War* (1857), 198–99.

33. Morrison, "Military Education and Strategic Thought," 118.

34. Ibid.

35. USMA Staff Records, USMA Archives, 6:178–79, 198–99; Morrison, "Military Education and Strategic Thought," 119.

36. Morrison, "Military Education and Strategic Thought," 119; Griess, "Dennis Hart Mahan," 239, 247. Mahan utilized Halleck's book in teaching the class in military science when Upton was a cadet. See Ambrose, *Halleck*, 7.

37. Williams, "Military Leadership of North and South," 27–28, 31–32, 43; Donald, *Lincoln Reconsidered*, 87–89. Russell Weigley provides a more balanced analysis in *American Way of War*, chap. 5.

38. Weigley, *American Way of War*, 82–83; Shy, "Jomini," 155, 162; Williams, "Military Leadership of North and South," 31–32.

39. Morrison, *"Best School in the World,"* 96–97, 153.

40. Griess, "Dennis Hart Mahan," 290, 310, 316–24, 326. See also Hattaway and Jones, *How the North Won*, 11–12.

41. Griess, "Dennis Hart Mahan," 217–18, 239; Skelton, *American Profession of Arms*, 247.

42. For example, see Morrison, "Military Education and Strategic Thought," 121.

43. Skelton, "Army in the Age of the Common Man," 98–99; Skelton, *American Profession of Arms*, 284–85; H. A. du Pont to "Dear Mama," Mar. 28, 1857, in Ambrose, "West Point in the Fifties," 306–7; E. Upton to Maria, Apr. 8, 1861, HLOM.

44. Skelton, "Army in the Age of the Common Man," 99. Even Walter Millis, who was not particularly sympathetic to the regulars' antimilitia rhetoric, recognized the militia's shortcomings. See *Arms and Men*, 135, 145.

45. Griess, "Dennis Hart Mahan," 290–91.

46. Mahan, *Elementary Treatise*; Mahan, *Treatise of Field Fortification*; Griess, "Dennis Hart Mahan," 290–92, 301–2.

47. E. Upton to "Dear brother," Feb. 2, 1861, HLOM; Hattaway and Jones, *How the North Won*, 11–12; Register of Merit, USMA Archives, 3:102, 107–12, 116, 122–28, 132, 138, 143, 149, 155, 157, 204–5; USMA Staff Records, ibid., 6:204–5, 262–63, 7:17, 50, 144–51, 161–63; E. Upton to John Upton, Feb. 1, 1857, GCHD. "Were it not for drawing," he wrote to his sister in June 1860, "I should, without doubt, better my last year's standing." E. Upton to "My Dear Sister," June 3, 1860, in *L&L*, 22.

48. Register of Merit, USMA Archives, 3:91, 96; Register of Delinquencies, 1856–61, ibid., 130; E. Upton to "My Dear Sister" [Maria], Sept. 7, 1857, in *L&L*, 13 (emphasis in original); Post Orders, USMA Archives, 5:323, 333, 337, 344, 364, 367, 375, 409. See also Sergent, *They Lie Forgotten*, 183–84. Upton earned these monthly privileges eight times in his final twenty-four months as a cadet. According to James Morrison, only fifteen to twenty cadets per month earned this privilege, roughly one-tenth of the corps. See *"Best School in the World,"* 122.

49. Post Orders, USMA Archives, 5:369; Morrison, *"Best School in the World,"* 73.

50. E. Upton to [Rachel Upton], June 24, 1856, GCHD (emphasis in original); E. Upton to "Dear Sister," Apr. 23, 1859, HLOM. Other cadets thought similarly.

51. U.S. Congress, Senate, *Report of the Board of Visitors to the United States Military Academy at West Point*, 34th Cong., 3rd sess., 1856, S. Exec. Doc. 2, 304; E. Upton to "My Dear Sister" [Maria], Apr. 12, 1857, in *L&L*, 13; O. Howard, *Autobiography*, 1:91–92.

52. E. Upton to "My Dear Sister," Feb. 9, 1859, in *L&L*, 15; E. Upton to "Dear Sister," Mar. 26, 1859, HLOM. Upton took twelve days' leave on March 12, 1859, in order to attend his brother's funeral See Post Orders, USMA Archives, 5:223.

53. E. Upton to "Cousin E—," May 1, 1859, in *L&L*, 16–17.

54. E. Upton to "My Dear Sister," Jan. 20, 1860, ibid., 19; E. Upton to "Dear Sister," Apr. 23, 1859, HLOM. Gardiner Shattuck has shown that during the Civil War, many northern evangelicals believed that "the best Christians are the best soldiers." See *Shield and Hiding Place*, 23–24.

55. E. Upton to "My Dear Sister," Jan. 20, 1860, HLOM.

56. Schaff, *Spirit of Old West Point*, 145–47. See also Gallagher, *Stephen Dodson Ramseur*, 25. Schaff's is the only firsthand account of this incident but does not provide the exact date it happened. Stephen Ambrose states that the duel was with swords. See *Duty, Honor, Country*, 160–61. Schaff, however, does not indicate what weapons, if any, were used.

57. Schaff, *Spirit of Old West Point*, 147–48; Pappas, *To the Point*, 311–14.

58. Schaff, *Spirit of Old West Point*, 164–65 (emphasis in original); Ambrose, *Duty, Honor, Country*, 169.

59. E. Upton to "My Dear Sister," Oct. 21, 1860, HLOM; Pappas, *To the Point*, 316–17.

60. E. Upton to "My Dear Sister," Dec. 1, 1860, HLOM; E. Upton to Maria, Jan. 12, 1861, ibid.

61. E. Upton to Julia, Mar. 27, 1861, ibid. (emphasis in original).

62. E. Upton to "Dear Sister," Dec. 21, 1860, ibid. (emphasis in original).

63. E. Upton to "Dear Brother" [John], Feb. 1, 1857, ibid.; E. Upton to Julia Upton, Feb. 16, 1879, ibid.

64. E. Upton to "My Dear Brother," Feb. 2, 1861, ibid. (emphasis in original); E. Upton to "My Very Dear Sister," Apr. 17, 1861, ibid.; E. Upton to "My Dear Sister," Dec. 1, 1860, HLOM (emphasis in original). For one example of a conflicted cadet, see Lake, "Crisis of Conscience."

65. The same order ended the five-year course of instruction. See USMA Staff Records, USMA Archives, 7:158–64; and Pappas, *To the Point*, 334–35.

66. USMA Staff Records, USMA Archives, 7:167; Post Orders, May 6, 1861, ibid., 6:14. See also Pappas, *To the Point*, 335–36.

Chapter 2

1. *L&L*, 42; E. Upton to "My Dear Sister," May 8, 1861, ibid., 44–45.

2. E. Upton to "My Dear Sister," May 8, 1861, ibid., 44–45; E. Upton to "My Dear Sister," May 24, 1861, ibid., 46.

3. E. Upton to "My Dear Sister," May 20, 1861, HLOM; E. Upton to Maria, July 1, 1861, ibid. (emphasis in original); E. Upton to Maria, July 9, 1861, ibid.

4. E. Upton to "Dear Sister," June 1, 1861, in *L&L*, 45; E. Upton to "My Dear Sister," June 6, 1861, HLOM; E Upton to Maria, July 9, 1861, ibid.

5. Stephen Ambrose writes, "Upton aimed and fired the opening gun of the battle." *Upton and the Army*, 18. Peter Michie simply states, "Upton had aimed the first gun." *L&L*, 53. I have seen no firsthand evidence to support either claim. The record regarding Upton's wounding is not terribly clear, either. Two firsthand accounts address it. The first is General Tyler's report of the battle. The second is a letter from Upton to a sister. See *OR*, 2:351; and E. Upton to "My Dear Sister," Nov. 25, 1861, in

L&L, 54. Neither detail the extent of the injury nor the circumstances under which it occurred.

6. E. Upton to "My Dear Sister," July 22, 1861, in *L&L*, 53; E. Upton to "My Dear Sister," Nov. 25, 1861, ibid., 54; *OR*, 2:348–57; W. T. Sherman to Mrs. Audenreid, Mar. 25, 1881, WSPLC.

7. E. Upton to "My Dear Sister," Sept. 30, 1861, in *L&L*, 57.

8. E. Upton to "My Dear Sister," Oct. 4, 1861, HLOM.

9. E. Upton to "My Dear Sister," Nov. 13, 1861, ibid. (emphasis in original).

10. E. Upton to "My Dear Sister," Nov. 18, 1861, ibid.

11. *L&L*, 55, 60–61; E. Upton to "My Dear Sister," Mar. 26, 1862, HLOM.

12. Sears, *To the Gates of Richmond*, 66–84.

13. Ibid., 85–86.

14. *OR*, 11(1):618–25.

15. Ibid., 11(2):434–36. For how Upton's actions fit into the campaign's larger context, see Burton, *Extraordinary Circumstances*, 109, 124, 336, 264–65.

16. *L&L*, 62.

17. E. Upton to "My Dear Sister," Sept. 26, 1862, in ibid., 63–64; *OR*, 19(1):176, 376–83, 409–10.

18. *L&L*, 66–67; Best, *121st New York*, 6–25.

19. Cilella, *Upton's Regulars*, 74, 77, 81. Regarding Franchot's unpopularity, see Best, *121st New York*, 31; Dr. Daniel Holt to "My dear Wife," Sept. [25], 1862, in Holt, *Surgeon's Civil War*, 29–30; and Greiner, *Subdued by the Sword*, 15. There is some confusion as to when Upton took command. Stephen Ambrose and Isaac Best give different accounts. See *Upton and the Army*, 20; and *121st New York*, 27–28. See also *L&L*, 66–67. Special Order No. 17, October 25, 1862, makes clear that Upton assumed command that day. See Regimental Books, 121st N.Y. Inf., RG 94, NARA. See also Cilella, *Upton's Regulars*, 74–83.

20. Best, *121st New York*, 30–31; Dr. Daniel Holt to "My dear Wife," Sept. [25], 1862, in Holt, *Surgeon's Civil War*, 29–30; Dr. Daniel Holt to "My dear Wife," Oct. 2, 1862, in Holt, *Surgeon's Civil War*, 32.

21. Dr. Daniel Holt to "My dear Wife," Sept. [25], 1862, ibid., 29–30; Best, *121st New York*, 29, 34–35; "Reminiscences of Major Douglas Campbell," in *L&L*, 68–69; Greiner, *Subdued by the Sword*, 16; E. Upton to the Ladies Aid Society, Little Falls, N.Y., Nov. 21, 1862, Regimental Books, 121st N.Y. Inf., RG 94, NARA; E. Upton to "Dear Sister," Dec. 7, 1862, in *L&L*, 69–70; E. Upton to Louisa Upton, Dec. 23, 1862, Emory Upton Collection, USMA Library Special Collections. For extended discussions of the regiment's health, see Cilella, *Upton's Regulars*, 89–96, 119–21. For the regiment's experiences at Belle Plain, see also Cilella, *Upton's Regulars*, 119–21; and Greiner, *Subdued by the Sword*, 24–25.40.

22. Best, *121st New York*, 33–34; General Order No. 3, 121st N.Y. Inf., May 31, 1863, Regimental Books, 121st N.Y. Inf., RG 94, NARA; Greiner, *Subdued by the Sword*, 21; Dean Pierce Diary, Civil War Collection, New York State Historical Association; Reminiscences of Maj. Douglas Campbell, in *L&L*, 68.

23. Reminiscences of Maj. Douglas Campbell, in *L&L*, 69; General Order No. 14, 121st N.Y. Inf., Dec. 18, 1862, Regimental Books, 121st N.Y. Inf., RG 94, NARA.

24. R. M. Caslen [asst. adj., 121st N.Y.], to Editor, *Herkimer County Journal*, Jan. 17, 1863, ibid. These soldiers probably deserted just prior to the Army of the Potomac's "Mud March" of January 1863.

25. Dr. Daniel Holt to "My dear Wife," Jan. 19, 1863, in Holt, *Surgeon's Civil War*, 68–69; General Order No. 40, 1st Div., 6th Army Corps, Feb. 19, 1863, Regimental Books, 121st N.Y. Inf., NARA; General Order No. 49, 1st Div., 6th Army Corps, Mar. 15, 1863, ibid. For details regarding the regiment's desertion problem, see Cilella, *Upton's Regulars*, 98–104, 139–44.

26. E. Upton to Dr. Bradley, medical director, 6th Corps, Nov. 15, 1862, Regimental Books, 121st N.Y. Inf., RG 94, NARA.

27. Dr. Daniel Holt to "My dear Wife," Jan. 19, 1863, in Holt, *Surgeon's Civil War*, 68; E. Upton to the Adjutant General [of New York], Jan. 27, 1863, Regimental Books, 121st N.Y. Inf., RG 94, NARA; Dr. Daniel Holt to "My dear Wife," Feb. 8, 1863, in Holt, *Surgeon's Civil War*, 75–76.

28. General Order No. 11, 121st N.Y. Inf., Nov. 25, 1862, Regimental Books, 121st N.Y. Inf., RG 94, NARA; General Order No. 10, 121st N.Y. Inf., Nov. 23, 1862, ibid.; Cilella, *Upton's Regulars*, 149–59.

29. E. Upton to Charles Evans, assistant adjutant general [of New York], Apr. 5, 1863, Regimental Books, 121st N.Y. Inf., RG 94, NARA.

30. The regiment's chief surgeon, Dr. Edward Walker, had been severely ill since December 1862 and resigned from the service in April 1863. See various letters in Holt, *Surgeon's Civil War*, 62, 84–86. See also Cilella, *Upton's Regulars*, 156–57.

31. Dr. Daniel Holt to "My dear Wife," June 5, 1863, in Holt, *Surgeon's Civil War*, 107 (emphasis in original).

32. Holt seems to have suffered from a near-chronic case of diarrhea, a common cause of death during the Civil War. See numerous letters written by Holt, ibid., 71, 75, 81, 106, 112.

33. Best, *121st New York*, 29.

34. Dr. Daniel Holt to "My dear Wife," Apr. 20, 1863, in Holt, *Surgeon's Civil War*, 90–91 (emphasis in original).

35. General Order No. 12, 121st N.Y. Inf., Nov. 27, 1862, Regimental Books, 121st N.Y. Inf., RG 94, NARA.

36. For excellent descriptions of the problems that beset the Army of the Potomac during the Fredericksburg Campaign, see Rable, *Fredericksburg! Fredericksburg!*, 63–99; O'Reilly, *Fredericksburg Campaign*, 19–33; Catton, *Army of the Potomac: Glory Road*, 19–65; and Wert, *Sword of Lincoln*, 183–204.

37. *OR*, 21:925–38; Rable, *Fredericksburg! Fredericksburg!*, 156–58, 190–203; O'Reilly, *Fredericksburg Campaign*, 135–65; Best, *121st New York*, 43–50; Greiner, *Subdued by the Sword*, 28–29; Cilella, *Upton's Regulars*, 122–29.

38. Best, *121st New York*, 51–52; Dr. Daniel Holt to "My dear Wife," Jan. 27, 1863, in Holt, *Surgeon's Civil War*, 69–72; Greiner, *Subdued by the Sword*, 37–38; Cilella, *Upton's Regulars*, 130–37. For more general accounts of the Mud March, see Rable, *Fredericksburg! Fredericksburg!*, 409–24; O'Reilly, *Fredericksburg Campaign*, 473–89; Wert, *Sword of Lincoln*, 214–15; and Catton, *Army of the Potomac: Glory Road*, 86–91.

39. Regarding the early stages of the Chancellorsville Campaign, see Ernest B. Furguson, *Chancellorsville, 1863*, chaps. 5–15; Wert. *Sword of Lincoln*, 231–46; and Catton, *Army of the Potomac: Glory Road*, 156–204.

40. *OR*, 25(1):579–81, 589; Cilella, *Upton's Regulars*, 168; Lansing Payne to Parents, May 4, 1863, Lansing Payne Papers, Civil War Collection, New York State Historical Association. See also Dr. Daniel Holt to "My dear Wife," May 17, 1863, in Holt,

Surgeon's Civil War, 103–6; Cilella, *Upton's Regulars*, 160–70; and Furgurson, *Chancellorsville*, 273–76. Ernest Furgurson addresses the actions of the Sixth Corps at Fredericksburg and Salem Church in ibid., chaps. 15–16.

41. *OR*, 25(1):189; Fox, *Regimental Losses*, 17, 32, 436. The Confederates released most of the 121st's captured soldiers within a few days. See Dr. Daniel Holt to "My dear Wife," May 15, 1863, in Holt, *Surgeon's Civil War*, 94–95. After the campaign had ended, Emory took ten days' leave to accompany his brother to Batavia. Henry was so severely wounded that he eventually was mustered out of the service. See E. Upton to Assistant Adjutant General, Army of the Potomac, May 22, 1863, 121st New York Personnel Records, Upton Personnel File, RG 15, NARA.

42. Dean Pierce Diary, May 3, 1862, Civil War Collection, New York State Historical Association; Dr. Daniel Holt to "My dear Wife," May 15, 1863, in Holt, *Surgeon's Civil War*, 92; Fox, *Regimental Losses*, 17, 32, 33, 436.

43. Greiner, *Subdued by the Sword*, 58; Best, *121st New York*, 76–78.

44. Best, *121st New York*, 84–86; Dr. Daniel Holt to "My dear Wife," various dates, in Holt, *Surgeon's Civil War*, 112–18.

45. Best, *121st New York*, 86–87; E. Upton to "My Dear Sister," July 4, 1863, HLOM.

46. *OR*, 27(1):671–73; Cilella, *Upton's Regulars*, 94–96, 196–98; E. Upton to "My Dear Sister," July 4, 1863, HLOM; Best, *121st New York*, 87–88. Upton's report in the *OR* stated that the regiment was in front of Round Top, but he was almost certainly mistaken, as he also stated that his right flank rested on a road that led to the Emmitsburg Pike. The only road in the area that met this requirement was one that ran from the north side of Little Round Top to the west through the Wheat Field to the Emmitsburg Pike. Upton thus had to have been in front of Little Round Top, not Round Top. The presence of a monument on the northern face of Little Round Top commemorating the 121st New York confirms this judgment. See *OR*, 27(1):671–73.

47. It is truly hazy as to when Upton left the 121st New York and took command of the Second Brigade on a permanent basis. Isaac Best cites July 4, 1864, as the end of his colonelcy with the regiment, but that was long after Upton had taken command of the brigade. The *OR* lists him as the commander of the 121st during the Gettysburg Campaign, and he submitted his after-action report in that capacity on August 6, 1863, yet it lists him as the brigade commander on July 31. The *OR* again lists Upton as the 121st's commander on October 10, but less than a month later, all accounts of the Battle of Rappahannock Station refer to him as the brigade commander, and the *OR* lists him as brigade commander on December 10. See E. Upton to "My Dear Sister," July 4, 1863, HLOM; Best, *121st New York*, 232; and *OR*, 27(1):163, 671, 27(3):801, 29(1):223, 605. Salvatore Cilella's history of the 121st New York does not provide a definitive date on which Upton gave up regimental command, noting that command of the 121st between Gettysburg and the start of the Overland Campaign alternated between Upton, Egbert Olcott, and Andrew Mather.

48. E. Upton to "My Dear Sister Minnie" [Maria?], July 4, 1863, HLOM; E. Upton to Louisa Upton, Dec. 23, 1862, Emory Upton Collection, USMA Library Special Collections. See also *OR*, 27(1):671.

49. E. Upton to "Dear Brother," Nov. 6, 1863, HLOM.

50. Ibid. (emphasis added); E. Upton to "My Dear Sister," July 4, 1863, ibid.

51. E. Upton to "My Dear Sister," July 4, 1863, ibid.; E. Upton to "My Dear Sister," Aug. 6, 1863, in *L&L*, 76; Certificate of Disability, Aug. 24, 1863, 121st New York Infantry

Records, Personnel File on Emory Upton, RG 15, NARA; E. Upton to the Adjutant General, Sixth Corps, Aug. 24, 1863, ibid.

52. E. Upton to "Dear Brother," Nov. 6, 1863, HLOM; E. Upton to "My Dearest Sister," July 4, 1863, ibid.; E. Upton to "My Dearest Sister," Aug. 2, 1863, ibid. Regarding Union generals' fixation on battle rather than on the prosecution of war, see Weigley, *American Way of War*, 135.

53. E. Upton to "My Dearest Sister," Aug. 2, 1863, HLOM; Dr. Daniel Holt to "My dear Wife," Aug. 2, 1863, in Holt, *Surgeon's Civil War*, 128–29; Dr. Daniel Holt to "My dear Wife," Aug. 20, 1863, ibid., 132–35. See also Greiner, *Subdued by the Sword*, 80–82; and Cilella, *Upton's Regulars*, 220–24.

54. *L&L*, 82. For numerous letters written in September 1863 that recommend Upton's promotion to brigadier general, see File 2666, 1881, Letters Received by the Appointments, Commission, and Personal Branch, 1871–1894, RG 94, NARA (hereafter cited as File 2666, RG94, NARA).

55. *OR*, 29(1):584, 587.

56. Ibid., 585–88, 592–93. Several sources verify this somewhat unbelievable account. See E. Upton to "My dear Sister," Nov. 15, 1863, in *L&L*, 86; Dr. Daniel Holt to "My dear Wife," Nov. 9, 1863, in Holt, *Surgeon's Civil War*, 154–55; Best, *121st New York*, 102; and John S. Kidder to "Dear Wife," Nov. 8, 1863, in Greiner, *Subdued by the Sword*, 91–92.

57. *OR*, 29(1):592–93; E. Upton to "My dear Sister," Nov. 15, 1863, in *L&L*, 82–86.

58. *OR*, 29(1):559, 610, 616; Freeman, *Lee's Lieutenants*, 3:264–69.

59. Brig. Gen. H. G. Wright to the Adjutant General, Nov. 19, 1863, File 2666, RG94, NARA; Maj. Gen. John Sedgwick to the Adjutant General of the Army, Nov. 19, 1863, ibid.; Maj. Gen. George Meade to the Adjutant General of the Army, Nov. 20, 1863, ibid.; E. Upton to "My Dear Sister," Apr. 10, 1864, HLOM.

60. E. Upton to "My Dear Sister," Apr. 18, 1864, in *L&L*, 89 (emphasis added); Starr, "General Emory Upton," 12; Maj. Gen. John Sedgwick to Abraham Lincoln, Feb. 1, 1864, File 2666, RG94, NARA.

61. E. Upton to Hon. Edwin D. Morgan, Apr. 11, 1864, ibid.

62. E. D. Morgan to E. M. Stanton, May 13, 1864, ibid.

63. Ambrose, *Upton and the Army*, 22.

64. E. Upton to Louisa Upton, Dec. 23, 1862, Emory Upton Collection, USMA Library Special Collections.

Chapter 3

1. Dr. Daniel Holt to "My dear Wife," Dec. 15, 1863, in Holt, *Surgeon's Civil War*, 165 (emphasis in original). See also Lyman, *Meade's Army*, 82 (Dec. 20, [1863]).

2. Best, *121st New York*, 111–13; Dr. Daniel Holt to "My dear Wife," Feb. 7, 1864, in Holt, *Surgeon's Civil War*, 171; Diary, May 3, 1864, in Holmes, *Touched with Fire*, 101–2. See also *OR*, 33:628, 786.

3. E. Upton to "My Dear Sister," Apr. 18, 1864, in *L&L*, 89; E. Upton to "My Dear Sister," Apr. 25, 1864, ibid., 91; E. Upton to "My Dear Sister," Apr. 10, 1864, HLOM. The Holland Land Office Museum has the first four pages of the April 25 letter but not the page from which the quote is taken.

4. Dr. Daniel Holt to "My dear Wife," May 5, 1864, in Holt, *Surgeon's Civil War*, 182; Rhea, *Battle of the Wilderness*, 54–59, 80–84; Wert, *Sword of Lincoln*, 237–38; Catton, *Army of the Potomac: A Stillness at Appomattox*, 56; R. Scott, *Into the Wilderness*, 44.

5. *OR*, 36(1):126, 665–66. For a good account of the role of Upton's brigade in the fighting in the Wilderness, see R. Scott, *Into the Wilderness*, 93–95, 174–76. See also Dr. Daniel Holt to "My dear Wife," May 6, 1864, in Holt, *Surgeon's Civil War*, 183; and Cilella, *Upton's Regulars*, 86–91.

6. Matter, *If It Takes All Summer*, 9–82; Rhea, *Battles for Spotsylvania*, 5–58; Wert, *Sword of Lincoln*, 343–45; Catton, *Army of the Potomac: A Stillness at Appomattox*, 93–98.

7. *OR*, 36(1):204, 666–67. For an account of Sedgwick's death, see Matter, *If It Takes All Summer*, 102.

8. *OR*, 36(1):660–61, 667; diary, Jan. 1, 1865, in Fisk, *Hard Marching Every Day*, 296–97.

9. The 95th Pennsylvania from Upton's brigade did not participate.

10. *OR*, 36(1):667–68; E. Upton to Adam Badeau, Dec. 26, 1873, Adam Badeau Papers, Library of Congress. The terminology concerning this assault can be confusing. The *OR* refers to Upton's command as an "assaulting column." It was not, however, a column as recognized in the late eighteenth and early nineteenth centuries. Rather, it was a column only when compared to the length of the entire Union line. More correctly, it was a mass attack conducted by infantry arrayed in several lines of battle.

11. *OR*, 36(1):667–88. Paddy Griffith incorrectly contends that Upton had given "special training as storm troops" to his brigade prior to the assaults at Rappahannock Station and at Spotsylvania. *Battle Tactics of the Civil War*, 66. The colonel did not employ special tactics in either battle, nor was there any special training ahead of time. At Spotsylvania three-quarters of the attacking regiments had been attached to Upton only a few hours beforehand; their "training" consisted of Upton briefing their officers.

12. Matter, *If It Takes All Summer*, 160–62.

13. *OR*, 36(1):667–68.

14. Ibid., 36(1):667–68, 36(2):602–3; Best, *121st New York*, 124–40; Matter, *If It Takes All Summer*, 159–61.

15. E. Upton to Adam Badeau, Dec. 26, 1873, Badeau Papers; Warner, *Generals in Blue*, 337–38, 575–76. William Matter echoes Upton's analysis. See *If It Takes All Summer*, 344. Regarding Mott's and Wright's actions that day, see *OR*, 36(1):67; Col. Theodore Lyman to [Unknown], May 10, 1864, in Lyman, *Meade's Headquarters*, 109–10; Lyman, *Meade's Army*, 150 (May 10, [1864]); Grant, *Memoirs*, 2:130–31; Badeau, *Military History of General U. S. Grant*, 2:164; and diary, May 10, [1864], in Holmes, *Touched with Fire*, 112–13.

16. Grant, *Memoirs*, 2:130–31; Badeau, *Military History of U. S. Grant*, 2:164–65.

17. *OR*, 36(1):144–45, 668–69.

18. E. Upton to G. Norton Galloway, Aug. 31, 1878, in *L&L*, 110–11; *OR*, 36(1):537, 669–70; Rhea, *Battles for Spotsylvania*, 276–77; Cilella, *Upton's Regulars*, 304–11; Matter, *If It Takes All Summer*, 216–22, 248–49.

19. *OR*, 36(1):669–70; Grant, *Memoirs*, 2:140; Dr. Daniel Holt to "My dear Wife," May 16, 1864, in Holt, *Surgeon's Civil War*, 190 (emphasis in original). See also *OR*, 36(1):70, 298; Best, *121st New York*, 141–52; Matter, *If It Takes All Summer*, 283–85; and Rhea, *To the North Anna River*, 78–80, 82–87.

20. *OR*, 36(1):144, 670; Vaill, *Second Connecticut*, 50; Fox, *Regimental Losses*, 178; Best, *121st New York*, 152.

21. Rhea, *Cold Harbor*, 182–87, 195–207; Trudeau, *Bloody Roads South*, 261–67; Catton, *Army of the Potomac: A Stillness at Appomattox*, 149–51.

22. *OR*, 36(1):172, 671; Vaill, *Second Connecticut*, 57–68; Cilella, *Upton's Regulars*, 314; Rhea, *Cold Harbor*, 238–47; Trudeau, *Bloody Roads South*, 267–74.

23. *OR*, 36(1):671; Best, *121st New York*, 157–58; Diary, June 8, 9, 1864, in Holt, *Surgeon's Civil War*, 199.

24. E. Upton to Maria, June 4, 1864, HLOM; Grant, *Memoirs*, 2:130–31; *OR*, 36(2):695; E. Upton to Brig. Gen. Lorenzo Thomas [adjutant general of the army], July 1, 1864, File 2666, RG94, NARA.

25. E. Upton to "My Dear Sister," June 7, 1864, HLOM.

26. E. Upton to "Brother" [John], Mar. 24, 1864, GCHD; E. Upton to "My Dear Sister," June 4, 1864, HLOM.

27. E. Upton to "My Dear Sister," June 5, 1864, in *L&L*, 109 (emphasis in original).

28. E. Upton to "My Dear Sister," June 18, 1864, HLOM (emphasis in original).

29. E. Upton to "My Dear Sister," Aug. 9, 1864, in ibid. The original letter is misdated June 9.

30. Dr. Daniel Holt to "My dear Wife," May 13, 1864, in Holt, *Surgeon's Civil War*, 188; *OR*, 40(1):493; Diary, June 1, 1864, in Holt, *Surgeon's Civil War*, 195 (emphasis in original).

31. E. Upton to "My Dear Sister," Sept. 2, 1864, HLOM. This letter is in *L&L*, but Michie substantially changed the text quoted here. The passage critical of Meade and Burnside reads therein: "Others I could mention are stumbling blocks." *L&L*, 123.

32. *OR*, 40(1):192–93, 492–93; Vaill, *Second Connecticut*, 69–79.

33. Diary, June 22, 1864, in Holt, *Surgeon's Civil War*, 209 (two entries, June 22, 1864). The 65th New York replaced the 5th Maine. Also, the 95th and 96th Pennsylvania had suffered so many casualties that they were combined into one command. See *OR*, 37(2):550; 40(2):547; 43(1):107; and Cilella, *Upton's Regulars*, 332–34.

34. It is a theme Upton often struck in his later work. For but two examples, see *MPUS*, 203–4, 211–13.

35. Diary, June 20, 21, 1864, in Holt, *Surgeon's Civil War*, 209 (emphasis in original).

36. *OR*, 40(1):193, 493, 40(3):106–7; Best, *121st New York*, 170–73; Vaill, *Second Connecticut*, 82–84; E. Upton to "My Dear Sister," July 19, 1864, HLOM.

37. *OR*, 43(1):709–10; E. Upton to "My Dear Sister," Aug. 24, 1864, HLOM; Catton, *Army of the Potomac: A Stillness at Appomattox*, 270–72, 279–80; Wilson, *Under the Old Flag*, 1:548.

38. *OR*, 43(1):696–97.

39. Wert, *From Winchester to Cedar Creek*, 29–37; *OR*, 43(1):63–65; Best, *121st New York*, 177–78; Patchan, *Last Battle of Winchester*, 105–8; Catton, *Army of the Potomac: A Stillness at Appomattox*, 284–86. For Wilson's view of Mosby's operations in the Shenandoah Valley, see *Under the Old Flag*, 1:548–49.

40. Patchan, *Last Battle of Winchester*, 204–5, 229–90; Wert, *From Winchester to Cedar Creek*, 43–44, 66–68.

41. *OR*, 43(1):25–26, 46–47, 54, 63–65, 173–74.

42. Ibid., 162–65, 173–74, 177–80; Vaill, *Second Connecticut*, 93–97; Best, *121st New York*, 181–82; Wert, *From Winchester to Cedar Creek*, 89–91; Patchan, *Last Battle of Winchester*, 390–91, 402–3.

43. Wilson, *Under the Old Flag*, 1:554; telegram, E. Upton to P. Upton, Sept. 22, 1864, File 2666, RG94, NARA. Wilson's account of Upton being carried around on a stretcher before relinquishing command may be a fabrication as the division's adjutant simply reported that command passed immediately to Colonel Edwards; nowhere does it mention Upton's "heroic" actions. See *OR*, 43(1):164. Salvatore Cilella, on the other hand, provides an entirely different narrative, one supported by soldiers' accounts. See *Upton's Regulars*, 337.

44. *L&L*, 136. Upton's promotion to major general was effective on October 19, 1864. See E. Upton to Brig. Gen. L. Thomas, Nov. 3, 1864, File 2666, RG94, NARA. See also Wilson, *Under the Old Flag*, 2:2–3.

45. *OR*, 39(3):442–445; S. Starr, *Union Cavalry*, 1:7–11. I have capitalized "Cavalry Corps" when referring to Wilson's command as that was its official designation.

46. S. Starr, *Union Cavalry*, 1:11–14, 21–22; Jones, *Yankee Blitzkrieg*, 6–8, 13–14.

47. Wilson, *Under the Old Flag*, 1:vi, 554; *OR*, 43(2):631, 637; E. Upton to "My dear Parents," Dec. 8, 1864, HLOM. Months later he still complained of acute pain from a "perverse nerve" that caused "a disagreeable sensation about the knee." See E. Upton to "My Dear Sister," Mar. 14, 1865, in *L&L*, 138.

48. *OR*, 45(2):171, 173, 190–91.

49. Ibid., 583, 49(1):586, 701, 712, 759. For a discussion of the logistical problems facing Wilson's command, see Jones, *Yankee Blitzkrieg*, 15–17. For those of Upton, see Fitzpatrick, "Misunderstood Reformer," 127–28.

50. W. Scott, *Story of a Cavalry Regiment*, 426–27; GDLC, Mar. 11, 1865. In 1908 E. N. Gilpin published what he alleged was his diary of Wilson's Raid. See "Last Campaign—A Cavalryman's Journal." It is, in fact, a very questionable account of the raid, one that recounts several incidents that are not in the original diary and that appear to be completely fictional. Apparently, General Wilson came to a similar conclusion. See E. N. Gilpin to J. H. Wilson, Sept. 18, 1907, WPLC.

51. GDLC, Mar. 13, 1865; W. Scott, *Story of a Cavalry Regiment*, 357.

52. GDLC, Mar. 16, 1865. Another measure of the loyalty Upton's soldiers felt toward their commander was the fact that either E. N. Gilpin or his brother, Tom, who was an officer in the division, named their daughter after him—Grace Upton Gilpin. See E. N. Gilpin to Tom Gilpin, June 6, 1878, E. N. Gilpin Papers, Library of Congress. The letter does not make clear which of the brothers was Grace's father.

53. *OR*, 49(2):29; Wilson, *Under the Old Flag*, 2:191–93; S. Starr, *Union Cavalry*, 1:27–29; Jones, *Yankee Blitzkrieg*, 52–53. Gilpin reported: "Good water, forage, and bee gums [honey]. Good supper. Ham and eggs." GDLC, Mar. 23, 1865.

54. GDLC, Mar. 26, 1865; *OR*, 49(1):472.

55. GDLC, Mar. 27, 1865.

56. *OR*, 49(1):472; Wilson, *Under the Old Flag*, 2:202–3.

57. GDLC, Mar. 28, 29, 30, 1865; Wilson, *Under the Old Flag*, 2:204–5, 207; *OR*, 49(1):472, 49(2):111–12.

58. *OR*, 49(1):472–73, 479, 490–91, 500–503; Wilson, *Under the Old Flag*, 2:207–8, 214–18; W. Scott, *Story of a Cavalry Regiment*, 436–37, 442–44; GDLC, Apr. 1, 1865.

59. E. F. Winslow, "Memoirs of the Civil War," WPUIL, ep. 1, pt. 1, 19; Wilson, *Under the Old Flag*, 2:221–22.

60. Wilson, *Under the Old Flag*, 2:222–26; *OR*, 49(1):351, 438, 473; W. Scott, *Story of a Cavalry Regiment*, 450–51.

61. A. Loughridge to E. F. Winslow, Feb. 27, 1885, WPUIL; Wilson, *Under the Old Flag*, 2:228. Winslow credits himself, not Upton, for attacking without orders. See E. F. Winslow to "Captain," Mar. 17, 1885, WPUIL.

62. GDLC, Apr. 2, 1865; *OR*, 49(1):473; E. Upton to "My dear Sister," Apr. 30, 1865, HLOM.

63. Wilson, *Under the Old Flag*, 2:232.

64. GDLC, Apr. 2, 4, 1865.

65. Jones, *Yankee Blitzkrieg*, 92; GDLC, Apr. 3, 4, 1865.

66. E. F. Winslow, "Memoirs of the Civil War," WPUIL, ep. 8, pt. 1, 32–33; GDLC, Apr. 3, 8, 1865; *OR*, 49(1):473; Wilson, *Under the Old Flag*, 2:237.

67. Jones, *Yankee Blitzkrieg*, 99–100; *OR*, 49(1):473; Wilson, *Under the Old Flag*, 2:245–46.

68. Wilson, *Under the Old Flag*, 2:251–52; GDLC, Apr. 13, 1865.

69. *OR*, 49(1):473; GDLC, Apr. 14, 15, 1865.

70. *OR*, 49(1):473–74; GDLC, Apr. 16, 1865.

71. *OR*, 49(1):474; Wilson, *Under the Old Flag*, 2:259–60.

72. E. F. Winslow, "Memoirs of the Civil War," WPUIL, ep. 8, pt. 2, 8–9; W. Scott, *Story of a Cavalry Regiment*, 491–92.

73. GDLC, Apr. 16, 1865 (emphasis in original); *OR*, 49(1):474–75, 480–82, 492–94, 498–99; E. Upton to "My dear Sister," Apr. 30, 1865, HLOM; J. H. Wilson to Adam Badeau, Apr. 22, 1865, WPLC; Wilson, *Under the Old Flag*, 2:263–65; Diary, Apr. 16, 1865, James H. Wilson Diaries and Papers, Historical Society of Delaware. See also Jones, *Yankee Blitzkrieg*, 134–38. For a book-length account of the action at Columbus, see Misulia, *Columbus, Georgia, 1865*.

74. Wilson had entered Macon ahead of Upton and had accepted the city's surrender. See GDLC, Apr. 20, 21, 1865; and *OR*, 49(2):415.

75. Weigley, *Great Civil War*, 451–52; Goldin and Lewis, "Economic Cost of the American Civil War." Some scholars have suggested that the number of dead was likely closer to 750,000 and might have been as high as 850,000. See J. David Hacker, "Recounting the Dead," *New York Times, Opionionator*, Sept. 20, 2011, http:// opinionator.blogs.nytimes.com/2011/09/20/recounting-the-dead/#more-105317, accessed July 27, 2015.

76. Royster, *Destructive War*.

77. E. Upton to "My dear Sister," Apr. 30, 1865, HLOM; E. Upton to "My Dear Sister," Mar. 14, 1865, in *L&L*, 138; E. Upton to Emily Upton, Dec. 15, 1868, TMFP.

Chapter 4

1. GDLC, Apr. 22, 24, 1865.

2. Ibid., May 5, 6, 1865; Wilson, *Under the Old Flag*, 2:306; *OR*, 49(2):527.

3. *L&L*, 173.

4. GDLC, May 8, 1865.

5. Ibid., May 10, 27, 1865; *OR*, 49(2):587, 604, 618–19, 655.

6. *OR*, 49(2):588, 685–86.

7. Ibid., 750, 788–90, 799, 802–3, 842.

8. Ibid., 617–18, 633–34; Wilson, *Under the Old Flag*, 2:306–8; Jones, *Yankee Blitzkrieg*, 170–79.

9. *OR*, 49(2):486, 616, 790, 817–18; GDLC, May 27, 1865. For an excellent account of the activities of Wilson's corps in postwar Georgia, see Pehrson, "James Harrison Wilson," 9–29.

10. Pehrson, "James Harrison Wilson," 30–31; Wilson, *Under the Old Flag*, 2:364–65; *OR*, 49(2):870, 873; *L&L*, 174–75.

11. GDLC, May 25, 1865; E. Upton to E. F. Winslow, July 7, 1865, WPUIL; E. Upton to Brig. Gen. E. D. Townsend [adjutant general of the army], May 24, 1865, File #2666, RG 94, NARA. Upton had been promoted to brevet major general, U.S. Volunteers, on October 19, 1864, and to brevet major general, U.S. Army, on March 13, 1865. See Cullum, *Biographical Register*, 2:774.

12. E. Upton to E. F. Winslow, July 7, 1865, WPUIL (emphasis in original); Marszalek, *Sherman*, 239–59. See also Warner, *Generals in Blue*, 296.

13. E. Upton to E. F. Winslow, July 7, 1865, WPUIL; *L&L*, 178, 181. Citing a 1918 interview Wilson gave to the *New York Times Magazine*, Stephen Ambrose argues that Wilson urged Upton to resign from the army at the end of the Civil War and to pursue a career in the railroad business. See *Upton and the Army*, 54. In the interview, however, Wilson simply states that he had tried to convince Upton to leave the army and enter the railroad business sometime after he himself had returned to civilian life, something that did not happen until 1870. See Richard Barry, "Emory Upton, Military Genius," *New York Times Magazine*, June 16, 1918, 12.

14. E. Upton to "My Dear Sister," Oct. 1, 1865, HLOM.

15. Ibid.; E. Upton to Maj. Gen. J. Pope, Oct. 14, 1865, in *L&L*, 187–88; E. Upton to "My Dear Sister," Apr. 10, 1864, HLOM.

16. E. Upton to W. T. Sherman, Nov. 8, 1867, WSPLC.

17. E. Upton to Brig. Gen. E. D. Townsend, Jan. 13, 1866, in *L&L*, 191–92; E. Upton to [a sister], Apr. 6, 1866, ibid., 193–94.

18. E. Upton to H. A. du Pont, Aug. 9, 1866, DPPHL; Col. H. B. Clitz to the Adjutant General, Jan. [?], 1867, and Gen. U. S. Grant to E. M. Stanton, Feb. 4, 1866, in *L&L*, 195–97; *ANJ*, Sept. 29, 1866. See also *L&L*, 194–95 (text).

19. Griffith, *Battle Tactics*, 100–101; Upton, *New System of Infantry Tactics*, 48–49, 57–63, 83–87, 98–104; Jamieson, *Crossing the Deadly Ground*, 101.

20. Casey, *Infantry Tactics*; *ANJ*, Sept. 29, 1866. See also Ambrose, *Upton and the Army*, 63.

21. Griffith, *Battle Tactics*, 100–101; E. Upton to Brig. Gen. E. D. Townsend, Jan. 13, 1866, in *L&L*, 191–92; Gen. U. S. Grant to E. M. Stanton, Feb. 4, 1866, ibid., 196–97.

22. Special Orders No. 300, War Department, June 11, 1867, in *L&L*, 197–98; Report of the Grant Board, July 15, 1867, ibid., 202–5; *ANJ*, July 20, 1867. Among those who testified in opposition were Henry Hunt and Silas Casey. The board received written testimony from Upton.

23. *ANJ*, Sept. 29, 1866, Feb. 2, 1867. The term "assimilated tactics" as it is used here and throughout the remainder of this work refers to the melding of infantry, cavalry, and artillery tactics.

24. Ibid., July 20, Aug. 10, 1867; Bigelow, *William Conant Church*, 125.

25. *ANJ*, Oct. 19, Nov. 9, 30, 1867, Sept. 5, 1868. Other, somewhat minor criticisms appeared in the *ANJ* on February 29 and March 21, 1868, and on June 4, 1870.

26. Ibid., June 6, 1868 (emphasis in original), Nov. 19, 1870.

27. Ibid., May 2, June 27, 1868 (emphasis in original), May 22, 1869.

28. Ibid., May 16, 23, 1868. For letters that offer similar analyses, see ibid., June 13, July 18, 1868.

29. E. Martin Upton to E. Upton, Feb. 1, 1869, DFP. After Emily's death, her mother transcribed her diary and letters into a letter book held by the Dickman Family. This and subsequent citations to the letters and diary are to that letter book, not to the original documents. The Emory Upton Collection in the USMA Library Special Collections contains a typed transcript of both.

30. *L&L*, 205; E. Upton to J. H. Wilson, Dec. 4, 1868, WPLC.

31. E. Upton to J. H. Wilson, Dec. 4, 1868, WPLC.

32. E. Upton to J. H. Wilson, Dec. 12, 1868, ibid.; *L&L*, 194, 243. The period between the adjournment of the Clitz Board in the summer of 1866 and Upton's engagement to Emily Martin in November 1867 remains a mysterious time in his life as I have found no correspondence from this period. It is apparent, however, that he was serving in some capacity at Paducah just prior to his engagement, presumably with the Twenty-Fifth Infantry. See E. Upton to J. H. Wilson, Nov. 21, 1867, WPLC.

33. E. Upton to J. H. Wilson, Feb. 27, 1869, WPLC. Ayres had graduated from West Point in 1847 and had served in the Army of the Potomac during the Civil War. See Warner, *Generals in Blue*, 14.

34. E. Upton to W. T. Sherman, Feb. 5, 1868, WSPLC.

35. The Upton Family Papers in the Genesee County History Department contains a handwritten manuscript entitled "Gibbon's Rome, A.D. 250."

36. E. Upton to J. H. Wilson, Apr. 21, 1869, WPLC; "Civil and Military Policy of Rome," chap. 30 of an unpublished manuscript of *MPUS*, Emory Upton Papers, USAMHI. This chapter and three others were not included in the edition of *MPUS* the War Department published in 1904. It seems likely that the book's editors had a particularly difficult time determining how the chapter on Roman policy fit into Upton's larger work. Chapter 8 will explore Upton's reasons for writing about Rome. Two other "missing" chapters, "Confederate Military Policy," and "Appropriations Made by the Confederate States Government from February, 1861, to June 14, 1864," are also located at the U.S. Army Military History Institute. The fourth "missing" chapter, "Command and Administration: Controversy between Genl. Scott and Jeffn. Davis," is located in the Du Pont Papers at the Hagley Museum and Library. See also Cooling, "Missing Chapters of Emory Upton."

37. E. Upton to J. H. Wilson, Oct. 27, 1869, WPLC.

38. *L&L*, 218–19. For a reference to an informal visit of "Fanny" Seward, one of William Seward's daughters, to the Willowbrook estate, see EMD, July 24, 1866, DFP. Also, William Seward Jr. served as a pallbearer at Emily's funeral. See Evelina Martin to Nelly Martin, Apr. 17, 1870, DFP.

39. *DAB*, 2(2):330–34, 346–47. Conkling and Blair sent letters of condolence to Emily's parents when she passed away in 1880. See transcripts of letters in the Dickman Family Papers. It is not clear whether the Martins were friends with Francis Blair Sr. or Francis Blair Jr. I have assumed the latter, given Blair's relationship with Horatio Seymour.

40. EMD, July 21, 22, 23, 1866, DFP.

41. See E. Martin Upton to E. Upton, Nov. 25, Dec. 6, 10, 25, 1867, Jan. 1, 1868, ibid.

42. EMD, Nov. 29, 1867, ibid. (emphasis added).

43. E. Martin Upton to E. Upton, Oct. 13, 1867, in *L&L*, 223–25; E. Martin Upton to E. Upton, Dec. 20, 1868, DFP.

44. E. Upton to Emily Upton, Aug. 3, 1868, TMFP; E. Upton to Emily Upton, Mar. 10, 1868, ibid.

45. EMD, Nov. 29, 1867, DFP; E. Upton to Emily Upton, Dec. 29, 1868, TMFP.

46. EMD, Nov. 29, 1867, DFP; E. Upton to J. H. Wilson, Nov. 21, 1867, WPLC.

47. E. Upton to W. T. Sherman, Feb. 5, 1868, WSPLC; E. Martin Upton to E. Upton, Feb. 12, 1868, DFP. Emily's sickness is a bit of a mystery. Scattered throughout her correspondence as well as that of her husband are references to neuralgia, yet it seems unlikely it could have caused her death. Based on many references to coughing and shortness of breath, as well as on the oft-stated belief that a warm climate (southern Europe, Arizona, Key West, Nassau) would aid her condition, it seems fairly clear she had tuberculosis. Nowhere, however, have I found any mention of tuberculosis or of consumption.

48. E. Martin Upton to E. Upton, Feb. 17, 1869, DFP. The date on this citation is correct. Many of Emily's letters to Emory recall what they were doing the previous year.

49. C. Martin to E. Martin Upton, Mar. 7, 1868, in *L&L*, 230–31. See also E. Upton to Emily Upton, Feb. 20, 1869, TMFP; and *L&L*, 229.

50. E. Upton to W. T. Sherman, Feb. 5, 1868, WSPLC; E. Upton to Emily Upton, Aug. 3, 1868, TMFP.

51. *L&L*, 233. For some idea of the places the couple visited, see *L&L*, 229. Various letters Upton wrote to the adjutant general of the army make it possible to trace the couple's path through Europe. See E. Upton to the Adjutant General, Apr. 1, June 1, July 1, 1868, Letters Received by the Office of the Adjutant General, RG 94, NARA; and E. Upton to J. Upton, May 7, 1868, GCHD.

52. Upton to J. H. Wilson, Feb. 27, 1869, WPLC; E. Upton to Emily Upton, Dec. 9, 1868, TMFP; E. Upton to Emily Upton, Dec. 15, 1868, closing "Your devoted husband," ibid.

53. E. Upton to Emily Upton, Dec. 9, 1868, ibid. (emphasis in original); E. Upton to Emily Upton, Dec. 15, 1868, closing "Your devoted husband," ibid.

54. E. Upton to Emily Upton, Jan. 24, Feb. 7, Mar. 8, 1869, ibid.

55. E. Upton to Emily Upton, Nov. 21, Dec. 14, 1868, Jan. 1, 2, 15, 19, Feb. 4, 10, 1869, ibid.

56. E. Upton to Emily Upton, Feb. 4, 9, 1869, ibid.

57. E. Upton to Emily Upton, Feb. 19, 1869, ibid. (emphasis added). This is one of numerous such letters.

58. E. Upton to Emily Upton, Dec. 25, 1868, Jan. 1, Feb. 9, 27, Mar. 10 (emphasis in original), 1869, ibid.

59. E. Upton to Emily Upton, Nov. 21, 1868, Jan. 3, Feb. 9, 14, 1869, ibid. Upton never refers to this Dodge by his first name. Richard I. Dodge, USMA Class of 1848, and Henry C. Dodge, Class of 1863, are the only contemporary academy graduates by this name, and according to George Cullum, neither was near Memphis at the time. See *Biographical Register*, 2:356–7, 3:7. Francis Heitman's entries in *Historical Register and Dictionary of the United States Army* are too vague to discern who else it might have been.

60. E. Upton to Emily Upton, Feb. 4, Dec. 15, 1869, closing with "Your affectionate husband," TMFP.

61. E. Upton to Emily Upton, Feb. 2, Mar. 1, 1869, ibid.

62. E. Upton to Emily Upton, Jan. 24, Feb. 2, 20 (emphasis in original), 1869, ibid.

63. E. Upton to Emily Upton, Dec. 1, 9, 1868, Feb. 11, 1869, ibid.; undated sketch, ibid.; E. Upton to Emily Upton, Feb. 20, 1869, ibid.

64. The correspondence often employs the initial "R," but twice the name "Rawles" appears. According to George Cullum, Rawles was stationed at Key West the winter of 1868–69. *Biographical Register*, 2:799. Upton implied that he was a classmate. See E. Upton to Emily Upton, Feb. 8, 1869, TMFP.

65. E. Upton to Emily Upton, Jan. 23, 27, Feb. 8, 1869, TMFP.

66. E. Upton to Emily Upton, Nov. 21, 1868, Mar. 4, 1869, ibid. Stewart never became secretary of the Treasury. See *DAB*, 9(2):3–5.

67. E. Upton to Emily Upton, Feb. 7, 1869, TMFP.

68. E. Upton to J. Upton, May 7, 1868, GCHD; E. Upton to J. H. Wilson, Oct. 15, 1868, WPLC (emphasis in original); E. Upton to Maria Upton, Mar. 4, 1868, HLOM. This last is one of several letters Upton wrote to his sister in French.

69. Wilson, *Life of John A. Rawlins*, chaps. 17–19; E. Upton to J. H. Wilson, Dec. 12, 1868, WPLC.

70. E. Upton to J. H. Wilson, Feb. 27, 1869, ibid.; E. Upton to J. Upton, May 7, 1868, GCHD; E. Upton to T. Jenckes, Jan. 14, 1869, Thomas A. Jenckes Papers, Library of Congress. Stephen Ambrose misidentifies Jenckes as Upton's congressman. Jenckes was from Rhode Island; Upton never lived in the state. See *Upton and the Army*, 69, 166n33.

71. E. Upton to Emily Upton, Jan. 27, Feb. 12, Dec. 4 (opening with "My dear Pet"), 1869, TMFP.

72. E. Upton to Emily Upton, Dec. 23, 24, 1868, Jan. 27, Feb. 4, 1869, ibid. Several other letters also express this concern.

73. E. Upton to Emily Upton, Dec. 15, 1868, closing "Your devoted husband," ibid.

74. E. Upton to Emily Upton, Jan. 26, Feb. 24, 1869, ibid. See also E. Upton to J. H. Wilson, Feb. 27, 1869, WPLC.

75. E. Upton to Emily Upton, Feb. 27, Mar. 4 (opening "My dear Emily"), 1869, TMFP.

76. E. Upton to J. H. Wilson, May 15, 1869, WPLC; E. Upton to [a sister], Mar. 28, 1869, in *L&L*, 233–34; E. Upton to J. H. Wilson, June 2, Dec. 31, 1869, WPLC.

77. E. Upton to J. H. Wilson, June 2, 1869, ibid.

78. See chapter 8.

79. E. Upton to J. H. Wilson, June 2, 1869, WPLC; Warner, *Generals in Gray*, 8.

80. Jamieson, *Crossing the Deadly Ground*, 6–9; E. Upton to J. H. Wilson, Sept. 21, 1869, WPLC. The Schofield Board did not formally adopt Upton's recommendations, but its product very much resembled his submission. The War Department, for reasons not altogether clear, did not endorse the board's findings. See Jamieson, *Crossing the Deadly Ground*, 7–9.

81. E. Upton to the Adjutant General of the Army, June 8, 1869, Letters Received by the Office of the Adjutant General, RG 94, NARA; Maj. Gen. Thomas H. Ruger to the Adjutant General, June 9, 1869, ibid. Sherman's handwritten reply is at the bottom of Adjutant General to Commanding General, June 12, 1869, ibid. See also Brig. Gen. E. D. Townsend to E. Upton, June 24, 1869, File 2666, RG94, NARA.

82. E. Upton to J. H. Wilson, July 17, 1869, WPLC.

83. E. Martin Upton to E. Upton, Mar. 3, 1870, DFP; E. Upton to J. H. Wilson, July 17, Sept. 21, Oct. 27, 1869, WPLC; E. Martin Upton to E. Upton, Oct. 18, 1869, DFP; E. Upton to the Adjutant General, Oct. 12, 1869, Letters Received by the Office of the Adjutant General, RG 94, NARA.

84. E. Upton to Emily Upton, Jan. 26, 1869, TMFP; E. Upton to J. H. Wilson, Dec. 31, 1869, Apr. 26, June 17, 1870, WPLC; Pehrson, "James Harrison Wilson," 70–72.

85. E. Martin Upton to E. Upton, Oct. 10, 1869, DFP. Emily wrote numerous letters to Upton that document her declining condition that are in the Dickman Family Papers.

86. Dr. Kirkwood to E. Upton, June 26, 1870, in *L&L*, 236–37 (emphasis in original); N. Martin to E. Upton, Mar. 31, 1870, DFP.

87. Elvina Martin to N. Martin, Apr. 17, 1870, DFP; E. Upton to "My Dear Parents," May 11, 1870, in *L&L*, 239–40; E. Upton to J. H. Wilson, Apr. 26, 1870, WPLC.

88. E. Upton to "My Dear Parents," May 11, 1870, in *L&L*, 239–40; E. Upton to "My Dear Sister," May 22, 1870, ibid., 240.

89. E. Upton to "My Dear Sister," May 22, 1870, ibid., 240; E. Upton to "My Dear Parents," May 11, 1870, ibid., 239–40. See also ibid., 246 (text).

Chapter 5

1. E. Upton to H. A. du Pont, June 20, 1870, DPPHL; E. Upton to J. H. Wilson, Aug. 21, 1870, WPLC; D. H. Mahan to W. T. Sherman, Sept. 13, 1869, WSPLC.

2. U.S. Congress, House, *Report of the Secretary of War* (1871), 2:441–42.

3. E. Upton to J. H. Wilson, Feb. 20, 1871, WPLC; General Orders No. 8, U.S. Corps of Cadets, July 18, 1870, USMA Archives; General Orders No. 10, U.S. Corps of Cadets, July 26, 1870, ibid.; General Orders No. 12, U.S. Corps of Cadets, Aug. 11, 1870, ibid.; General Orders No. 18, U.S. Corps of Cadets, Sept. 9, 1870, ibid.; General Orders No. 19, U.S. Corps of Cadets, Sept. 11, 1870, ibid.

4. E. Upton to J. H. Wilson, Aug. 21, 1870, WPLC; *L&L*, 275. Technically, hazing was not permitted, yet it was tolerated.

5. E. Upton to J. H. Wilson, Aug. 21, 1870, WPLC. At that time the academy's Dialectic Society was a cadet debate club. See Ambrose, *Duty, Honor, Country*, 137–38.

6. O. Howard, *Autobiography*, 1:92; *L&L*, 278.

7. E. Upton to "Dear Mother" [Mrs. Martin], June 1, 1873, in *L&L*, 282–83.

8. E. Upton to "My Dear Father and Mother," Jan. 28, 1872, ibid., 280; E. Upton to [Daniel and Electa Upton?], May 25, 1873, ibid., 280–81.

9. U.S. Congress, House, *Expulsion of Cadets*, 2–4, 7, 42–44; *L&L*, 257–60.

10. Dillard, "United States Military Academy," 85; U.S. Congress, House, *Expulsion of Cadets*, 14, 26; *L&L*, 261–62; Dillard, "United States Military Academy," 85–86.

11. U.S. Congress, House, *Expulsion of Cadets*, 7–8 (emphasis added).

12. T. Pitcher and E. Upton to "the inspector of the Academy," Feb. 9, 1871, in *L&L*, 266–70; E. Upton to J. H. Wilson, Feb. 24, 1871, WPLC (emphasis in original); Dillard, "United States Military Academy," 86–87.

13. *L&L*, 271; U.S. Congress, House, *Expulsion of Cadets*, 44.

14. U.S. Congress, House, *Expulsion of Cadets*, 50–51; Pappas, *To the Point*, 363–65.

15. E. Upton to J. H. Wilson, Feb. 20, 1871, WPLC.

16. Pappas, *To the Point*, 365; *L&L*, 271. See also Ambrose, *Duty, Honor, Country*, 278–79; Dillard, "United States Military Academy," 87–88; and Crackel, *West Point*, 216–17.

17. Dillard, "United States Military Academy," 192–96; U.S. Congress, House, *Report of the Secretary of War* (1870), 2:301.

18. Cadet J. W. Smith to E. Upton, June 25, 1871 [two letters], Adjutant Letters Received, 1853–72, USMA Archives; Cadet C. R. Tyler to E. Upton, June 21, 1871, ibid.; Cadet F. R. Rice to E. Upton, June 28, 1871, ibid.; E. Upton to Capt. E. L. Boynton, June 30,

1871, ibid. Even then the controversy did not die. In August 1874 the *New National Era* demanded an investigation of the manner in which Smith had been examined in those two subjects. For accounts of Smith's travails, see Dillard, "United States Military Academy," 193–202; and Pappas, *To the Point*, 373–77.

19. Flipper, *Colored Cadet*, 120–22, 265. Lowell D. and Sara H. Black, editors of Flipper's autobiography, attribute to Upton other contacts with Flipper, but they have their dates confused, describing incidents that happened in 1876 when Upton had departed the academy in the summer of 1875. Also, the Blacks state that Upton "frequently" counseled the cadet, but their source for this information, a magazine article reprinted in Flipper's autobiography, tells of only one time that it happened, that being when Upton thought he was about to quit. See Flipper, *Colored Cadet*, 143–44, 158–60; and Black and Black, *Officer and a Gentleman*, 69–72, 71n36.

20. Flipper, *Colored Cadet*, 134, 321–22.

21. Upton's correspondence is silent on this issue, but this seems a reasonable conclusion, especially given that Flipper had concluded that Smith was responsible for much of what had happened to him. See *Colored Cadet*, 164–65. For a brief account of Smith's and Flipper's experiences, see Crackel, *West Point*, 145–46.

22. E. Upton to H. A. du Pont, Mar. 14, 1873, DPPHL; *L&L*, 274; Reed, *Cadet Life*, 195–96.

23. *New York Times*, Mar. 3, 5, 1873; General Orders No. 5, U.S. Corps of Cadets, Mar. 4, 1873, USMA Archives.

24. General Orders No. 6, U.S. Corps of Cadets, Mar. 5, 1873, USMA Archives; Reed, *Cadet Life*, 196, 200–201; *New York Times*, Mar. 6, 7, 1873.

25. E. Upton to H. A. du Pont, Mar. 7, 14, 1873, DPPHL.

26. General Orders No. 10, U.S. Corps of Cadets, Mar. 7, 1873, USMA Archives (emphasis in original).

27. E. Upton to Superintendent, USMA, Mar. 7, 1873, Register of Letters Received, Adjutant USMA, ibid.

28. U.S. Congress, House, *Report of the Secretary of War* (1872), 2:795. Pitcher believed, almost certainly correctly, that he had been removed due to the January 1871 honor incident. See Pitcher to the Secretary of War, May 11, 1871, Superintendent's Letter Book, USMA Archives, vol. 5.

29. E. Upton to J. H. Wilson, June 2, 1869, WPLC; E. Upton to H. A. du Pont, Jan. 18, 1872, DPPHL (emphasis in original); U.S. Congress, House, *Report of the Secretary of War* (1871), 2:429.

30. E. Upton to J. H. Wilson, Feb. 20, 24, 1871, WPLC; Pappas, *To the Point*, 377–78, 388; E. Upton to "Dear General" [Sherman], Oct. 15, 1871, Upton Collection, USMA Library Special Collections. The academy's board of visitors concurred with Upton's analysis regarding the need for "new blood" on the Academic Board. See U.S. Congress, House, *Report of the Secretary of War* (1871), 2:438–39.

31. E. Upton to H. A. du Pont, June 30, 1870, Apr. 7, 1871, DPPHL. See also E. Upton to W. T. Sherman, Apr. 15, 1873, WSPLC.

32. E. Upton to H. A. du Pont, Apr. 7, 1871, DPPHL.

33. Ibid.; Ambrose, *Upton and the Army*, 78.

34. E. Upton to H. A. du Pont, Mar. 15, Apr. 7, 1871, Dec. 24 [28?], 1872, DPPHL; *L&L*, 206–7; Ambrose, *Upton and the Army*, 77.

35. E. Upton to H. A. du Pont, Mar. 7, 13, 14, June 17, 19, 1873, DPPHL.

36. E. Upton to H. A. du Pont, Aug. 12, 1873, ibid. See also E. Upton to H. A. du Pont, Aug. 2, 1873, ibid.

37. E. Upton to H. A. du Pont, Aug. 23, 1873, ibid.; Ambrose, *Upton and the Army*, 78–79.

38. E. Upton to H. A. du Pont, Aug. 23, 1873, DPPHL; Upton, *Infantry Tactics*; U.S. War Department, *Cavalry Tactics*; U.S. War Department, *Artillery Tactics*; E. Upton to H. A. du Pont, Oct. 31, 1874, DPPHL. Stephen Ambrose has confused the publication dates of the three manuals. See *Upton and the Army*, 79, 166n25. Based upon the comments in the *Army and Navy Journal*, it is clear that the infantry and cavalry manuals came out in the spring of 1874, while Upton's letter to du Pont of October 31, 1874, (cited below) states that the artillery manual had just been published. The copyright for both artillery and cavalry manuals were held by the War Department, but Upton kept the credit for the infantry manual and hence the copyright and royalties.

39. E. Upton to H. A. du Pont, Feb. 24, 1875, DPPHL; E. Upton to W. T. Sherman, Feb. 6, 1875, WSPLC; W. T. Sherman to W. H. Morris, Aug. 17, 1882, cited in Jamieson, *Crossing the Deadly Ground*, 9.

40. *ANJ*, Apr. 4, 1874. The journal mentions "two arms" rather than "three" because the artillery manual was not published until the following October.

41. E. Upton to W. C. Church, Apr. 7, 1874, CPLC; *ANJ*, July 4, 11, 1874. Despite the relative lack of opposition to the cavalry tactics in letters published by the *Journal*, the debate over the role of cavalry in future conflicts persisted into the early years of the twentieth century. Maj. Gen. Wesley Merritt's article in the initial issue of the *Journal of the Military Service Institution of the United States*, though not attacking Upton by name, assailed his concept of cavalry operations. See "Cavalry: Its Organization and Armament," *JMSIUS* 1, no. 1 (1880): 42–52.

42. E. Upton to J. H. Wilson, May 4, 1874, WPLC.

43. E. Upton to W. T. Sherman, May 29, 1875, WSPLC; E. Upton to J. H. Wilson, May 29, 1875, WPLC.

44. E. Upton to W. C. Church, Mar. 7, 1874, CPLC; E. Upton to W. T. Sherman, May 7, 1875, WSPLC; E. Upton to W. C. Church, May 10, 1875, CPLC.

45. E. Upton to H. A. du Pont, Oct. 31, 1874, DPPHL; Upton, "Prussian Company Column," 307–9. The *International Review* was a highly respected journal that specialized in topics on politics, economics, history, and the military. Among its editors were Henry Cabot Lodge and Henry Gannett.

46. Upton, "Prussian Company Column," 313.

47. E. Upton to J. H. Wilson, Aug. 21, 1870, WPLC.

48. Philip H. Sheridan, *Personal Memoirs*, 2:451–52; Upton, *Infantry Tactics*, viii (emphasis added).

49. E. Upton to W. T. Sherman, Feb. 3, 1873, WSPLC. It is not clear how many times and for how long Sara stayed at West Point. Many of Upton's letters to du Pont state, "Miss Sara sends her regards." In December 1872 he told du Pont that she had left for the winter: "I am entirely alone." Six months later he again told his friend that she sent her regards. See E. Upton to H. A. du Pont, Dec. 27, 1872, Aug. 12, 1873, DPPHL.

50. For example, see Dillard, "United States Military Academy," 174–75.

51. E. Upton to J. H. Wilson, June 17, 1870, WPLC. The annual reports of the Board of Visitors, the secretary of war, and the superintendents during this period make

clear that there was a substantial struggle not only within the academy but also between politicians and the army staff regarding the course of study and admission standards at West Point. See also Ambrose, *Duty, Honor, Country*, 198–202.

52. Pappas, *To the Point*, 413–14; Crackel, *West Point*, 144–45, 188–95; E. Upton to Maria, Aug. 16, 1875, HLOM.

53. E. Upton to W. T. Sherman, Sept. 3, 1874, Letters Received by Headquarters of the Army, 1800–1899, RG 108, NARA; E. Upton to W. T. Sherman, Sept. 23, 1874, WSPLC.

54. E. Upton to W. T. Sherman, Sept. 10, 1874, May 7, 1875, WSPLC.

55. William W. Belknap to E. Upton, June 23, 1875, Letters Sent by the Secretary of War, Military Affairs, 1800–1899, RG 107, NARA; W. T. Sherman to E. Upton, July 12, 1875, File 2666, RG 94, ibid.; Upton to W. T. Sherman, Sept. 3, 1874, Letters Received by Headquarters of the Army, 1800–1899, RG 108, ibid. It is not clear what Upton meant by the "Asiatic problem." Almost every issue of the *Army and Navy Journal* during this period detailed the British struggles in Afghanistan, and as outlined in chapter 4, Upton was somewhat familiar with developments in China.

56. William W. Belknap to E. Upton, June 23, 1875, Letters Sent by the Secretary of War, Military Affairs, 1800–1899, RG 107, ibid.; *Who Was Who in America*, 1:414; *New York Times*, Sept. 13, 1915. See also Utley, *Frontier Regulars*, 147–48.

57. *Who Was Who in America*, 1:1078; *National Cyclopedia of American Biography*, 27:311–12; *New York Times*, Mar. 16, 1926.

58. Upton to Maria, July 27, 1875, HLOM. This letter provides a vivid account of Upton's journey through Nevada and California and especially of his experiences at Yosemite. It implies that he wrote others as he crossed the United States, but these are now missing.

Chapter 6

1. W. T. Sherman to "Governor General of Calcutta," July 12, 1875, WSPLC; W. T. Sherman to "Commander-in-Chief of Her Majesty's Forces in India," July 12, 1875, ibid.; W. T. Sherman to "His Imperial Highness, The Grand Duke," July 12, 1875, ibid. I have been unable to find the letter Fish wrote; Upton, however, mentions it in his correspondence. See E. Upton to the Adjutant General, Dec. 24, 1876, Letters Received by the Office of the Adjutant General, RG 94, NARA.

2. W. T. Sherman to "Whom it may concern," July 12, 1875, WSPLC.

3. E. Upton to [unknown family member], Aug. 15, 1875, in *L&L*, 309–10; E. Upton to Maria Upton, Aug. 16, 1875, HLOM; E. Upton to W. T. Sherman, Sept. 10, 23, 1874, WSPLC; E. Upton to H. A. du Pont, Nov. 23, 1874, DPPHL.

4. E. Upton to Maria Upton, Aug. 16, 1875, HLOM.

5. E. Upton to [unknown family member], Aug. 27, 1875, in *AAE*, 374; Various letters, *L&L*, 315–17; E. Upton to [unknown family member], Sept. 23, 1875, in *AAE*, 382; E. Upton to [unknown family member], Aug. 27, 1875, ibid., 374; E. Upton to [unknown family member], Sept. 7, 1875, in *L&L*, 314; E. Upton to [unknown family member], Sept. 23, 1875, in *AAE*, 380.

6. E. Upton to [unknown family member], Sept. 7, 1875, in *L&L*, 312–13; E. Upton to [unknown family member], Aug. 31, 1875, in *AAE*, 375–77.

7. *AAE*, 12; E. Upton to J. H. Wilson, Feb. 9, 1876, WPLC. For a description of the foundries, arsenals, and factories the Americans visited, see Joseph Sanger, "Artillery in the East," *JMSIUS* 1, no. 2 (1880): 228–29.

8. E. Upton to [unknown family member,] Sept. 23, 1875, in *AAE*, 378–79, 383.

9. E. Upton to [unknown family member], Sept. 7, 1875, in *L&L*, 313–14; E. Upton to [unknown family member], Sept. 23, 1875, in *AAE*, 381; E. Upton to J. H. Wilson, Feb. 9, 1876, WPLC.

10. E. Upton to [unknown family member], Oct. 5, 1875, in *L&L*, 387–92; E. Upton to Maria Upton, Oct. 24, 1875, HLOM. Sanger agreed with Upton's evaluation of recently built forts, though he praised older fortifications. See "Artillery in the East," 238–44. The letter to Maria cited here is another example of Peter Michie's editing of Upton's correspondence misrepresenting fact. An excerpt of the letter can be found in *L&L*, 318–22. Its opening paragraph gives the impression that Upton is describing events in Shanghai. This is because Michie deleted the letter's opening paragraphs, which make clear that the arsenal and the dinner were in Tientsin.

11. E. Upton to [unknown family member], Oct. 1, 1875, in *AAE*, 387; E. Upton to [unknown family member], Nov. 13, 1875, in *L&L*, 323; E. Upton to J. H. Wilson, Feb. 9, 1876, WPLC. The quality of the individual artillery pieces and the caliber of Chinese fortifications impressed Sanger, though. See "Artillery in the East," 232–47.

12. *AAE*, 19–20.

13. Ibid., 26–29.

14. Ibid., 29–30.

15. Sanger came to a similar conclusion. See "Artillery in the East," 251.

16. E. Upton to J. H. Wilson, Feb. 9, 1876, WPLC; *AAE*, 32.

17. *AAE*, 29, 31–32.

18. William H. Seward to Mr. [Frederick] Low (American Minister to China), Oct. 31, 1871; and Mr. [Frederick] Low to "one of General Upton's friends," Feb. 29, 1872, in *L&L*, 284–89.

19. E. Upton to [unknown family member], Aug. 15, 1875, in *L&L*, 309–10. It seems likely that the "Mr. Stewart" mentioned was Alexander Stewart, Grant's failed nominee for secretary of the Treasury. See chapter 4, note 60.

20. E. Upton to Maria Upton, Aug. 16, 1875, HLOM; E. Upton to Mr. Shepard, Oct. 28, 1876, in *L&L*, 290–98; E. Upton to J. H. Wilson, Feb. 9, 1876, WPLC; William H. Belknap to Hamilton Fish, Feb. 3, 1876, Letters Sent by the Secretary of War, Military Affairs, 1800–1899, RG 107, NARA.

21. For an analysis of the Mexican-American War, in which Upton compares the actual costs of fighting the war with a mixed force of volunteers and regulars to the hypothetical costs of fighting the war with a "properly" maintained regular army, see *MPUS*, 218–21.

22. E. Upton to J. H. Wilson, Apr. 19, 1878, WPLC. This statement ignores entirely the scandals that had engulfed the Grant administration, but elsewhere Upton was not silent on that issue. Chapter 8 will address this is some detail. The Chinese nature of American military policy is a common theme in Upton's writing. For other examples, see *MPUS*, vii–viii; and E. Upton to J. A. Garfield, May 6, 1878, GPLC.

23. E. Upton to [unknown family member], Nov. 13, 1875, in *L&L*, 322–26; E. Upton to [unknown family member], Dec. 10, 1875, ibid., 328–31.

24. E. Upton to [unknown family member], Dec. 17, 1875, ibid., 331–36; E. Upton to [unknown family member], Dec. 23, 1875, ibid., 336–40; E. Upton to [unknown family member], Jan. 9, 1876, in *AAE*, 407–8; E. Upton to [unknown family member], Jan. 20, 1876, ibid., 409–12; E. Upton to [unknown family member], Jan. 27,

1876, in *L&L*, 343–47; E. Upton to [unknown family member], Feb. 20, 1876, ibid., 348; E. Upton to [unknown family member], Feb. 6, 1876, in *AAE*, 415–16. Upton's party spent almost twice as much time in India than in any other nation visited on the journey. They were in Japan for four weeks, China for four weeks, Persia for six weeks (a large portion of which was spent crossing that nation on horseback), Italy for four weeks, Russia for eight weeks, Austria-Hungary and Serbia combined for four weeks, Germany for four weeks, and France and Great Britain combined for three weeks.

25. E. Upton to J. H. Wilson, Feb. 9, 1876, WPLC (emphasis added); E. Upton to [unknown family member], Jan. 9, 1876, in *AAE*, 408–9; E. Upton to [unknown family member], Jan. 16, 1876, in *L&L*, 341; E. Upton to [unknown family member], Feb. 8, 1876, ibid., 415; E. Upton to Maria Upton, Jan. 2, 1876, HLOM.

26. E. Upton to J. H. Wilson, Feb. 9, 1876, WPLC; E. Upton to [unknown family member]. Dec. 10, 1875, in *L&L*, 330–31. The parable of the mustard seed can be found in Matthew 13:31–32. The King James Version reads: "Another parable he put forth unto them, saying, The kingdom of heaven is like to a grain of mustard seed, which a man took, and sowed in his field: Which indeed is the least of all seeds: but when it is grown, it is the greatest among herbs, and becometh a tree, so that the birds of the air cometh and lodge in the branches thereof."

27. E. Upton to [unknown family member], Feb. 6, 1876, in *AAE*, 416.

28. Ibid., 75–77.

29. E. Upton to [unknown family member], Dec. 17, 1875, in *L&L*, 331–32; *AAE*, 77.

30. E. Upton to [unknown family member], Jan. 20, 1876, ibid., 411 (emphasis added).

31. E. Upton to Maria Upton, Jan. 2, 1876, HLOM; *MPUS*, 235–36. Regarding the decision not to employ a cadre system at the start of the Civil War, see Weigley, *History of the United States Army*, 287.

32. *AAE*, 35, 80–81.

33. Ibid., viii, 319.

34. Chapter 8 addresses a circumstance that likely provoked this complaint.

35. *AAE*, 52–53. A large part of Upton's *Military Policy of the United States* is dedicated to an examination of Stanton's actions during the Civil War.

36. See S. Cohen, *Indian Army*, 4–29.

37. Ibid., 7; Mason, *Matter of Honour*, 83, 277–78; S. Cohen, *Indian Army*, 33–34, 54–55; *AAE*, 77; Farwell, *Armies of the Raj*, 39, 174–77. Philip Mason provides a detailed discussion of the failures of British leadership. See *Matter of Honour*, chaps. 11–12.

38. E. Upton to [unknown family member], Feb. 20, Mar. 6, 1876, in *L&L*, 348–59; E. Upton to [unknown family member], Mar. 19, 1876, ibid., 359–67; E. Upton to [unknown family member], Mar. 20, 1876, ibid., 369.

39. E. Upton to [unknown family member], Mar. 25, 1876, in *AAE*, 430–34.

40. Ibid., 90–92, 93.

41. E. Upton to [unknown family member], Mar. 19, 1876, in *L&L*, 362, 367; E. Upton to [unknown family member], Apr. 15, 1876, in *AAE*, 435; E. Upton to [unknown family member], Mar. 20, 1876, in *L&L*, 368.

42. *ANJ*, Aug. 17, 1878.

43. E. Upton to W. C. Church, Aug. 16, 1878, CPLC.

44. E. Upton to [unknown family member], Mar. 20, 1876, in *L&L*, 370. For a brief description of the Belknap scandal, see Weigley, *History of the United States Army*, 287.

45. E. Upton to [unknown family member], May 7, 1876, in *L&L*, 372–73. In editing Upton's correspondence, Peter Michie often omitted the names of people Upton mentioned. In the letter cited here, he deleted the name of the person who "sinned deeply." But this letter's content, as well as his March 20, 1876, correspondence with a family member (cited above) and his July 19, 1876, letter to Wilson (cited below) and events transpiring at the time, strongly suggest the "sinner" was William Belknap.

46. E. Upton to J. H. Wilson, July 19, 1876, WPLC.

47. See, among many others, Ambrose, *Upton and the Army*, 88–89, 98; Weigley, *Towards an American Army*, 100–126; Andrews, "Years of Frustration," 267.

48. *AAE*, 75; W. T. Sherman to J. A. Garfield, Feb. 9, 1878, GPLC.

49. E. Upton to [unknown family member], Apr. 15, 1876, in *AAE*, 434–37. Sanger observed that Persia seemed to be "infested by roving bands of robbers." "Artillery in the East," 250.

50. E. Upton to [unknown family member], Apr. 30, 1876, in *AAE*, 437–40. For reasons that are not clear, there is far less correspondence available from the European portion of Upton's trip than its Asian phase. As a result, much less can be known about his exact itinerary, who he met, and what he observed.

51. E. Upton to John Upton, May 7, 1868, GCHD; E. Upton to [unknown family member], June 4, 1876, in *L&L*, 378.

52. *AAE*, 140–41.

53. Various letters, in *L&L*, 377–80. In his correspondence Upton refers to a Mr. Atkinson as the chargé d'affaires in St. Petersburg. Almost certainly this was Col. Hoffman Atkinson. See Atkinson's obituary, *New York Times*, Nov. 29, 1901.

54. E. Upton to Maj. Gen. E. Townsend, Aug. 27, 1876, Letters Received by the Office of the Adjutant General, 1871–80, RG 94, NARA; E. Upton to [unknown family member], Aug. 20, 1876, in *L&L*, 382–83. Atkinson was a close friend of Wilson's and may have opened a few doors for Upton because of that friendship. See E. Upton to J. H. Wilson, Oct. 12, 1876, WPLC.

55. E. Upton to J. H. Wilson, July 19, 1876, WPLC; E. Upton to [Unknown family member], Aug. 20, 1876, in *L&L*, 382. Upton was not unaware of the class nature of the struggle that would ensue in Russia. See E. Upton to [unknown family member], July 16, 1876, in *L&L*, 380.

56. E. Upton to [Unknown family member], Aug. 20, 1876, in *L&L*, 383.

57. Ibid., 384.

58. Upton, *AAE*, 160. Regarding the importance of the Russian army's education system, see Menning, *Bayonets before Bullets*, 33–38.

59. Upton dedicated twelve pages to his report on Japan, nineteen to China, fifty-four to India, seven to Persia, forty-seven to Italy, fourteen to Russia, twenty-nine to Austria, thirty-three to Germany, twenty-four to France, and nineteen to Britain.

60. For an excellent discussion of the substance of the Miliutin Reforms and their consequences, particularly as they affected the larger organization, see Menning, *Bayonets before Bullets*, chap. 1. John L. H. Keep is more interested in the manner in which these changes affected individual soldiers. See *Soldiers of the Tsar*, chap. 15.

61. E. Upton to Maj. Gen. E. Townsend, Sept. 11, 1876, Letters Received by the Office of the Adjutant General, 1871–1880, RG 94, NARA.

62. *AAE*, 183–190.

63. Ibid., 169–81.

64. Deák, *Beyond Nationalism*, 156–64, 187–89. For a discussion of the Honvédség and Landwehr, see Rothenberg, *Army of Francis Joseph*, 75–77.

65. Rothenberg, *Army of Francis Joseph*, 78–80.

66. Deligrad is a small town on the Morava River approximately ninety-five miles south of Belgrade. The nearest large town, Alexinatz (modern Aleksinac), is another six miles up the Morava and at the time was the location of the advance guard of the Serbian army.

67. E. Upton to the Adjutant General, Sept. 25, 1876, Letters Received by the Office of the Adjutant General, 1871–80, RG 94, NARA.

68. Anderson, *Eastern Question*, 186–87; E. Upton to the Adjutant General, Sept. 25, 1876, Letters Received by the Office of the Adjutant General, 1871–80, RG 94, NARA; E. Upton to "My dear [Hoffman] Atkinson," Oct. 12, 1876, WPLC.

69. E. Upton to the Adjutant General, Sept. 25, 1876, Letters Received by the Office of the Adjutant General, 1871–80, RG 94, NARA; E. Upton to "My dear Atkinson," Oct. 12, 1876, WPLC; E. Upton to J. H. Wilson, Oct. 19, 1876, ibid.

70. Ekmecic, "Serbian Army in the Wars of 1876–1878," 287–95; Stokes, "Serbian Military Doctrine and the Crisis of 1875–1878" Stokes, "Social Role of the Serbian Army"; Anderson, *Eastern Question;* Castellan, *History of the Balkans*, chap. 12; Jelavich, *Russia's Balkan Entanglements*, chap. 4; E. Upton to "My dear Atkinson," Oct. 12, 1876, WPLC; and E. Upton to J. H. Wilson, Oct. 19, 1876, ibid.

71. E. Upton to the Adjutant General, Oct. 1, 1876, File 2666, RG 94, NARA; E. Upton to [unknown family member], Oct. 8, 1876, in *L&L*, 385–86; E. Upton to Maria Upton, Oct. 27, 1876, HLOM.

72. E. Upton to the Adjutant General, Dec. 27, 1876, Letters Received by the Office of the Adjutant General, 1871–80, RG 94, NARA; J. C. Bancroft Davis to E. Upton, July 21, 22, 23, 1876, ibid.

73. E. Upton to J. C. Bancroft Davis, July 26, 1876, ibid.

74. J.C. Bancroft Davis to E. Upton, July 29, 1876, ibid.

75. E. Upton to J. C. Bancroft Davis, Aug. 2, 1876, ibid.; N. Fish to E. Upton, Aug. 17, 1876, ibid.; E. Upton to the Adjutant General, Dec. 27, 1876, ibid.; E. Upton to W. T. Sherman, Aug. 26, 1876, ibid.; W. T. Sherman to U. S. Grant, Aug. 26, 1876, ibid.; U. S. Grant to W. T. Sherman, Aug. 26, 1876, ibid.; W. T. Sherman to E. Upton, Aug. 26, 1876, ibid.

76. E. Upton to N. Fish, Aug. 28, 1876, ibid.; N. Fish to E. Upton, Aug. 30, 1876, ibid.

77. E. Upton to the Adjutant General, Dec. 27, 1876, ibid.; E. Upton to J. H. Wilson, Oct. 19, 1876, WPLC.

78. E. Upton to Maria Upton, Oct. 22, 1876, HLOM; E. Upton to the Adjutant General, Dec. 27, 1876, Letters Received by the Office of the Adjutant General, 1871–80, RG 94, NARA.

79. *DAB*, 3(1):134–35, 3(2):406; H. Fish to J. D. Cameron, Jan. 13, 1877, Letters of the Department of State, 1784–1906, RG 59, NARA.

80. Memo, George W. McCrary to the Adjutant General, [n.d., May 1877], Letters Sent by the Secretary of War, Military Affairs, 1800–1899, RG 107, NARA.

81. E. Upton to "My dear General" [W. T. Sherman?], July 6, 1877, Upton Papers, USAMHI.

82. E. Upton to [unknown family member], Oct. 8, 1876, in *L&L*, 385–86.

83. *AAE*, 195–202.

84. Ibid., 198, 201.

85. Ibid., 207–13, 223–24.

86. Ibid., 203–5, 213–18.

87. Ibid., 219. It is a conclusion with which Michael Howard agrees. See *Franco-Prussian War*, 455. See also Wawro, *Franco-Prussian War*, 80–84.

88. *AAE*, 218–21.

89. Rosinski, *German Army*, 96–99, 114–16; Demeter, *German Officer Corps*, 20–32, 86–87.

90. *AAE*, 219; Craig, *Politics of the Prussian Army*, 136–59. For discussions of the tension that developed between Moltke and Bismarck as the war dragged on, see M. Howard, *Franco-Prussian War*, esp. 350–57; and Wawro, *Franco-Prussian War*, 278–80, 290–92, 304–5. Gordon Craig describes the manner in which Manteuffel "engineered" the fall of Minister of War Eduard von Bonin in 1859. See *Politics of the Prussian Army*, 139–43.

91. Craig, *Politics of the Prussian Army*, 215.

92. E. Upton to Julia Upton, Feb. 16, 1879, GCHD. Upton saw little difference between a dictatorship and a monarchy and used the two words interchangeably.

93. Only two pieces of evidence suggest Upton visited France. The first is a letter he wrote to James Wilson while in Berlin in which he gives a forwarding address in Paris. See E. Upton to James Wilson, Oct. 19, 1876, WPLC. The second is a letter to his sister in which he states: "I shall go to Paris via . . . Brussels, and hope to arrive there about November 5th. If possible I shall sail so as to spend Christmas at Willowbrook." See E. Upton to Maria Upton, Oct. 22, 1876, HLOM. This last letter makes no mention of Britain, and given the time constraints Upton imposed upon himself here, he left himself little time to visit that country. It therefore seems likely that he visited France but briefly before departing for the United States and Britain perhaps not at all. If this is what happened, he likely based his report on the French army almost entirely on his observation of its maneuvers while on his honeymoon in 1868. As for Britain, his report on its army is not very informative and could have been written based upon what he had read as well as on his observations in India.

94. *AAE*, 248, 249.

95. Ibid., 250, 254, 255–60.

96. Ibid., 253–54, 268–69. This is almost exactly what happened after the British Expeditionary Force's virtual destruction in the campaigns of 1914 and 1915.

97. Beckett, *Amateur Military Tradition*, 182. For an excellent discussion of the purchase system and the reasons for its elimination, see Harries-Jenkins, *Army in Victorian Society*, chap. 3. See also Huntington, *Soldier and the State*, 47.

98. Harries-Jenkins, *Army in Victorian Society*, 114, 128–29; Bond, *Victorian Army and the Staff College*, 133–35, 141; Huntington, *Soldier and the State*, 43–44, 49–50.

99. E. Upton to Maria Upton, Nov. 25, 1875, HLOM.

100. *AAE*, 270–316; E. Upton to the Adjutant General, Sept. 25, Dec. 27, 1876, Letters Received by the Office of the Adjutant General, 1871–80, RG 94, NARA; E. Upton to "My dear Atkinson," Oct. 12, 1876, WPLC; E. Upton to J. H. Wilson, Oct. 19, 1876, ibid.

Chapter 7

1. E. Upton to J. H. Wilson, Jan. 4, 1877, WPLC; E. Upton to Maria, Jan. 22, 1877, HLOM; E. Upton to H. A. du Pont, Apr. 1, 1877, DPPHL.

2. E. Upton to J. H. Wilson, May 19, 1877, WPLC; Annual Report, Artillery School, Ft. Monroe, Va., Nov. 14, 1878, Letters Received by the Office of the Adjutant General, RG 94, NARA; E. Upton to H. A. du Pont, Apr. 1, 1877, DPPHL.

3. E. Upton to H. A. du Pont, Apr. 1 (emphasis added), Sept. 30 (emphasis in original), 1877, DPPHL.

4. E. Upton to W. T. Sherman, Nov. 22, 1877, WSPLC. Stephen Ambrose argues that Upton changed his mind due to pressure from Sherman. "Congress had paid for Upton's European trip so that he could report his observations," according to Ambrose, "not so that he could attack the government." See *Upton and the Army*, 97–98. Ambrose cites a February 9, 1878, letter from Sherman to Upton in the Sherman Papers in the Library of Congress to support this assertion. Based on the letter cited here, it is obvious that long before the general's letter had arrived, Upton had concluded that he would not publish "Military Policy" as part of his report and that Sherman was aware of this decision. Rather than an effort to change Upton's mind, the February 1878 letter likely was an effort to provide him with justification for his decision to delay publication. Moreover, one week before Sherman had written the letter cited above, Upton had written to James Wilson that he would publish the originally conceived last chapter as a separate work. See E. Upton to J. H. Wilson, Feb. 2, 1878, WPLC.

5. E. Upton to H. A. du Pont, Jan. 13, 1878, DPPHL; E. Upton to J. H. Wilson, May 19, July 29, Nov. 15, 1877, Feb. 2, 1878, WPLC.

6. W. T. Sherman to J. A. Garfield, Feb. 9, 1878, GPLC; E. Upton to F. V. Greene, Jan. 25, 1879, GPNYPL; *ANJ*, Feb. 3, 1877; *The Nation*, June 6, 1878; Brown, "General Emory Upton," 126. James Wilson wrote a favorable review of the book for an unknown publication, but I have been unable to locate it. See E. Upton to J. H. Wilson, Mar. 21, 1878, WPLC.

7. *AAE*, 317–20.

8. Ibid., 323–24, 327–37, 353–54, 367.

9. Ibid., 360–61, 366. He does not specifically reference the act, but it is clear that is his meaning.

10. E. Upton to H. A. du Pont, Apr. 1, 1877, DPPHL; *AAE*, 362–63, 367.

11. Ibid., 337–53.

12. Ibid., 323.

13. Ibid., 367–69 (emphasis in original).

14. Ambrose, *Upton and the Army*, 101–2; Weigley, *Towards an American Army*, 109, 124–25.

15. E. Upton to W. A. Johnson, Aug. 6, 1880, GCHD.

16. *AAE*, 337; Cooper, "Army's Search for a Mission," 188; Millis, *Arms and Men*, 146–49; Jamieson, *Crossing the Deadly Ground*, 119; E. Upton to H. A. du Pont, Apr. 11, 1878, DPPHL; E. Upton to J. H. Wilson, Mar. 21, 1878, WPLC.

17. *AAE*, 96–99.

18. Upton, *Tactics for Non-Military Bodies*, 5–6.

19. Ibid., 13 (emphasis added).

20. Ibid., preface (n.p.); E. Upton to W. T. Sherman, Jan. 30, 1880, WSPLC.

21. E. Upton to J. A. Garfield, July 5, 1878, GPLC. See also *AAE*, 368.

22. Ambrose, *Upton and the Army*, 105–6.

23. E. Upton to J. A. Garfield, July 5, 1878, GPLC; E. Upton to J. H. Wilson, July 19, 1876, WPLC. Regarding the army's perception that the Indian wars were far from over, see Jamieson, *Crossing the Deadly Ground*, 120–21.

24. For example, see Ambrose, *Upton and the Army*, 105.

25. E. Upton to J. H. Wilson, Aug. 11, 1877, WPLC. The remainder of the post's garrison, along with its commander, Col. George Getty, had left Fort Monroe to help quell the labor unrest. See Annual Report, Artillery School at Ft. Monroe, Va., Nov. 14, 1878, Letters Received by the Office of the Adjutant General, RG 94, NARA; and E. Upton to F. V. Greene, Aug. 18, 1877, GPNYPL.

26. E. Upton to J. H. Wilson, Feb. 6, 1878, WPLC; E. Upton to Julia Upton, Feb. 16, Oct. 19, 1879, Feb. 1, 1880, GCHD.

27. Pehrson, "James Harrison Wilson," 98–102; Cooper, *Army and Civil Disorder*, 254–58; Katz, *From Appomattox to Montmartre*, 161–83; Messer-Kruse, *Yankee International*, 100–101; Bernstein, *First International in America*, 73–90, 294.

28. E. Upton to "Dear Sister," Dec. 21, 1860, in *L&L*, 30; E. Upton to "Dear Brother" [John], Feb. 1, 1857, GCHD; *MPUS*, xiii, xiv.

29. For an account of the violence in Pittsburgh precipitated by employment of ill-prepared and poorly led militia, see Bruce, *1877*, 144–48, 164–71, 309.

30. E. Upton to H. A. du Pont, June 20, 1878, DPPHL; E. Upton to J. A. Garfield, July 5, 1878, GPLC.

31. Weigley, *Towards an American Army*, 124–25; *AAE*, 323–24; W. T. Sherman to E. Upton, Nov. 18, 1878, WSPLC (emphasis in original). Other army officers were more blunt in their advocacy of a system of conscription. For one example, see John Schofield, "Report and Observations upon the Manœuvres of the French Army and the Military Systems of France and Other Nations of Europe," *JMSIUS* 3, no. 12 (1882): 158.

32. E. Upton to W. T. Sherman, Nov. 22, 1877, WSPLC; E. Upton to H. A. du Pont, Mar. 6, [1879], DPPHL. Upton strikes this theme repeatedly. "The abuse for my pains," he wrote in an earlier letter to du Pont, "will be unlimited." See E. Upton to H. A. du Pont, Nov. 19, 1878, ibid.

33. E. Upton to H. A. du Pont, Jan. 13, 1878, DPPHL; E. Upton to J. A. Garfield, May 6, 1878, GPLC. See also E. Upton to J. A. Garfield, May 18, June 26, July 24, 1878, GPLC.

34. *MPUS*, vii, xii, xiii.

35. Ibid., viii, xi.

36. Ibid., xiv–xv.

37. Ibid., 61–62, 229, 232–33, 394, 423–31; E. Upton to H. A. du Pont, Nov. 19, 1878, DPPHL.

38. *MPUS*, xi. This is a common theme in Upton's correspondence. See E. Upton to W. T. Sherman, Nov. 6, 1879, WSPLC; and E. Upton to H. A. du Pont, Jan. 13, 1878, Oct. 31, Dec. 31, 1879, Feb. 28, Mar. 16, 1880, DPPHL.

39. *MPUS*, 305.

40. Ibid., 397.

41. Ibid., 85, 105, 228.

42. Ibid., 203–5, 215.

43. Ibid., 256–57, 258. During the summer of 1864, the term of service expired for 455 of the Union's 956 volunteer infantry regiments, 81 of 158 artillery batteries, and "approximately one-half of the cavalry regiments." See Castel, *Decision in the West*, 9.

44. *MPUS*, 258–60.

45. Ibid., 364, 390–92, 400. Certainly, the extreme nature of Upton's charges regarding the actions of the Joint Committee on the Conduct of the War are unwarranted, but there is substance to his belief that the committee did much to discredit and undermine McClellan. See Sears, *George B. McClellan*, 352; and Williams, *Lincoln and the Radicals*, 245–56.

46. *MPUS*, 284, 287, 395.

47. Ibid., 286.

48. Ibid., 400.

49. Ibid., 293, 303, 377, 405. Upton provides numerous other examples of Stanton's "meddling." See ibid., esp. 287, 300, 306–7, 366–68, 397.

50. The Hapsburg Empire's Aulic Council "had often stood for over-centralized control." See Hattaway and Jones, *How the North Won*, 123.

51. *MPUS*, 291–93; E. Upton to H. A. du Pont, Dec. 18, 1879, DPPHL. For an extended discussion of this "war council" and of Upton's evaluation of it, see Hattaway and Jones, *How the North Won*, 101–7, 123–24.

52. *MPUS*, 315, 394.

53. Ibid., 267–68, 439. Upton pursued a similar analysis for all of America's earlier wars. See ibid., 141–42, 190–92, 221.

54. Upton believed it possible to be a "politician" without ever achieving the distinction of "statesman." See ibid., xii–xiii.

55. Ibid., xiv–xv, 202, 208–10, 222.

56. Ibid., 259, 261, 402.

57. Ibid., vii, xi, xiii, xiv, 395.

58. Weigley, *Towards an American Army*, 110–11; Williams, *Americans at War*, 94; E. Upton to J. H. Wilson, Dec. 26, 1878, WPLC; E. Upton to H. A. du Pont, Jan. 13, 1878, DPPHL.

59. Thomas and Hyman, *Stanton*, 534–46, 577; Ekirch, *Civilian and the Military*, 109–11; Hyman, "Ulysses Grant I," 187–89.

60. E. Upton to H. A. du Pont, Feb. 28, 1880, DPPHL; E. Upton to H. A. du Pont, Jan. 13, 1878, ibid. (emphasis in original); E. Upton to H. A. du Pont, June 20, 1878, ibid. The secretary of war's ability to combine the powers of the purse and sword is a recurring theme in Upton's correspondence. See E. Upton to J. A. Garfield, Jan. 4, 1878, GPLC; and E. Upton to W. T. Sherman, Aug. 9, 1878, WSPLC.

61. E. Upton to J. H. Wilson, July 17, 1869, WPLC; E. Upton to H. A. du Pont, Oct. 12, Dec. 18, 1879, DPPHL. See also E. Upton to H. A. du Pont, Oct. 31, 1879, ibid.

62. *MPUS*, chaps. 19–25.

63. Ambrose argues otherwise. See *Upton and the Army*, 132.

64. Upton used the term "usurper" in reference to Lincoln only once, charging that Lincoln had "usurped" Congress's war powers and had assumed near-dictatorial powers. See *MPUS*, 229.

65. An excellent biography of Palmer is I. B. Holley's *General John M. Palmer, Citizen Soldiers, and the Army of Democracy*. The book is a combination of biography and

autobiography, roughly 40 percent of it having been written or outlined by General Palmer.

66. Upton had relied on Jared Sparks's *Writings of Washington*, which omitted several key documents. See Palmer, *Washington, Lincoln, Wilson*, 3–5.

67. Palmer, *Washington, Lincoln, Wilson*, 20–21, 27, 267. R. M. Cheseldine, a lieutenant colonel in the Ohio National Guard, argued similarly in "Where Upton Made His Big Mistake."

68. Flexner, *George Washington in the American Revolution*, 192–3, 370, 520.

69. Ambrose, *Upton and the Army*, 108, 126. See also Weigley, *Towards an American Army*, 124.

70. For one example, see E. Upton to J. H. Wilson, Apr. 1, 1878, WPLC.

71. Ambrose admitted as much when he acknowledged that Upton did not propose conscription as a means to provide manpower to the army. See *Upton and the Army*, 102.

72. E. Upton to J. H. Wilson, Aug. 11, 1877, Dec. 26, 1878, WPLC; E. Upton to J. Schofield, July 28, 1877, JSPLC.

73. E. Upton to W. C. Church, July 28, 1877, CPLC; E. Upton to J. A. Garfield, July 5, 1878, GPLC. The belief that Upton approved of large yet empty organizations is one of the enduring legacies of the Weigley-Ambrose school of scholarship. For a continuation of this intellectual thread, see E. Cohen, *Making Do with Less*, 7–8.

74. J. A. Garfield to W. T. Sherman, June 2, 1878, WSPLC.

Chapter 8

1. E. N. Gilpin to Tom Gilpin, June 6, 1878, E. N. Gilpin Papers, Library of Congress. See Ambrose, *Upton and the Army*, 137, regarding Upton being a hermit.

2. E. Upton to Maria Upton, Apr. 29, 1879, HLOM; *L&L*, 466; Francis H. Parker Diary, Feb. 18, 1879, USAMHI; E. Upton to F. V. Greene, Jan. 25, 1879, GPNYPL; T. N. Benjamin to H. A. du Pont, Sept. 13, 1878, DPPHL.

3. Annual Reports, Artillery School at Ft. Monroe, Va., Nov. 14, 1878, ., Oct. 18, 1879, Letters Received by the Office of the Adjutant General, 1871–80, RG 94, NARA.

4. Annual Report, Artillery School at Ft. Monroe, Va., Oct. 18, 1879, ibid.; Reardon, *Soldiers and Scholars*, 13–14. Interestingly, there is no mention in the report of the breach-loading rifle or, for that matter, of the rifled musket.

5. E. Upton to the Adjutant General, Oct. 22, 1878, Letters Received by the Office of the Adjutant General, 1871–80, RG 94, NARA; Annual Report, Artillery School at Ft. Monroe, Va., Nov. 14, 1878, ibid.

6. For but two examples of Upton's correspondence that indicate the depth of his research, see E. Upton to W. T. Sherman, Oct. 18, 1878, WSPLC; and E. Upton to J. Schofield, Oct. 3, 1877, JSPLC.

7. E. Upton to J. A. Garfield, Oct. 14, Nov. 16, 1878, GPLC.

8. E. Upton to J. A. Garfield, June 26, 1878, ibid.; E. Upton to W. T. Sherman, Aug. 9, 1878, WSPLC; E. Upton to J. H. Wilson, Oct. 21, 1878, WPLC; E. Upton to H. A. du Pont, n.d. [fall 1878], Nov. 6, 1878, DPPHL; E. Upton to W. T. Sherman, Oct. 18, 1878, WSPLC; W. T. Sherman to J. A. Garfield, June 23, 30, 1878, GPLC; J. A. Garfield to E. Upton, June 28, July 27, 1878, in *L&L*, 450–51.

9. E. Upton to W. T. Sherman, Oct. 18, 1878, WSPLC. See also E. Upton to J. A. Garfield, May 18, 1878, GPLC.

10. Andrews, "Years of Frustration," 25–31, 93–124, 196–205; Thomas, "Army Reform in America," 230; Utley, *Frontier Regulars*, 10–18; Smith, *Life and Letters of James Abram Garfield*, 1:420–22. Logan's feud with Sherman was due largely to Sherman's appointment of Maj. Gen. O. O. Howard rather than Logan to the command of the Army of the Tennessee after the death of Maj. Gen. James McPherson at the Battle of Atlanta in July 1864, a move, according to Ezra Warner, that "caused Logan to hate West Pointers from the bottom of his heart." *Generals in Blue*, 282–83. See also Lewis, *Sherman*, 388–89; and Marszalek, *Sherman*, 278–79, 430, 441. A vitriolic attack on West Point and Annapolis is Logan, *Volunteer Soldier*, chaps. 6–8.

11. James A. Garfield, "The Army of the United States, Part I," *North American Review* 126 (Mar.-Apr. 1878): 194–95.

12. Ibid., 197 (emphasis added).

13. Ibid., 202–3, 210–11.

14. Warner, *Generals in Blue*, 155–56; James A. Garfield, "The Army of the United States, Part II," *North American Review* 126 (May–June 1878): 442–49.

15. Ibid., 450–61.

16. Ibid., 463–65.

17. E. Upton to J. A. Garfield, May 6, 1878, GPLC; W. T. Sherman to J. A. Garfield, Apr. 24, 1878, ibid. It is not clear if or to what degree Upton aided Garfield in the article's preparation. See E. Upton to J. H. Wilson, Apr. 19, 1878, WPLC.

18. Thomas, "Ambrose E. Burnside," 7–9; Thomas, "Army Reform in America," 231–42.

19. U.S. Congress, Senate, *Reorganization of the Army*, 2:78, 503–4. The bill and all supporting documentation can be found in this Senate report.

20. Ibid., 1:1–4. Donna Thomas points out that the exact deliberations of the committee are impossible to know since it conducted its business in closed session. See "Army Reform in America," 243.

21. U.S. Congress, Senate, *Reorganization of the Army*, 2:7–8 (emphasis added).

22. U.S. Senate, 45th Cong., 3rd sess., 1878, *Congressional Record*, 8(1):298–300.

23. U.S. Congress, Senate, *Reorganization of the Army*, 2:4, 504; E. Upton to W. T. Sherman, Mar. 21, 1878, WSPLC; E. Upton to J. H. Wilson, Mar. 21, Apr. 1, 1878, WPLC; E. Upton to W. T. Sherman, Dec. 19, 1878, WSPLC.

24. Andrews, "Years of Frustration," 213–14; Thomas, "Army Reform in America," 252. Several authors have addressed the legislative history of the Burnside Bill. For a brief account, see Thomas, "Ambrose E. Burnside," 9–12. For longer, more detailed descriptions, see Thomas, "Army Reform in America," 248–55; and Andrews, "Years of Frustration," 208–17.

25. Weigley, *Towards an American Army*, 109–10; Ambrose, *Upton and the Army*, vii–viii; John Pope to W. T. Sherman, Jan. 2, 1879; Phil Sheridan to W. T. Sherman, Jan. 4, 1879; and Irvin McDowell to the House Subcommittee on Military Affairs, May 21, 1878, in U.S. Congress, Senate, *Papers in Relation to the Reorganization of the Army*, 11, 27–29. See also U.S. Congress, House, *Reduction of Army Officers' Pay, Reorganization of the Army, and Transfer of the Indian Bureau*, 19, 21.

26. Andrews, "Years of Frustration," 240–41; Skirbunt, "Prologue to Reform," 176; Huntington, *Soldier and the State*, 235.

27. For accounts of the influence of German universities on their American counterparts, see Diehl, *Americans and German Scholarship;* Herbst, *German Historical School in American Scholarship;* and Turner and Bernard, "Prussian Road to University?"

28. Long, *Literary Pioneers;* Hofstadter, *Social Darwinism in American Thought*, 172–79.

29. Jonas, *United States and Germany*, 21–23; Gatzke, *Germany and the United States*, 32.

30. *The Nation*, July 28, 1870; Jonas, *United States and Germany*, 21–23, 28–31; Schieber, *Transformation of American Sentiment toward Germany*, 3–6, 14–37; Dobson, *Politics in the Gilded Age*, 53–54. This is not to say that all Americans viewed the Franco-Prussian War in so sanguine a manner. See Ekirch, *Civilian and the Military*, 121.

31. The measure's convoluted legislative history complicates understanding the February 20 vote. A "nay" vote meant the Burnside Bill would remain a part of the appropriations bill, likely ensuring its passage. A "yay" vote removed the bill from the appropriations measure, thereby all but ensuring its defeat.

32. U.S. Senate, 45th Cong., 3rd sess., 1879, *Congressional Record*, 8(2):1760. Unfortunately, the *Record* does not specify the party affiliations of the senators. For that data, see *Congressional Quarterly's Guide to U.S. Elections*, 785–811.

33. *The Nation*, May 30, 1878; Andrews, "Years of Frustration," 188–92; Ekirch, *Civilian and the Military*, 112–23; Huntington, *Soldier and the State*, 222–26.

34. *ANJ*, Dec. 28, 1878.

35. Ibid., Dec. 7, 28, 1878.

36. *The Nation*, May 30, 1878, Jan. 16, 1879.

37. Thomas, "Army Reform in America," 254; Andrews, "Years of Frustration," 221. See also Marszalek, *Sherman*, 435–36.

38. U.S. Senate, 45th Cong., 3rd sess., 1879, *Congressional Record*, 8(2),1758; Thomas, "Ambrose E. Burnside," 11; Andrews, "Years of Frustration," 212.

39. U.S. Congress, Senate, *Reorganization of the Army*, 2:265–72.

40. Ibid., 276–77.

41. Thomas, "Ambrose E. Burnside," 10.

42. Several of the names in this stanza are misspelled. It is not clear if they are mistakes or if Parker took poetic license. Orlando Poe and Joseph Audenried were aides to Sherman. William Hazen, commander of the Sixth Infantry, had written to the Burnside Committee to recommend that Uptonian reform of the staff be adopted; he had been outspoken in his criticisms of the sutler system in the early 1870s. "Sangree" is probably Upton's traveling companion, Joseph Sanger, who also wrote to the committee. "Miles" could be either Nelson or Evan Miles, both of whom were serving on the western frontier at the time. "Marrow" is almost certainly either Albert or Henry A. Morrow, who also were serving in the West. It is not clear who Parker was referring to with "Murkook." A notation on the poem indicates that "Lieutenant Trowel, Rice and Company" refers to the Providence Tool Company. See Heitman, *Historical Register and Dictionary of the United States Army*, 1:175, 517, 708–9, 729, 795, 859–60; and *Who Was Who in American History— The Military*, 247, 445.

43. A copy of "Upton's Lament" is in the Francis H. Parker Papers, USAMHI. Parker's diary, also at USAMHI, notes on January 16, 1879, "Wrote U—Lament."

44. Parker's low opinion of Upton's proposals did not prevent him from socializing with his nemesis, for his diary indicates that he spent an evening at Upton's quarters. See Francis H. Parker diary, Feb. 18, 1879, USMHI.

45. Greene, *Present Military Situation in the United States*, 7–8. Joseph Sanger had made the same observation more than thirty years earlier. In an article for the *United*

Service he noted: "In this country and England we have small regular armies and a reserve of militia and volunteers. Why? Because we do not fear sudden invasion." "Duties of Staff Officers," *United Service* 2 (June 1880): 754–55.

46. Ekirch, *Civilian and the Military*, 112–23; Garraty, *New Commonwealth*,, 225, 240–41.

47. U.S. Senate, 45th Cong., 3rd sess., 1878, *Congressional Record*, 8(1):299–300 (emphasis added); Thomas, "Army Reform in America," 251.

48. Dobson, *Politics in the Gilded Age*, 54. Regarding civil-service reform in this era, see Hogenboom, *Outlawing the Spoils*, 111–97. See also Garraty, *New Commonwealth*, 251–58.

49. E. Upton to Julia Upton, Feb. 16, 1879, GCHD (emphasis added).

50. E. Upton to Julia Upton, Feb. 1, 1880, ibid.

51. Ibid.

52. E. Upton to Julia Upton, Oct. 19, 1879, ibid.

53. Upton had written *Military Policy of the United States* in chronological order, yet "Civil and Military Policy of Rome," as chapter 33, appears after those that addressed the Civil War campaigns of 1862. He provided no explanation as to why he placed it there, nor did he make it clear how Roman military policy related to that of the United States. Upton's "Civil and Military Policy of Rome" therefore appears to be a very strange document taken at face value. The War Department apparently thought so too, for it omitted that chapter when it published the book in 1904.

54. Emory Upton, "Civil and Military Policy of Rome," unpublished chapter of *Military Policy of the United States*, USAHMI, 7, 19–22, 44, 49.

55. Summary drawn from ibid., 58–69 (quotes, 63, 64–65, 68–69; emphasis in original). Upton was far from the first to draw parallels between Rome and the United States. See Weigley, *History of the United States Army*, 92.

56. Marszalek, *Sherman*, 448–49; Jamieson, *Winfield Scott Hancock*, 165–66; E. Upton to H. A. du Pont, June 26, 1880, DPPHL.

57. *Harper's Weekly*, July 27, 1878.

58. *The Nation*, Apr. 17, 1879 (emphasis in original).

59. T. O. Howe, "Is the Republican Party in Its Death Struggle," *North American Review* 126 (May–June 1878): 381–403; George W. Julian, "The Death-Struggle of the Republican Party," ibid. (Mar.–Apr. 1878): 262–92; T. O. Howe, "The Third Term," ibid. 130 (Feb. 1880): 116–29; E. W. Stoughton, "The Third Term: Reasons for It," ibid. (Mar. 1880): 224–35; George S. Boutwell, "General Grant and a Third Term," ibid. (Apr. 1880): 370–87; J. S. Black, "The Third Term: Reasons against It," ibid. (Mar. 1880): 197–223; J. S. Black, "General Grant and Strong Government," ibid. (May 1880): 417–37; E. Upton to J. H. Wilson, Oct. 19, 1876, WPLC.

60. Pehrson, "James Harrison Wilson," 125–31; E. Upton to J. H. Wilson, Dec. 26, 1878, WPLC. See also E. Upton to J. H. Wilson, Nov. 23, [1878], ibid. Nowhere in his correspondence was Upton explicitly critical of Grant. There are any number of possible explanations for this, the most likely being that Peter Michie altered some letters and omitted others. Michie was loyal both to Grant and to Upton and likely did not wish to publish material that might bring either into disrepute. Given his known alterations of Upton's correspondence as well as the content of Upton's correspondence with Julia, which was very critical of the era's politics and none of which is in *Life and Letters*, it is very likely this is exactly what happened.

61. Francis Parkman, "The Failure of Universal Suffrage," *North American Review* 127 (July–Aug. 1878): 1–20; E. Upton to Julia Upton, Nov. 9, 1879, Feb. 1, 1880, GCHD.

62. James Madison, "Federalist No. 10," in Rossiter, *Federalist Papers*, 77, 80–84. For a brief synopsis of the debate at the Constitutional Convention about the merits of republicanism versus those of democracy, see Beeman, *Plain, Honest Men*, 122–23.

63. Circumstantial evidence suggests the Uptons were Whigs, likely very committed ones. Rep. Benjamin Pringle, who gave Upton his appointment to West Point, was a Whig, while two of his older brothers who moved to Michigan in the 1850s became deeply involved in Republican Party politics there. According to Michael F. Holt, concerns about executive usurpation of power, the maintenance of a balance of power between the branches of government, and efforts to defend republican government and values defined the Whig Party's ideology. See "Pringle, Benjamin (1807–1887)," Biographical Directory of the United States Congress, http://bioguide.congress.gov/scripts/biodisplay.pl?index=P000543 (accessed July 2, 2015); and Holt, *Rise and Fall of the American Whig Party*, 26–34.

64. Ambrose claims otherwise in *Upton and the Army*, 142.

65. Sherman quoted in Thomas, "Ambrose E. Burnside," 9; E. Upton to F. V. Greene, Dec. 11, 1877, GPNYPL.

66. Upton had received assignment to the Fourth Artillery while he was serving at the artillery school.

67. E. Upton to W. C. Church, Aug. 18, 1879, CPLC.

68. E. Upton to W. C. Church, Feb. 27, Mar. 3 (emphasis in original), 1880, ibid.

69. E. Upton to H. A. du Pont, Feb. 28, 1880, DPPHL.

70. Emory Upton, "Facts in Favor of Compulsory Retirement," *United Service* 2 (Mar. 1880): 269–81. For parts 2 and 3 of this article, see *United Service* 3 (Dec. 1880): 649–66; and 4 (Jan. 1881): 19–32.

71. *ANJ*, Mar. 6, 1880. E. Upton to W. C. Church, Mar. 3, 1880, ibid. After the defeat of the Burnside Bill, Upton may have condensed *The Military Policy of the United States* and published it in *Atlantic Monthly*. The November 1879 issue of that periodical contains an article entitled "Our Military Past and Future" written by an anonymous author. In language that sounds much like that of Upton, the author employs military history to advocate the establishment of national volunteers, abolition of the militia, maintenance of a sufficient regular army, and establishment of "a system of popular instruction in the elements of the art and science of war." See "Our Military Past and Future," *Atlantic Monthly* 44 (Nov. 1879): 561–75.

72. E. Upton to the Adjutant General, July 6, 1880, File 2666, RG 94, NARA.

Chapter 9

1. E. Upton to the Adjutant General, June 23, Sept. 7, 11, Nov. 5 (with endorsements), 1880, File 2666, RG94, NARA; Adjutant General of the Army to E. Upton, Sept. 9, 1880, ibid.

2. Dr. Saunders to [Peter Michie?], [n.d., after Upton's death], in *L&L*, 481–83.

3. E. Upton to [Miss Martin], Feb. 1, 1880, ibid., 478; E. Upton to H. A. du Pont, July 6, Sept. 22, 1880, DPPHL; Hyson et al., "Suicide of General Emory Upton," 447; E. Upton to Maria Upton, Sept. 22, 1880, HLOM.

4. E. Upton to [Miss Martin], Feb. 1, 1880, in *L&L*, 477 (emphasis in original).

5. Rachel, one of Emory's older sisters, had died in 1856, and Le Roy, a younger brother, died while Emory was a cadet at West Point. See W. Upton, *Upton Family Records*, 252.

6. E. Upton to Electa Upton, Aug. 27, 1880, in *L&L*, 478.

7. E. Upton to W. A. Johnson, Aug. 6, 1880, GCHD (emphasis added).

8. E. Upton to H. A. du Pont, June 10, 1880, DPPHL. Regarding Garfield's apparent embrace of the Stalwarts, see Allan Peskin, *Garfield*, 483–84.

9. Eisenschiml, *Celebrated Case of Fitz-John Porter*, 212–50, 255–56. James McPherson concludes that Porter's inaction "deserved at least mild censure." See *Battle Cry of Freedom*, 529n. For a more recent account of the events of August 29, 1862, see Hennessy, *Return to Bull Run*, 224–308, 464–65. For an account of the Schofield Board, see Connelly, *John M. Schofield*, 249–61.

10. Eisenschiml, *Celebrated Case of Fitz-John Porter*, 214; *MPUS*, 341–45; E. Upton to J. A. Garfield, Dec. 8, 1879, in *L&L*, 458–63. Byng had been accused of cowardice but was found innocent of that charge. He was found guilty, however, of "failing to 'do his utmost.'" See Potter and Nimitz, *Sea Power*, 48–51.

11. J. A. Garfield to B. Hinsdale, Apr. 21, 1880, in Hinsdale, *Garfield-Hinsdale Letters*, 449. See also numerous diary entries in Garfield, *Diary*, 4:362–80.

12. Eisenschiml, *Celebrated Case of Fitz-John Porter*, 255; J. A. Garfield to J. Pope, Dec. 22, 1869, in Smith, *Life and Letters of James Abram Garfield*, 1:268–69; Garfield, *Diary*, 365 (Feb. 13, 1880).

13. J. A. Garfield to E. Upton, Dec. 10, 1879, in *L&L*, 464–65. For critical assessments of the court-martial proceedings and of Garfield's role in them, see Peskin, *Garfield*, 162–63; and Eisenschiml, *Celebrated Case of Fitz-John Porter*, 255, 262.

14. Regimental Orders No. 85, Headquarters, 4th Artillery, Dec. 23, 1880, Regimental Order Book, RG 391, NARA; E. Upton to the Adjutant General, Jan. 22, 1881, Letters Received by the Office of the Adjutant General, RG 94, ibid.; Regimental Orders No. 87, Headquarters, 4th Artillery, Dec. 29, 1880, Regimental Order Book, RG 391, ibid.

15. E. Upton to the Adjutant General, Aug. 25, 1880, Letters Received by the Office of the Adjutant General, RG 94, ibid. For Upton's opinion regarding the conflict with American Indians, see E. Upton to F. V. Greene, Oct. 3, 1879, GPNYPL. Upton had corresponded with Greene concerning the tactical lessons of the 1877–78 Russo-Turkish War, taking great interest in the siege of Plevna. He found Greene's reports so insightful that he distributed copies to officers in his class on strategy at Fortress Monroe. See E. Upton to F. V. Greene, Aug. 18, Dec. 11, 1877, GPNYPL.

16. E. Upton to W. T. Sherman, Jan. 30, Feb. 2, 1880, WSPLC.

17. E. Upton to W. T. Sherman, Feb. 2, June 26, 1880, ibid.; E. Upton to H. A. du Pont, June 10, 19, 1880, DPPHL; E. Upton to Maria, Nov. 22, 1879, HLOM; E. Upton to Julia Upton, Nov. 9, 1879, GCHD.

18. E. Upton to H. A. du Pont, June 19, 1880, DPPHL.

19. E. Upton to W. T. Sherman, Feb. 2, 1880, WSPLC; E. Upton to F. V. Greene, Oct. 3, 1879, GPNYPL; Lt. E. J. McClernand to the War Department, n.d. [after Upton's death], in *L&L*, 469–72.

20. E. Upton to F. V. Greene, Apr. 15, 1878, GPNYPL.

21. H. C. Hasbrouck to [Peter Michie?], Feb. 10, 1882, in *L&L*, 491–92.

22. Adjutant, 4th Artillery Regiment, to the Assistant Adjutant General, Mar. 15, 1881, File 2666, NARA; clipping, *San Francisco Evening Bulletin*, Mar. 16, 1881, ibid.

23. E. Upton to Sara Upton, Mar. 13, 1881, HLOM.

24. E. Upton to the Adjutant General, n.d. [Mar. 13 or 14, 1881], Mar. 14, 1881, in *L&L*, 495.

25. I. McDowell to the Adjutant General, Mar. 16, 1881, Letters Received by the Office of the Adjutant General, RG 94, NARA; W. T. Sherman to I. McDowell, Mar. 18, 1881, ibid.; Diary, Mar. 29, 1881, James H. Wilson Diaries and Papers, Historical Society of Delaware; *ANJ*, Mar. 26, 1881; John C. Tidball Manuscript, "Memoirs, 1882–1884," 166–82, Special Collections, USMA Library.

26. J. H. Wilson to H. A. du Pont, Mar. 16, 1881, DPPHL (emphasis in original).

27. John C. Tidball, "Memoirs, 1882–1884," Special Collections, USMA Library, 166–82.

28. I. McDowell to the Adjutant General of the Army, Mar. 17, 1881, File 2666, NARA; A. J. Alexander to I. McDowell, Mar. 19, 1881, ibid.; *ANJ*, Mar. 26, 1881.

29. Not having the medical background required to make such a diagnosis, I am deeply indebted to the research conducted by John M. Hyson Jr., DDS; William H. Mosberg Jr., MD; George E. Sanborn, MD; and Lt. Col. Joseph W. A. Whitehorne, U.S. Army (ret.). For a detailed analysis of Upton's symptoms based on his medical records and letters written by friends, family, and attending doctors as well as on Upton's degenerating handwriting, see "Suicide of General Emory Upton," 445–52.

30. S. Upton to H. A. du Pont, June 9, 1881, DPPHL; Ambrose, *Upton and the Army*, 151–52. Stephen Ambrose implies that much of the correspondence sent to Michie for use in *Life and Letters* can be found in the du Pont Papers at the Hagley Museum and Library. Neither I nor the archivists there have been able to uncover them. See ibid., 177–78.

31. P. S. Michie to H. A. du Pont, Apr. 9, 17, 1881, DPPHL; Sara Upton to H. A. du Pont, May 6, 16, 1884, ibid.; W. T. Sherman to P. S. Michie, [n.d.], enclosure to W. Appleton to H. A. du Pont, Dec. 2, 1885, ibid. Upton's siblings' efforts to get du Pont to finish the manuscript went on for several years as evidenced by the nearly two-dozen letters (most but not all of them from Sara Upton) that in some manner ask about his progress on *The Military Policy of the United States*.

32. John Upton to A. S. Root, Dec. 11, 1894, John Upton File, Former Student Files, Alumni Records, Oberlin College Archives. For a discussion and analysis of the shortcomings encountered by the army during the "splendid little war," see Cosmas, *Army for Empire*.

33. Millett and Maslowski, *For the Common Defense*, 304, 330; Roberts, "Reform and Revitalization," 210–14; Weigley, *History of the United States Army*, 324–25.

34. Roberts, "Reform and Revitalization," 212–14.

35. Jessup, *Elihu Root*, 1:242–43; Wilkinson, *Brain of an Army*. See also Weigley, "Elihu Root Reforms and the Progressive Era"; Roberts, "Reform and Revitalization," 207–8; and Williams, *Americans at War*, 102, 106–7.

36. Root, *Military and Colonial Policy of the United States*, 108–9, 125.

37. Ibid., 109.

38. Among the editors of the War Department's edition of Upton's work was Joseph Sanger. See *MPUS*, iv.

39. Schofield, *Forty-Six Years in the Army*, 407–8, 421–22; Weigley, *Towards and American Army*, 173; E. Root to P. Jessup, Jan. 23, 1934, cited in Jessup, *Elihu Root*, 1:242–43. Also see Connelly, *John M. Schofield*, 333–34.

40. Weigley, *Towards an American Army*, passim. See also Lane, *Armed Progressive*, 150–51, 173–74.

41. Vagts, *History of Militarism*, 13–14.

42. Ibid., 14.

43. Ritter, *Sword and the Scepter*, 2:5.

44. John Logan and Leonard Wood are but two examples. See Logan, *Volunteer Soldier*, 604–9; and Wood, *America's Duty*, 236. The latter is a virtually unchanged version of Wood's earlier *Our Military History: Its Facts and Fallacies* except that the former publication included a chapter entitled "Lessons of the World War."

45. Weigley, *Towards and American Army*, 156–59.

46. James S. Pettit, "How Far Does Democracy Affect the Organization and Discipline of Our Armies, and How Can Its Influence Be Most Effectively Utilized," *JMSIUS* 38 (Jan.–Feb., 1906): 10. The contest year versus that of the winning essays' publication can be confusing: The winning essays always were published in the year following the contest.

47. Ibid., 2, 4.

48. Pettit might be forgiven for never having read Upton's chapter on Rome, as the War Department never published it.

49. "How Far Does Democracy Affect the Organization and Discipline of Our Armies, and How Can Its Influence Be Most Effectively Utilized: Discussion," *JMSIUS* 38 (Mar.–Apr. 1906): 339, 340.

50. Ibid., 334, 359. Russell Weigley evaluates Steele differently. See *Towards an American Army*, 159.

51. A. C. Sharpe, "Organization and Training of a National Reserve for Military Service," *JMSIUS* 10 (Mar. 1889): 18. Upton would have rejected Sharpe's willingness to allow these citizen-soldiers to elect their officers. See ibid., 19.

52. William Cary Sanger, "Organization and Training of a National Reserve for Military Service," *JMSIUS* 10 (Mar. 1889): 34, 35, 39.

53. For similar sentiments, see Arthur L. Wagner, "An American War College," *JMSIUS* 10 (July 1889): 287–304; John W. Gibbon, "The Danger to the Country from the Lack of Preparation for War," *JMSIUS* 11 (Jan. 1890): 16–28; Joseph B. Bachelor, "A United States Army," *JMSIUS* 10 (Jan. 1892): 54–74; and Elmer W. Hubbard, "The Military Academy and the Education of Officers," *JMSIUS* 16 (Jan. 1895): 1–24.

54. Sidney E. Stuart, "The Army Organization, Best Adapted to a Republican Form of Government, Which Will Insure [*sic*] an Effective Force," *JMSIUS* 14 (Mar. 1893): 233–34, 254–55, 276–77.

55. E. L. Zalinski, "The Army Organization, Best Adapted to a Republican Form of Government, Which Will Insure [*sic*] an Effective Force," *JMSIUS* 14 (Sept. 1893): 940.

56. Ibid., 941.

57. Ibid., 968–969.

58. W. Cary Sanger, "The Army Organization, Best Adapted to a Republican Form of Government, Which Will Insure [*sic*] an Effective Force," *JMSIUS* 14 (Nov. 1893): 1147. This is the same Sanger cited above. This article lists his title as "Ass't Chief of Art'y, N.G.S.N.Y."

59. Ibid., 1148, 1151, 1164, 1165. Regarding his proposal for depots, see Upton, *Armies of Asia and Europe*, 367–69.

60. Sanger, "Army Organization," 1166, 1180.

61. Louis C. Scherer, "Limitations of the National Guard," *JMSIUS* 18 (Mar. 1896): 267–84; J. G. Harbord, "The Necessity of a Well Organized and Well Trained Infantry at the Outbreak of War, and the Best Means to Be Adopted by the United States for Obtaining Such a Force," *JMSIUS* 21 (July 1897): 1–27; Howard A. Giddings, "How to Improve the Condition and Efficiency of the National Guard," *JMSIUS* 21 (July 1897): 61–75; Arthur Williams, "Readiness for War," *JMSIUS* 21 (Sept. 1897): 225–56; R. K. Evans, "The Infantry of Our Regular Army: Its History, Possibilities, and Necessities," *JMSIUS* 22 (May 1898): 449–70.

62. Charles Rhodes, "The Experiences of Our Army since the Outbreak of the War with Spain: What Practical Use Has Been Made of Them and How They May Be Further Utilized to Improve Its Fighting Efficiency," *JMSIUS* 36 (Mar.–Apr. 1905): 192; Linn, *Philippine War*, 125–26, 326 (emphasis added).

63. Alfred C. Sharpe, "Our Autumn Maneuvers," *JMSIUS* 34 (Jan.–Feb. 1904): 65 (emphasis added).

64. William H. Johnston, "A Military Chautauqua," *JMSIUS* 34 (Jan.–Feb. 1904): 98, 100.

65. Arthur L. Wagner, "Combined Maneuvers of the Regular Army and Organized Militia," *JMSIUS* 36 (Jan.–Feb. 1905): 82–83. For more detail regarding Wagner's experiences with the National Guard in various maneuver exercises, see Brereton, *Educating the U.S. Army*, 99–100, 111–15.

66. Wagner, "Combined Maneuvers of the Regular Army and Organized Militia," 87 (emphasis added); Weigley, *Towards an American Army*, 149.

67. Logan, *Volunteer Soldier*, 116–20, 156; Schofield, *Forty-Six Years in the Army*; Huidekoper, *Military Unpreparedness of the United States*. See also Weigley, *Towards an American Army*, 163, 170–73; and Roberts, "Reform and Revitalization," 200–201. For a discussion of Logan's ideas, see Weigley, *Towards an American Army*, chap. 8.

68. U.S. War Department, *Epitome of Upton's Military Policy of the United States*, 3; U.S. Senate, 64th Cong., 1st sess., 1916, *Congressional Record*, 53(6):5499–5505.

69. Weigley, *History of the United States Army*, 345–49.

70. Chambers, *To Raise an Army*, 103; Kreidberg and Henry, *Military Mobilization in the United States Army*, 191–92. Regarding the Plattsburg Movement, see Clifford, *Citizen Soldiers*.

71. Palmer, *Statesmanship or War*, 37–79.

72. Weigley, *Towards an American Army*, 199–200.

73. U.S. House, 64th Cong., 1st sess., 1916, *Congressional Record*, 53(5):4303.

74. Nowhere is Upton mentioned in Palmer's first work, *Statesmanship or War*. If, however, Palmer's advocacy in *Statesmanship or War* of a citizen-soldier army is combined with his anti-Uptonian strictures in *Washington, Lincoln, Wilson*, it is clear that his earlier work is an argument against what he perceived were Upton's proposals.

75. Bacevich, "Emory Upton," 22; E. Cohen, *Making Do with Less*, 6–9.

76. Upton, *Armies of Asia and Europe*, 323–24.

Bibliography

Primary Sources

Manuscripts

Dickman Family Papers (Privately Held), Auburn, N.Y.
    Emily Upton Diary and Letters
Genesee County Courthouse, Batavia, N.Y.
    Emory Upton Last Will and Testament
Genesee County History Department, Office of the County Historian, Batavia, N.Y.
    Upton Family Papers
    Emory Upton, "A New System of Infantry Tactics. . . ."
Historical Society of Delaware, Wilmington, Del.
    James H. Wilson Diaries and Papers
Holland Land Office Museum, Batavia, N.Y.
    Emory Upton Letters
Library of Congress, Manuscript Division, Washington, D.C.
    Adam Badeau Papers
    William C. Church Papers
    James A. Garfield Papers
    E. N. Gilpin Papers
    Thomas A. Jenckes Papers
    John M. Schofield Papers
    William T. Sherman Papers
    James H. Wilson Papers
National Archives and Records Administration, Washington, D.C.

Record Group 15	Records of the Veteran's Administration
Record Group 59	Records of the Department of State
Record Group 94	Records of the Office of the Adjutant General
Record Group 107	Records of the Office of the Secretary of War
Record Group 108	Records of the Office of the Headquarters of the Army
Record Group 391	Records of Regular Army Mobile Units, 1821–1942
Record Group 393	Records of US Army Continental Commands, 1821–1920

New York Public Library, New York City
    Francis V. Greene Papers
New York State Historical Association, Civil War Collection, Cooperstown
    Samuel French Papers
    Lansing Paine Papers
    Dean Pierce Diary
    Charles West Papers
Oberlin College Archives, Oberlin, Ohio
    Alumni Records
    General College Records

Princeton University Library and Archives, Department of Rare Books and Special Collections, Princeton, N.J.
  Throop and Martin Family Papers, 1693–1951
U.S. Army Military History Institute, Carlisle Barracks, Pa.
  Francis H. Parker Papers
  David Russell Papers and Diary
  Emory Upton Papers
    Emory Upton, "The Military Policy of the United States" (manuscript version)
U.S. Military Academy Archives, West Point, N.Y.
  Adjutant's Letter Book
  Adjutant's Letters Received
  Annual Report of the Superintendant
  Cadets Admitted Book
  Circumstances of the Parents of Cadets
  Descriptive Lists of New Cadets
  Orders Received From Commandant of Cadets
  Orders, United States Corps of Cadets
  Post Orders
  Register of Delinquencies
  Register of Letters Received, USMA
  Register of Merit
  Reports of the Board of Visitors to the United States Military Academy
  Superintendant's Letter Book
  USMA Staff Records
U.S. Military Academy Library Special Collections, West Point, N.Y.
  Henry A. Dupont Collection
  Peter S. Michie Collection
  Emory Upton Collection
  John C. Tidball Collection
University of Iowa Libraries, Iowa City
  Edward F. Winslow Papers
University of Michigan Alumni Records, Ann Arbor
  Jospeh Sanger File
University of Notre Dame Archives, Notre Dame, Ind.
  William T. Sherman Papers
Upton Family Papers (Privately Held), Placerville, Calif.
  Emory Upton Letters
William L. Clements Library, University of Michigan, Ann Arbor
  Isaac O. Best Papers
Winterthur Manuscripts, Hagley Museum and Library, Wilmington, Del.
  Henry A. du Pont Papers
  Emory Upton, "The Military Policy of the United States" (manuscript version)

U.S. Government Documents

U.S. Congress. *Congressional Record.* 1876–81. Vols. 4–12. Washington, D.C.
———. House. *Expulsion of Cadets from Military Academy.* 41st Cong., 3rd sess., 1871. H. Rpt. 28.

———. *The Military Policy of the United States during the Mexican War.*, 63rd Cong., 2nd sess., 1914. H. Doc. 972.

———. *Reduction of Army Officers' Pay, Reorganization of the Army, and Transfer of the Indian Bureau.* 44th Cong., 1st sess., 1876. H. Rpt. 354.

———. *Reorganization of the Militia.* 46th Cong., 2nd sess., 1880. H. Rpt. 763.

———. *Report of a Sub-Committee of the Committee on Military Affair Relating to the Reorganization of the Army.* 45th Cong., 2nd sess., 1878. H. Misc. Doc. 56.

———. *Report of the Secretary of War.* 35th Cong., 2nd sess., 1858. H. Exec. Doc. 2.

———. *Report of the Secretary of War.* 41st Cong., 3rd sess., 1870. H. Exec. Doc. 1.

———. *Report of the Secretary of War.* 42nd Cong., 2nd sess., 1871. H. Exec. Doc. 1.

———. *Report of the Secretary of War.* 42nd Cong., 3rd sess., 1872. H. Exec. Doc. 1.

———. Senate. *Creation of the American General Staff.* 68th Cong., 1st sess., 1924. S. Doc. 119.

———. *The Military Policy of the United States, by Bvt. Maj. Gen. Emory Upton.* 62nd Cong., 2nd sess., 1912. S. Doc. 494.

———. *Papers in Relation to the Reorganization of the Army.* 46th Cong., 1st sess., 1879. S. Misc. Doc. 14.

———. *Preparedness for National Defense.* 64th Cong., 1st sess., 1916. S. Doc. 442.

———. *Reorganization of the Army.* 45th Cong., 3rd sess., 1879. S. Rpt. 555, 2 pts.

———. *Report of the Commission on West Point.* 36th Cong., 2nd sess., 1860. S. Misc. Doc. 3.

———. *Report of the Secretary of War.* 34th Cong., 3rd sess., 1856. S. Exec. Doc. 7.

———. *Report of the Secretary of War.* 35th Cong., 1st sess., 1857. S. Exec. Doc. 2.

———. *Report of the Secretary of War.* 36th Cong., 1st sess., 1859. S. Exec. Doc. 2.

U.S. Military Academy. *Official Register of the Officers and Cadets of the U.S. Military Academy, West Point, NY.* Published Annually.

———. *Regulations for the United States Military Academy at West Point, New York.* New York: John F. Trow, 1857.

———. *Resume of Existing Orders, U.S. Corps of Cadets.* New York: D. Van Nostrand, 1874.

U.S. War Department. *Artillery Tactics, United States Army, Assimilated to the Tactics of Infantry and Cavalry.* 1874. Reprint, New York: D. Appleton, 1889.

———. *Cavalry Tactics, United States Army, Assimilated to the Tactics of Infantry and Artillery.* New York: D. Appleton, 1874.

———. *Epitome of Upton's Military Policy of the United States.* Washington, D.C.: Government Printing Office, 1916.

———. *Report of the Secretary of War.* Washington, D.C.: Government Printing Office, 1866–81.

———. *The War of the Rebellion: A Compilation of the Official Records of the Union and Confederate Armies.* 128 vols. Washington, D.C.: Government Printing Office, 1880–1901.

Periodicals

Army and Navy Journal.
Atlantic Monthly.
Batavia (N.Y.) Daily News.
Harper's Weekly.

International Review.
Journal of the Military Service Institution of the United States.
Morning Daily News [Batavia, N.Y.].
The Nation.
The New York Times.
The North American Review
Progressive Batavian [Batavia, N.Y.].
Republican Advocate [Batavia, N.Y.].
Spirit of the Times [Batavia, N.Y.].
United Service.

Published Sources

Ambrose, Stephen E., ed. "West Point in the Fifties: The Letters of Henry A. du Pont." *Civil War History* 10 (September 1964): 291–309.

Badeau, Adam. *Military History of General U. S. Grant.* 3 vols. New York: D. Appleton, 1885.

Best, Isaac. *History of the 121st New York State Infantry.* Chicago: J. H. Smith, 1921.

Casey, Silas. *Infantry Tactics for the Instruction, Exercise, and Manœuvres of the Soldier, a Company, Line of Skirmishers, Battalion, Brigade, or Corps D'Armée.* 3 vols. New York: D. Van Nostrand, 1862.

Combination Atlas Map of Genesee County, New York. Philadelphia: Everts, Ensign, and Everts, 1876.

Corbin, Henry C., and Raphael P. Thian. *Legislative History of the General Staff of the Army of the United States.* Washington, D.C.: USGPO, 1901.

Cullum, George W. *Biographical Register of the Officers and Graduates of the U.S. Military Academy at West Point, N.Y.* 3 vols. Boston: Houghton, Mifflin, 1891.

Fisk, Wilbur. *Hard Marching Every Day: The Civil War Letters of Private Wilbur Fisk, 1861–1865.* Edited by Emil Rosenblatt and Ruth Rosenblatt. Lawrence: University Press of Kansas, 1992.

Flipper, Henry O. *The Colored Cadet at West Point: Autobiography of Lieutenant Henry Ossian Flipper, U.S.A.* New York: Homer Lee, 1878.

Forsyth, George A. *Thrilling Days in Army Life.* New York: Harper and Brothers, 1900.

Fox, William F. *Regimental Losses in the American Civil War, 1861–1865.* Albany: Albany Publishing, 1889.

Garfield, James A. *The Diary of James A. Garfield.* Edited by Harry J. Brown and Frederick D. Williams. 4 vols. East Lansing: Michigan State University Press, 1967–81.

———. *The Works of James Abram Garfield.* Edited by Burke A. Hinsdale. 2 vols. Boston: J. R. Osgood, 1882–83.

Gilpin, E. N. "The Last Campaign—A Cavalryman's Journal." *Journal of the U.S. Cavalry Association* 18 (April 1908): 617–75.

Grant, Ulysses S. *The Personal Memoirs of Ulysses S. Grant.* 2 vols. New York: Charles L. Webster, 1885.

Greene, Francis V. *The Present Military Situation in the United States.* New York: Charles Scribner's Sons, 1915.

Halleck, Henry W. *Elements of Military Art and Science.* New York: D. Appleton, 1846.

Hardee, W. J. *Rifle and Light Infantry Tactics for the Exercise and Manœuvres of Troops When Acting as Light Infantry or Riflemen.* Philadelphia: Lippincott, Graneloff, 1855.

Heitman, Francis B., ed. *Historical Register and Dictionary of the United States Army from Its Organization, September 29, 1879, to March 2, 1903.* 2 vols. 1903. Reprint, Baltimore: Geneological Publishing, 1994.

Hinsdale, Mary L., ed. *Garfield-Hinsdale Letters: Correspondence between James Abram Garfield and Burke Adams Hinsdale.* 1947. Reprint, New York: Kraus, 1969.

Holmes, Oliver Wendall. *Touched with Fire: Civil War Letters and Diary of Oliver Wendall Holmes, Jr., 1861–1864.* Edited by Mark DeWolf Howe. Cambridge, Mass.: Harvard University Press, 1946.

Holt, Daniel M. *A Surgeon's Civil War: The Letters and Diary of Daniel M. Holt, M.D.* Edited by James M. Greiner, Janet L. Coryell, and James R. Smither. Kent, Ohio: Kent State University Press, 1994.

Howard, Oliver Otis. *Autobiography of General O. O. Howard.* 2 vols. New York: Baker and Taylor, 1908.

Huidekoper, Frederic L. *The Military Unpreparedness of the United States: A History of American Land Forces from Colonial Times until June 1, 1915.* New York: Macmillan, 1915.

Jones, James P., ed. "'Your Left Arm:' James H. Wilson's Letters to Adam Badeau." *Civil War History* 12 (September 1966): 230–45.

Lake, Virginia T., ed. "A Crisis of Conscience: West Point Letters of Henry A. du Pont, Oct. 1860–June 1861." *Civil War History* 25 (March 1979): 55–65.

Logan, John A. *The Volunteer Soldier of America.* Chicago: R. S. Peale, 1887.

Lyman, Theodore. *Meade's Army: The Private Notebooks of Lt. Col. Theodore Lyman.* Edited by David W. Lowe. Kent, Ohio: Kent State University Press, 2007.

———. *Meade's Headquarters, 1863–1865: Letters of Colonel Theodore Lyman from Wilderness to Appomattox.* Edited by George R. Agassiz. Boston: Atlantic Monthly Press, 1922.

Mahan, Dennis H. *An Elementary Treatise on Advanced Guard, Out-Post, and Detachment Service of Troops, and the Manner of Posting and Handling Them in Presence of an Enemy. With a Historical Sketch of the Rise and Progress of Tactics, &c. &c.* New York: J. Wiley, 1853.

———. *A Treatise of Field Fortifications, Containing Instructions on the Methods of Laying Out, Constructing, Defending, and Attacking Intrenchments, with the General Outlines also of the Arrangement, the Attack, and Defence of Permanent Fortifications.* 3rd ed. New York: J. Wiley, 1856.

Michie, Peter S. *General McClellan.* New York: D. Appleton, 1901.

———. *Life and Letters of Emory Upton.* New York: D. Appleton, 1885.

Porter, Horace. *Campaigning with Grant.* New York: Century, 1897.

Powell, William H., ed. *List of Officers of the Army of the United States from 1779 to 1900.* New York: L. R. Hamersly, 1900.

Reed, Hugh T. *Cadet Life at West Point.* 3rd ed. Richmond, Ind.: Irwin Reed and Son, 1911.

Ridpath, John C. *The Life and Works of James A. Garfield.* Hartford, Conn.: James Betts, 1881.

Rodenbough, Theophilus F., and William L. Haskins, eds. *The Army of the United States: Historical Sketches of Staff and Line.* New York: Maynard, Merrill, 1896.

Root, Elihu. *The Military and Colonial Policy of the United States: Addresses and Reports by Elihu Root.* Edited by Robert Bacon and James B. Scott. Cambridge, Mass.: Harvard University Press, 1916

Rossiter, Clinton, ed. *The Federalist Papers.* New York: Praeger, 1961.

Schaff, Morris. *The Spirit of Old West Point.* Boston: Houghton Mifflin, 1912.

Schofield, John M. *Forty-Six Years in the Army.* New York: Century, 1897.

Scott, William F. *The Story of a Cavalry Regiment: The Career of the Fourth Iowa Veteran Volunteers, from Kansas to Georgia, 1861–1865.* New York: G. P. Putnam's Sons, 1893.

Sheridan, Philip H. *Personal Memoirs of P. H. Sheridan.* 2 vols. New York: Charles Webster, 1888.

Sherman, William T. *Home Letters of General Sherman.* Edited by Mark A. DeWolfe Howe. New York: Charles Scribner's Sons, 1909.

———. *Memoirs of General William T. Sherman, Written by Himself.* 2 vols. New York: D. Appleton, 1875.

Smith, Theodore C. *The Life and Letters of James Abram Garfield.* 2 vols. New Haven, Conn.: Yale University Press, 1925.

Thorndike, Rachel S., ed. *The Sherman Letters: Correspondence between General and Senator Sherman, from 1837 to 1891.* New York: Charles Scribner's Sons, 1894.

Upton, Emory. *The Armies of Asia and Europe: Embracing Official Reports of the Armies of Japan, China, India, Persia, Italy, Russia, Austria, Germany, France, and England.* New York: D. Appleton, 1878.

———. "Facts in Favor of Compulsory Retirement." *United Service* 2 (March 1880): 269–88; 3 (December 1880): 649–66; 4 (January 1881): 19–32.

———. *Infantry Tactics, Double and Single Rank, Adapted to American Topography and Improved Firearms.* New York: D. Appleton, 1874.

———. *The Military Policy of the United States.* Washington: Government Printing Office, 1904.

———. *A New System of Infantry Tactics, Double and Single Rank, Adapted to American Topography and Improved Fire-arms.* New York: D. Appleton, 1867.

———. "The Prussian Company Column." *International Review* 3 (May 1875): 302–17.

———. *Tactics for Non-military Bodies, Adapted to the Instruction of Political Associations, Police Forces, Fire Organizations, Masonic, Odd-Fellows, and Other Civic Societies.* New York: D. Appleton, 1870.

Upton, William Henry. *Upton Family Records.* London: Mitchell and Hughes, 1893.

Vaill, Theodore. *History of the Second Connecticut Volunteer Heavy Artillery.* Winsted, Conn.: Winsted Printing, 1868.

Vinton, John W. *The Upton Memorial: A Geneological Record of the Descendants of John Upton of North Reading, Mass.* Bath, Maine: E. Upton and Son, 1874.

Wagner, Arthur. *Organization and Tactics.* London: B. Westerman, 1895.

———. *The Service of Security and Information.* 1893. Reprint, Kansas City: Hudson-Kimberly, 1903.

Wilson, James H. *The Life and Services of Brevet Brigadier-General Andrew Jonathan Alexander.* New York: [s.n.], 1887.

———. *The Life of John A. Rawlins: Lawyer, Assistant Adjutant-General, Chief of Staff, Major General of Volunteers, and Secretary of War.* New York: Neale, 1916.

———. *Under the Old Flag.* 2 vols. New York: D. Appleton, 1912.

Wood, Leonard. *America's Duty as Shown by Our Military History: Its Facts and Fallacies.* Chicago: Reilly and Lee, 1921.

———. *Our Military History: Its Facts and Fallacies.* Chicago: Reill and Britton, 1916.

Secondary Sources

Abrahamson, James L. *America Arms for a New Century.* New York: Free Press, 1981.

———. "The Military and American Society, 1881–1922." Ph.D. diss., Stanford University, 1977.

Ambrose, Stephen E. *Duty, Honor, Country: A History of West Point.* Baltimore: The Johns Hopkins University Press, 1966.

———. "Emory Upton and the Armies of Asia and Europe." *Military Affairs* 28 (Spring 1964): 27–32.

———. *Halleck: Lincoln's Chief of Staff.* Baton Rouge: Louisiana State University Press, 1962.

———. "A Theorist Fights: Emory Upton in the Civil War." *Civil War History* 9 (December 1963): 341–64.

———. "Upton and the Army." Ph.D. diss., University of Wisconsin–Madison, 1963.

———. *Upton and the Army.* Baton Rouge: Lousiana State University Press, 1964.

Anderson, M. S. *The Eastern Question, 1774–1923: A Study in International Relations.* New York: St. Martin's, 1966.

Andrews, Richard Allen. "Years of Frustration: William T. Sherman, the Army, and Reform, 1869–1883." Ph.D. diss., Northwestern University, 1968.

Bacevich, Andrew J. "Emory Upton: A Centenial Assessment." *Military Review* 61 (December 1981): 21–28.

———. "Progressivism, Professionalism, and Reform." *Parameters* 9 (March 1979): 66–71.

Barnard, John. *From Evangelicism to Progressivism at Oberlin College, 1866–1917.* Columbus: Ohio State University Press, 1969.

Barr, Ronald J. *The Progressive Army: U.S. Army Command and Administration, 1870–1914.* New York: St. Martin's, 1998.

Bassford, Christopher. *Clausewitz in English: The Reception of Clausewitz in Britain and America, 1815–1945.* New York: Oxford University Press, 1994.

Beckett, Ian F. W. *The Amateur Military Tradition, 1558–1945.* New York: Manchester University Press, 1991.

Beeman, Richard. *Plain, Honest Men: The Making of the American Constitution.* New York: Random House, 2009.

Bernstein, Samuel. *The First International in America.* New York: Augustus M. Kelley, 1962.

Bigelow, Donald N. *William Conant Church and the Army and Navy Journal.* 1952. Reprint, New York: AMS, 1968.

Black, Lowell D., and Sara H. Black. *An Officer and a Gentleman: The Military Career of Lieutenant Henry O. Flipper.* Dayton, Ohio: Lora, 1988.

Bond, Brian. *The Victorian Army and the Staff College, 1854–1914.* London: Eyre Methuen, 1972.

Brereton, T. R. *Educating the Army: Arthur L. Wagner and Reform, 1875–1905.* Lincoln: University of Nebraska Press, 2000.

Brown, Richard G. "General Emory Upton: The Army's Mahan." *Military Affairs* 17 (Fall 1953): 125–31.

Bruce, Robert V. *1877, Year of Violence.* 1959. Reprint, Chicago: Quadrangle Books, 1970.

Bruscino, Thomas. "Naturally Clausewitzian: U.S. Army Theory and Education from Reconstruction to the Interwar Years." *Journal of Military History* 77 (October 2013): 1251–75.

Burton, Brian K. *Extraordinary Circumstances: The Seven Days Battles.* Bloomington: Indiana University Press, 2001.

[Byrns, James F., et al.]. *The Golden Years: Margaret and Frederick S. Upton.* St. Joseph, Mich.: Privately printed, 1967.

Castel, Albert. *Decision in the West: The Atlanta Campaign of 1864.* Lawrence: University Press of Kansas, 1992.

Castellan, Georges. *History of the Balkans: From Mohammed the Conqueror to Stalin.* Translated by Nicholas Bradley. New York: Columbia University Press, 1992.

Catton, Bruce. *The Army of the Potomac: Glory Road.* New York: Doubleday, 1952.

———. *The Army of the Potomac: Mr. Lincoln's Army.* New York: Doubleday, 1951.

———. *The Army of the Potomac: A Stillness at Appomattox.* New York: Doubleday, 1953.

Challener, Richard. *The French Theory of the Nation in Arms, 1866–1939.* New York: Russell and Russell, 1965.

Chambers, John W. *To Raise an Army: The Draft Comes to Modern America.* New York: Free Press, 1987.

Cheseldine, R. M. "Where Upton Made His Big Mistake." *Infantry Journal* 36 (March 1930): 279–88.

Cilella, Salvatore G., Jr. *Upton's Regulars: The 121st New York Infantry in the Civil War.* Lawrence: University Press of Kansas, 2009.

Clifford, John G. *The Citizen Soldiers: The Plattsburg Training Camp Movement, 1913–1920.* Lexington: University Press of Kentucky, 1972.

Coakley, Robert W. *The Role of Federal Military Forces in Domestic Disorders, 1789–1878.* Washington, D.C.: U.S. Army Center of Military History, 1988.

Coburn, Mark. *Terrible Innocence: General Sherman at War.* New York: Hippocrene Books, 1993.

Codington, Edwin B. *The Gettysburg Campaign: A Study in Command.* New York: Charles Scribner's and Sons, 1968.

Coffman, Edward M. *The Old Army: A Portrait of the American Army in Peacetime.* New York: Oxford University Press, 1986.

———. *The Regulars: The American Army, 1898–1941.* Cambridge, Mass.: Harvard University Press, 2004.

Cohen, Eliot A. *Making Do with Less, or Coping with Upton's Ghost.* Carlisle Barracks, Pa.: U.S. Army War College, 1995.

Cohen, Stephen P. *The Indian Army: Its Contribution to the Development of a Nation.* Delhi, India: Oxford University Press, 1990.

Colby, Elbridge. "Elihu Root and the National Guard." *Military Affairs* 23 (Spring 1959): 28–34.

Connelly, Donald B. *John M. Schofield and the Politics of Generalship.* Chapel Hill: University of North Carolina Press, 2006.

Cooling, Benjamin F. "The Missing Chapters of Emory Upton: A Note." *Military Affairs* 37 (February 1973): 13–15.

Cooper, Jerry M. *The Army and Civil Disorder: Federal Military Intervention in Labor Disputes.* Westport, Conn.: Greenwood, 1978.

———. "The Army's Search for a Mission, 1865–1890." In *Against All Enemies: Interpretations of American Military History from Colonial Times to the Present,* edited by Kenneth J. Hagen and William R. Roberts, 173–95. New York: Greenwood, 1986.

———. *The Rise of the National Guard: The Evolution of the American Militia, 1865–1920.* Lincoln: University of Nebraska Press, 1997.

Cosmas, Graham A. *An Army for Empire: The United States Army in the Spanish-American War.* Columbia: University of Missouri Press, 1971.

———. "Military Reorganization after the Spanish-American War." *Military Affairs* 35 (February 1971): 12–17.

Crackel, Theodore J. *West Point: A Bicentential History.* Lawrence: University Press of Kansas, 2002.

Craig, Gordon A. *The Politics of the Prussian Army, 1640–1945.* New York: Oxford University Press, 1955.

Cross, Whitney R. *The Burned-over District.* New York: Harper and Row, 1965.

Cunliffe, Marcus. *Soldiers and Civilians: The Martial Spirit in America.* New York: Free Press, 1968.

Deák, István. *Beyond Nationalism: A Social and Political History of the Habsburg Officer Corps, 1848–1918.* New York: Oxford University Press, 1990.

Dearing, Mary R. *Veterans in Politics: The Story of the G.A.R.* Baton Rouge: Lousiana State University Press, 1952.

Demeter, Karl. *The German Officer Corps in Society and State, 1650–1945.* New York: Praeger, 1965.

Derthick, Martha. *The National Guard in Politics.* Cambridge, Mass.: Harvard Univeristy Press, 1965.

The Dictionary of American Biography. New York: Scribner, 1959.

Diehl, Carl. *Americans and German Scholarship, 1770–1870.* New Haven, Conn.: Yale University Press, 1978.

Dillard, Walter S. "The United States Military Academy, 1865–1900: The Uncertain Years." Ph.D. diss., University of Washington, 1972.

Dobson, John M. *Politics in the Gilded Age.* New York: Praeger, 1972.

Donald, David. *Lincoln Reconsidered.* 2nd ed. New York: Alfred A. Knopf, 1966.

Ecelbarger, Gary. *Black Jack Logan: An Extraordinary Life in Peace and War.* Guilford, Conn.: Lyons, 2005.

Eggert, Gerald G. *Railroad Labor Disputes: The Beginnings of Federal Strike Policy.* Ann Arbor: University of Michgan Press, 1967.

Eisenschiml, Otto. *The Celebrated Case of Fitz-John Porter: An American Dreyfus Affair.* Indianapolis: Bobbs-Merrill, 1950.

Ekirch, Arthur A. *The Civilian and the Military: A History of the American Antimilitarist Tradition.* New York: Oxford University Press, 1956.

Ekmecic, Milorad. "The Serbian Army in the Wars of 1876–78: National Liability or National Asset?" In *Insurrections, War, and the Eastern Crisis in the 1870s,* edited by Béla Király and Gale Stokes, 276–304. New York: Columbia University Press, 1985.

Fairchild, James H. *Oberlin: The Colony and the College, 1833–1883.* Oberlin, Ohio: E. J. Goodrich, 1883.

Farwell, Byron. *Armies of the Raj: From the Mutiny to Independence, 1858–1947.* New York: Norton, 1989.

Fitzpatrick, David J. "Emory Upton: The Misunderstood Reformer." Ph.D. diss., University of Michigan, 1996.

———. "Emory Upton and the Army of a Democracy." *Journal of Military History* 77 (April 2013): 463–90.

———. "Emory Upton and the Citizen-Soldier." *Journal of Military History* 65 (April 2001): 355–90.

Fletcher, Robert S. *A History of Oberlin College from Its Foundation through the Civil War.* 2 vols. Oberlin, Ohio: Oberlin College, 1943.

Flexner, James T. *George Washington in the American Revolution, 1775–1783.* Boston: Little, Brown, 1968.

Foner, Jack D. *The United States Soldier between Two Wars: Army Life and Reforms, 1865–1898.* New York: Humanities, 1970.

Freeman, Douglas S. *Lee's Lieutenants: A Study in Command.* 3 vols. New York: Charles Scribner's Sons, 1942–44.

Furgurson, Ernest B. *Chancellorsville, 1863: The Souls of the Brave.* New York: Alfred A. Knopf, 1992.

Gallagher, Gary W. *Stephen Dodson Ramseur: Lee's Gallant General.* Chapel Hill: University of North Carolina Press, 1985.

Ganoe, William A. *History of the United States Army.* New York: Appleton, 1933.

Garraty, John. *The New Commonwealth, 1877–1890.* New York: Harper and Row, 1968.

Gates, John M. "The Alleged Isolation of U.S. Army Officers in the Late Nineteenth Century." *Parameters* 10 (September 1980): 32–45.

Gatzke, Hans W. *Germany and the United States: A Special Relationship?* Cambridge, Mass.: Harvard University Press, 1980.

Gazely, John G. *American Opinion of German Unification, 1848–1871.* New York: N.p., 1926.

Glatthaar, Joseph T. *Partners in Command: The Relationships between Leaders in the Civil War.* New York: Free Press, 1994.

Goldin, Claudia D., and Frank J. Lewis. "The Economic Cost of the American Civil War: Estimates and Imlication." *Journal of Economic History* 35 (June 1975): 299–326.

Goss, Thomas J. *The War within the Union High Command: Politics and Generalship during the Civil War.* Lawrence: University Press of Kansas, 2003.

Greiner, James M. *Subdued by the Sword: A Line Officer with the 121st New York Volunteers.* Albany: State University of New York Press, 2003.

Griess, Thomas E. "Dennis Hart Mahan: West Point Professor and Advocate of Professionalism, 1830–1871." Ph.D. diss., Duke University, 1969.

Griffith, Paddy. *Battle Tactics of the Civil War.* New Haven, Conn.: Yale University Press, 1989.

Harries-Jenkins, Gwyn. *The Army in Victorian Society.* Toronto: University of Toronto Press, 1977.

Hattaway, Herman, and Archer Jones. *How the North Won: A Military History of the Civil War.* Urbana: University of Illinois Press, 1983.

Hennessy, John. *Return to Bull Run: The Campaign and Battle of Second Manassas.* New York: Simon and Schuster, 1993.

Herbst, Jurgen. *The German Historical School in American Scholarship: A Study in the Transfer of Culture.* Ithaca, N.Y.: Cornell University Press, 1965.

Hess, Earl J. *Trench Warfare under Grant & Lee: Field Fortification in the Overland Campaign.* Chapel Hill: University of North Carolina Press, 2007.

Hill, Jim D. *The Minute-Man in Peace and War: A History of the National Guard.* Harrisburg, Pa.: Stackpole, 1963.

Hofstadter, Richard. *Anti-Intellectualism in American Life.* New York: Alfred A. Knopf, 1963.

———. *Social Darwinism in Ameircan Thought.* Philadelphia: University of Pennsylvania Press, 1944.

Hogenboom, Ari. *Outlawing the Spoils: A History of the Civil Service Reform Movement, 1865–1883.* Urbana: University of Illinois Press, 1961.

Holley, I. B. *General John M. Palmer, Citizen-Soldiers, and the Army of Democracy.* Westport, Conn.: Greenwood, 1982.

Holt, Michael F. *The Political Crisis of the 1850s.* New York: John Wiley and Sons, 1978.

———. *The Rise and Fall of the American Whig Party: Jacksonian Politics and the Onset of the Civil War.* New York: Oxford University Press, 1999.

Howard, Michael. *The Franco-Prussian War.* 1961. Reprint, London: Routledge, 1991.

———. "Jomini and the Classical Tradition in Military Thought." In *The Theory and Practice of War,* edited by Michael Howard, 5–20. Bloomington: Indiana University Press, 1965.

Huntington, Samuel P. *The Soldier and the State: The Theory and Politics of Civil-Military Relations.* Cambridge, Mass.: Harvard University Press, 1957.

Hutton, Paul Andrew. *Phil Sheridan and His Army.* Norman: University of Oklahoma Press, 1985.

Hyman, Harold M. "Ulysses Grant I, Emperor of America?: Some Civil-Military Continuities and Strains of the Civil War and Reconstruction." In *The United States Military under the Constitution of the United States, 1789–1989,* edited by Richard H. Kohn, 175–92. New York: New York University Press, 1991.

Hyson, John M., Jr., et al. "The Suicide of General Emory Upton: A Case Report." *Military Medicine* 155 (October 1990): 445–52.

Jamieson, Perry D. *Crossing the Deadly Ground: United States Army Tactics, 1865–1899.* Tuscaloosa: University of Alabama Press, 1994.

———. *Winfield Scott Hancock: Gettysburg Hero.* Abilene, Tex.: McWhiney Foundation Press, 2003.

Janowitz, Morris. *The Professional Soldier: A Social and Political Portrait.* New York: Free Press, 1960.

Jelavich, Barbara. *Russia's Balkan Entanglements, 1806–1914.* New York: Cambridge University Press, 1991.

Jessup, Philip C. *Elihu Root.* 2 vols. New York: Dodd, Mead, 1938.

Johnson, James E. "Charles G. Finney and a Theology of Revivalism." *Church History* 38 (September 1969): 338–58.

Johnson, Paul E. *A Shopkeeper's Millennium: Society and Revivals in Rochester, New York, 1815–1937.* New York: Hill and Wang, 1978.

Jonas, Manfred. *The United States and Germany: A Diplomatic History.* Ithaca, N.Y.: Cornell University Press, 1984.

Jones, James P. *John A. Logan: Stalwart Republican of Illinois.* Tallahassee: University Press of Florida, 1982.

———. *Yankee Blitzkrieg: Wilson's Raid through Alabama and Georgia.* Athens: University of Georgia Press, 1976.

Karsten, Peter. "Armed Progressives: The Military Reorganizes for the American Century." In *The Military in America,* edited by Peter Karsten, 229–71. New York: Free Press, 1980.

Katz, Philip M. *From Appomattox to Montmartre: Americans and the Paris Commune.* Cambridge, Mass.: Harvard University Press, 1998.

Keep, John L. H. *Soldiers of the Tsar: Army and Society in Russia, 1462–1874.* New York: Oxford University Press, 1985.

Koistinen, Paul A. C. *Mobilizing for Modern War: The Political Economy of American Warfare, 1865–1919.* Lawrence: University Press of Kansas, 1997.

Kreidberg, Marvin A., and Merton G. Henry. *History of Military Mobilization in the United States Army, 1775–1945.* Washington, D.C.: USGPO, 1955.

Lane, Jack C. *Armed Progressive: General Leonard Wood.* San Rafael, Calif.: Presidio, 1978.

Langly, Lester. "The Democratic Tradition and Military Refrom, 1878–1885." *Southwestern Social Science Quarterly* 48 (September 1967): 192–200.

Lewis, Lloyd. *Sherman, Fighting Prophet.* New York: Harcourt, Brace, 1958.

Linderman, Gerald F. *Embattled Courage: The Experience of Combat in the American Civil War.* New York: Free Press, 1987.

Linn, Brian McAllister. *The Echo of Battle.* Cambridge, Mass.: Harvard University Press, 2007.

———. *The Philippine War, 1899–1902.* Lawrence: University Press of Kansas, 2000.

Long, E. B. *The Civil War Day by Day.* Garden City, N.Y.: Doubleday, 1971.

Long, Orie. *Literary Pioneers: Early American Explorers of European Culture.* 1935. Reprint, New York: Russell and Russell, 1963

Luvaas, Jay. *The Military Legacy of the Civil War: The European Inheritance.* Chicago: University of Chicago Press, 1959.

Machoian, Ronald G. *William Harding Carter and the American Army: A Soldier's Story.* Norman: University of Oklahoma Press, 2006.

Marszalek, John F. *Sherman: A Soldier's Passion for Order.* New York: Free Press, 1993.

Marvel, William. *Burnside.* Chapel Hill: University of North Carolina Press, 1991.

Masland, John W., and Laurence I. Radway. *Soldiers and Scholars: Military Education and National Policy.* Princeton, N.J.: Princeton University Press, 1957.

Mason, Philip. *A Matter of Honour: An Account of the Indian Army, Its Officers and Men.* London: Jonathan Cape, 1974.

Matloff, Maurice, ed. *American Military History.* Washington, D.C.: Government Printing Office, 1989.

Matter, William D. *If It Takes All Summer: The Battle of Spotsylvania.* Chapel Hill: University of North Carolina Press, 1988.

McConnell, Stuart. *Glorious Contentment: The Grand Army of the Republic, 1865–1900.* Chapel Hill: University of North Carolina Press, 1992.

McPherson, James M. *Battle Cry of Freedom: The Civil War Era.* New York: Oxford University Press, 1988.

McWhiney, Grady, and Perry D. Jamieson. *Attack and Die: Civil War Military Tactics and the Southern Heritage.* Tuscaloosa: University of Alabama Press, 1982.

Menning, Bruce W. *Bayonets before Bullets: The Imperial Russian Army, 1861–1914.* Bloomington: University of Indiana Press, 1992.

Merrill, James M. *William Tecumseh Sherman*. Chicago: Rand McNally, 1971.

Messer-Kruse, Timothy. *The Yankee International: Marxism and the American Reform Tradition, 1848–1876*. Chapel Hill: University of North Carolina Press, 1998.

Millett, Allan R. "The Constitution and the Citizen Soldier." In *The United States Military under the Constitution of the United States, 1789–1989*, edited by Richard H. Kohn, 97–119. New York: New York University Press, 1991.

———. *Military Professionalism and Officership in America*. Columbus: Ohio State University Press, 1977.

Millett, Allan R., and Peter Maslowski. *For the Common Defense: A Military History of the United States of America*. Rev. ed. New York: Free Press, 1994.

Millis, Walter. *Arms and Men*. New York: G. P. Putnam and Sons, 1956.

———. *The Martial Spirit*. Boston: Houghton, Mifflin, 1931.

Misulia, Charles A. *Columbus, Georgia, 1865: The Last True Battle of the Civil War*. Tuscaloosa: University of Alabama Press, 2010.

Mitchell, Allan. *The German Influence in France after 1870: The Formation of the French Republic*. Chapel Hill: University of North Carolina Press, 1979.

Morgan, H. Wayne. *From Hayes to McKinley: National Party Politics, 1877–1896*. Syracuse, N.Y.: Syracuse University Press, 1969.

Morrison, James L., Jr. *"The Best School in the World": West Point, the Pre–Civil War Years, 1833–1866*. Kent, Ohio: Kent State University Press, 1986.

———. "Military Education and Strategic Thought, 1846–1861." In *Against All Enemies: Interpretations of American Military History from Colonial Times to the Present*, edited by Kenneth J. Hagen and William R. Roberts, 113–31. New York: Greenwood, 1986.

———. "The United States Military Academy, 1833–1866: Years of Progress and Turmoil." Ph.D. diss., Columbia University, 1970.

The National Cyclopedia of American Biography.

Nenninger, Timothy. "The Army Enters the Twentieth Century, 1904–1917." In *Against All Enemies: Interpretations of American Military History from Colonial Times to the Present*, edited by Kenneth J. Hagen and William R. Roberts, 219–34. New York: Greenwood, 1986.

———. *The Leavenworth Schools and the Old Army*. Westport, Conn.: Greenwood, 1978.

O'Reilly, Francis A. *The Fredericksburg Campaign: Winter War on the Rappahannock*. Baton Rouge: Lousiana State University Press, 2003.

Palmer, John M. *America in Arms: The Experience of the United States with Military Organization*. New Haven, Conn.: Yale University Press, 1941.

———. *Statesmanship or War*. Garden City, N.Y.: Doubleday, 1927.

———. *Washington, Lincoln, Wilson: Three War Statesmen*. Garden City, N.Y.: Doubleday, 1930.

Pappas, George S. *To the Point: The United States Military Academy, 1802–1902*. Westport, Conn.: Praeger, 1993.

Parker, Russell D. "The Philosophy of Charles G. Finney." *Ohio History* 82 (Summer–Autumn, 1973): 142–53.

Patchan, Scott C. *The Last Battle of Winchester: Phil Sheridan, Jubal Early, and the Shenandoah Valley Campaign, August 7–September 19, 1864*. El Dorado Hills, Calif.: Savas Beatie, 2013.

Pehrson, Paul C. "James Harrison Wilson: The Post-War Years, 1865–1925." Ph.D. diss., University of Wisconsin–Madison, 1993.

Perkins, E. J. "The Military Staff: Its History and Development." *Military Review* 243 (September 1953): 81–88.

Perlmutter, Amos. *The Military and Politics in Modern Times: On Professionals, Praetorians, and Revolutionary Soldiers.* New Haven, Conn.: Yale University Press, 1977.

Peskin, Allan. *Garfield.* Kent, Ohio: Kent State University Press, 1978.

Porch, Douglas. *The March to the Marne: The French Army, 1871–1914.* New York: Cambridge University Press, 1981.

Potter, E. B., and Chester W. Nimitz, eds. *Sea Power.* Englewood Cliffs, N.J.: Prentice-Hall, 1960.

Rable, George C. *Fredericksburg! Fredericksburg!* Chapel Hill: University of North Carolina Press, 2002.

Rafuse, Ethan. *McClellan's War: The Failure of Moderation in the Struggle for the Union.* Bloomington: Indiana University Press, 2005.

Reardon, Carol. *Soldiers and Scholars: The U.S. Army and the Uses of Military History, 1865–1920.* Lawrence: University Press of Kansas, 1990.

Reichley, Marlin S. "Federal Military Intervention in Civil Disturbances." Ph.D. diss., Georgetown University, 1939.

Reinhardt, George C., and William R. Kintner. *The Haphazzard Years: How America Has Gone to War.* Garden City, N.Y.: Doubleday, 1960.

Rhea, Gordon. *The Battle of the Wilderness, May 5–6, 1864.* Baton Rouge: Lousiana State University Press, 1994.

———. *The Battles for Spotsylvania Court House and the Road to Yellow Tavern, May 7–12, 1864.* Baton Rouge: Louisiana State University Press, 1997.

———. *Cold Harbor: Grant and Lee, May 26–June 3, 1864.* Baton Rouge: Lousisana State University Press, 2002.

———. *To the North Anna River: Grant and Lee, May 13–25, 1864.* Baton Rouge: Lousiana State University Press, 2000.

Riker, William H. *Soldiers of the States: The Role of the National Guard in American Democracy.* Washington, D.C.: Public Affairs, 1957.

Ritter, Gerhard. *The Sword and the Scepter: The Problem of Militarism in Germany.* 4 vols. Translated by Heinz Norden. Coral Gables, Fla.: University of Miami Press, 1969.

Roberts, William R. "Reform and Revitalization, 1890–1903." In *Against All Enemies: Interpretations of American Military History from Colonial Times to the Present,* edited by Kenneth J. Hagen and William R. Roberts, 198–218. New York: Greenwood, 1986.

Rosinski, Herbert. *The German Army.* New York: Praeger, 1966.

Rothenberg, Gunther E. *The Army of Francis Joseph.* West Lafayette, Ind.: Purdue University Press, 1976.

Royster, Charles. *The Destructive War: William Tecumseh Sherman, Stonewall Jackson, and the Americans.* New York: Alfred A. Knopf, 1991.

Russ, William A., Jr. "Was There Danger of a Second Civil War during Reconstruction?" *Mississippi Valley Historical Review* 25 (June 1938): 3–38.

Sarkesian, Sam C. *The Professional Army Officer in a Changing Society.* Chicago: Nelson-Hall, 1975.

Schieber, Clara E. *The Transformation of American Sentiment toward Germany, 1870–1914.* 1923. Reprint, New York: Russell and Russell, 1973.

Scott, Robert G. *Into the Wilderness with the Army of the Potomac.* Bloomington: University of Indiana Press, 1985.

Sears, Stephen W. *George B. McClellan: The Young Napoleon.* New York: Ticknor and Fields, 1988.

———. *Landscape Turned Red: The Battle of Antietam.* New York: Ticknor and Fields, 1983.

———. *To the Gates of Richmond: The Peninsula Campaign.* New York: Ticknor and Fields, 1992.

Semsch, Philip L. "Elihu Root and the General Staff." *Military Affairs* 27 (Spring 1963): 16–27.

Sergent, Mary E. *They Lie Forgotten: The United States Military Academy, 1856–1861, Together with a Class Album for the Class of May 1861.* Middletown, N.Y.: Prior King, 1986.

Shattuck, Gardiner H. *A Shield and Hiding Place: The Religious Life of Civil War Armies.* Macon, Ga.: Mercer University Press, 1987.

Shy, John. "Jomini." In *Makers of Modern Strategy: From Machiavelli to the Nuclear Age,* edited by Peter Paret, 143–85. Princeton, N.J.: Princeton University Press, 1986.

Skelton, William B. *An American Profession of Arms: The Army Officer Corps, 1784–1861.* Lawrence: University Press of Kansas, 1992.

———. "The Army in the Age of the Common Man, 1815–1845." In *Against All Enemies: Interpretations of American Military History from Colonial Times to the Present,* edited by Kenneth J. Hagen and William R. Roberts, 91–112. New York: Greenwood, 1986.

Skirbunt, Peter D. "Prologue to Reform: The 'Germanization' of the United States Army, 1865–1898." Ph.D. diss., Ohio State University, 1983.

Spaulding, Oliver L. *The United States Army in War and Peace.* New York: Putnum, 1937.

Spiers, Edward M. *The Late Victorian Army, 1868–1902.* New York: Manchester University Press, 1992.

Starr, Merritt. "General Emory Upton—His Brothers, His Career." *Oberlin Alumni Magazine* 18 (May 1922): 12–15, 31–36.

Starr, Stephen Z. *The Union Cavalry in the Civil War.* 3 vols. Baton Rouge: Lousiana State University Press, 1979–85.

Stillman, Richard J., II. *Creating the American State: The Moral Reformers and the Modern Administrative World They Made.* Tuscaloosa: University of Alabama Press, 1998.

Stohlman, Robert F., Jr. *The Powerless Position: The Commanding General of the Army of the United States, 1864–1903.* Manhattan, Kans.: Military Affairs, 1975.

Stojanovic, Mihailo D. *The Great Powers and the Balkans, 1875–1878.* Cambridge, Eng.: Cambridge University Press, 1939.

Stokes, Gale. "Serbian Military Doctrine and the Crisis of 1875–78." In *Insurrections, War, and the Eastern Crisis in the 1870s,* edited by Béla Király and Gale Stokes, 261–75. New York: Columbia University Press, 1985.

———. "The Social Role of the Serbian Army before World War I: A Synthesis." In *Essays on War and Society in East Central Europe, 1740–1920,* edited by Stephen Fischer-Galati and Béla Király, 105–16. New York: Columbia University Press, 1987.

Symonds, Craig L. "An Improvised Army at War, 1861–1865." In *Against All Enemies: Interpretations of American Military History from Colonial Times to the Present,* edited by Kenneth J. Hagen and William R. Roberts, 155–71. New York: Greenwood, 1986.

Taaffe, Stephen R. *Commanding the Army of the Potomac.* Lawrence: University Press of Kansas, 2006.

Taylor, John M. *Garfield of Ohio.* New York: W. W. Norton, 1970.

Thomas, Benjamin P., and Harold M. Hyman. *Stanton: The Life and Times of Lincoln's Secretary of War.* New York: Alfred A. Knopf, 1962.

Thomas, Donna. "Ambrose E. Burnside and Army Reform, 1850–1881." *Rhode Island History* 37 (February 1978): 2–13.

———. "Army Reform in America: The Crucial Years, 1876–1881." Ph.D. diss., University of Florida, 1980.

Trudeau, Noah A. *Bloody Roads South: The Wilderness to Cold Harbor, May–June 1864.* Boston: Little, Brown, 1989.

Turner, James, and Paul Bernard. "The Prussian Road to University?: German Models and the University of Michigan, 1837–c.1895." In *Rackham Reports,* 6–52. Ann Arbor: Univeristy of Michigan, 1989.

Utley, Robert M. *Frontier Regulars: The United States Army and the Indian, 1866–1891.* Lincoln: University of Nebraska Press, 1973.

Vagts, Alfred. *A History of Militarism: Romance and Realities of a Profession.* New York: W. W. Norton, 1937.

Walker, Wallace E. "Emory Upton and the Army Officer's Creed." *Military Review* 61 (April 1981): 65–68.

Walters, Ronald G. *American Reformers, 1815–1860.* New York: Hill and Wang, 1978.

Warner, Ezra. *Generals in Blue: The Lives of Union Commanders.* Baton Rouge: Lousiana State University Press, 1964.

———. *Generals in Gray: The Lives of the Confederate Commanders.* Baton Rouge: Lousiana State University Press, 1959.

Wawro, Geoffrey. *The Franco-Prussian War: The German Conquest of France in 1870–1871.* New York: Cambridge University Press, 2003.

Weigley, Russell F. "The American Civil-Military Cultural Gap: A Historical Perspective, Colonial Times to the Present." In *Soldiers and Civilians: The Civil-Military Gap and American National Security,* edited by Peter D. Feaver and Richard H. Kohn, 215–46. Cambridge, Mass.: MIT Press, 2001.

———. "The American Military and the Principle of Civilian Control from McClellan to Powell." *Journal of Military History* 57 (October 1993): 27–58.

———. *The American Way of War.* New York: Macmillan, 1973.

———. "The Elihu Root Reforms and the Progressive Era." In *Command and Commanders in Modern Warfare,* edited by William Geffen, 11–30. Colorado Springs: U.S. Air Force Academy, 1969.

———. "The End of Militarism." In *The Military and Society: The Proceedings of the Fifth Military History Symposium, United States Air Force Academy, 5–6 October 1972,* edited by Maj. David MacIsaac, 3–14. Colorado Springs: U.S. Air Force Academy, 1972.

———. *A Great Civil War: A Military and Political History, 1861–1865.* Bloomington: Indiana University Press, 2000.

———. *History of the United States Army.* New York: Macmillan, 1967.

———. "The Interwar Army." In *Against All Enemies: Interpretations of American Military History from Colonial Times to the Present,* edited by Kenneth J. Hagen and William R. Roberts, 257–78. New York: Greenwood, 1986.

———. "The Long Death of the Indian-Fighting Army." In *Soldiers and Civilians: The U.S. Army and the American People,* edited by Garry D. Ryan and Timothy K. Nenninger, 27–39. Washington, D.C.: National Archives and Records Administration, 1987.

———. *Towards an American Army: Military Thought from Washington to Marshall.* New York: Columbia University Press, 1962.

Wert, Jeffry D. *From Winchester to Cedar Creek: The Shenandoah Valley Campaign of 1864.* Mechanicsburg, Pa.: Stackpole, 1987.

———. *The Sword of Lincoln: The Army of the Potomac.* NewYork: Simon and Schuster, 2005.

Who Was Who in America, 1897–1942. Chicago: Marquis, 1966.

Who Was Who in American History—The Military. Chicago: Marquis, 1975.

Wilkinson, Spenser. *The Brain of an Army: A Popular Account of the German General Staff.* Westminster, Eng.: Archibald Constable, 1895.

Williams, T. Harry. *Americans at War: The Development of the American Military System.* Baton Rouge: Lousiana State University Press, 1960.

———. "The Attack upon West Point during the Civil War." *Mississippi Valley Historical Review* 25 (March 1939): 491–504.

———. *The History of American Wars.* New York: Alfred A. Knopf, 1981.

———. *Lincoln and the Radicals.* Madsion: University of Wisconsin Press, 1941.

———. "The Military Leadership of North and South." In *Why the North Won the Civil War,* edited by David H. Donald, 23–47. Baton Rouge: Lousiana State University Press, 1960.

Zais, Barrie. "The Struggle for a 20th Century Army." Ph.D. diss., Duke University, 1981.

Index

Page numbers in *italics* denote illustrative matter.